WE FILIPINOS LIVING
CONDEMN THE FASC
OF MARCOS AND HIS GANG
OF HOODLUMS — PUPPETS OF
U.S. IMPERIALISM.
THE MASS-MURDERS OF
MEN, WOMEN AND CHILDREN,
COMMITTED IN COLD BLOOD
BY MARCOS AND HIS GESTAPO THUGS,
ARE CRIMES AGAINST HUMANITY.
YOU, MARCOS, — YOUR WIFE IMELDA,
AND YOUR HANDFUL OF FASCIST
GANGSTERS, — WILL SURELY MEET
YOUR DOOM, IN THE HANDS OF THE
FILIPINO PEOPLE. WE PROCLAIM
SOLIDARITY WITH OUR
FILIPINO BROTHERS AND SISTERS
MABUHAY ANG MASANG PILIPINO!

INTERNATIONAL COMMITTEE FOR FREEDOM IN THE PHILIPPINES.

Edited by
Aram Moshayedi

With contributions by
Magalí Arriola
CJ Salapare
Nyah Ginwright

Hammer Museum
University of California
Los Angeles

DelMonico Books • D.A.P.
New York

David Medalla

In Conversation with the Cosmos

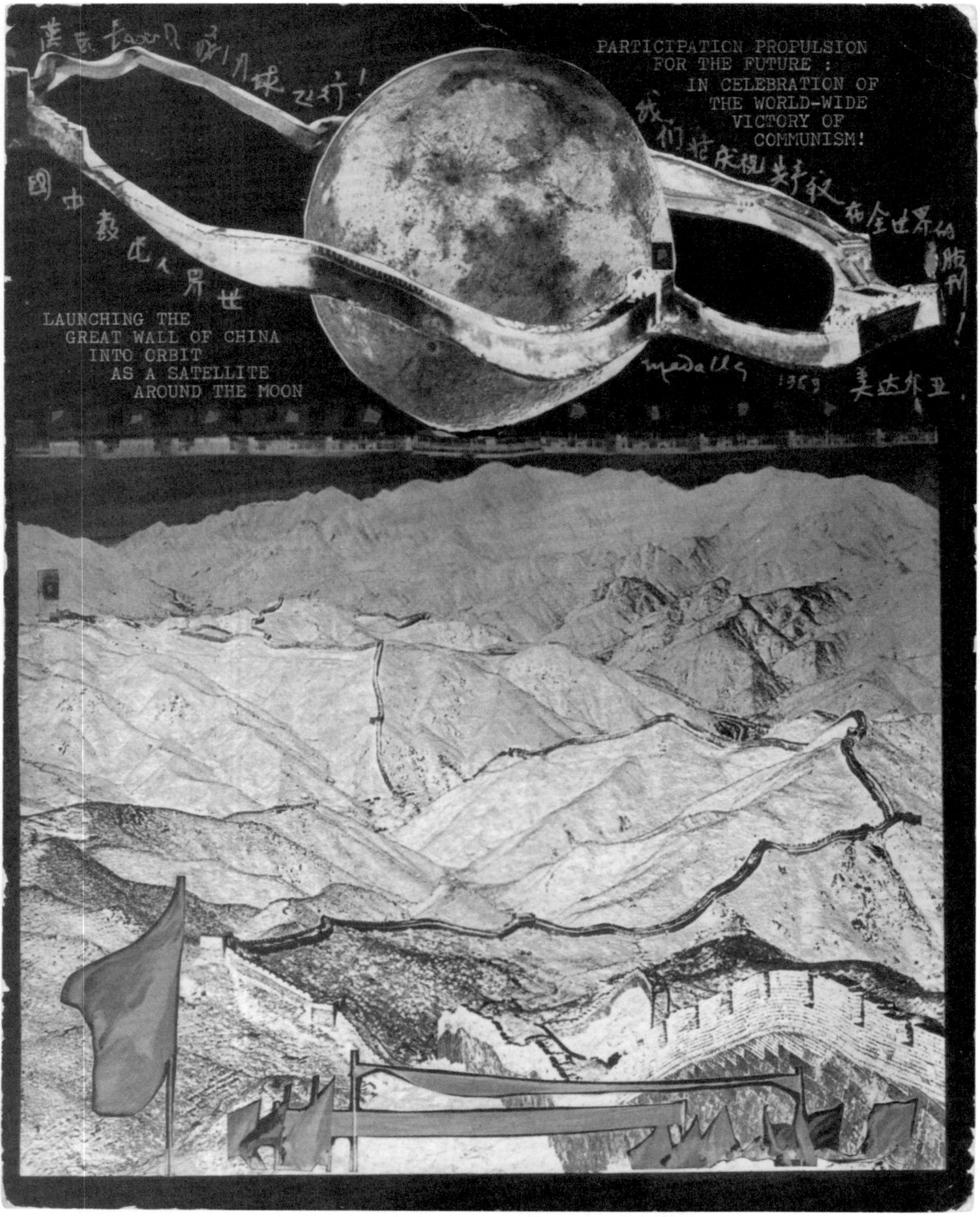
PARTICIPATION PROPULSION FOR THE FUTURE : IN CELEBRATION OF THE WORLD-WIDE VICTORY OF COMMUNISM!
LAUNCHING THE GREAT WALL OF CHINA INTO ORBIT AS A SATELLITE AROUND THE MOON

Director's Foreword

Ann Philbin

David Medalla: In Conversation with the Cosmos was initiated after an encounter I had with Aram Moshayedi in the exhibition *An Opera for Animals* at Para Site in Hong Kong in the spring of 2019. Aram and I were traveling together on one in a series of research trips to cities in East and Southeast Asia to broaden the scope of the Hammer Museum's collection, exhibitions, and programs. We found ourselves in front of *Sirens* (2019), a suite of photographs by Adam Nankervis of his longtime partner and collaborator, David Medalla. Medalla appeared in the images frail and ill, gripped by the aftereffects of a recent stroke. His contorted facial expressions were adorned by an array of fantastical masks constructed from the flotsam and jetsam of daily life, much like the ones he had worn in various contexts throughout the long arc of his decades-long artistic career. The pair produced the series while Nankervis cared for Medalla, and this manifestation of the intimacy they shared would be their final collaboration. The haunting and tender photographs persuaded Aram to pursue an idea that had been lingering in the back of his mind.

Aram already had been tracking Medalla in his research. Two years earlier, he had traveled to Manila with Steven Song, a member of the Hammer's board of directors, in order to better understand the artist's relationship to the Philippines, where he was born but lived only intermittently. Medalla began traveling internationally at a young age and moved to London in the early 1960s. Aram wondered how artists in the Philippines regarded Medalla and how much influence he had over subsequent generations, given the extent to which his career took place abroad. After his experience with Nankervis's photographs in Hong Kong, Aram decided to follow his instincts and explore whether an exhibition of Medalla's work might be possible.

The conversations that followed with Nankervis were encouraging, but Medalla's failing health and the conditions of a global pandemic made the pursuit challenging. In the end, Aram was not able to meet Medalla before he passed away in December 2020, and this reality has shaped the exhibition and publication in the years since. The research informing the project relies on both Medalla's historical biography and the mythology around his self-construction and inhabitation of multiple artistic personae.

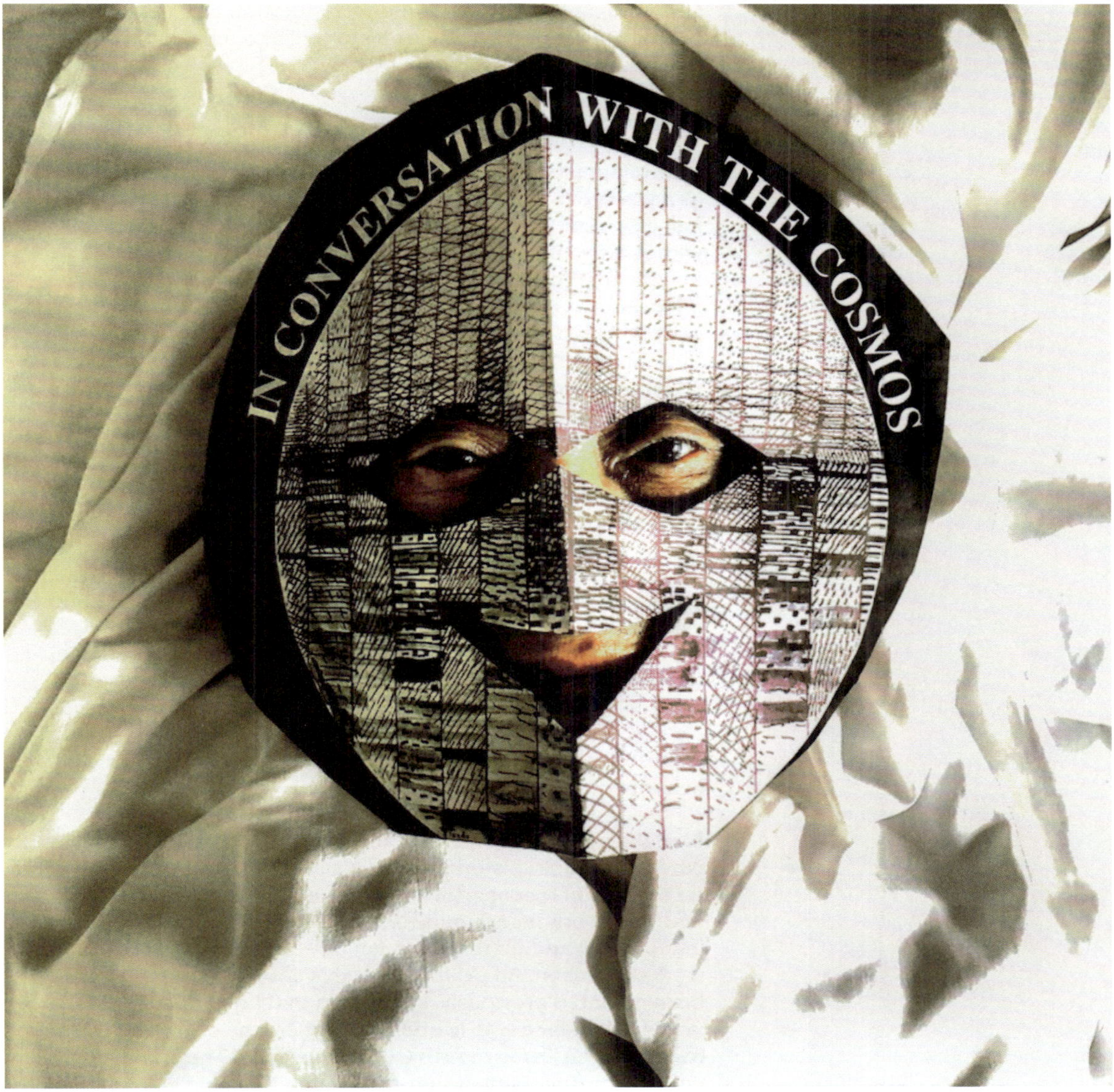

previous
Four Easy Steps, based on the original paper collage *Building the Great Wall of China around the Moon*, 1969/96. Enlarged photocopy. 32 3/8 × 25 11/16 in. (82.2 × 65.3 cm).

above
Adam Nankervis, *David Medalla in conversation with the cosmos*, 2017. C-print. 31 7/16 × 23 5/8 in. (79.8 × 60 cm).

Given Medalla's anti-institutional reputation and the degree to which his works evade art historical and museological constraints, the question of whether an exhibition can adequately represent an art practice that proved difficult to contain during his lifetime endures.

Aram's approach has been guided by those who knew Medalla and who collaborated with him at various moments over the last fifty or so years. Many of the insights come from Nankervis, without whom this undertaking would not be possible. His herculean efforts to preserve what he can of Medalla's legacy have made it possible for the Hammer to mount this exhibition of artworks, artefacts, ephemera, and scraps of documentation. The exhibition is archival in nature, meaning that it constructs a historical context for thinking about the artist's body of work. Without David's physical presence or direction, it would be brazen to assume it is possible to recreate the experience of his art—which was elusive, immaterial, and fleeting even while he was actively producing it. Instead, the exhibition constructs a portrait of an artist who never comes fully into focus.

Though the lion's share of material in the exhibition was loaned by the David Medalla Archive, overseen by Nankervis and another vacant space in Berlin, others who have preserved Medalla's art in their private and public collections have also enabled the telling of this story. On behalf of the Hammer Museum, I am grateful to the lenders for temporarily parting with their cherished objects and thus providing an opportunity for audiences to experience firsthand the artist's curious trajectories and self-described "cosmic propulsions."

Medalla holds a legendary status among a small cadre of artists, curators, and art historians, and his influence can be felt in many tendencies of recent artmaking. Yet representations of his diverse and varied practice in museums and institutions are woefully inadequate, and there have been few opportunities to view his works in person. An exhibition of this scope and density has not been mounted previously. I am proud that Los Angeles will share in this experience with Mexico City, where the exhibition will travel to the Museo Tamayo Arte Contemporáneo. The Tamayo was an early partner in the tour of this exhibition, and we couldn't be happier that Medalla's artistic output will be on offer to audiences there on such an expansive scale.

I am also appreciative of the Hammer Museum's staff, whose unwavering dedication allows for challenging projects such as this one to be realized. Aram remained invested in this exhibition and publication despite unforeseen obstacles and delays, and I am impressed by his devotion to Medalla's work and history throughout. He has led this exhibition alongside a truly inspiring team that helps all the curators of the museum realize their ideas and give shape to their thinking with and on behalf of artists. Curatorial assistant Nyah Ginwright inherited the project from former curatorial assistant Nicholas Barlow, and both undertook the heavy lifting that was required of them at various stages of its organization with equanimity and grace. I remain ever thankful for the guidance provided by the Hammer's deputy directors—Cynthia Burlingham, deputy director of curatorial affairs; Michael Harrison, deputy director of finance; and Fred Yeries, deputy director of external affairs—whose deep knowledge and understanding have helped contribute to the overall identity of the Hammer Museum as a steadfast and nimble institution. The museum's board of directors also contributes greatly to this reputation, and I cannot thank them enough for their individual commitments. The Hammer's board of advisors plays a sizable role in the growth of the museum's contemporary collection; their understanding of contemporary art helps inform how we shape the collection as part of an ongoing dialogue with the art of today.

We are deeply grateful to the exhibition funders The Andy Warhol Foundation for the Visual Arts, Karen Hillenburg, Christine Meleo Bernstein and Armyan Bernstein, the E. Rhodes and Leona B. Carpenter Foundation, David Regan and Edgar Cervantes, John Auerbach and Edward Tang, Beth and Ken Karmin, and Edward Lee. Their financial contributions have helped to make this endeavor possible.

Lastly, although David Medalla is no longer here to receive our gratitude, I am compelled to thank him for the sprawling and nebulous body of work that he has left in his wake. My sense is that his commitments to the merging of art and life and to otherworldly pursuits can only ever be represented as fragments. I am honored knowing that the Hammer is a place where an experimental exhibition of this nature can happen. We make no claims that *In Conversation with the Cosmos* provides a comprehensive view of Medalla's life and work, but we do hope it inspires audiences and artists alike to pursue the unimaginable.

Inspired by poet Octavio Paz's remark that,
'it is easier to discover a new planet than to find
a new way of making love,'
Artist David Medalla
will give an original
work of art and a full
body massage.
to anyone who can
invent a new way
of making love
that has not been
portrayed in the
sculptures of Khajuraho
in India, in the
<u>shunga</u> scrolls &
woodcuts of Japan,
in the ivory & wave
paintings of China,
in the Tantric images of
Tibet & Nepal, and in other
erotic artworks
in the world. Please send
your entries (drawings,
paintings, sculptures,
photos, videos, films, etc.)
to David Medalla
(address below) together with
self-addressed stamped envelope,
any time before the year 2000

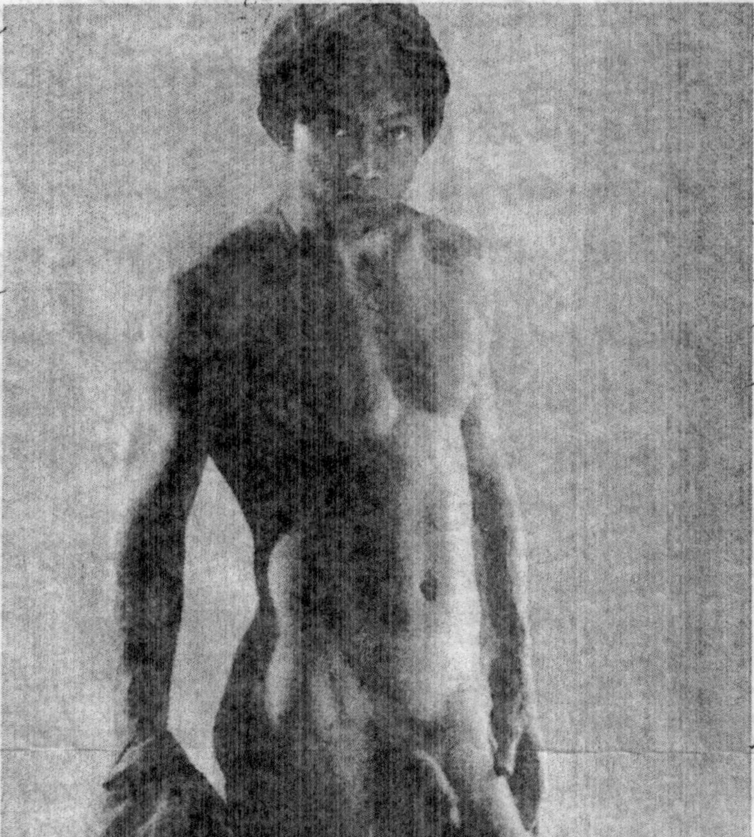

DAVID MEDALLA © 1994
23 LEXINGTON AVENUE, APT. #320
NEW YORK, NY 10010
TEL (212) 505-2542

A Love That Leaves No Traces

Aram Moshayedi

David Medalla dreamt of sculptures that would, in his words, "breathe, perspire, cough, laugh, yawn, smirk, wink, pant, dance, walk, crawl ... and move among people as shadows move among people."[1] Over the course of his life, Medalla seemed to have many dreams like these, which redefined the relationship between art and lived experience and the very nature of what is possible. Under the title "MMMMMMM ... MANIFESTO (a fragment)" (1965), Medalla outlines his expansive sculptural ambitions for an active, kinetic future at a moment of heightened conservativism and reductivist thinking. The manifesto appeared in the *Signals Newsbulletin*, which was published by Signals London, a gallery Medalla cofounded in 1964 with artists Gustav Metzger and Marcello Salvadori, critics Guy Brett and Christopher Walker, and curator Paul Keeler. The gallery ushered in a new era of experimental artmaking and provided an outpost for international artists such as Mathias Goeritz, Lygia Clark, Alejandro Otero, Takis, Otto Piene, Liliane Lijn, and Mira Schendel, whose innovative kinetic and interactive art fell outside of the mainstream British art establishment. Medalla's "auto-creative" biokinetic Cloud Canyons, known informally as "bubble machines," took shape at Signals. These ever-changing works mobilized an arsenal of tiny soap bubbles that slowly seeped and oozed from clear plastic tubes and makeshift wooden structures. They are arguably Medalla's most accessible contributions to twentieth-century art, and the clearest articulation of the dreams laid out in his manifesto.

Medalla recounted his inspiration for using soap bubbles in formative, visceral memories from his childhood that reveal the artist's penchant for self-mythologizing. He also once described his Cloud Canyons as "a cloud in trousers," borrowing from the title of a 1914 poem by the Russian Futurist Vladimir Mayakovsky.[2] While there may be nothing overtly sexual about the idea of a sculpture wearing pants, the mental image it evokes provides an early example of the sublimated desire that permeates Medalla's sixty-plus years of practice. Clay Perry's closely cropped photograph from 1964 captures one of the Cloud Canyons in the act of discharging foam that undeniably resembles the head, shaft, and base of a penis. The image makes explicit the eroticism of Medalla's practice, even as the framework he proposed for the sculpture at the time obscured that dimension.

Medalla's identity and sexual orientation seem to have been at the core of his artistic thinking from a young age. On a self-portrait rendered in paint and sand in a style reminiscent of Art Brut and the brand of Abstract Expressionism imported to the Philippines by artist Alfonso Ossorio, the artist wrote the name "Gaybriel." Hardly a coded reference, the title asserts Medalla's gay subjectivity, providing a lens through which his art can be better understood as an embodiment of desire. This claim is offered here not to recuperate Medalla as a "gay artist." This quality has been ever-present in his work, although it has been elided by critics, historians, and curators. Rather, it is important to consider how his sexuality shaped his artistic life and political objectives. Many

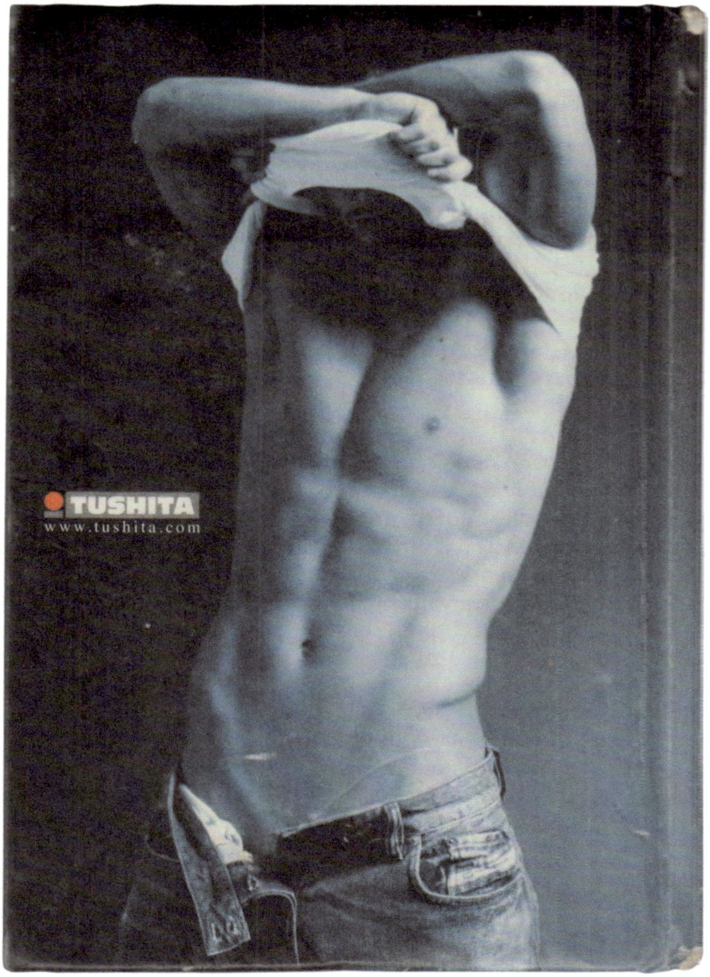

accounts of his life convey his charisma. His relationships with friends and lovers—many of whom he recorded in drawings and writing and with whom he made important collaborative works—were perhaps his most essential artistic materials.

Medalla often made art in homage to the artist and writer heroes from the European canon whose voices informed his identity. Their presence in his work indicates his own aspirations and the context of which he longed to be a part, even before he began traveling abroad. His artistic biography is peppered with names like Arthur Rimbaud, Piet Mondrian, Constantin Brâncuși, Vladimir Tatlin, and Kazimir Malevich. In clipped and collaged photographs of their faces, poems dedicated to their memories, ritual actions performed for a camera at their graves and monuments, and in many other instances, he dedicated himself to the legacies of his intellectual crushes. With these historical

previous
Inspired by poet Octavio Paz's remark that "it is easier to discover a new planet than to find a new way of making love…", 1994. Photocopy and ballpoint pen on paper. 10 ½ × 8 3⁄16 in. (26.7 × 20.8 cm).

above
Cover of *I am an enigma even to myself—An Artist's Archives*, 2009. Book. 6 1⁄8 × 4 5⁄16 × ½ in. (15.5 × 11 × 1.3 cm).

figures, he had lively imaginary conversations that were similar to the ones he shared in real life with his contemporaries—Marcel Duchamp, Louis Aragon, Gaston Bachelard, and James Dean among them. A handful of his early paintings and drawings depict creative figures from a non-European genealogy—namely Filipino painter Fernando Zóbel de Ayala and Filipino poet José Garcia Villa—but these instances are overshadowed by the abundance of men whose names uphold the Eurocentric view of Modernism that they themselves fashioned. Medalla's seduction by men of historical import was not without self-awareness. In a business card he carried during his time at the DAAD Artists-in-Berlin residence program in the late 1990s, he cheekily refers to himself as the originator and chairman of the "Endangered Species Foundation for the protection & preservation of single straight male artists."

The countless photo clippings that fill the pages of his many scrapbooks and notebooks evince the visual contours of Medalla's desire. Beneath a photo of an unnamed model donning perfectly parted, straight blond hair, a relatively recent tribal tattoo, and a pair of exotic swim briefs, the artist has added the caption: "My ideal lover and his mysterious tattoo." The notebooks that Medalla maintained throughout his lifetime are crammed with page after page of oiled and chiseled bodies, mostly white, mostly bare chested and shaved or waxed, in magazines and printed advertisements. While some faces are recognizable—River Phoenix, Justin Bieber, Rob Lowe, and other celebrity heartthrobs—anonymous underwear and swimwear models show just how ready-made Medalla's sexual fantasies could be.

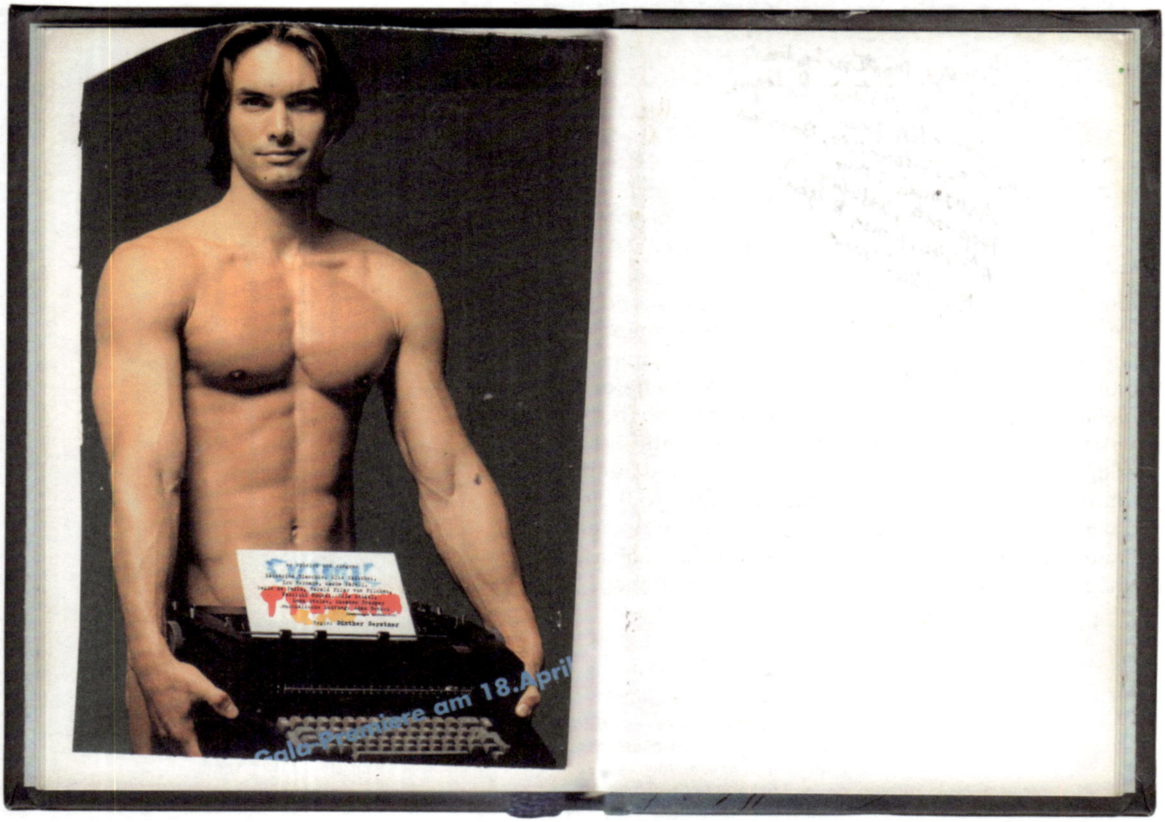

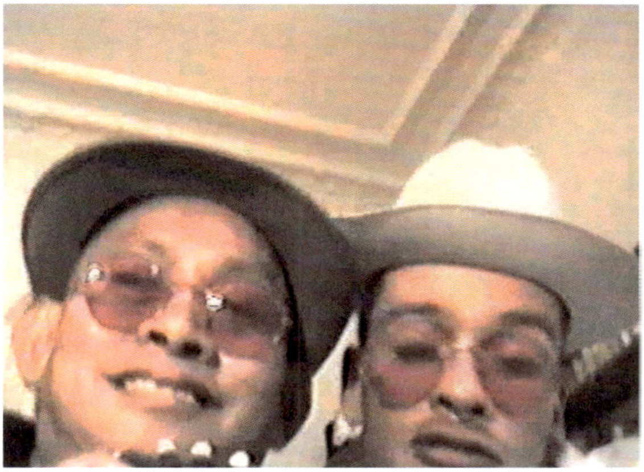
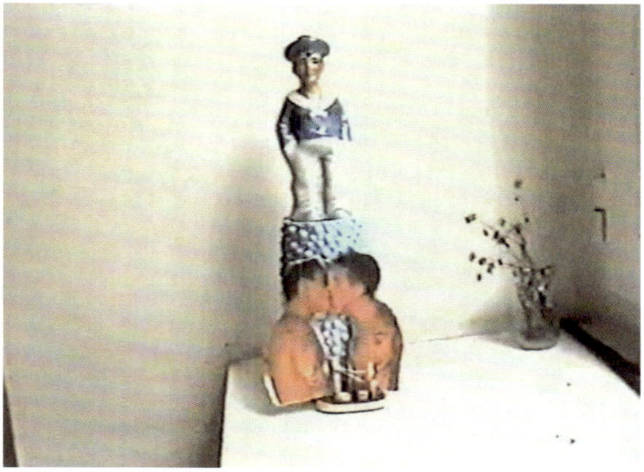

Medalla wrote and rewrote the story of his life onto pages that were simultaneously populated by his many infatuations from the annals of art history and mail-order catalogues. His poems, inner thoughts, and proposals for an unrealized autobiography and other publications were scrawled in the artist's ornate handwriting throughout his many notebooks. He also crossed out the title pages of existing books and handwrote his own name and other personal information in their place, as if they were books about him. Medalla's mode of writing and artmaking on top of existing materials is more than an economical byproduct of his experiences in the 1960s counterculture and the Maoist ideals he carried with him throughout the 1970s. The density of his output reveals how the artist was preoccupied, in equal measure, by his own professional narrative and the personal pleasures that seemed to guide it. The art and writing that Medalla left behind embody the spirit of a palimpsest—a biography of the artist that can be understood only according to its proximity to, and by being on top of, others. In documents and artworks, Medalla's contradictory and enigmatic biography emerges through the names and faces that captured his attention, as different as they often were from his own.

In an interview for the critical journal *Black Phoenix* in 1979, the artist Rasheed Araeen pressed Medalla about a critic who characterized the artist's status as marginal. Responding to Araeen's question about how Medalla had not been considered British despite a decades-long relationship with London, the Filipino artist replied, "I don't want to be a British artist, whatever that means."[3] He continued, "Well, whether I like it or not, I'm not going to be part of that central tradition of European culture. But that's not really my problem; that's a problem for Europe. This may sound arrogant on my part, but it's never been my problem. Having worked here off and on for nearly 20 years, I don't even have one drawing in an English art collection. That's not my problem; it's their problem."[4] The exchange with Araeen—an artist who was also no stranger to the regime of marginalization

opposite
Interior spread from *I am an enigma even to myself—An Artist's Archives*, 2009. Book. 6 1/8 × 4 5/16 × 1/2 in. (15.5 × 11 × 1.3 cm).

above
David Medalla and Adam Nankervis, *Colour Blind*, 1997. Stills from digital video, color, sound. 24:03 min.

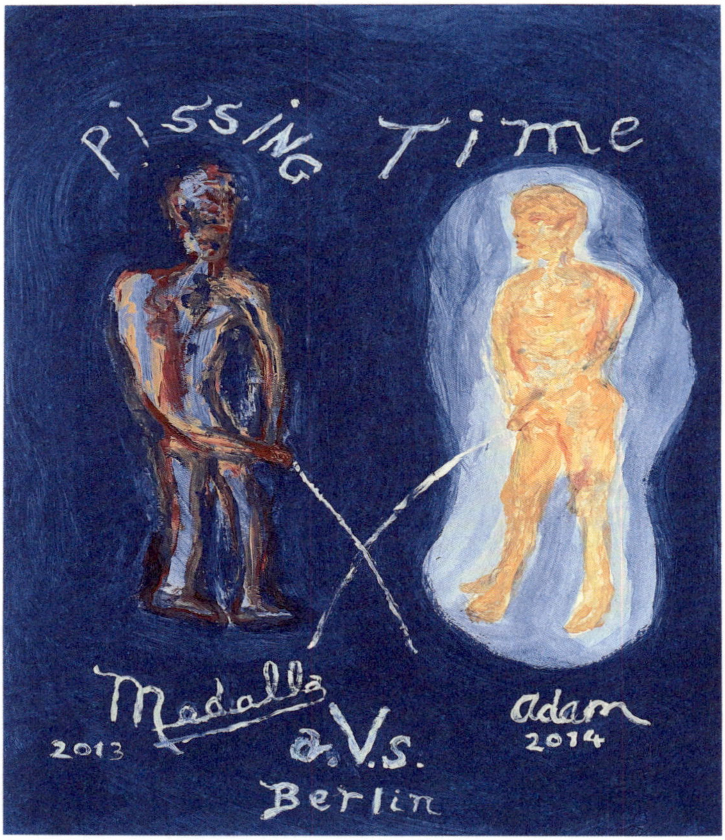

imposed by British and Western art traditions—indicates Medalla's ambivalence about his desire to belong to a context that denied him.

Perhaps in response to his estrangement from the mainstream art world that Araeen's line of questioning alludes to, Medalla seemed to pursue gratification in the shared spaces of political artmaking and collectivity. Throughout the period he spent living and working in London, he maintained a relationship with the cultural scenes of Manila. Particularly in the years that Ferdinand Marcos ruled by martial law from 1972 to 1981, Medalla remained emphatic in his criticisms of the dictatorship and the American empire that supported it. In September 1969, at the opening of the Cultural Center of the Philippines, a monument to Western culture that was sponsored by Imelda Marcos, Medalla appeared in protest with a small group of Filipino artists. "Stop prostituting the arts" read one demonstrator's sign; "We want a home not a fascist tomb," read another. The same year, curator Harald Szeemann invited Medalla to participate in *Live in Your Head: When Attitudes Become Form*, the influential exhibition of groundbreaking artworks from 1960s art movements, including

Postminimalism, Arte Povera, Land art, and Conceptual art. Medalla was at his most politically active in the late 1960s and early 1970s. As part of the Exploding Galaxy commune and collective, which he cofounded in London, he staged dance performances against the war in Vietnam. With Cecilia Vicuña, John Dugger, and Guy Brett, he launched Artists for Democracy, an organization "giving material and cultural support to liberation movements worldwide." And he produced performances and related artworks dedicated to the independence of African nations in the aftermath of colonial rule.

From an early age, Medalla produced participatory artworks that facilitated intimate exchanges through shared experience and audience participation. In *A Stitch in Time* (1968–2019), which was inspired by handkerchiefs he had embroidered and given to departing lovers, the artist invited visitors to sit together and stitch something of their own choosing onto a large swath of fabric. The process focused the attention of the performer/viewer on the closeness of a relatively small encounter and formed a direct line of communication between the artist and his fellow contributors. While his participatory works may have been driven in part by a desire to ameliorate the alienation he likely felt from the dominant art world, some of his drawings, sketches, collages, and notebooks indicate that he was also motivated by the fantasies, erotic connections, and sexual encounters that appear in his more private artmaking practice—in works that were rarely, if ever, exhibited publicly during his lifetime. To see these documents teeming with ejaculating penises and phallic protrusions alongside Medalla's more outward-facing production—the one aligned with collectivity, participatory artmaking, and a dematerialized art object—is to reconsider his practice along the lines of desire and difference. His interest in bringing people together in shared spaces appears to have been on a continuum with how he imagined bodies interacting in the privacy of his scrapbooks.

Medalla's use of the phrase "Cosmic Propulsion" to describe his biokinetic artworks after the 1960s takes on new meaning in the context of his more clandestine, inward-facing practice. Guy Brett, Medalla's most acquainted biographer, characterized this category of propositional art as "foci for imaginative reverie, which could both take a verbal and/or physical form."[5] The many erotic allusions that appear in Medalla's drawings offer another explanation of what Cosmic Propulsion might mean. The comparison between Medalla's formal experiments and his erotic sensibilities seems to have evaded even his closest interlocutors, who may have been in pursuit of a more nuanced argument couched in the conventions and methodologies of art history to better position Medalla among artists and artistic movements that came before him. With the benefit of distance, his works appear to be as much a result of his travels and encounters with collaborators and strangers who shared in his love of art, ideas, and the men—it was almost always, for him, men—who produce them. Evoking Medalla's sexual life as a

Pissing Time, 2013/14. Acrylic paint and felt marker on paper. 39 3/8 × 27 1/2 in. (100 × 70 cm).

defining aspect of his art offers an opportunity to liberate his work from the art historical categories and geographical styles that he was determined to dismantle.

Medalla's meaningful collaboration with his romantic partner Adam Nankervis, which lasted for nearly thirty years, has thus far evaded art historical investigation, likely because of the discipline's limitations. The personal and professional lives of the artists were intertwined in the Mondrian Fan Club, which they cofounded as a nebulous homage to Piet Mondrian. Comprising performances, photographs, videos, ephemera, merchandise, and more, the collaborative project emerged from their mutual admiration for the late Dutch painter. Even more so, the Mondrian Fan Club is the outgrowth of Medalla and Nankervis's love for one another. The quantity of photographs and videos that document their Mondrian-inspired "Impromptus" (spontaneous performative actions) in various urban and rural settings represent a travelogue of experiences they shared. The images that depict their time together under the pretense of Mondrian's legacy are tender and endearing, the byproduct of an intimate exchange between two people that was made public in the form of art.

It is difficult to characterize the nature of Medalla and Nankervis's exchange, but it is not solely a collaborative art venture. Love and affection are typically outside of the purview of art historical discourse. The vocabulary at our disposal is unsatisfying, and the fear of being overly sentimental leads one to take a more "rational" and "objective" perspective. But the desirous longing that pulses through Medalla's art is undeniable, and the love that he found in Nankervis is palpable in the works they produced side by side. In their video *Colour Blind* (1997), the two artists are warm with one another, their eyes sparkle, they are sweet and silly, and they are vulnerable, while the camera bears quiet witness. The dreams Medalla had for a sculpture that breathes, perspires, winks, and pants came to life in the collaborative bond he shared with Nankervis and other fellow artists. Perhaps his dreams for sculptural impossibilities were destined to materialize in the intimacy and love he found along the way.

Artists' Liberation Front leaflet, ca. 1971.

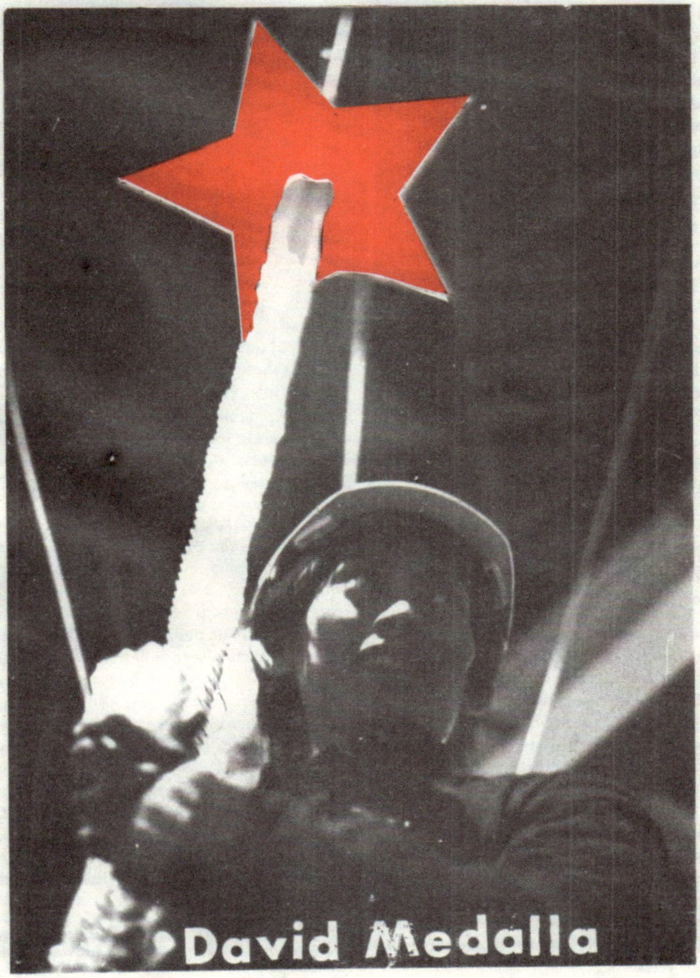

Socialist Art through Socialist Revolution!

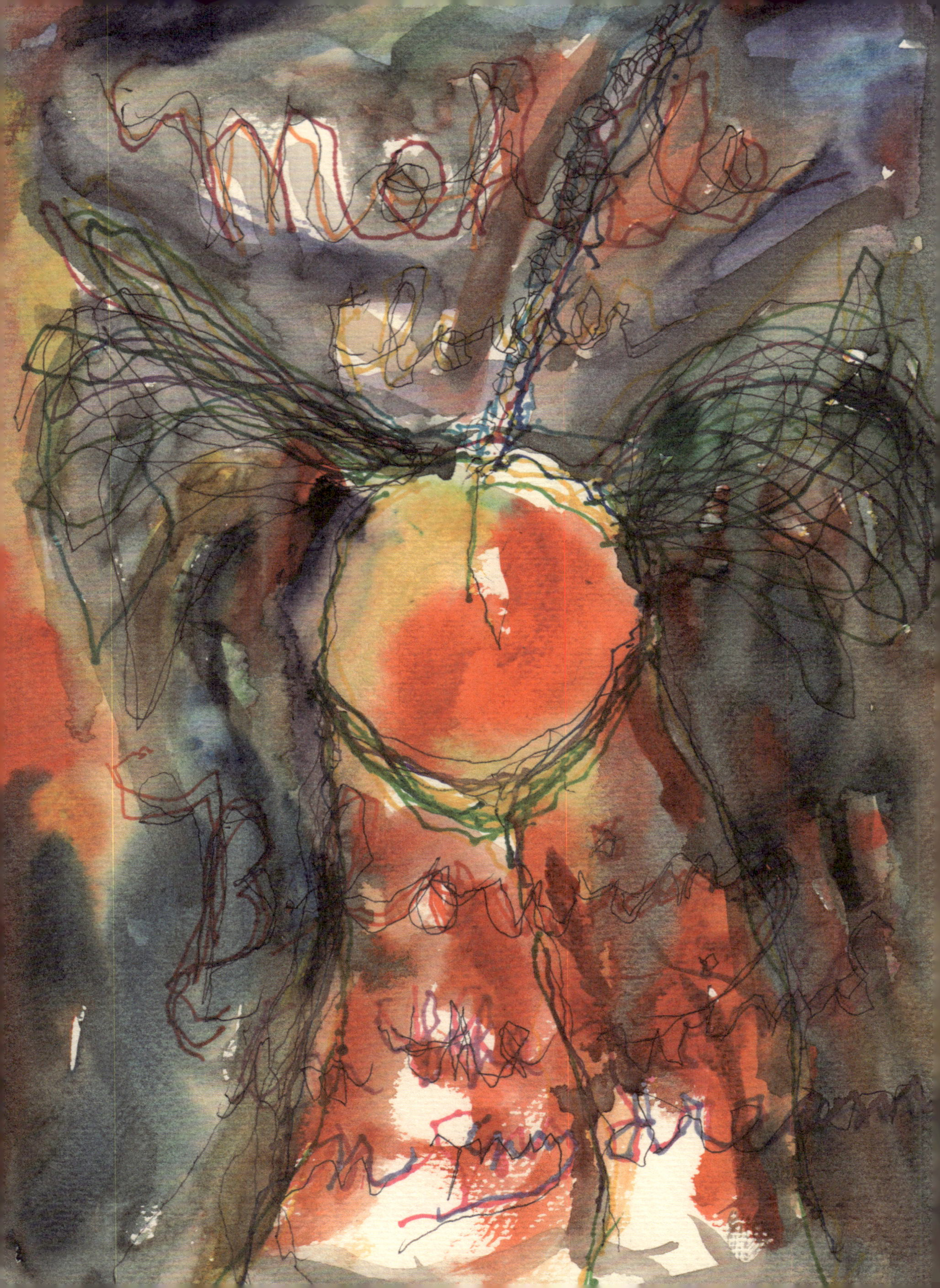

And then, and then, and then . . . David Medalla: A short tale about a flower, a letter, an egg, a monkey, and an artist

Magalí Arriola

> Was the subject dreaming? Or was it the artist who dreamt the subject of the portrait?
>
> David Medalla, *The Secret Portrait of...* (1954)

In 1965, David Medalla posed to himself a query: "Mmmmmmm... Mmmedalla! What do you dream of?"[1] This call draws out both the first letter of his last name and the moment of reflection that precedes the answer to a question. The pause also alludes to the images, thoughts, and sensations that occur in a person's mind during sleep, as well as to one's cherished aspirations in life. Medalla's response, in what he titled "MMMMMMM... Manifesto (a fragment)," outlined his dearest ambitions as an artist. He wrote, "I dream of the day when I shall create sculptures that breathe, perspire, cough, laugh, yawn, smirk, wink, pant, dance, walk, crawl... and move among people as shadows move among people.... Sculptures that will retain a shadow's secret dimensions without a shadow's obsequious behaviours.... Sculptures without hope, with waking and sleeping hours.... Sculptures that, on certain seasons, will migrate *en masse* to the North Pole."[2] His personal answer aimed to liberate his work, instead of following the dogmatic style of many manifestos of the historical avant-garde.

When Medalla wrote his manifesto using the authorial detachment of the third person, he wasn't far from reaching his goal of breathing life into sculpture. He was already working on his Cloud Canyons, soft plumes of soap foam generated by bubble machines, which he described as manifesting "the deepest possibilities of art in motion."[3] The everchanging sensuous forms came from his memories of "the waves of Manila's Sea, the oozing saliva of a dying Japanese soldier, the clouds over [the] Grand Canyon, ... [and] Marcel Duchamp's shaving cream."[4] He also aspired for the works to explore "how normally invisible forces could be made tangible, visible to the naked eye."[5] The movement and shapes of the soap foam were the result of the material's reaction to outside influences, such as temperature, gravity, atmospheric pressure and, not least, the presence of spectators. Medalla called these sculptures "biokinetic," a term he also applied to other works he produced between 1963 and 1967, including *Mud Machine* and the Sand Machine series. He saw these works as transformative, self-creating art situated at the crossover between nature and science.

The artist repeated the question "Mmmmmmm... Mmmedalla! What do you dream of?" and his answer came in the form of narrating a speculative voyage to the center of the earth. There he would place a sculpture, "a Mohole flower... [with] its petals curled like the crest of a tidal wave approaching the shore." Through the Mohole Flower series (1964–2019), he envisioned a "bio-thermal" mechanical sculpture that would wake at repeated intervals to light its center and unfold its petals,[6] to "re-emerge in various shapes from different parts of the world."[7] The various existing sketches, which both precede and follow the realization

previous
Mohole Flower Blowing in the Wind in my Dreams, 2019. Watercolor, ink pen, and felt-tip marker on watercolor paper. 14 ¼ × 10 ⁹⁄₁₄ in. (36.2 × 27 cm).

opposite
Announcement for *Biokinetics*, Indica Gallery, London, 1967.

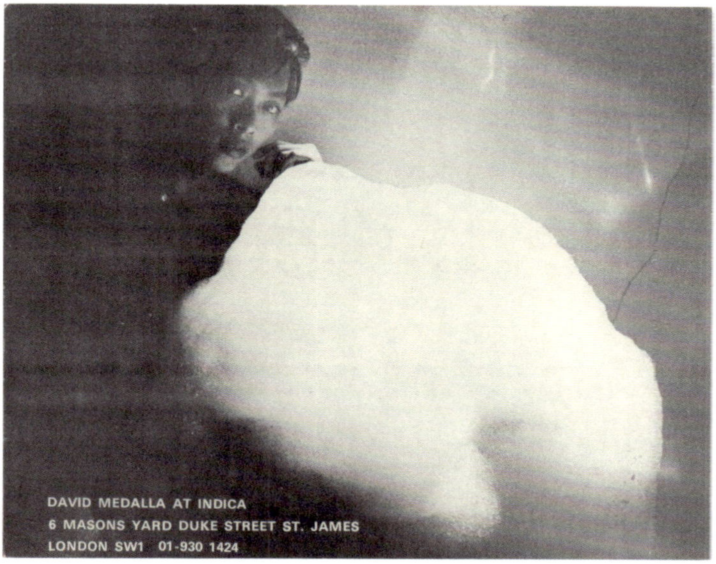

of the sculpture, depict it as a phallic-shaped organ ready to fertilize the center of the earth. The work took its name from Project Mohole, a utopian scientific investigation, started in 1957 and aborted in 1966, that consisted of digging to the core of our planet in order to extract a fragment of its crust. Many considered the project to be the result of a mid-twentieth-century space program in search of an intra-terrestrial frontier. Medalla conceived of "interior space and exterior space ... [as] mutually interchangeable,"[8] and he devised this and other projects as "cosmic propulsions"—initiatives that could be produced, performed, or simply exist as ideas that transcended time and art history, as "foci for imaginative reverie which could both take a verbal and/or physical form."[9] The planetary scale of Mohole Flower and the monumental proportions of other unrealized projects, such as *Peelable Sculpture*, a lush and layered organic shape the artist sketched in 1967, speak of Medalla's creativity as an expandable conceptual and poetic energy cross-pollinating art, technology, and nature. The artist viewed these forces as being in dialogue with the sociopolitical context of the era—the Cold War, post-colonialism, and the Vietnam War. Medalla believed the artist to be "merely an initiator ... of certain ideas that contain the seeds or the nuclei of new creative actions."[10] However, he would also reveal himself to be a conveyer or transmitter of an experimental and socially engaged collaborative energy, as the participatory projects that he would soon put into practice reveal.

For Medalla, art was "a living process in which one, two or several people formulate suggestions that others take up and develop in different directions.... Why not create a situation," he proposed, "where dance, poetry, singing, painting and sculpture

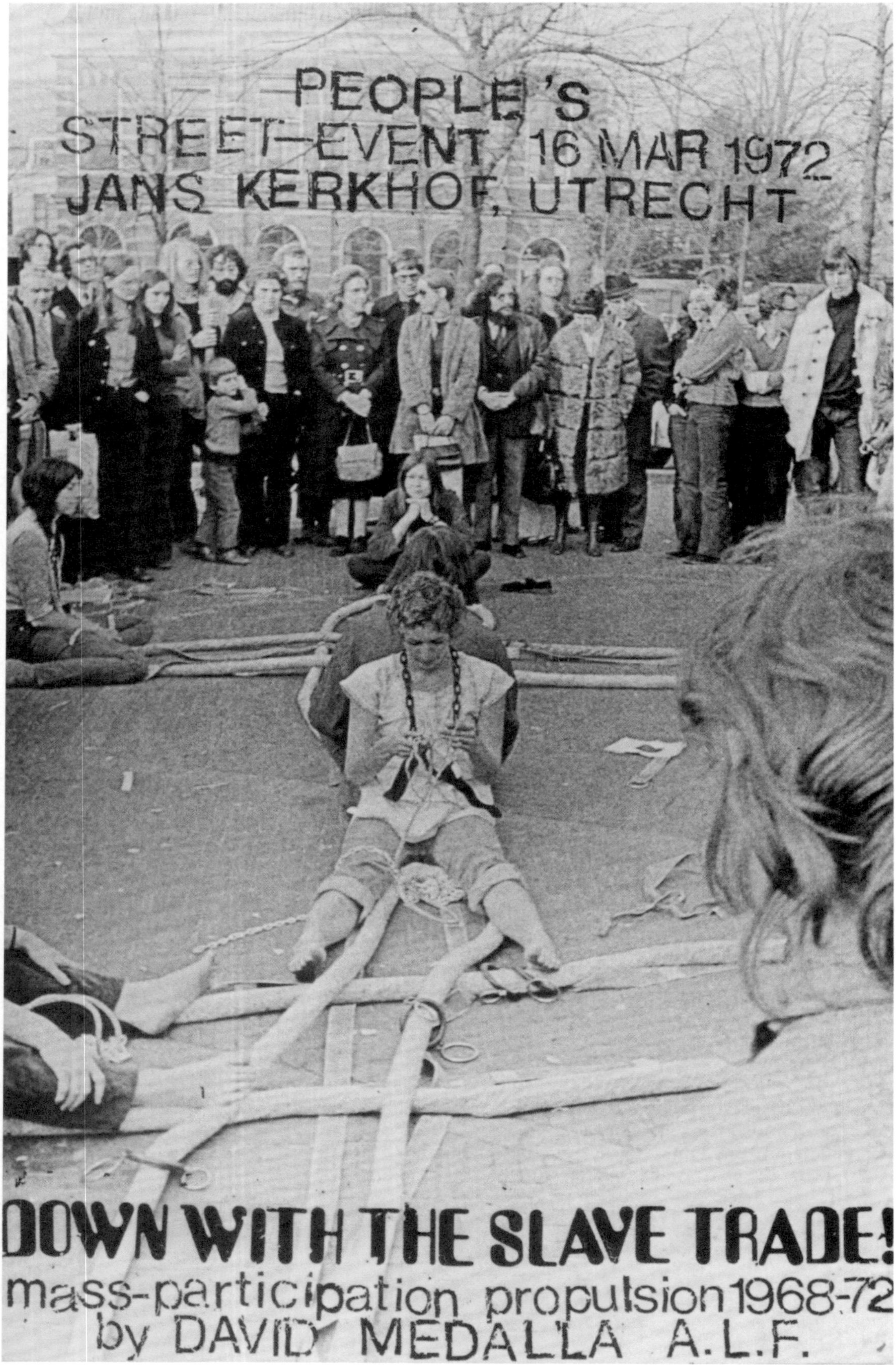
PEOPLE'S
STREET-EVENT 16 MAR 1972
JANS KERKHOF, UTRECHT
DOWN WITH THE SLAVE TRADE!
mass-participation propulsion 1968-72
by DAVID MEDALLA A.L.F.

could cooperate and penetrate each other?"[11] In order to bring these conditions into existence, Medalla opened a short-lived communal space called the Exploding Galaxy (1967–68). There, all kinds of participatory events and multidisciplinary performances took place, aiming to overcome the divide between the artist and the spectator, art and everyday life. In these "mass participation propulsions," each person's creative energy could be a catalyst for the transformation of society—eclipsing social norms, embracing counterculture, and transcending political barriers. *Down with the Slave Trade!* (1972) was one of these early participatory events. People were invited to insert themselves into a massive tangle of chains, plastic tubes, and color pennants. The web's configuration held participants together, making them rely on each other to move. Its structure was inspired by the organizing principles of Piet Mondrian (one of Medalla's preferred artists) and Georges Vantongerloo, who both searched for spiritual equilibrium through abstraction by stripping things bare from their formal appearance. Metaphorically, Medalla sought to free the chains and fetters from their association with slavery and oppression (just like, years before, he aspired to free sculpture from the servile behavior of its own shadow), and instead to celebrate communion by "link[ing] all the people in the world together."[12] As the curator Guy Brett stated, "What Medalla was clearly attempting to do [with propulsions] was to bring together an emancipatory social and political consciousness with an emancipatory notion of artistic structure, into a kind of reciprocal relationship."[13] The artist claimed, "Seizing the traditional symbol of slavery (chains) and discarding its conventional connotations [leads to] its paradoxical transformation."[14]

A decade later, the artist turned to using parables in his paintings to illustrate moral or spiritual lessons. In *Parables of Friendship: Myself and Lovato Guerrino at Castello in Venice* (1983), the first of the Parables of Friendship series, the artist portrayed, from memory, a moment on the eve of his performance *Voyages and Somersaults of the Pilgrim Monkey* (1981) at the Grand Salon Academy of Venice. Medalla recounted these origins of the painting in a letter written to its owner, Michael Adams, in 1985: "Guerrino entered the room [of the apartment in which he was hosting Medalla] in the moonlight bringing an egg from his parent's farm in Vicenza."[15] In the painting, Medalla tied the anecdote to many of the topics, characters, fables, metaphors, and concepts that comprise the cosmogony of his work.

As Medalla recalls, painting *Myself and Lovato Guerrino* was an "exhilarating experience, for it enabled [him] to capture in a relatively stable form an ephemeral and beautiful moment."[16] It also allowed him to resolve "synoptically" a composition that synthetized two of his major interests in painting—Mondrian's dynamic balance between the horizontal and the vertical and Henri Matisse's use of the arabesque—while incorporating various objects in the room that were to be utilized as props for his *Voyages and Somersaults* performance. *Myself and Lovato*

Poster for *Down with the Slave Trade!*, Utrecht, the Netherlands, March 16, 1972.

Guerrino encapsulated the artist's idea of synoptic-realism, which incorporated, in Brett's words, "the visual, understood in its contemporary form as a complex mosaic spanning everything from optical sensation to paravisual phenomena and dreams, together with the level of subjective sensations, volitions, desires, aspirations, memories, in their complex interactions with the conditions (historical, economic, cultural, linguistic) in which people live."[17] In this and other works, Medalla's synoptic-realism collapsed time and space and brought together personal acquaintances, historical characters, different cultures, and various geographies in order to articulate a multisensorial approach to the trivial but meaningful events that constitute everyday life.

In *Voyages and Somersaults*, Medalla performed wearing a mask while weaving together spoken anecdotes and allusions to his personal and artistic universe: the connection between the Portuguese explorer Ferdinand Magellan and the artist's native Philippines; an improbable meeting between Renaissance painters Antonello da Messina and Giorgione di Castelfranco; and the interplay between actor James Dean—to whom the artist dedicated *The Secret Portrait of…* in 1954—and a toy monkey.[18]

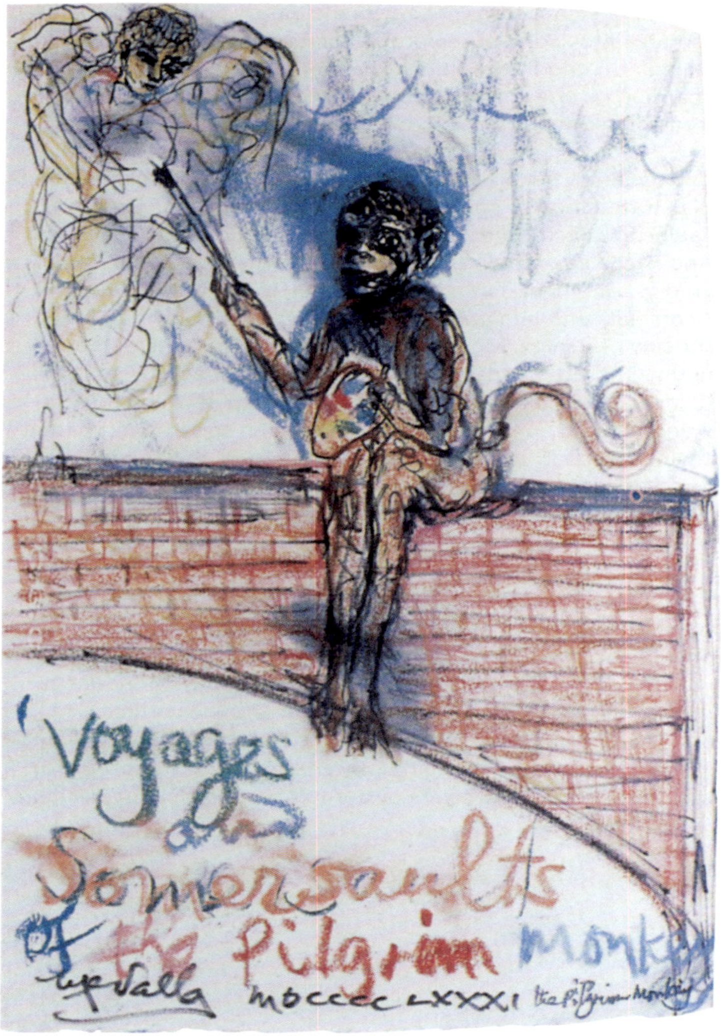

This monkey, who was the main character of the performance and Medalla's alter ego, had the ability to somersault through space and time, transcending social, cultural, and historical borders. In the performance, "every somersault involves a meeting with another animal and each refers to an artistic problem."[19] The monkey encounters a boxing kangaroo acting in a circus in Toulouse-Lautrec's nineteenth-century Paris, a rhinoceros painted by the Italian art historian and curator Roberto Longhi, and *King Kong* projected in a movie theater at the height of Abstract Expressionism in New York. In this and many other works, Medalla demonstrated a profound interest in art history through various means, including imaginary rendezvous with historical characters, such as the painter Johannes Vermeer, in his first performance from 1975, *Johannes Vermeer of Delft*, and his formation of the Mondrian Fan Club, with the artist Adam Nankervis in 1991. In the 1990s and 2000s, the Mondrian Fan Club performed spontaneous actions that Medalla called "Impromptus." These ephemeral works contemplated the figure of the Dutch painter Piet Mondrian and the nature of creation as an emancipatory force. Like his more elaborated narrative mise-en-scènes, these poetic interventions frequently involved masquerade and were meant to quietly unsettle the social fabric and playfully re-signify public space.

Medalla's 1985 letter about *Myself and Lovato Guerrino* created a sort of mise en abîme. By zooming into a canvas that described the making of a performance, which hinted at meaningful encounters and events in the artist's life, the letter revealed how deeply interlaced staging, storytelling, and painting were in his practice. It also referred to a series of concepts and notions that were at the core of his writings, installations, paintings, Impromptus, and performances during the span of his career: the transiency of memory, time and space travel, the magnetism of chance meetings, and the charm of long-term friendship. All of these themes concatenate to give substance to what Yve-Alain Bois described as "the sense of the infinite unfolding that [his work] entails (the 'and then, and then' of David's narration)."[20] Medalla perceived life as a continual stream of change; he was constantly on the move, recasting cultural, racial, and sexual identity. He enacted figures of speech as poetic mechanisms to emancipate things and concepts from their literal denotation and to liberate sensuousness and desire from the restricting boundaries of heteronormativity. Having left his Philippine homeland at an early age, he nevertheless kept evoking his childhood memories, conjuring cultural histories and traditions, and supporting political, sexual, and artistic dissidence. He believed in dreams and narratives as creative and transgressive strategies that allowed him to explore the relationship between the self and the collective and to mediate the individual experience within the public realm. Undoubtedly, Medalla captured "that fleeting, magical moment of the kind that matters only to the individual,"[21] but he always transfigured it into an experience relevant to others too.

Title page of the script for *Voyages and Somersaults of the Pilgrim Monkey*, 1981.

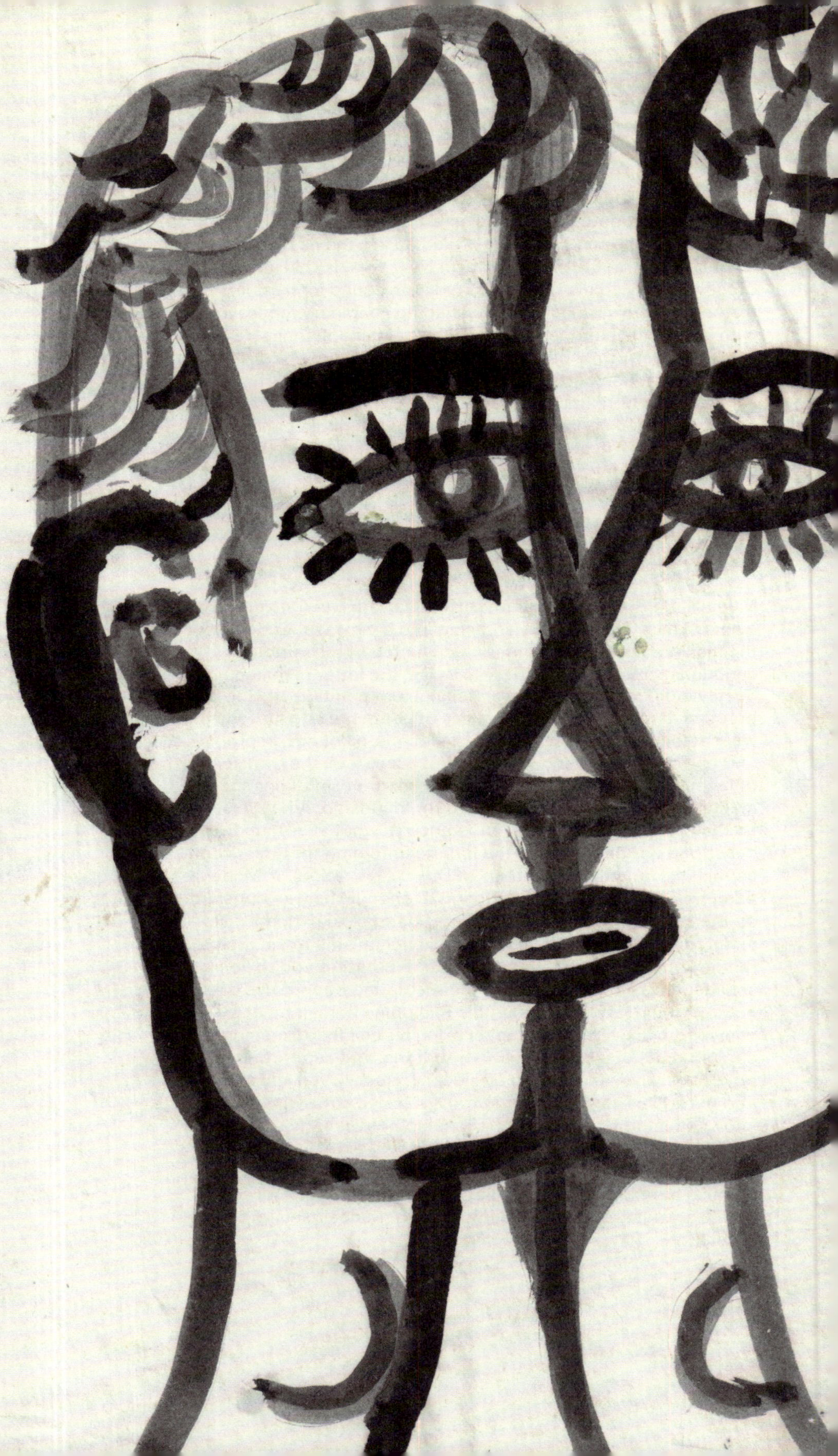

What the Wind Carries

CJ Salapare

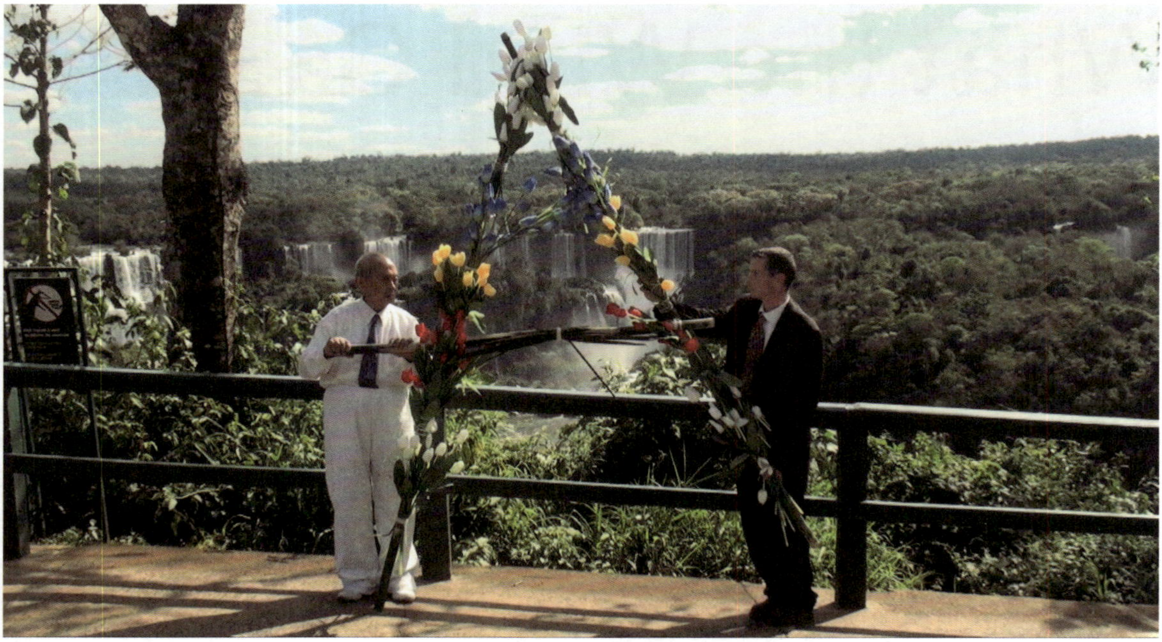

In what ways can artists be present when they are no longer present in body, when only the objects they made remain: how can they continue to exert a spiritual, a creative, an emancipatory force?

Guy Brett, *Exploding Galaxies: The Art of David Medalla*

If our lot is mutability of form, then why be surprised that our energies might not be refracted and recurrent in the world . . . ?

Mark Doty, *What Is the Grass: Walt Whitman in My Life*

In 1911, in Paris, Dutch artist Piet Mondriaan dropped a letter from his last name.[1] Nearly a century later, in São Paulo, David Medalla and his partner, Adam Nankervis, wondered why. Following Mondrian's example, they elided the city's name twice over, resulting in *so pulo*, which they were pleasantly surprised to learn means "I jump" in Portuguese. *So Pulo* became the subtitle for the third part of Medalla and Nankervis's exhibition *The Secret History of the Mondrian Fan Club*, which took place at Baró Galeria in São Paulo in 2010.[2]

The letter did not disappear entirely. In Medalla and Nankervis's Impromptu performance *Tulips for Iguazu* (2010), the *A* reappears in wooden form, festooned with silk tulips and framed by the Iguazu Falls, a natural wonder sited at the border of Argentina and Brazil. Mondrian's iconic grids give way to the lush greenery of local flora; the painter's characteristic primary colors are transposed from plane to petal; and his crisply contained surface is brought

previous
Untitled, ca. 1957. Graphite and China ink on paper. 11 × 8 7/16 in. (28 × 21.5 cm).

above and opposite
Renata Padovan, *Tulips for Iguazu*, 2010. Still from digital video, color, sound. 7:35 min.

into communion with the world—waterfall, tourists, and all. Renata Padovan's film of the performance records its ritual-like proceedings. Items are gathered and the oversized letter is made and carried to the site. A banner and other participants appear; a metallic flower is taken apart and reconstructed. Instead of spoken word, a soundscape fills the ear: a knife's whittling, rushing water, a ringing bell.

The modest components of *Tulips for Iguazu* seem at odds with the lofty connotations of "cosmic graffiti," the artists' term for their whimsically crafted letters based on Mondrian's name (and coincidentally, their own), which they displayed over time in locales familiar and far-flung. As legend has it, the sequence of letters was intended to spell out a sentence: A signal in the sky.[3] Though this string of words did not fully materialize, its letters are not merely stranded moments in time. A part can illuminate the whole—and the world. Within this frame, the *A* moves fluidly across signification and scale—miniscule one instant, larger than life the next.

This recurring meeting of the quotidian and the quixotic gives Medalla's art its confounding beauty. These qualities often merge through stray details and moments of digression, as we see in the glimpses of life that intercut *Tulips for Iguazu*. A bird rests; a caterpillar slithers on a rock; the Iguazu Falls roar. Mid-performance, we behold a chance meeting: a butterfly lands on Medalla's hand, and he offers it to his partner. A bridge forms where their fingers touch, and the butterfly changes hands. What elsewhere seems extraneous here feels essential. This fleeting exchange could be a metaphor or a crafty allusion, a world of meaning unto itself, or a glimmer of beauty and no more. Everything commingles within Medalla's conditions of creation; nothing appears individual or isolated. The matter at hand for us, then, is to divine how interconnected such entities are—and could be.

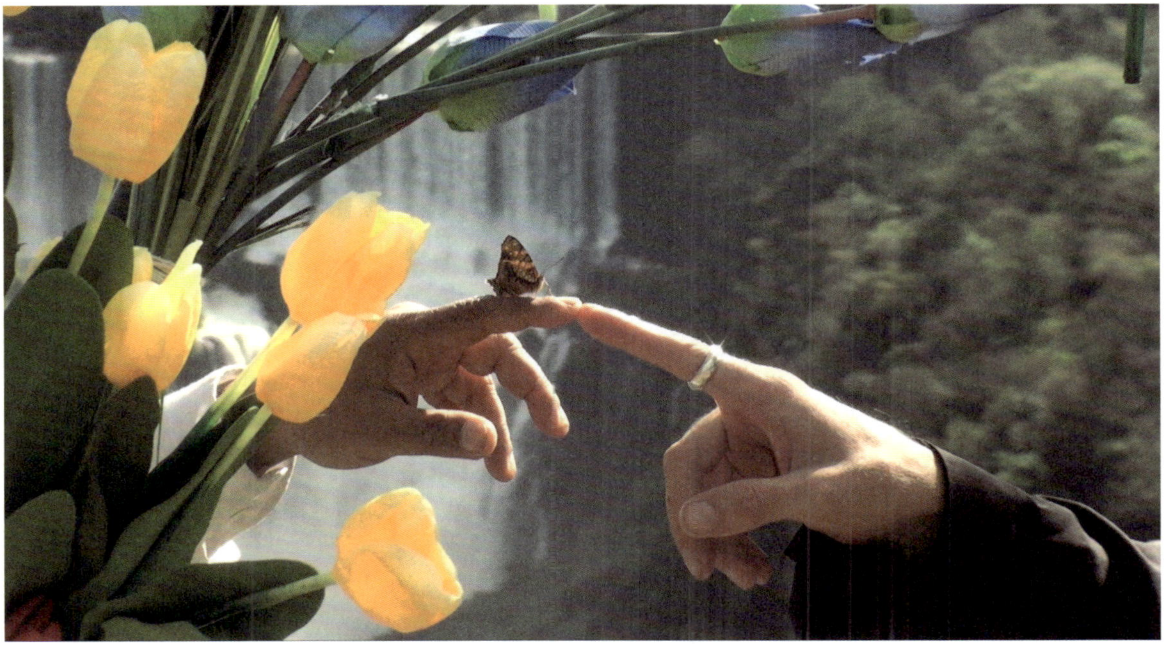

"He comes with the wind."[4]

In her foreword to *Exploding Galaxies*, Dore Ashton looks up to Medalla. "Every once in a while he alights like a mythical bird, flutters about doing serious reconnaissance, and departs, leaving a feather or two."[5] Pinning down his elusive presence seems like a futile task. Do we capture the bird, or map its landings and patterns of flight? Should we try to catch what the wind carries, like a feather or birdsong? I often wonder if we could just feel and follow the wind itself.

Since Medalla's passing in 2020, we are beginning to revisit the artist's transdisciplinary—often ephemeral, unrealized, or even utopian—works from a bird's-eye view, without the artist and the dual fashioning of self and art that propelled his practice. This way of making involved an entanglement of means: narrating, catalyzing, living, connecting. To try and unspool these threads reveals Medalla as a serpentine spinner of tales, a delightfully capricious narrator of "life as it is, [and] life as it ought to be."[6]

A story of love's loss and its serendipitous return inspired *A Stitch in Time* (1968–2019). In 1968, Medalla gifted two departing lovers with needles, spools of thread, and handkerchiefs, each stitched with the artist's name and "a brief message of love." Both recipients left London for opposite sides of the world, never to be seen again by the artist. Years later, at Schiphol Airport in Amsterdam, Medalla spotted one of his stitched handkerchiefs sewn to a larger piece of cloth adorning a stranger's backpack. The artist recalled, "The young man said someone in Bali gave him the column of cloth and told him he could stitch anything on it.... I handed [it] back... but I did not tell him that [it] started as my 'stitch in time.'"[7]

Like its originary tale, the iterative installation *A Stitch in Time* begins with exchange. People are invited to sew items of their choosing—trash, treasure, or trifle—onto a sweeping swath of fabric; above, spools of multicolored thread are held aloft by a ladderlike apparatus of wood and rope. Together, they craft collective tapestries of memory, with each unique iteration bearing the labor of a different assembly of hands. As the work continues, conventions of time, space, subject, and signifier are made porous, almost playful. For the artist, one pleasure of stitching was the privacy of mind it afforded, even with neighboring sitters close by.[8] To stitch in time, therefore, is to illuminate how creation itself is relational, co-constitutive, and ongoing: making as always *in medias res*.

Along these lines, many have noted how affect and affection are integral to *A Stitch in Time*'s architecture of relations.[9] The boundary is always blurred between giver and recipient within these circuits of reciprocity, and this push and pull serves as a

David Medalla and participants working on *A Stitch in Time* in the exhibition *A Survey of the Avant Garde in Britain*, Gallery House, London, 1972.

metabolizing force. What one gives, no matter how simple or brief, is the catalyst; whatever one takes away becomes another seed[10]

What has David Medalla given us?

A life's work; an ongoing case of vertigo; trails of fragments, unruly memories, and fractal-like thoughts; an incomplete history; an archive befitting the artist's anti-institutional leanings; an example of resourcefulness in the face of ascriptive conditions—economic, racial, sexual, and otherwise; a case of Peter Pan syndrome; a baron in the trees;[11] a limiting case in art history; a dead end to be enlivened; an ongoing philosophy on the mutability of form; a primer on identity's flux and fixity; a manifesto on the liberty of imagination; a modern-day oral tradition (anyone who knew him personally will regale you with a tale or two); parables of friendship (and friction) amounting to a life made, lived, and told.[12]

What we experience in this incomplete accounting is what Yve-Alain Bois described as the "'and then, and then' of David's narration."[13] Bois revisited Medalla's work while writing a dual obituary-cum-memoir on him and their dear friend Guy Brett. While leafing through the artist's notebooks and listening to him rhapsodize, Bois recalls how "complexly sedimented all his

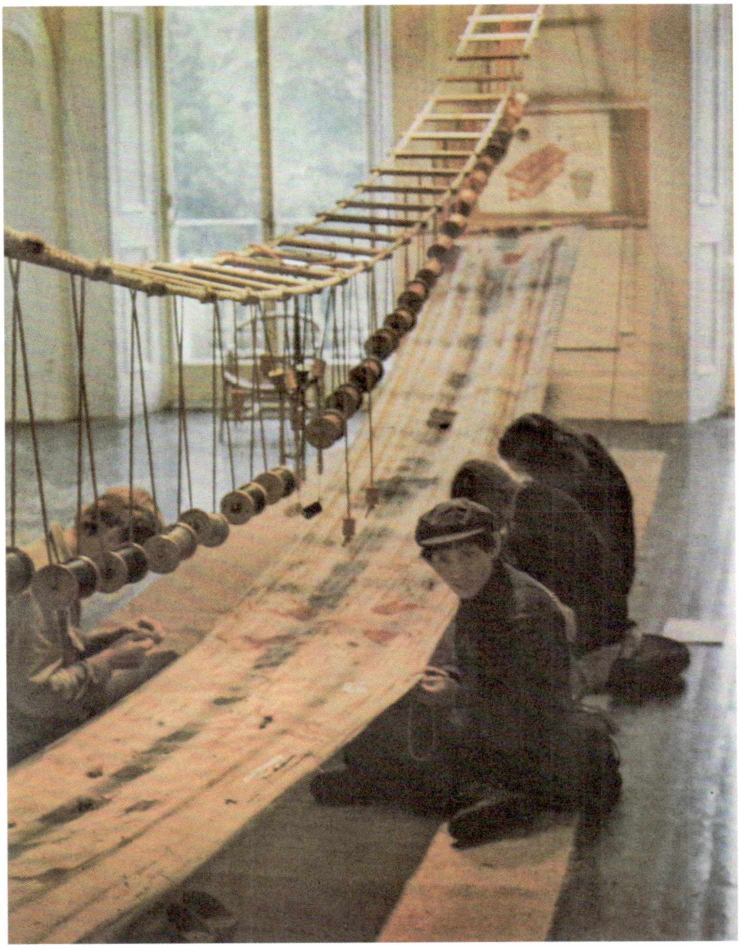

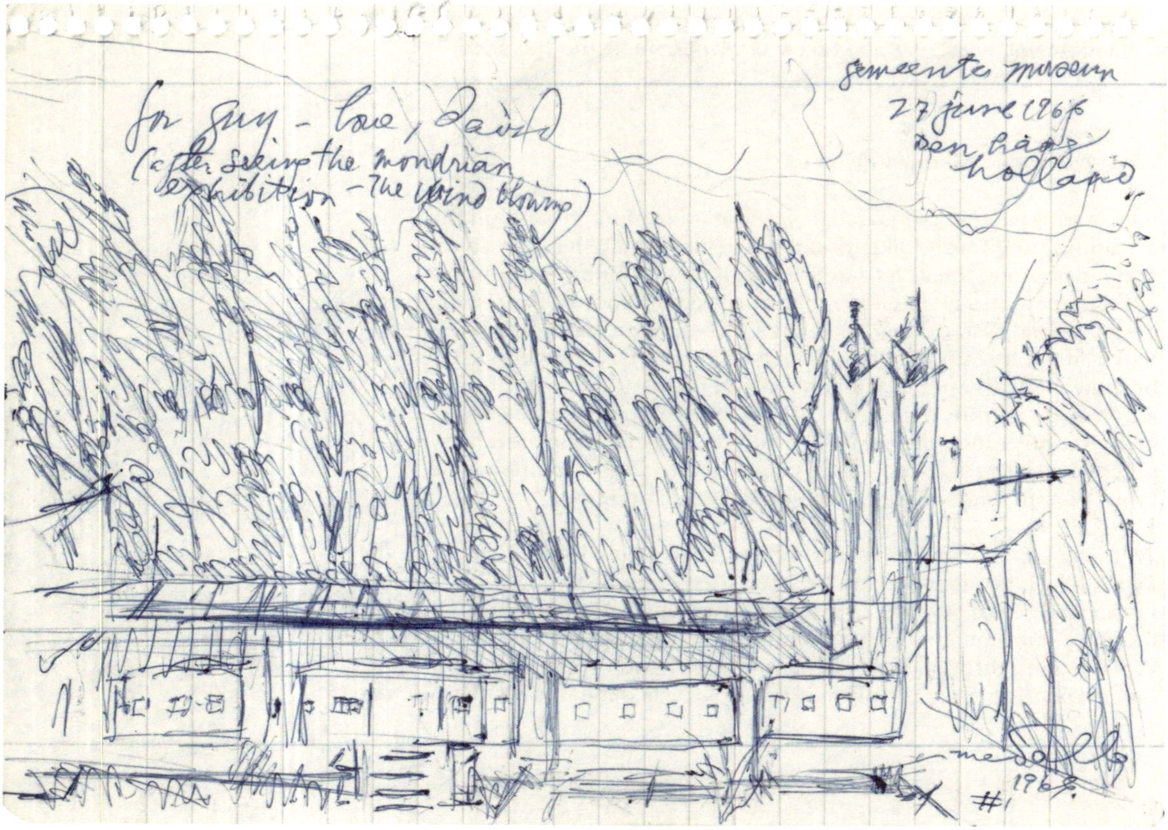

projects already were at the embryonic level. There were always at least three or four historical and cultural narratives, both local and global, intertwined in any single project, always several possible points of entry, always multiple levels of potential interpretation."[14]

Across time, Bois seems to commune with Medalla, who coined the term "synoptic-realism" in 1979 to describe his works and their synthesis of methods. In the artist's words, these works "articulate in coherent, vibrant, imaginative and organic ways [one's own] multiple experiences of reality, and ... construct the forms most appropriate to these experiences of reality."[15] For Medalla, these registers cannot be cleanly separated or categorized, insofar as these actions imply a sense of closure. A "work" is a world unto itself; the atomic doubles as the cosmic. The artist mingled poetry and physics because their pursuits share a vital impulse: to dilate as they distill.

This multivalence presents a challenge for anyone writing about Medalla, which Rasheed Araeen likened to "putting an elephant in a birdcage."[16] I wonder if there are ways of writing that can approximate the registers of synoptic-realism, which partly

for guy—love, david #1, 1966. Ballpoint pen on ruled paper. 5 7⁄8 × 8 1⁄16 in. (15 × 20.5 cm).

entails moving from a logic of containment to one of artistic consonance. What vessels—words, concepts, affect, and sentiment—can channel an artist's sensibility and convey a multiplicity of experience? To make sense of things, the art historian's recourse is to interpret and explain: to get under the skin, uncover a hidden schema, and inch toward a mastery of understanding. Of course, such an approach is useful and at times necessary. However, for an artist like Medalla, other modes might be more fitting—and potentially freeing.

What we talk about when we talk about Medalla is neither precision nor certainty. *What*, then? To narrate or describe his work is more difficult than it appears, for the arts of ekphrasis and metamorphosis are an incommensurable pair. As such, description's stakes could not be higher: its aim, which Sharon Marcus, Heather Love, and Stephen Best term *robust realism* (echoing Medalla's own designation of synoptic-realism), insists on marginalia, errant detail, and their means of interrelation.[17] How we connect these wayward threads can animate that which has permanently changed: the experience of Medalla's art, a shared reality now defined by degrees of remove rather than through one's direct interaction and collaboration. For those "sensitive strangers" to the artist's work, how might these gaps be bridged when he is nowhere to be found?[18] It's a leading question, since the artist can also be present everywhere, depending on what we bring and how openly we look.

To carry something of his spirit and to create in his manner—perhaps these are means of conjuring his presence and continuing his tales.

On June 27, 1966, Medalla was inspired to catch the wind. His tools of choice were spiral-bound paper and a blue pen. In the resulting drawing, blue lines of scribbles skew diagonally to our left, rising, at times swirling, shifting erratically between horizontal and vertical leanings. Together, they envelop much of the paper's surface; its evenly spaced printed lines seem to fade into the wind's thickets. Between the wind and the paper's edges, the artist's characteristic handwriting offers some context, including the location ("outside the Gemeente Museum in Den Haag [Netherlands]") and the moment in time ("after seeing the Mondrian exhibition—the wind blowing"). That Medalla was gripped not only by Mondrian's masterworks of dynamic equilibrium but also by what lay outside the museum is apt: wind eludes sight but cannot escape sense.

Additional text on the drawing shows that the artist did not simply want to commit a memory to paper but also to share it with another: "for guy—love, david." Medalla's companion during this trip to Holland was Guy Brett, who was his close collaborator and became a lifelong friend. Together with Gustav Metzger, Marcello Salvadori, Christopher Walker, and Paul Keeler, they cofounded

Signals London, an experimental gallery in postwar Britain for artists working at the crossroads of interdisciplinarity and internationalism. The drawing is part of a set of eight works on paper that offers an intimate view of their friendship's quarters. Here we see not the manifestos, moving sculptures, and heady debates that we associate with Signals' and kinetic art's histories,[19] but rather quiet and fleeting moments spent in one another's thrall. Another rendering in the series depicts the contents of their luggage, which Medalla drew five minutes before the pair departed for London. Souvenirs abound, including Van Gogh postcards, catalogues on Vermeer and Mondrian, and tulip seeds. At Schiphol Airport, Brett would soon add one more item to his suitcase: a sealed brown envelope with the eight drawings inside, a gift from Medalla.[20]

In *Some Reflections on the Random in Life and Art* (1985), Medalla opined, "The invisible is the totality of what we call life in all its manifest forms: the unity of the micro-cosmos and the macro-cosmos. We apprehend this unity only at certain inspired moments."[21] Until his passing, the artist opened himself up to these

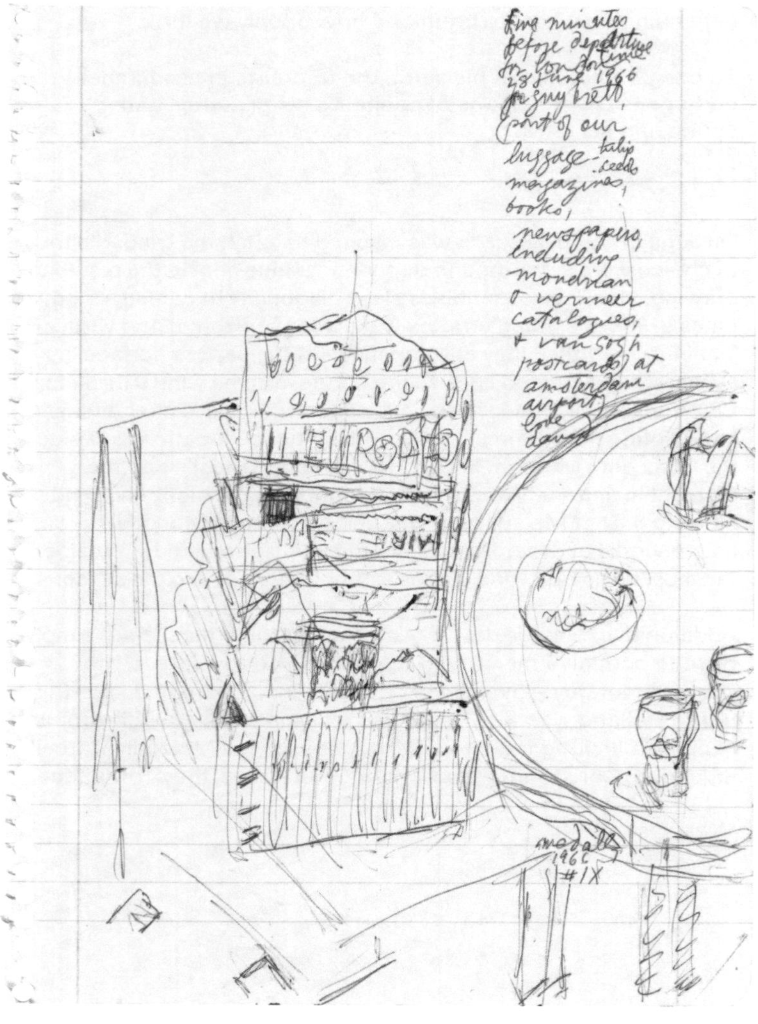

moments of chance and coincidence, a perpetual exercise in wonder. What we are left with is one possible raison d'être: an enduring drive for drawing forth life's invisible yet interconnected dimensions through art—beyond the confines of one's life and a lifetime.

Perhaps this explains why the artist was fascinated with the solitary tulip in Mondrian's studio—"preserved" mid-bloom, encased in metal, and symmetrically arranged—that Medalla had seen in André Kertész's iconic 1926 photograph.[22] Kertész recollected how he "instinctively tried to capture in [his] photographs the spirit of [Mondrian's] paintings... He had a vase with a flower, but the flower was artificial. It was colored by him with the right color to match the studio."[23] Medalla never met Mondrian. He knew of this tulip only through Kertész's black-and-white photograph and presumably from stories told and overheard. With no certainty on the flower's color or material composition, the artist resorted to wonder. On the exhibition page for *The Secret History of the Mondrian Fan Club: So Pulo*, he wrote, "I like to imagine Mondrian painting his solitary tulip a different primary colour with the changes of the season in a given year: yellow in spring, red in summer, blue in autumn, and white in winter."[24] Once again, metaphor is subject to metamorphosis.

In 1991, Medalla and Nankervis founded the Mondrian Fan Club in New York, with Guy Brett as one of its first members.[25] For the group, the modernist painter was a source of inspiration but also caution. They considered him a misunderstood and often overlooked hero during his lifetime, while also viewing his posthumous fame as suspect, given the deadening "forces of commerce, museology, and academic art history."[26] Their goal of reviving Mondrian called for a synthesis of approaches: performances, unrealized and unrealizable plans, drawings, even cosmic graffiti.

Today, little of this work remains. Scant documentation was made, the filmed Impromptu at Iguazu being a rare exception. Nankervis's website for another vacant space, which is in part dedicated to Medalla's archive, offers a disclaimer: "Given the ethereal nature of the actions ... much is lost in archiving, both films and images are scarce."[27] Nankervis admits that this scarcity was due largely to a lack of funds, but also, sometimes, they ended up "doing things for the sake of doing things and then leaving documentation to the wind."[28]

I am reminded of a bird in flight, ethereal in essence.

five minutes before departure for london, for guy brett, 1966. Ballpoint pen on ruled paper. 8 1/16 × 5 7/8 in. (20.5 × 15 cm).

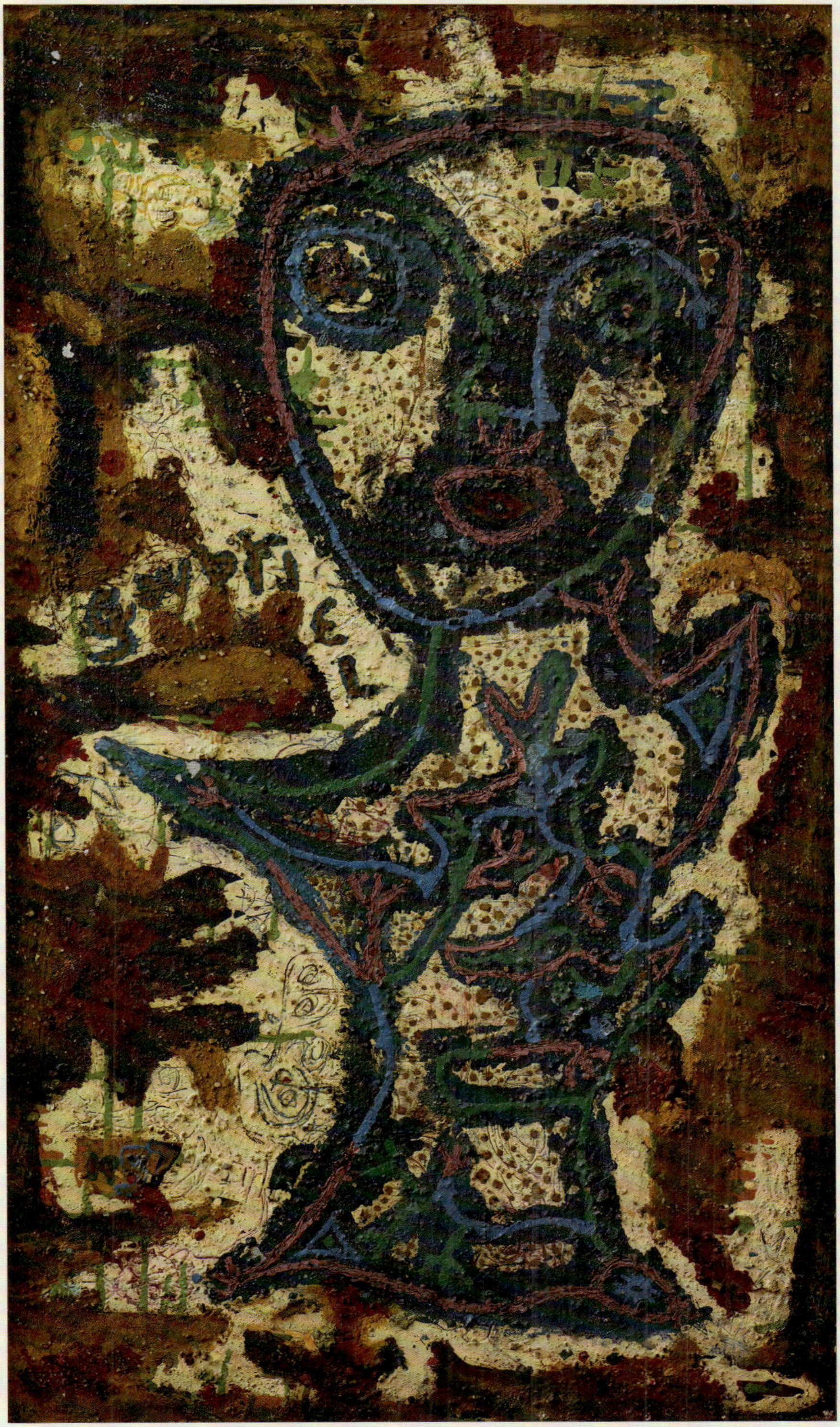

1

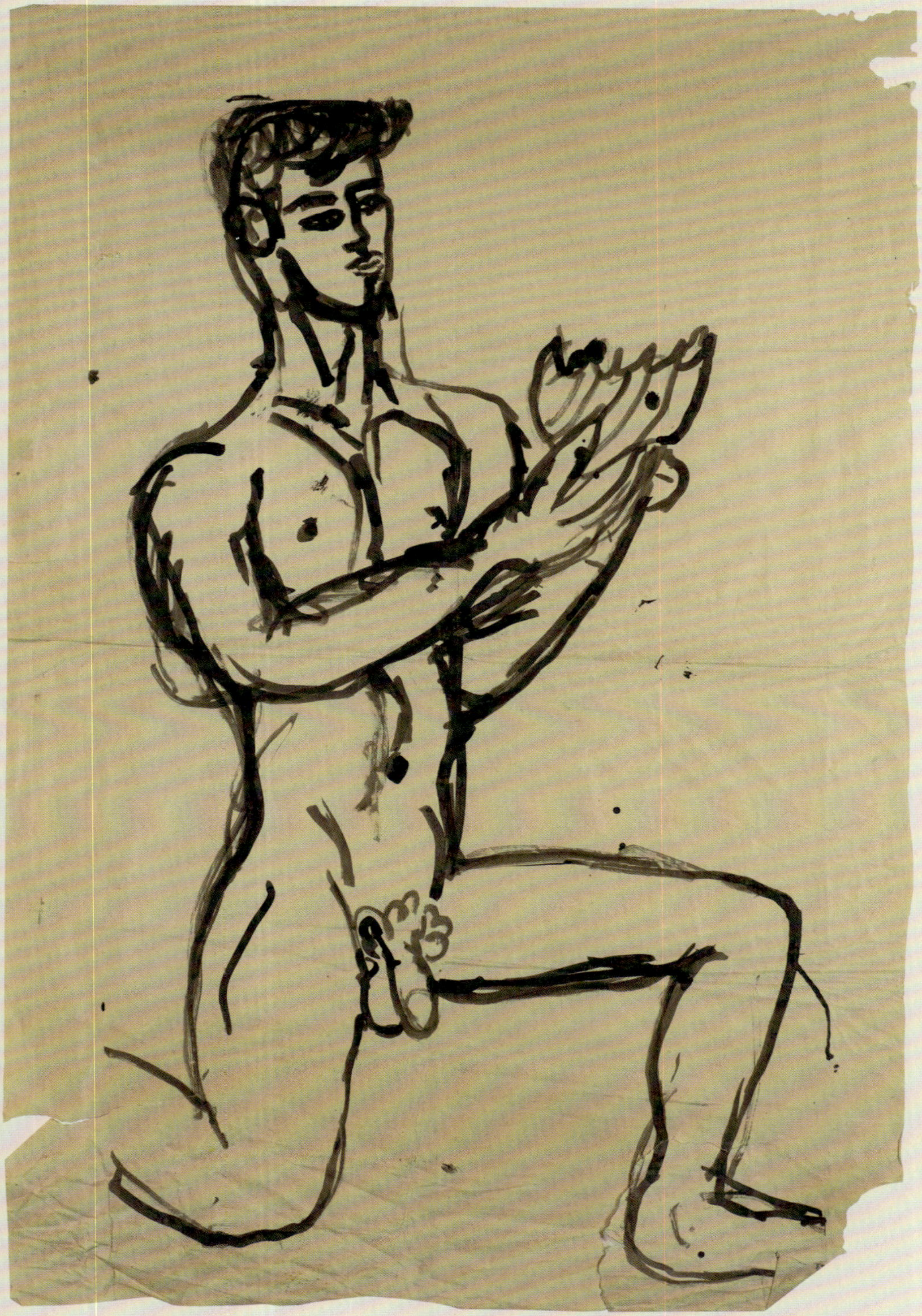

2

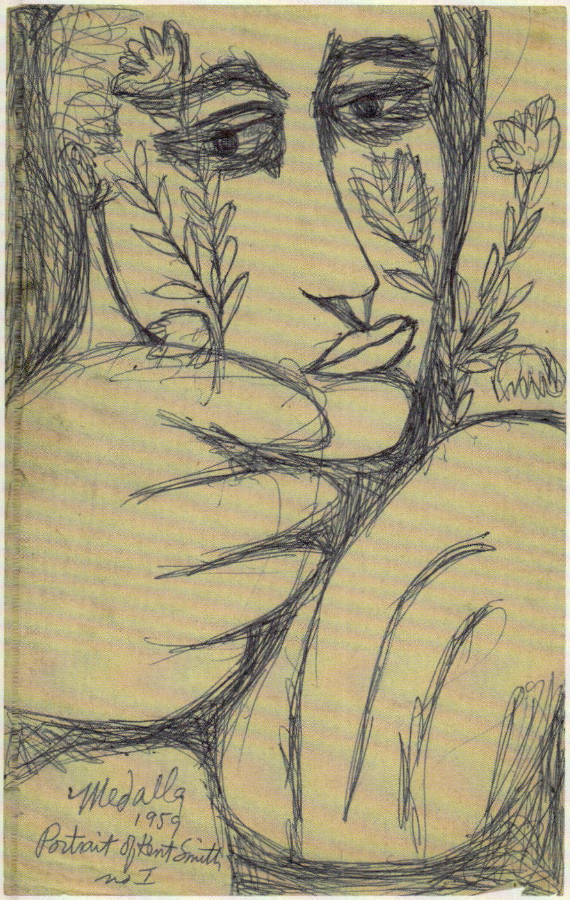

3

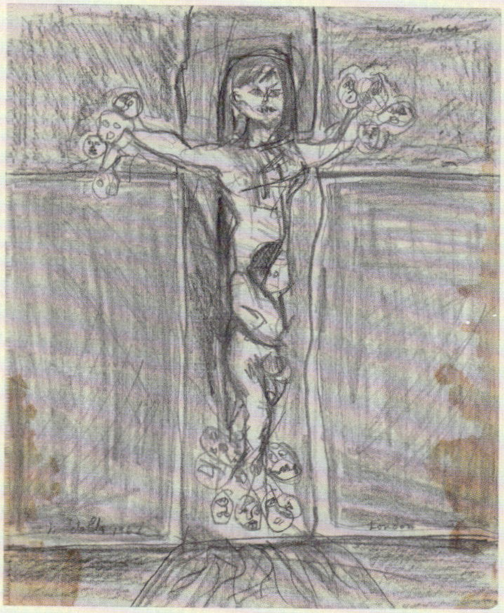
4

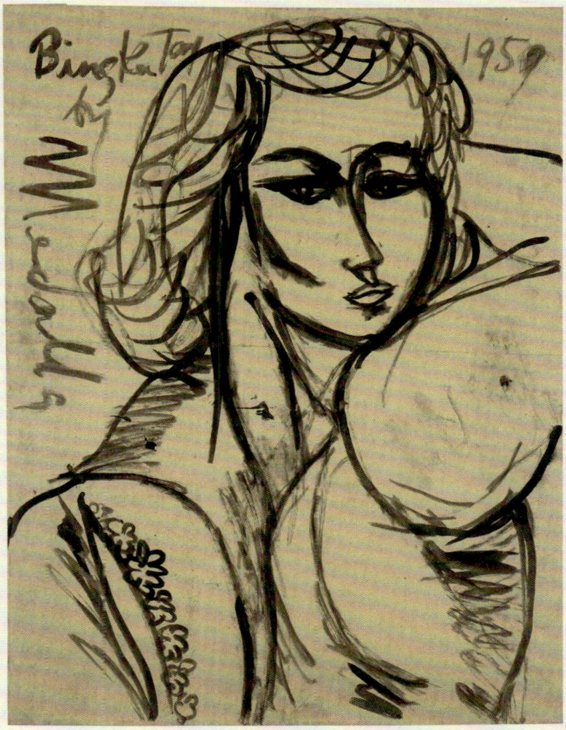

5

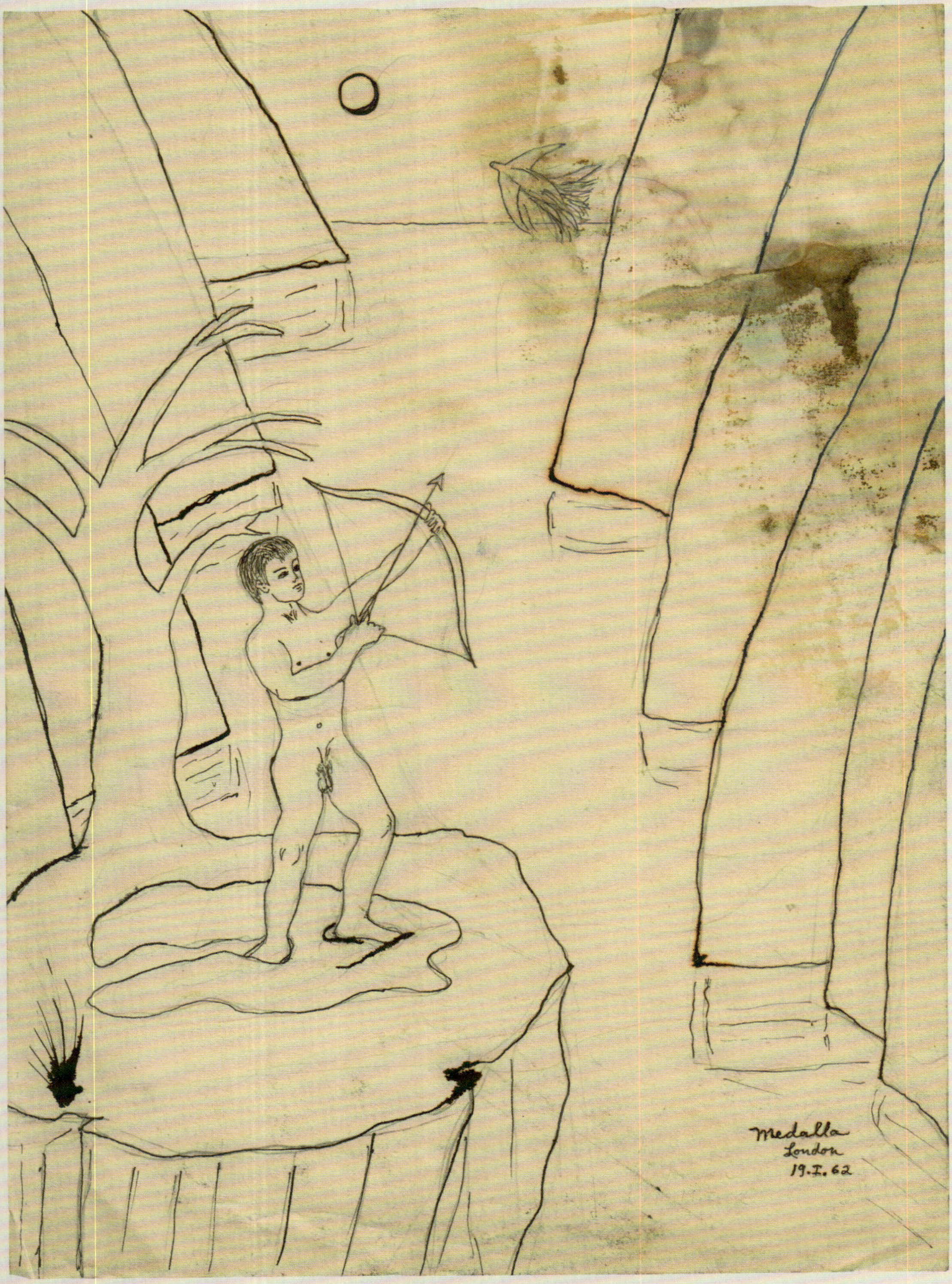

6

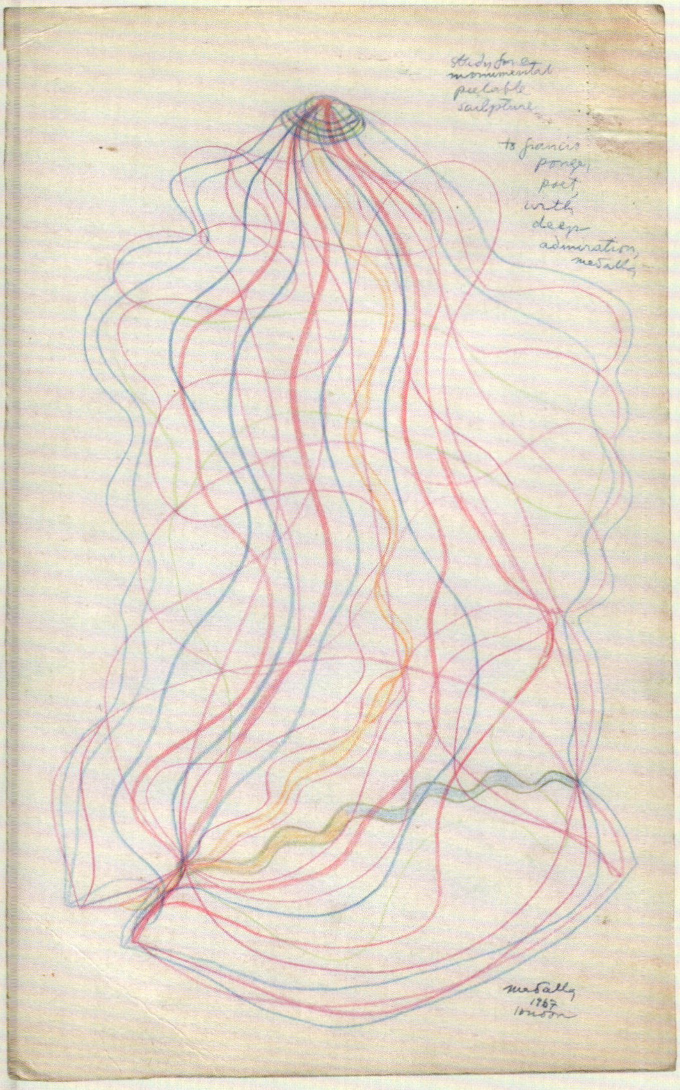
study for a
monumental
peelable
sculpture
to francis
ponge,
poet
with
deep
admiration,
medalla
medalla
1967
london

7

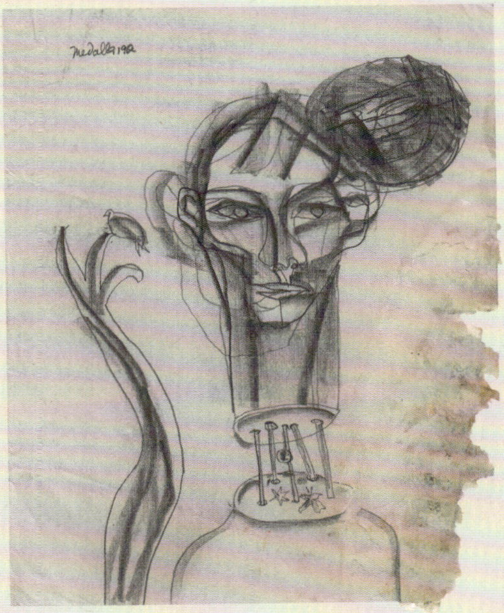

8

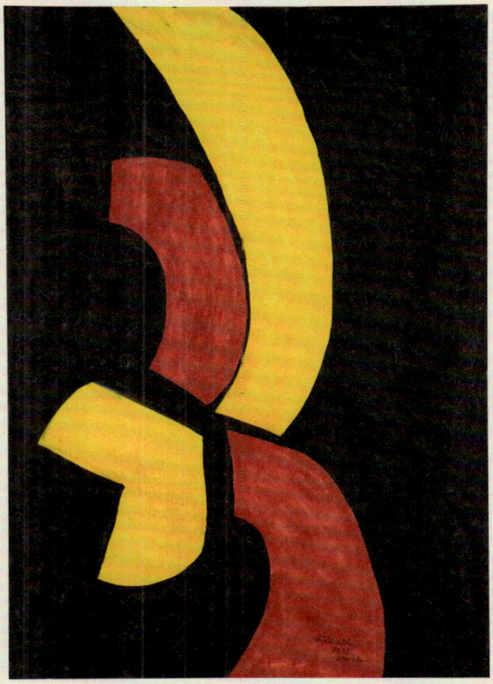

9

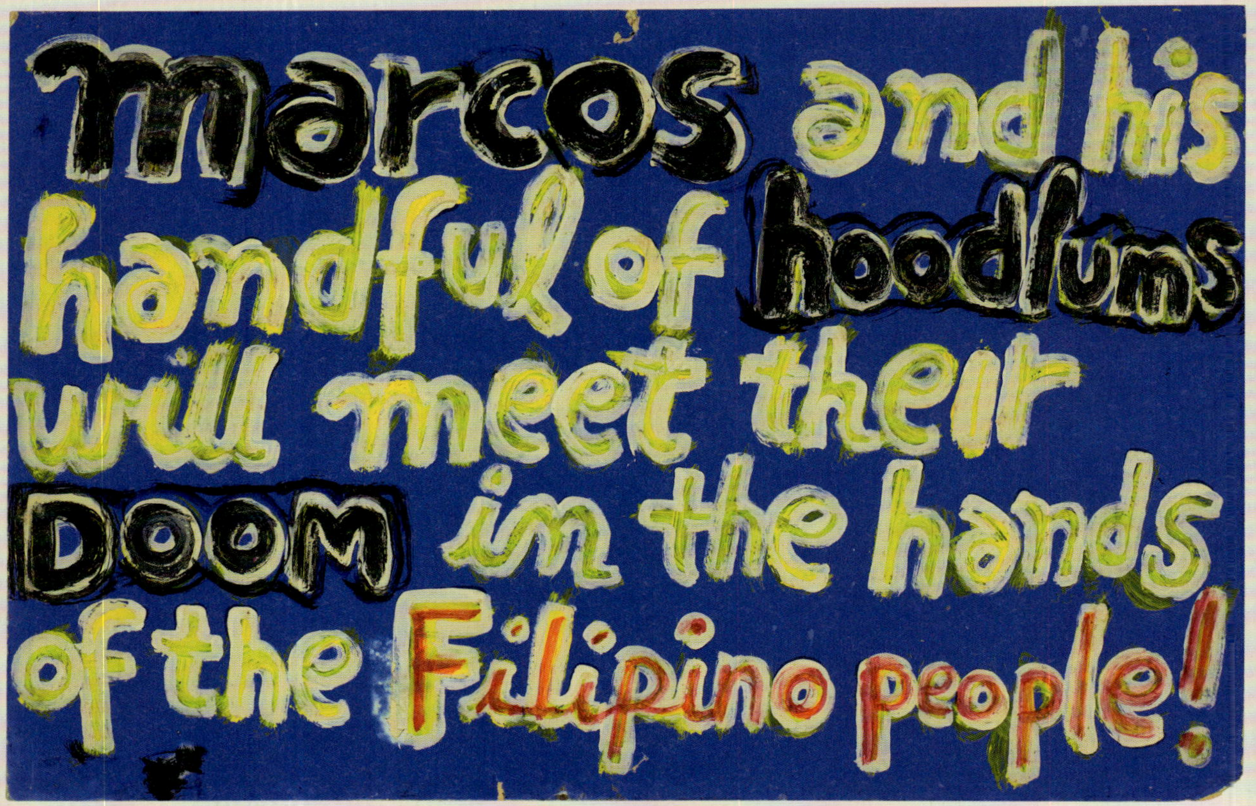
marcos and his
handful of hoodlums
will meet their
DOOM in the hands
of the Filipino people!

10

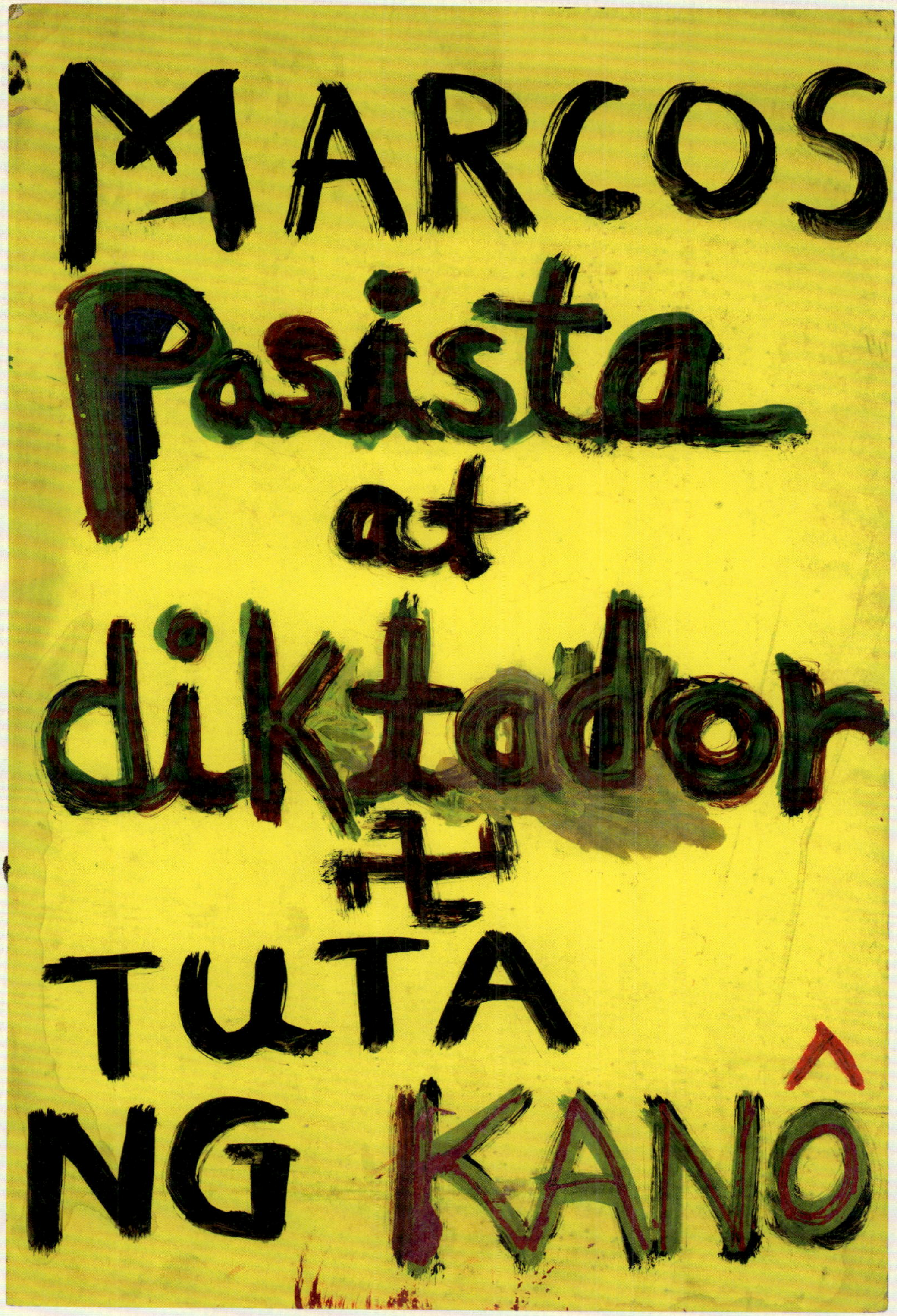

11

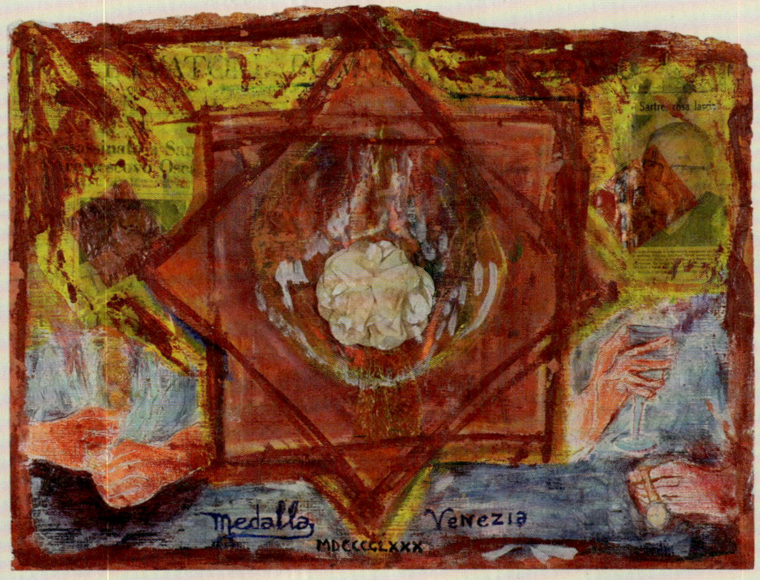
Medalla
Venezia
MDCCCCLXXX

12

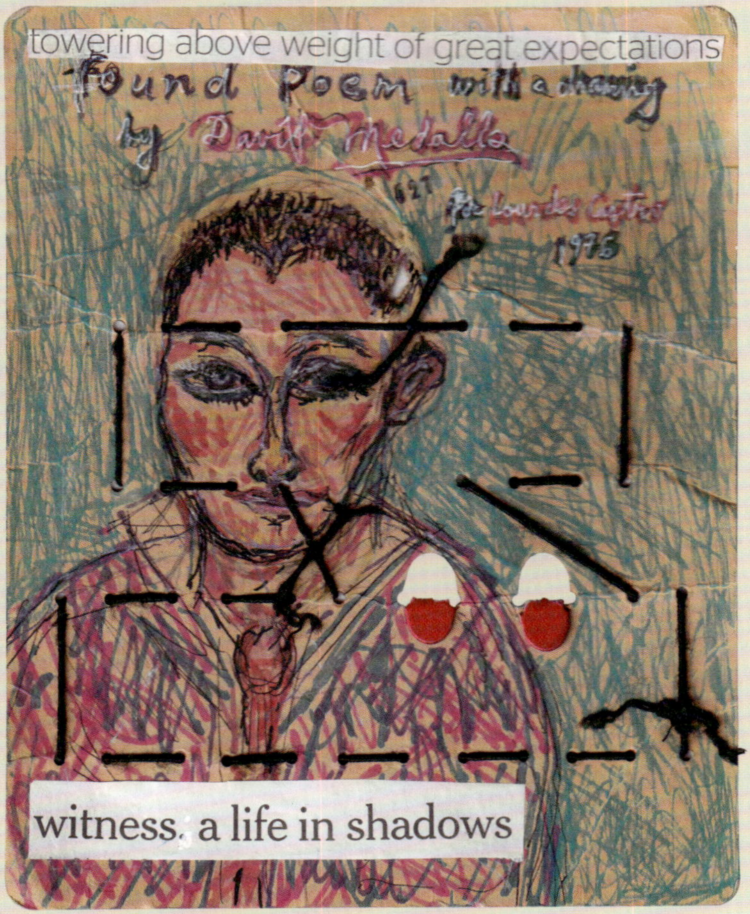
towering above weight of great expectations
found poem with a drawing
by David Medalla
for Lourdes Castro
witness. a life in shadows

13

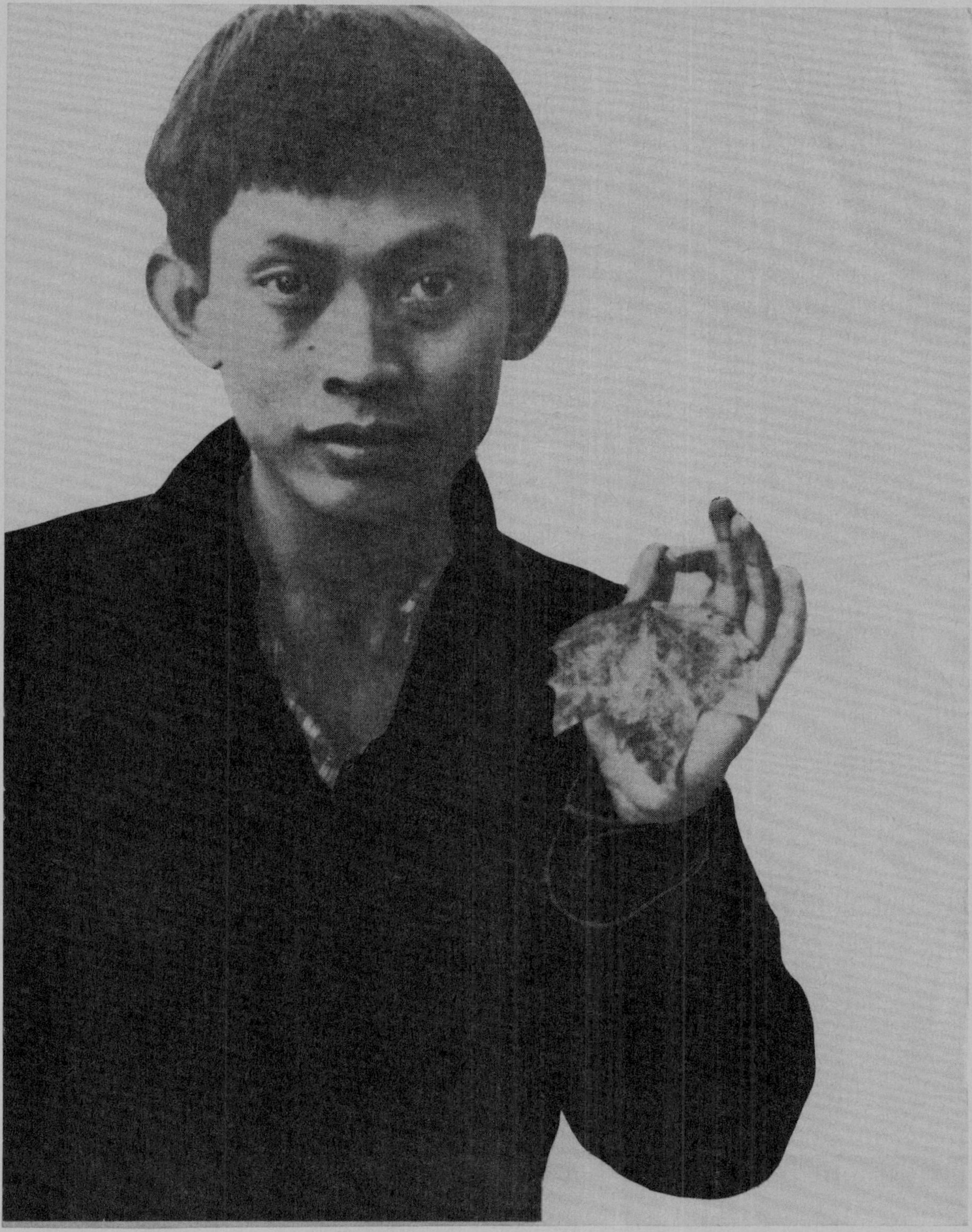

Lava Machine
1962–64

In Medalla's "biokinetic" sculptures, which he initiated in the early 1960s, the artist aspired to materialize intangible and energetic forms. His most notable biokinetic works include Lava Machine, Sand Machine (1963–2015), Cloud Canyons (1963–2017), and *Mud Machine* (1964–67). Among those series, Lava Machine stands out for the ways that it aspired to test the limits of material possibility. Medalla's proposals for this unrealized work describe a machine that oozes lava, akin to a human-made volcano. His abstract renderings blur the visual distinction between the "lava" and the machine that produces it, creating an undifferentiated and unctuous whole. At the start of the 1960s, kinetic works of art were barely garnering mainstream attention, in part because they defied institutional standards for the presentation and preservation of art. Lava Machine, in particular, would have harnessed variability and change to a degree that no museum at the time would have been willing to accommodate.

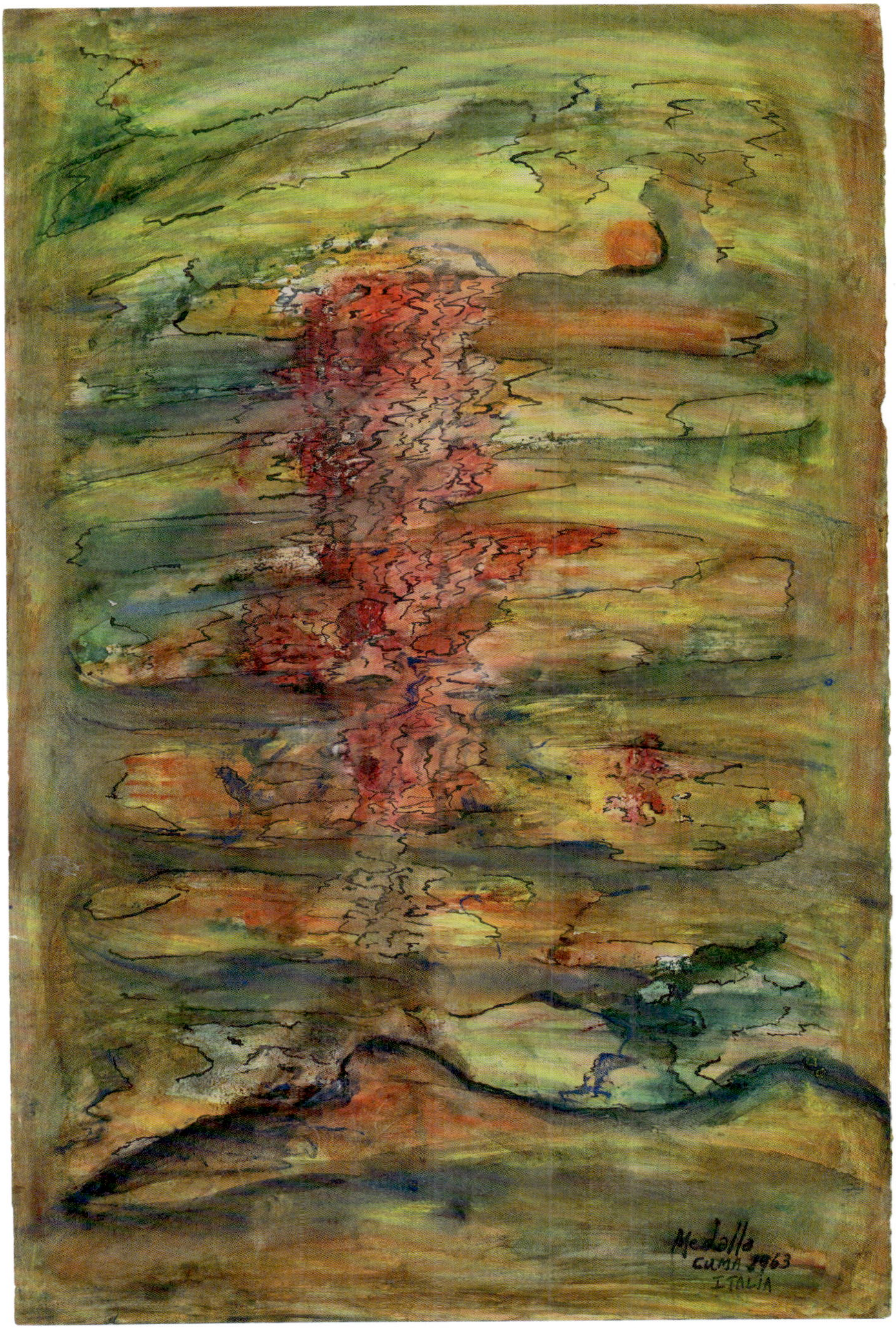

previous
Announcement for *David Medalla—Drawings and Watercolours*, Mercury Gallery, London, 1965.

above
CUMA—Study for Lava Machine, 1963. Watercolor on paper. 18 15⁄16 × 12 5⁄8 in. (48 × 32 cm).

MMMMMMM . . . MANIFESTO

(a fragment)

Mmmmmmm . . . Mmmedalla! What do you dream of?

I dream of the day when I shall create sculptures that breathe, perspire, cough, laugh, yawn, smirk, wink, pant, dance, walk, crawl, . . . and move among people as shadows move among people. . . . Sculptures that will retain a shadow's secret dimensions without a shadow's obsequious behaviour. . . . Sculptures without hope, with waking and sleeping hours. . . . Sculptures that, on certain seasons, will migrate *en masse* to the North Pole. Sculptures with a mirror's translucency minus the memory of a mirror!

Mmmmmmm . . . Mmmedalla! What do you dream of?

I dream of the day when I shall go to the centre of the earth and in the earth's core place a flower-sculpture. . . . Not a lotus, nor a rose, nor a flower of metal, . . . nor yet a flower of ice and fire. . . . But a *mohole*-flower, its petals curled like the crest of a tidal wave approaching the shore. . . .

Mmmmmmm . . . Mmmedalla! What do you dream of?

I dream of a day when, from the capitals of the world, London Paris New York Madrid Rome, I shall release missile-sculptures. . . . to fly — at nine times the speed of sound . . . to fall — slim as a stork on a square in Peking . . . bent, crushed — like a soldier's boot after an explosion — on an airport in Ecuador . . . in splinters — on the fields of Omaha. . . . A few — to cross interstellar space . . . accumulating, as they wing along, asteroids, meteorites, magnetic fields, interstellar germs . . . of a new life . . . on their way from our galaxy to the Spiral Nebula. . . . *Mmmmmmmmmmmmmmmmmmmm. . . .*

David Medalla

London, 1965

above
"MMMMMMM . . . Manifesto (a fragment)," first published in *Signals Newsbulletin* 8 (June 1965).

opposite
Lava Machine, 1962. Acrylic on paper. 19 11⁄16 × 12 13⁄16 in. (50 × 32.5 cm).

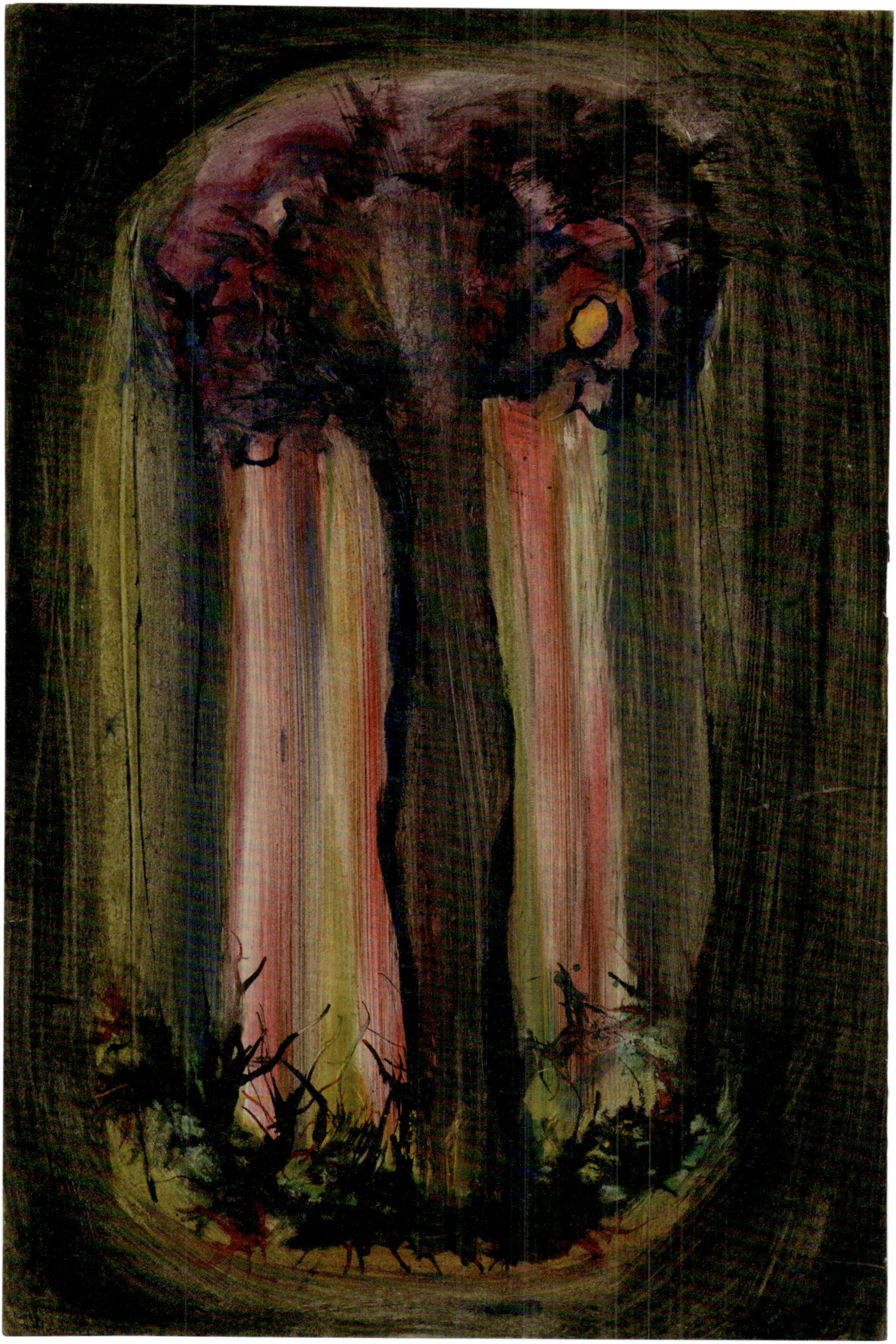

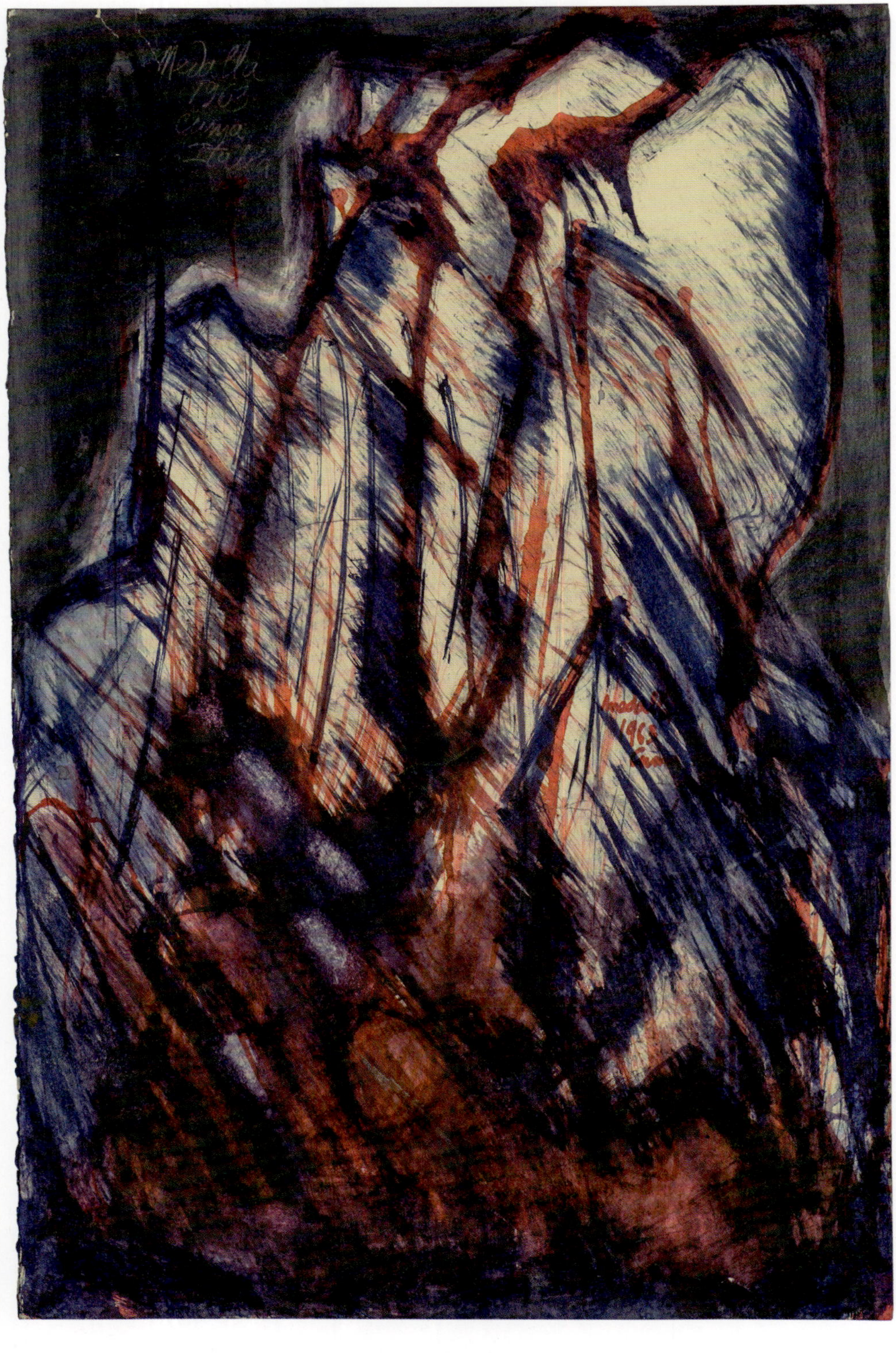

CUMA—Study for Lava Machine, 1963. China ink, graphite, and felt-tip marker on paper. 19 ⅝ × 12 ¹³⁄₁₆ in. (49.9 × 32.5 cm).

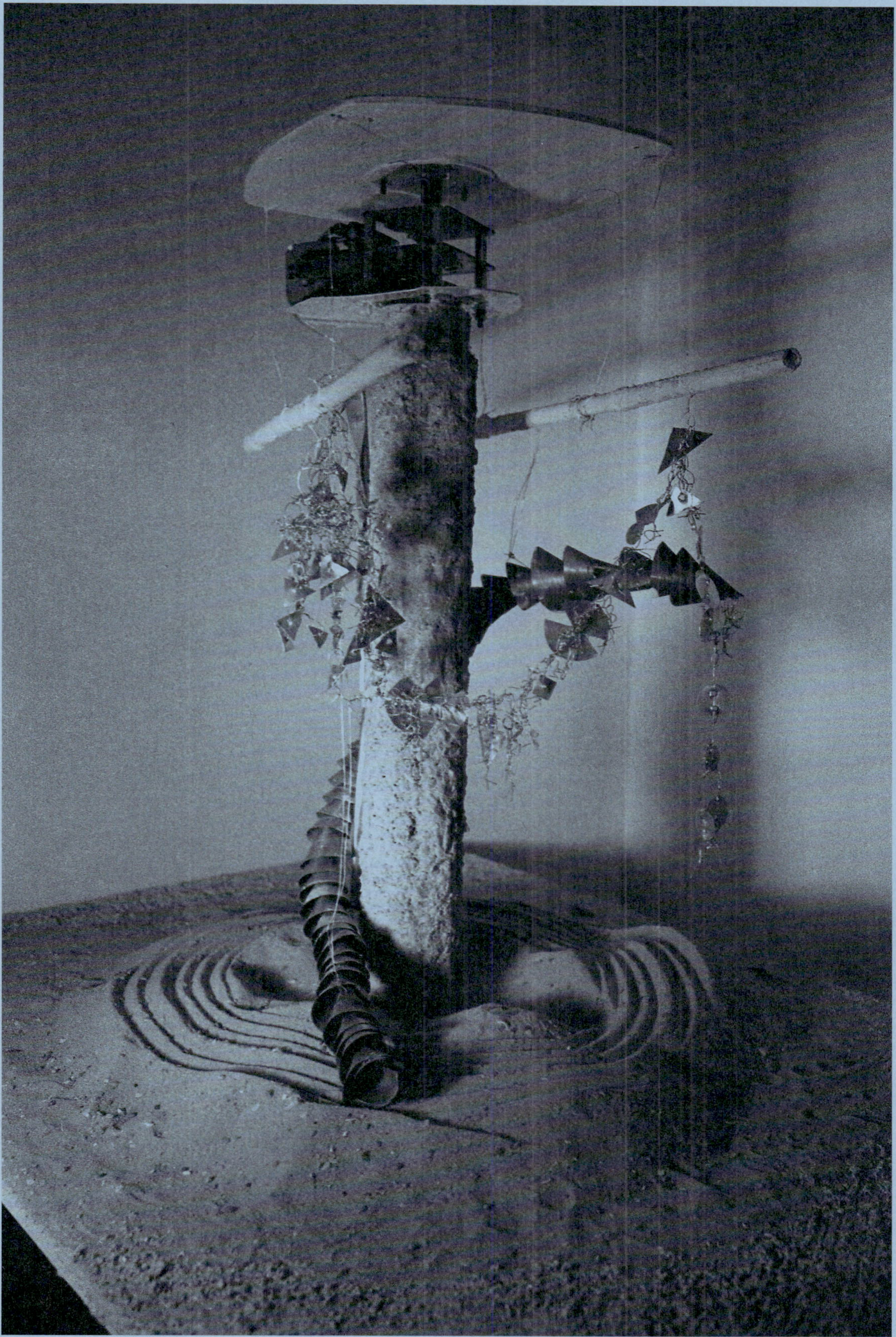

Sand Machine
1963–2015

Medalla's small-scale Sand Machine assemblages are powered by a motor, which rotates a central protrusion that leisurely drags a metal helix through a box containing dry sand. The movement creates intricate circular rings in the sand. Medalla likened these forms to a three-dimensional mandala—a geometric configuration of symbols, often drawn with colored sand, that can be used as a guide for meditation. The shape of the helix reappears in many of the artist's other works, where it is sometimes interpreted as a snake and as a symbol for eroticism. Compared to the dramatic movement in Cloud Canyons (1963–2017) and Lava Machine (1962–64), the Sand Machine's gestures are slow and contemplative. The artist has described the Sand Machine works as metaphors for a future in which solar energy and sand are utilized to cultivate fertile terrain in the Earth's deserts.

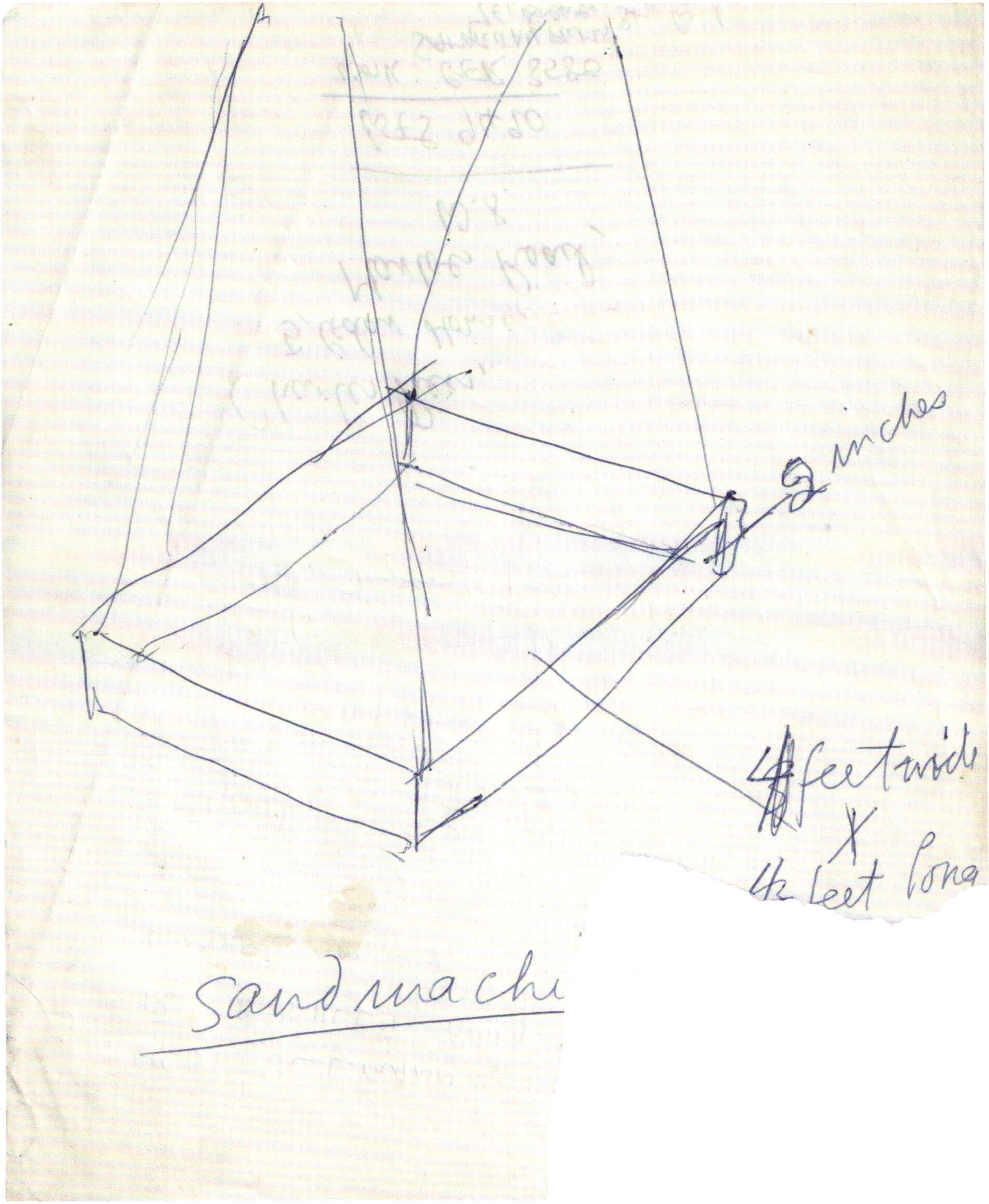

previous
Clay Perry, *David Medalla's Sand Machine*, ca. 1963.

above
Sand Machine, ca. 1963. Ballpoint pen on paper. 9 15⁄16 × 7 15⁄16 in. (25.3 × 20.3 cm).

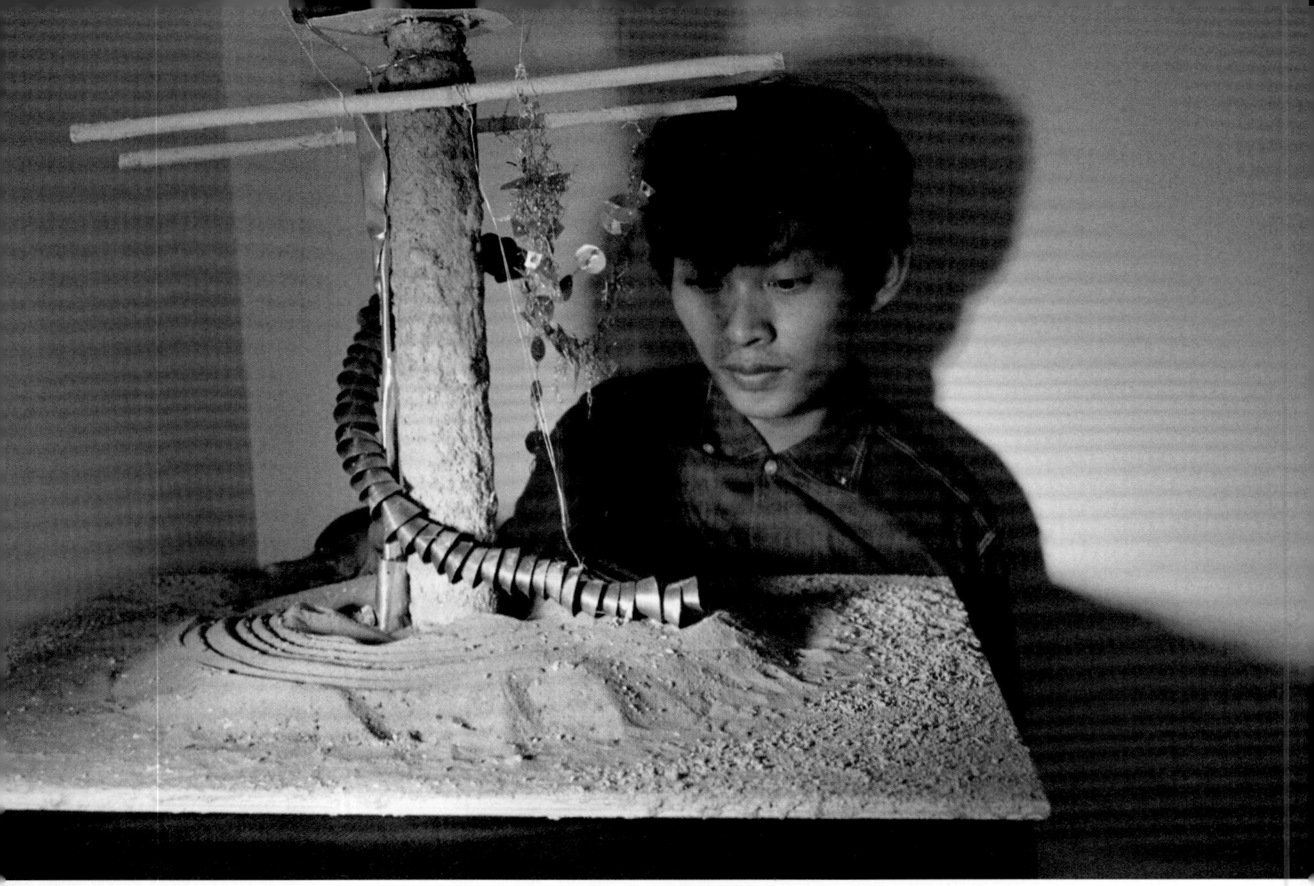

Clay Perry, *David Medalla with his Sand Machine*, ca. 1963.

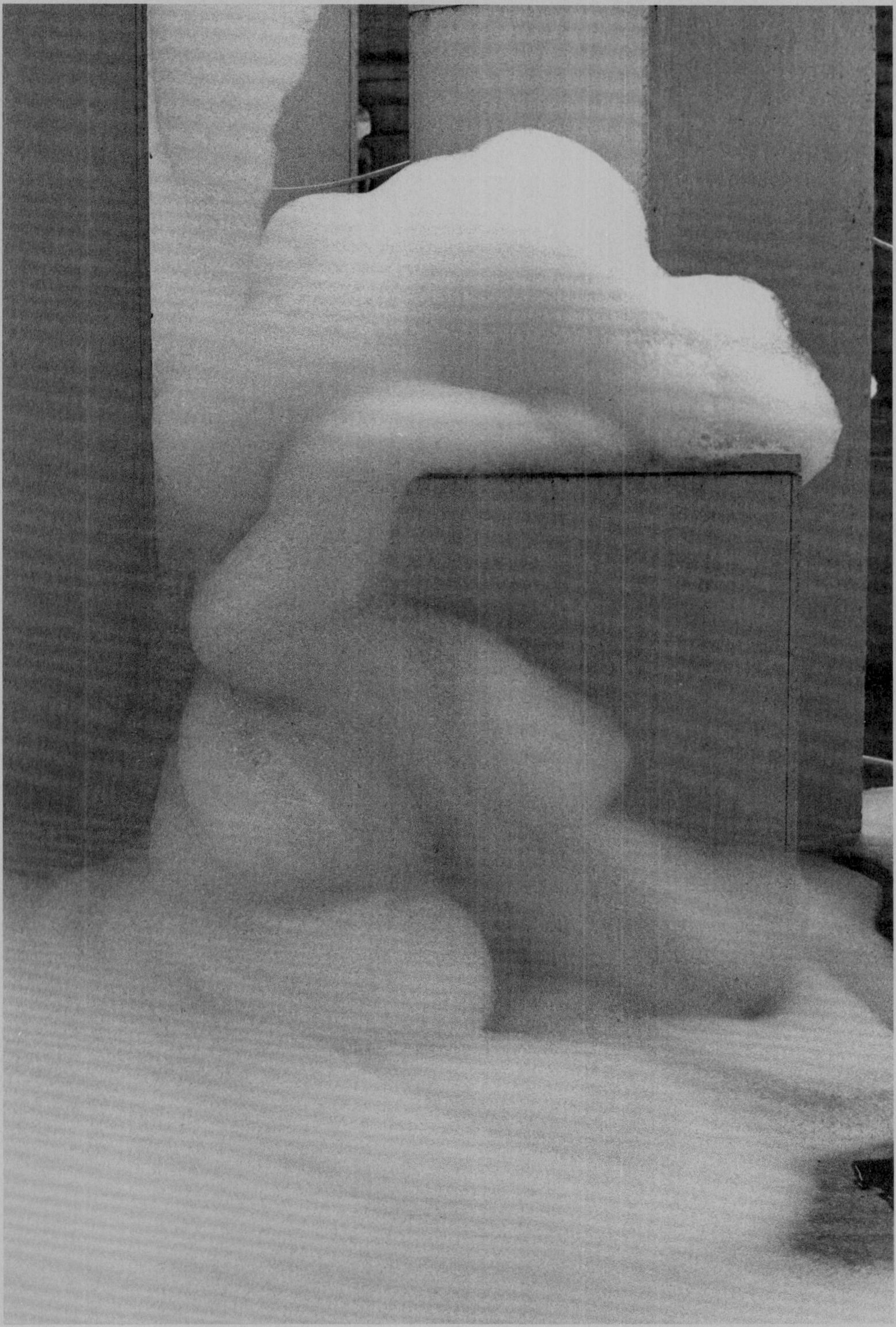

Cloud Canyons 1963–2017

Medalla first exhibited his Cloud Canyons at Signals London in 1964. Colloquially named "bubble machines," the works primarily consist of soft columns of soap foam oozing from wooden bases and clear acrylic tubes. The self-generating forms of Medalla's Cloud Canyons undermine the fixity of sculpture and represent a unique collaboration between human and machine in art. The Cloud Canyons are both autonomous and malleable, as the presence of bodies in the room changes the air currents and temperature, thus altering the shape and consistency of the foam. Among his many sources of inspiration for the series, the artist cited a frothy rice dessert his mother would prepare for him as a child in the Philippines, sudsy beer in copper cauldrons at a brewery, and blood foaming from the mouth of an injured soldier lying outside of his house in Manila during the Second World War. The works, which challenged the established protocols of exhibition and historical preservation, garnered both acclaim and controversy in the art establishment of the 1960s.

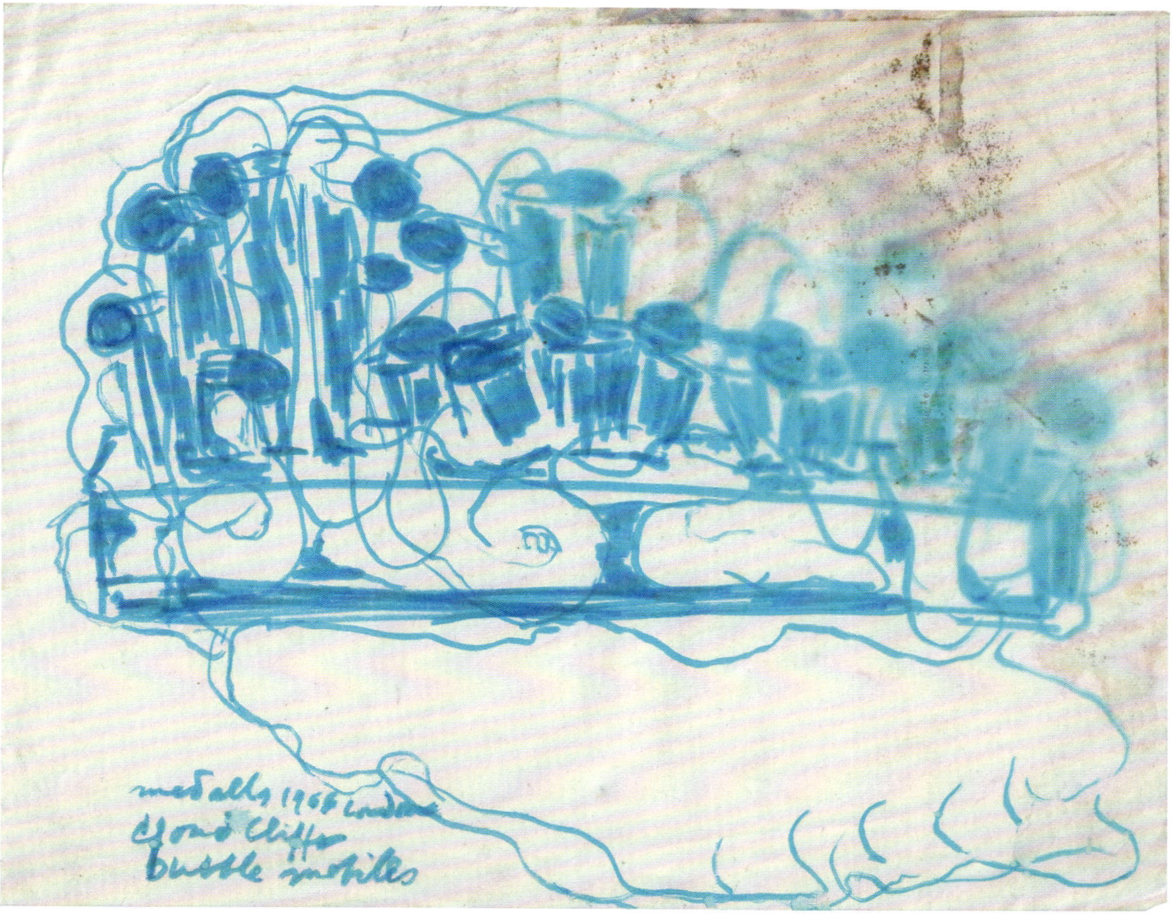

previous
Clay Perry, *David Medalla's Cloud Canyons*, 1964.

above
Cloud Cliffs bubble mobiles, 1968. Felt-tip marker on paper. 8 × 9 15/16 in. (20.3 × 25.3 cm).

Cloud Canyon, 2020–21. Wood, acrylic, foam. Installation view, *David Medalla: Parables of Friendship*, Bonner Kunstverein, Bonn, Germany, September 18, 2021–January 30, 2022.

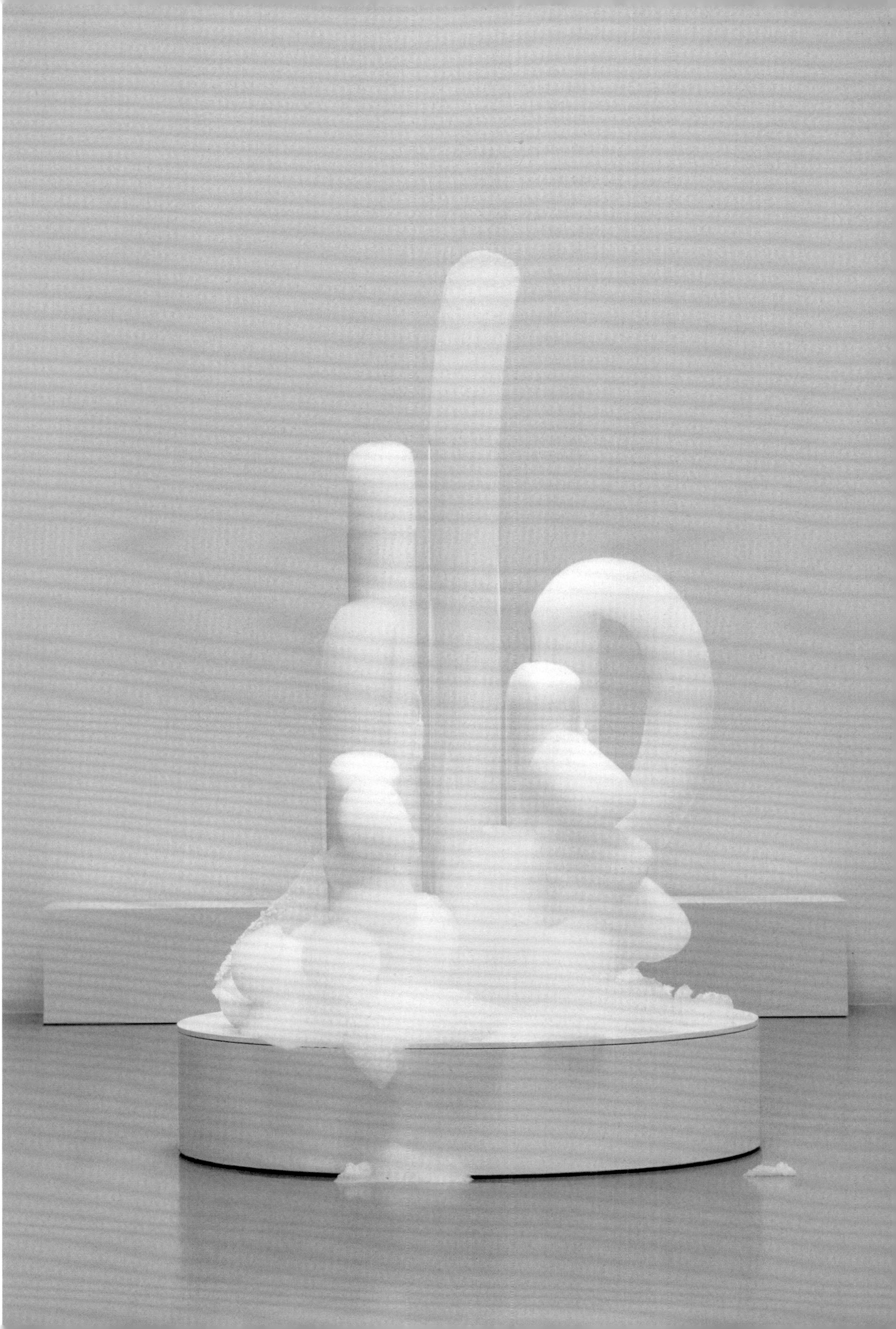

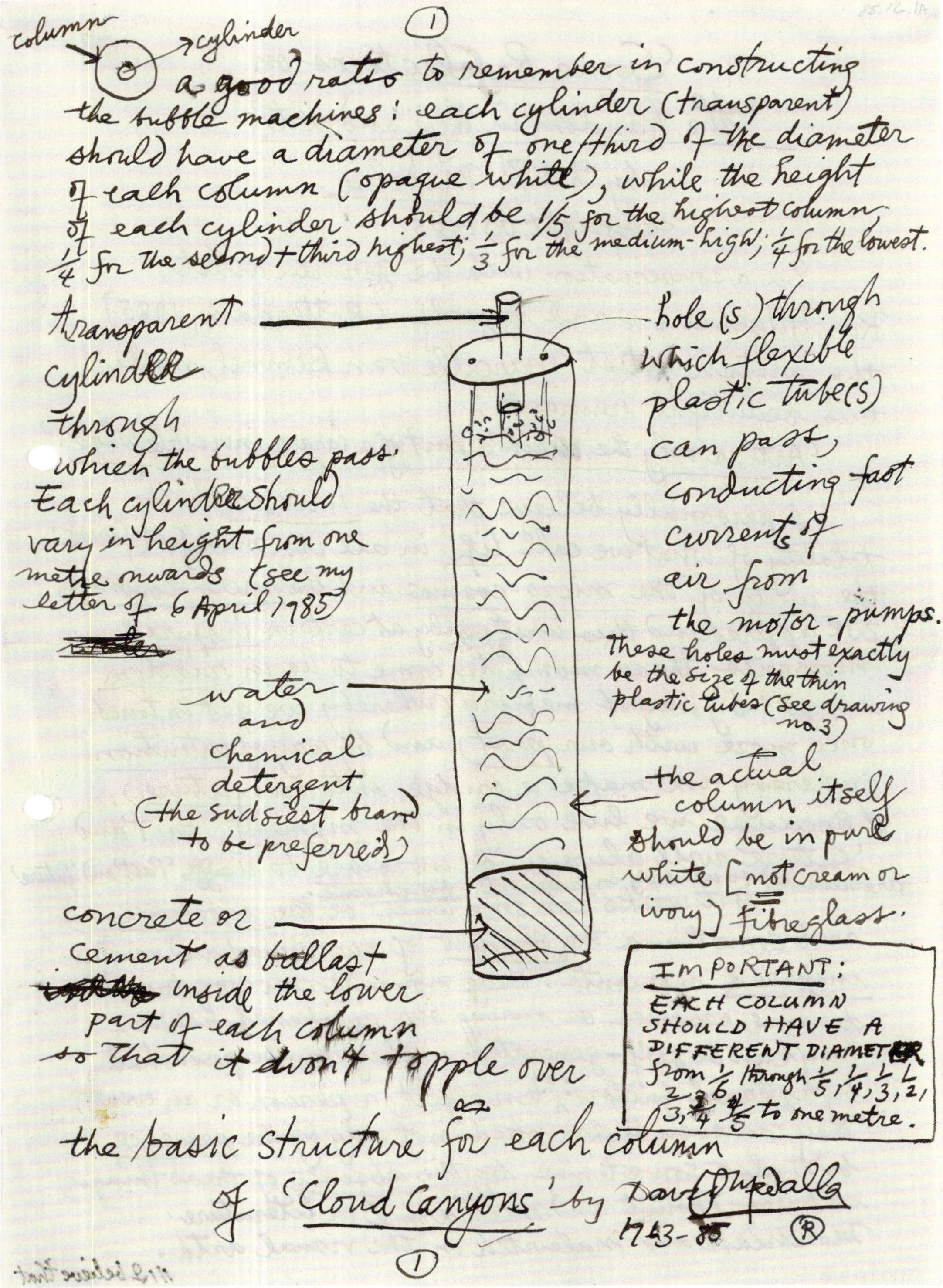
85.16.1A

(1)

column → cylinder

a good ratio to remember in constructing the bubble machines: each cylinder (transparent) should have a diameter of one third of the diameter of each column (opaque white), while the height of each cylinder should be 1/5 for the highest column, 1/4 for the second + third highest; 1/3 for the medium-high; 1/4 for the lowest.

transparent cylinder through which the bubbles pass. Each cylinder should vary in height from one metre onwards (see my letter of 6 April 1985)

hole(s) through which flexible plastic tube(s) can pass, conducting fast currents of air from the motor-pumps. These holes must exactly be the size of the thin plastic tubes (see drawing no. 3)

water and chemical detergent (the sudsiest brand to be preferred)

the actual column itself should be in pure white [not cream or ivory] fibreglass.

concrete or cement as ballast inside the lower part of each column so that it don't topple over

IMPORTANT: EACH COLUMN SHOULD HAVE A DIFFERENT DIAMETER from 1/2 through 1/6, 1/5, 1/4, 1/3, 1/2, 1/3, 3/4, 4/5 to one metre.

as the basic structure for each column of 'Cloud Canyons' by David Medalla 1963-85 ®

(1)

Cloud Canyons and Some Reflections on the Random in Life and Art, 1985. Ink on paper. Two of three sheets, 11¾ × 8¼ in. (29.8 × 21 cm) each.

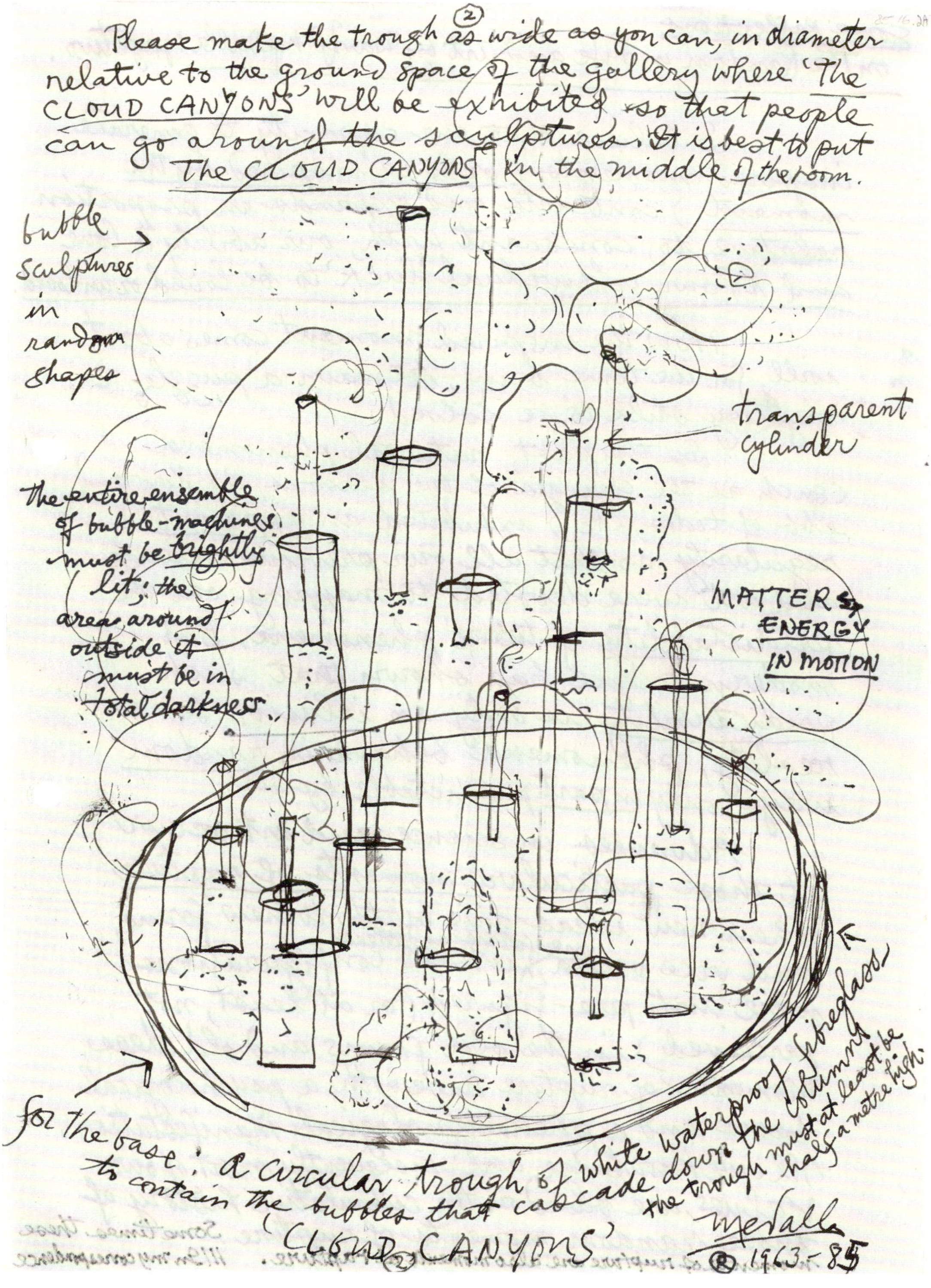

2
Please make the trough as wide as you can, in diameter relative to the ground space of the gallery where 'The CLOUD CANYONS' will be exhibited, so that people can go around the sculptures. It is best to put The CLOUD CANYONS in the middle of the room.
bubble sculptures in random shapes
transparent cylinder
The entire ensemble of bubble-machines must be brightly lit; the area around/outside it must be in total darkness
MATTER & ENERGY IN MOTION
for the base: a circular trough of white waterproof fibreglass to contain the bubbles that cascade down the columns
the trough must at least be half a metre high.
'CLOUD CANYONS'
2
Medalla
® 1963-85

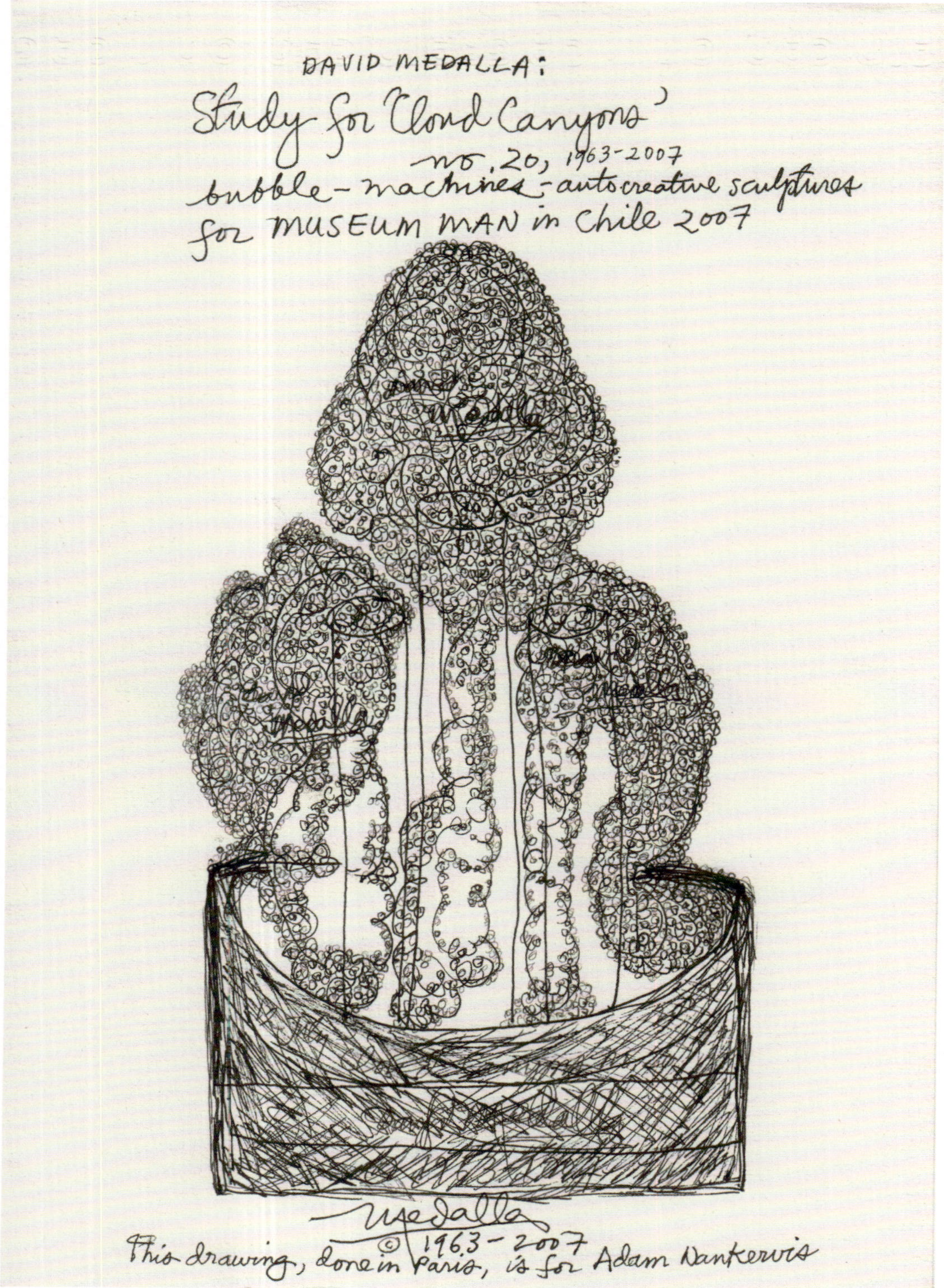

Study for Cloud Canyons no. 20, 2007. Ink pen on paper. 11¾ × 8¼ in. (29.8 × 20.9 cm).

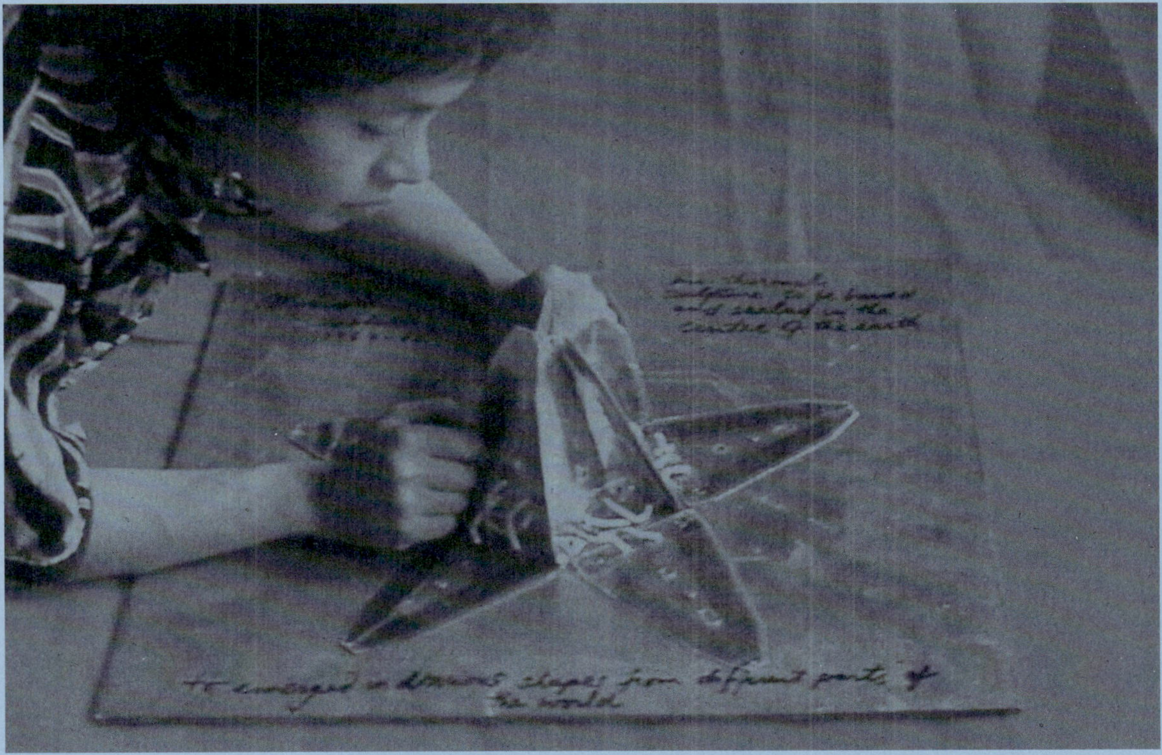

centre of the earth
the world

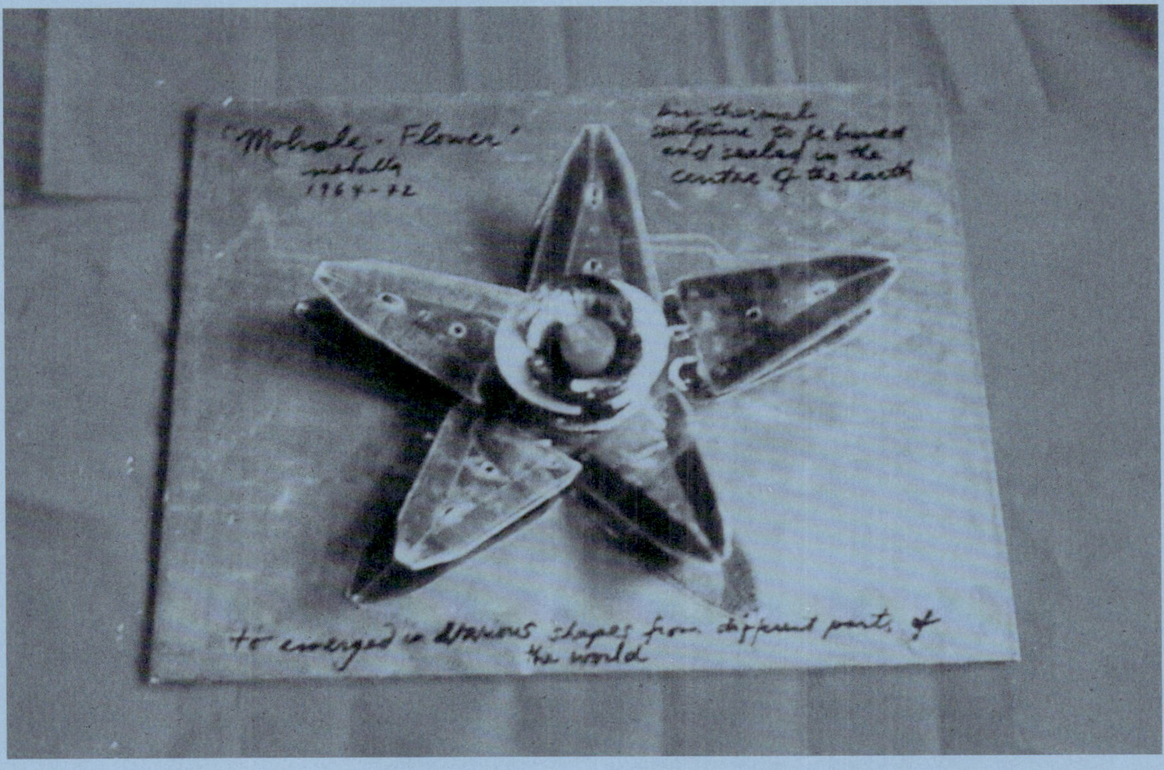

"Mohole - Flower"
1964-72
centre of the earth
shapes from different parts of
the world

Mohole Flower
1964–2019

Mohole Flower occupied a central place in Medalla's practice for over five decades, recurring in the form of sculptures, drawings, and preparatory sketches. The series was inspired by Project Mohole, a scientific study initiated in the 1950s by Walter Munk of the Scripps Institution of Oceanography. The study sought to drill a hole through the Earth's crust to obtain samples from the Mohorovičić discontinuity (Moho), the boundary that separates the Earth's crust and mantle, with the goal of obtaining vital information about the history and composition of the planet. Medalla created his first Mohole Flower drawing in 1964 as an artistic and poetic extension of the scientific endeavor. Through the years, his drawings became increasingly descriptive of his dream of replicating the study through art.

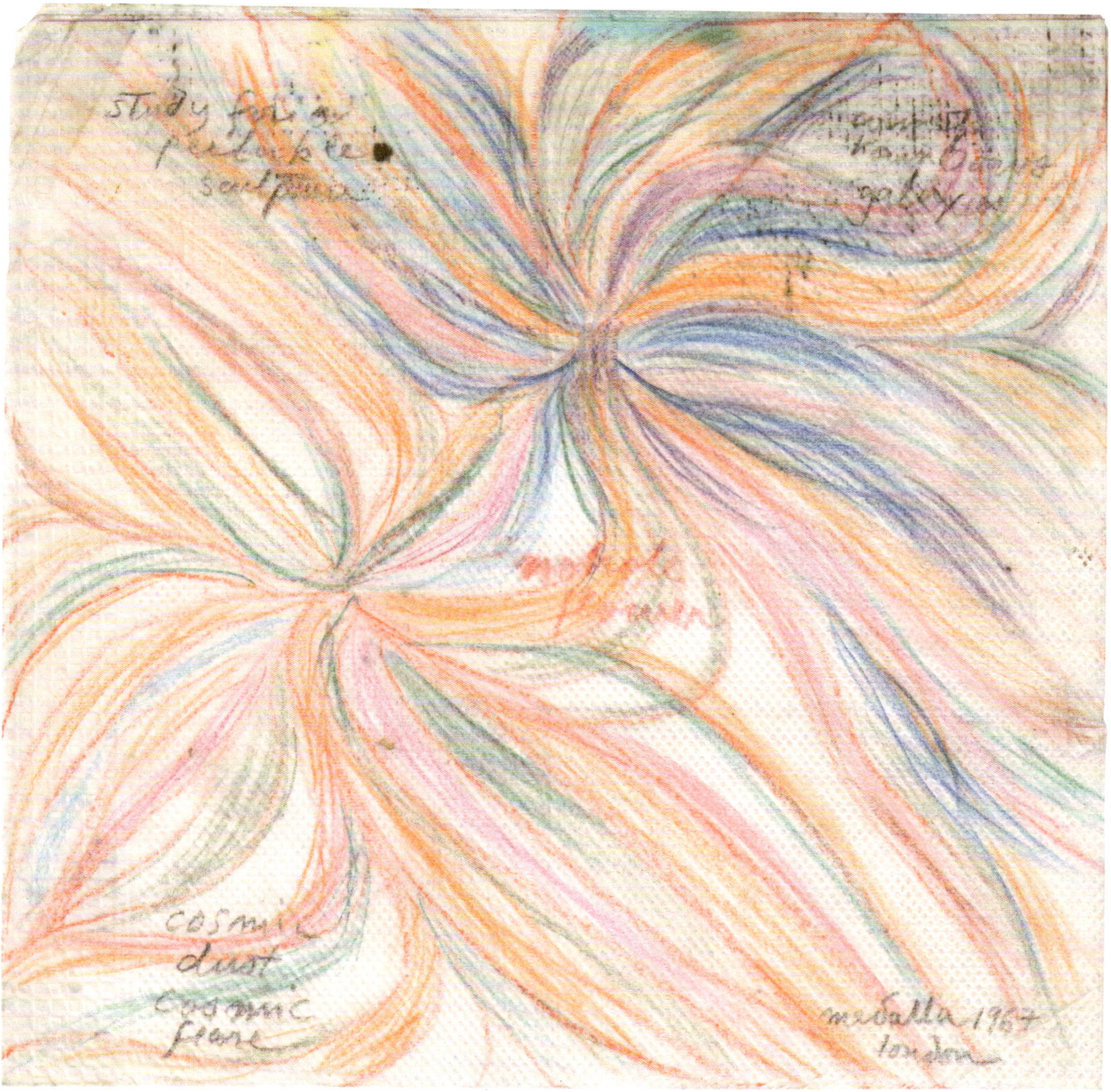

previous, top and bottom
David Medalla with *Mohole Flower*, 1964–72.

above
Mohole Flower, 1967. Colored pencil on paper napkin. 6½ × 6½ in. (16.5 × 16.5 cm).

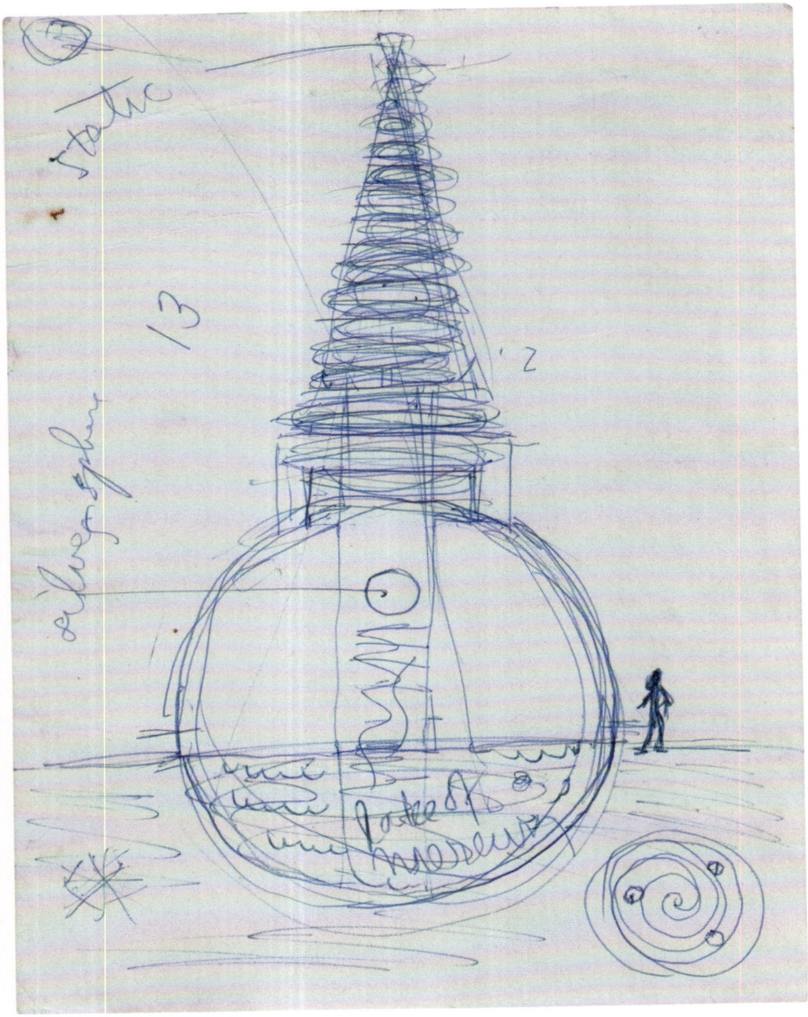

above
Study for mohole flower, 1963. Ballpoint pen on paper. 7 × 5 7⁄16 in. (17.8 × 13.8 cm).

opposite
Mohole Sculpture, 1968. Ink on paper. 12 5⁄8 × 8 1⁄16 in. (32 × 20.5 cm).

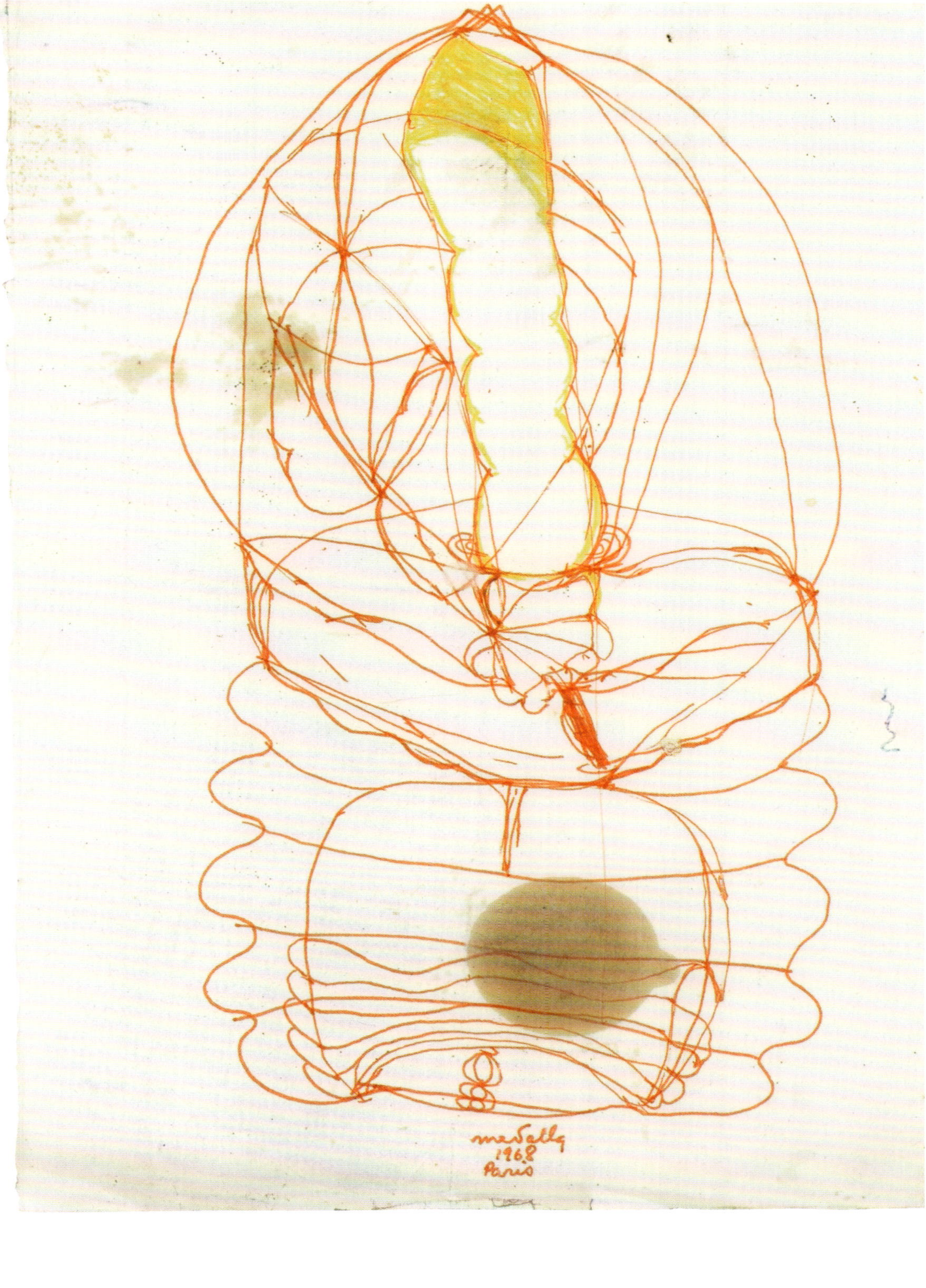
1968
Paris

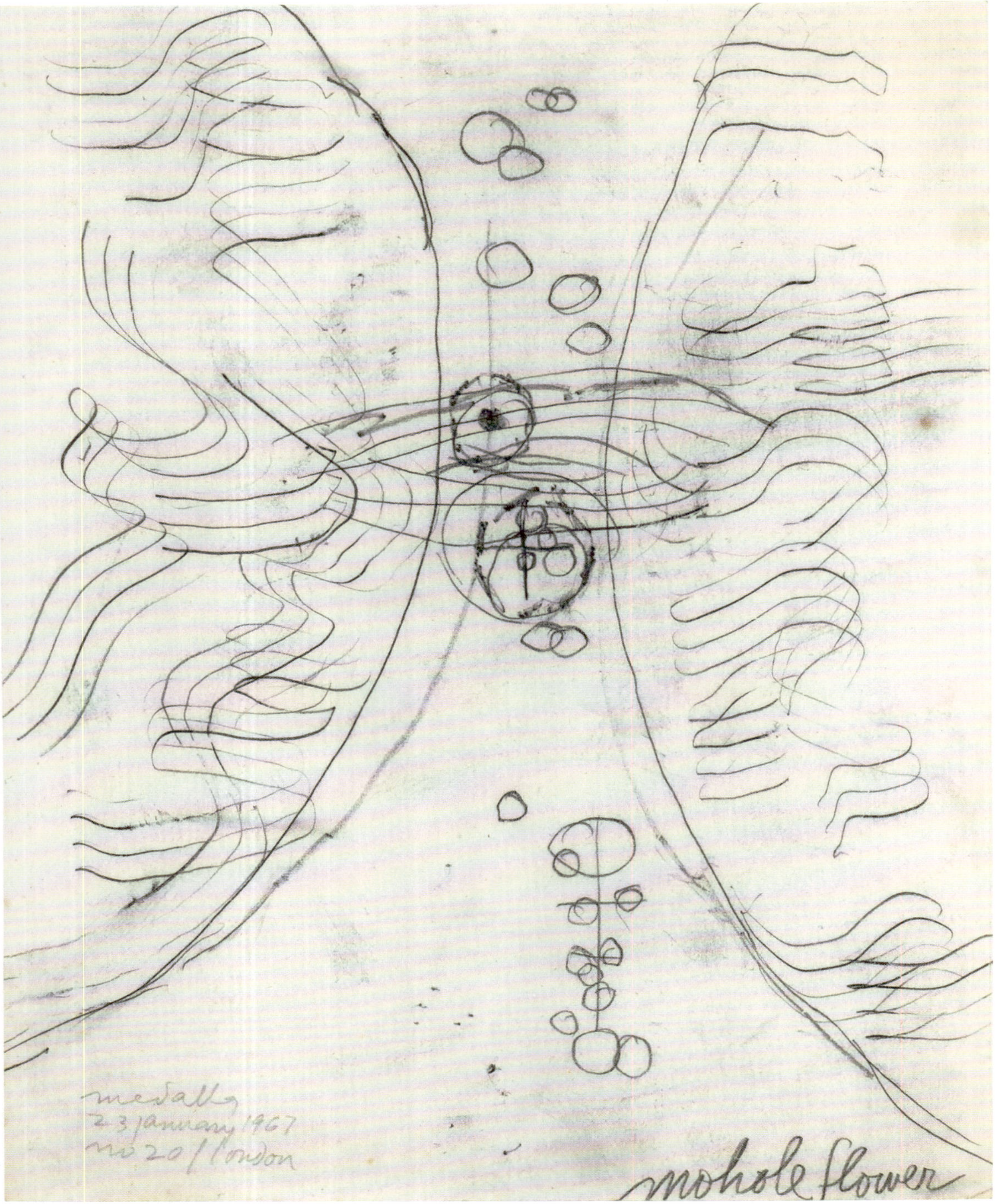

Mohole flower no. 20, 1967. Graphite and ballpoint pen on paper. 10 ¼ × 7 ⅞ in. (26 × 20 cm).

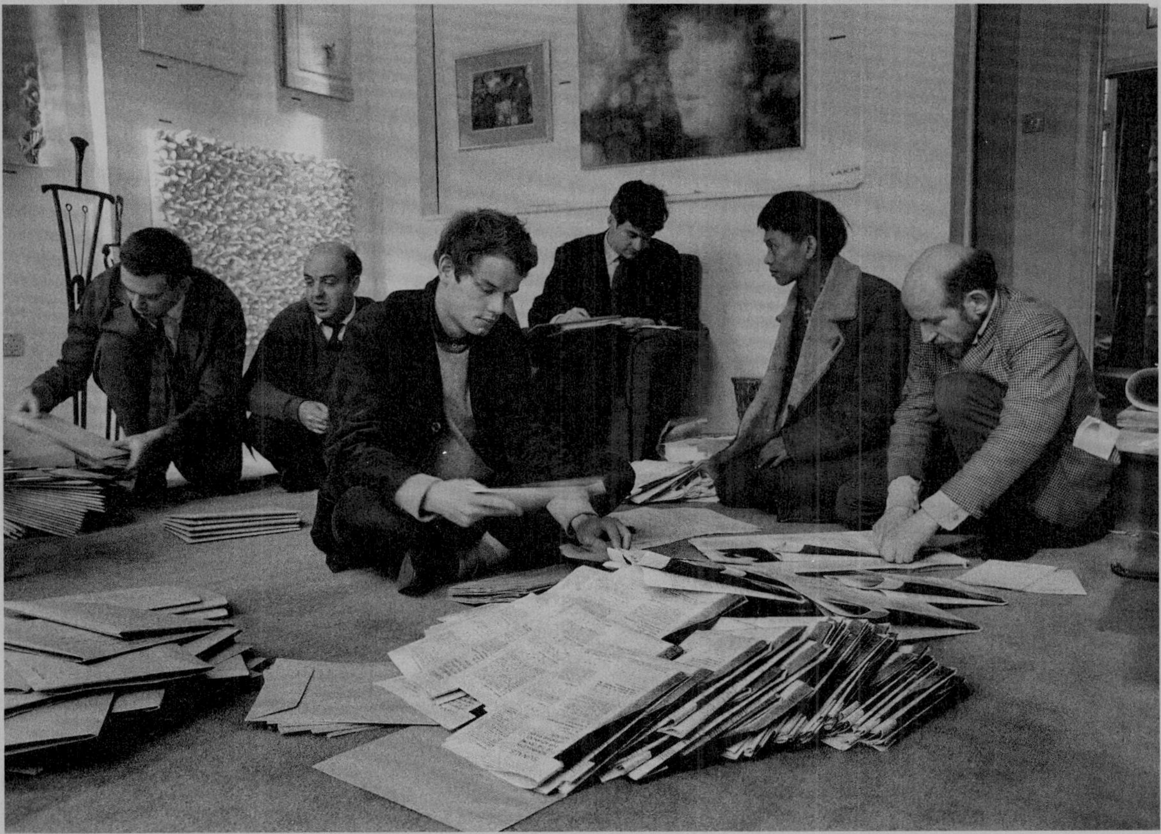

Signals London 1964–66

In 1964, a group of artists and art critics comprised of Guy Brett, Paul Keeler, David Medalla, Gustav Metzger, Marcello Salvadori, and Christopher Walker founded Signals London in a studio space on Wigmore Street in London's West End. Originally called the Centre for Advanced Creative Study, the gallery was renamed Signals after a series of electronic works with blinking lights by the artist Takis. Signals acted as an incubator for artists such as Sérgio de Camargo, Lygia Clark, Li Yuan-chia, Soto, and Takis, who were encouraged to experiment in ways that more prominent London galleries did not embrace. The gallery also published *Signals Newsbulletin*, which focused on politics, poetry, scientific discoveries, and exhibitions in the gallery. The gallery supported the work of artists who engaged unconventional materials and alternative paradigms, including artists hailing from Asia and Latin America. Signals is now recognized for having played a crucial role in the diversification of Britain's gallery landscape.

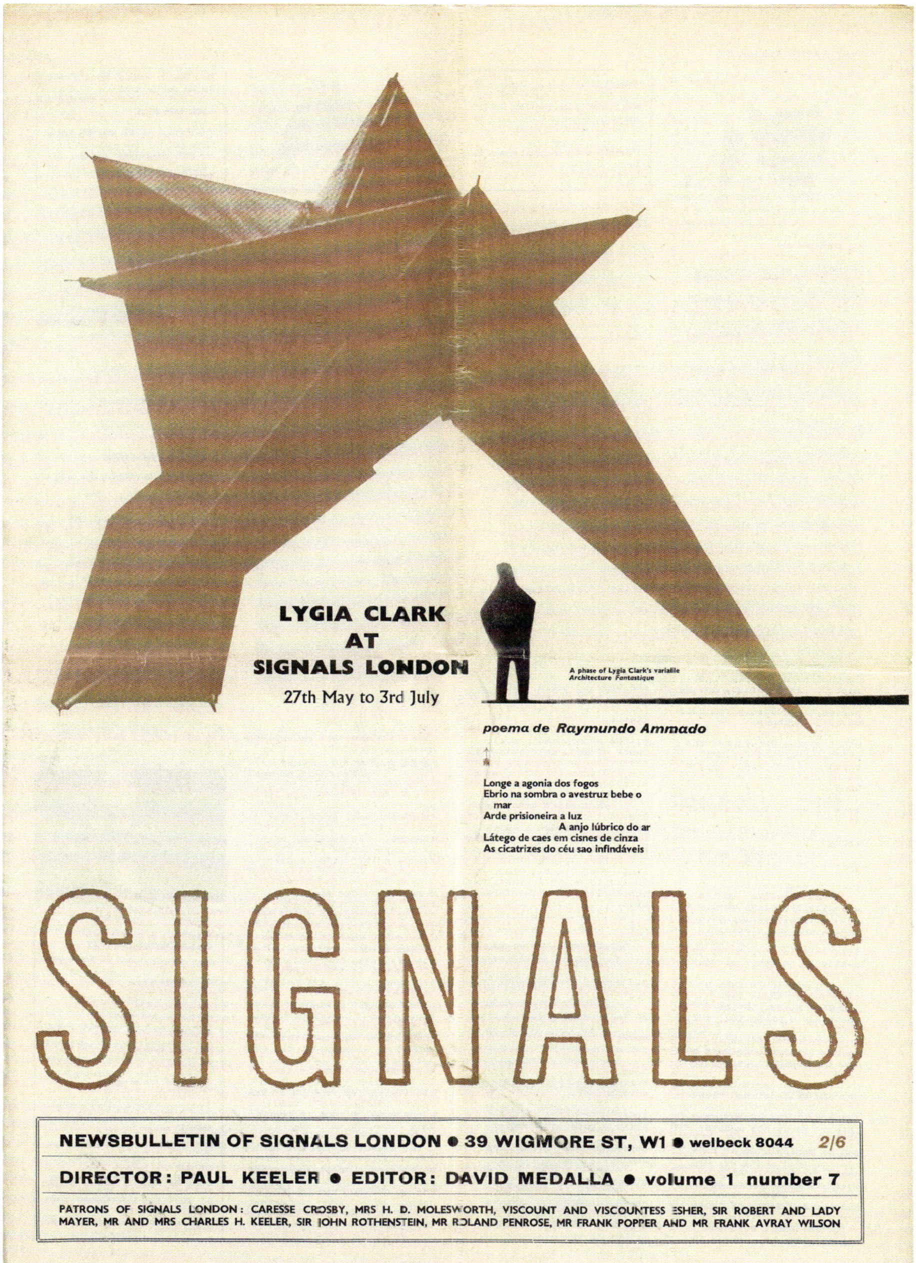

LYGIA CLARK
AT
SIGNALS LONDON
27th May to 3rd July

A phase of Lygia Clark's variable *Architecture Fantastique*

poema de Raymundo Ammado

Longe a agonia dos fogos
Ebrio na sombra o avestruz bebe o
mar
Arde prisioneira a luz
A anjo lúbrico do ar
Látego de caes em cisnes de cinza
As cicatrizes do céu sao infindáveis

SIGNALS

NEWSBULLETIN OF SIGNALS LONDON • 39 WIGMORE ST, W1 • welbeck 8044 2/6

DIRECTOR: PAUL KEELER • EDITOR: DAVID MEDALLA • volume 1 number 7

PATRONS OF SIGNALS LONDON: CARESSE CROSBY, MRS H. D. MOLESWORTH, VISCOUNT AND VISCOUNTESS ESHER, SIR ROBERT AND LADY MAYER, MR AND MRS CHARLES H. KEELER, SIR JOHN ROTHENSTEIN, MR ROLAND PENROSE, MR FRANK POPPER AND MR FRANK AVRAY WILSON

previous
Clay Perry, *Mailing Signals Newsbulletin*, 1964.

above
Signals Newsbulletin 7 (April–May 1965).

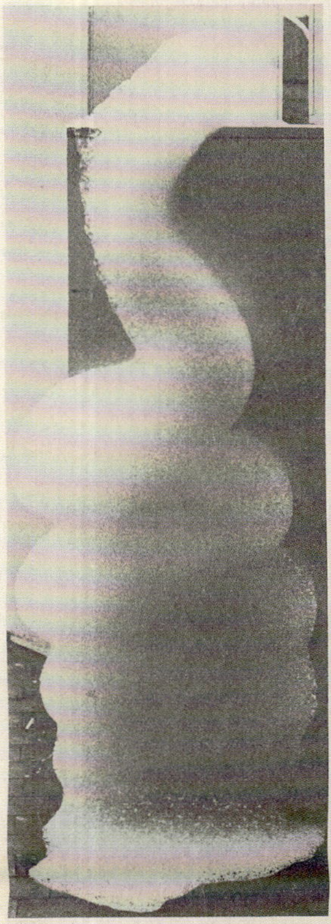

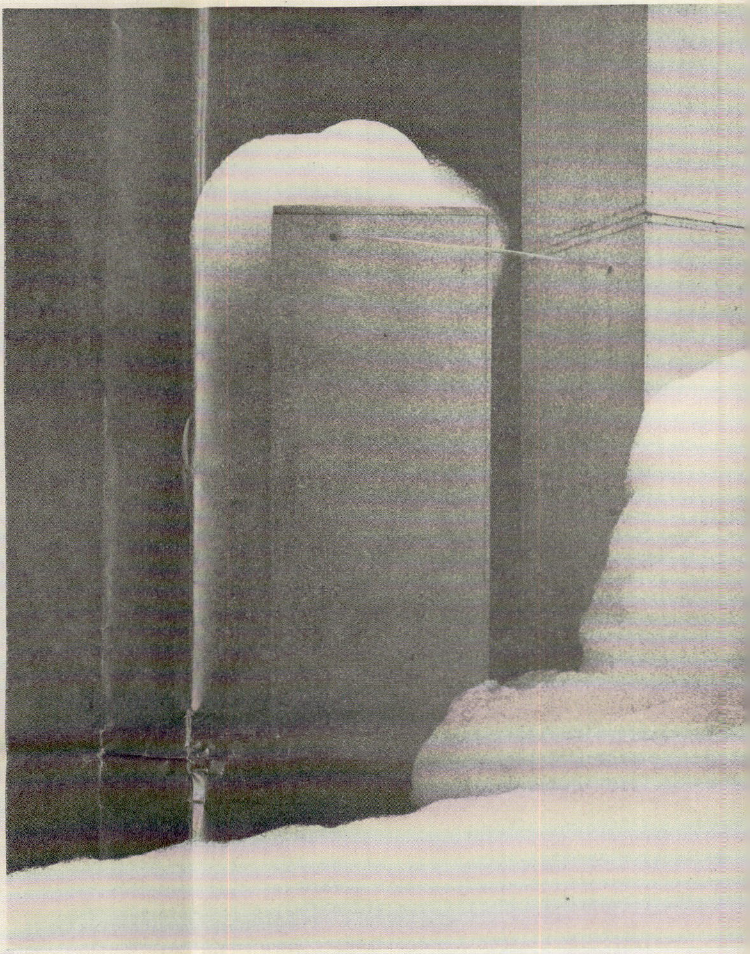

DAVID MEDALLA: CLOUD CANYONS: BUBBLE MOBILES 1964.

PHCTOGRAPHS BY CLAY PERRY.

". . . the universe begins to look more like a great thought than like a great machine . . The old dualism of mind and matter . . . seems likely to disappear, not through matter becoming in any way more shadowy or insubstantial than heretofore, or through mind becoming resolved into a function of the working of matter, but through substantial matter resolving itself into a creation and manifestation of mind . . .
A soap bubble with irregularities and corrugations on its surface is perhaps the best representation, in terms of simple and familiar materials, of the new universe revealed to us by the theory of relativity."

—Sir James Jeans.

"IF YOU LIKE I SHALL GROW IRREPROACHABLY GENTLE, NOT A MAN, BUT A CLOUD IN TROUSERS. . ."

Vladimir Mayakovsky.

With the five bubble machines exhil year in London **David Medalla** has a leading position in art.
A quarter million forms continuo sly reflecting, growing, disintegrating
Random activity is at present among crucial questions in art.
Apart from other contributions his w made, **Medalla** has shown con lusi random activity in material/transform capable of achieving not only the mos forms and motions but also an aesthet of the highest order.

—Gustav M

Bubbles in flight over Cornwall Gardens

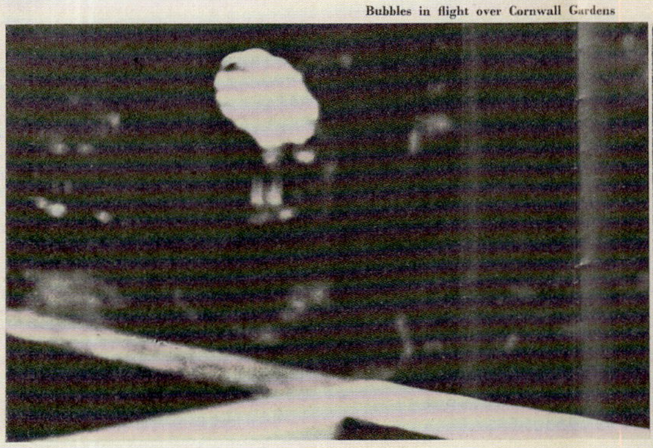

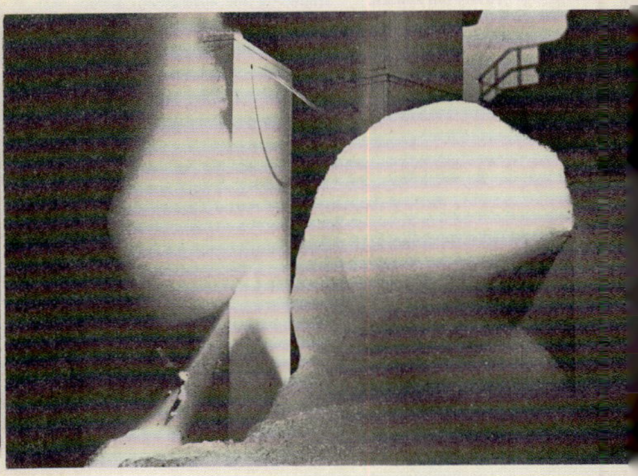

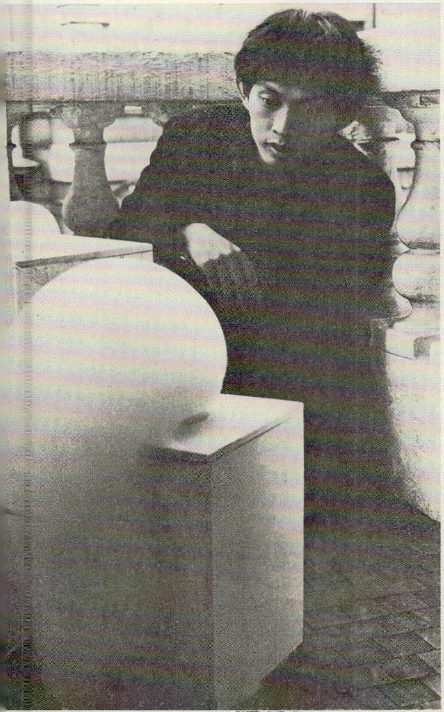

Portrait of David Cortez de Medalla by Clay Perry

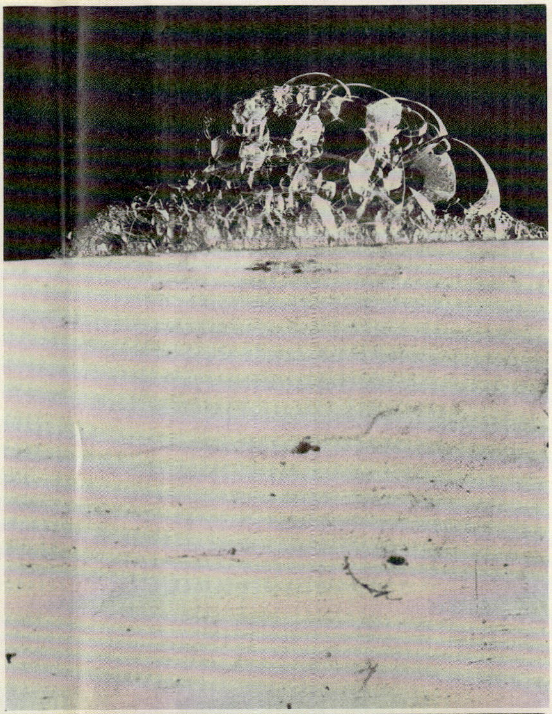

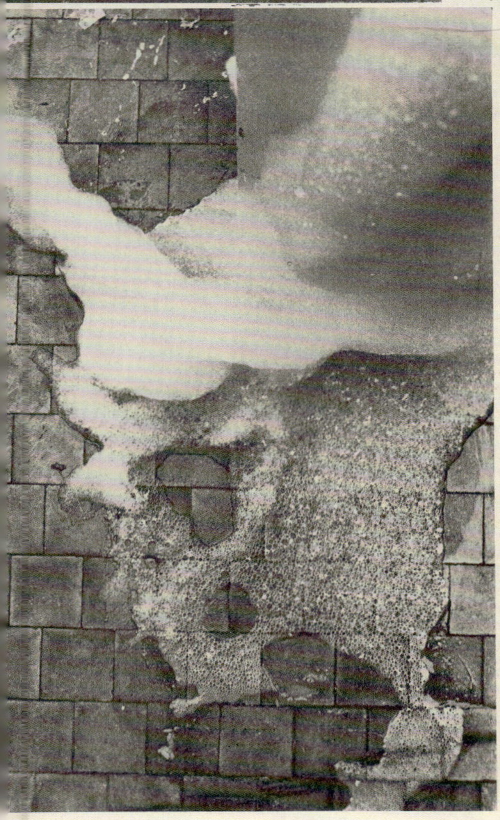

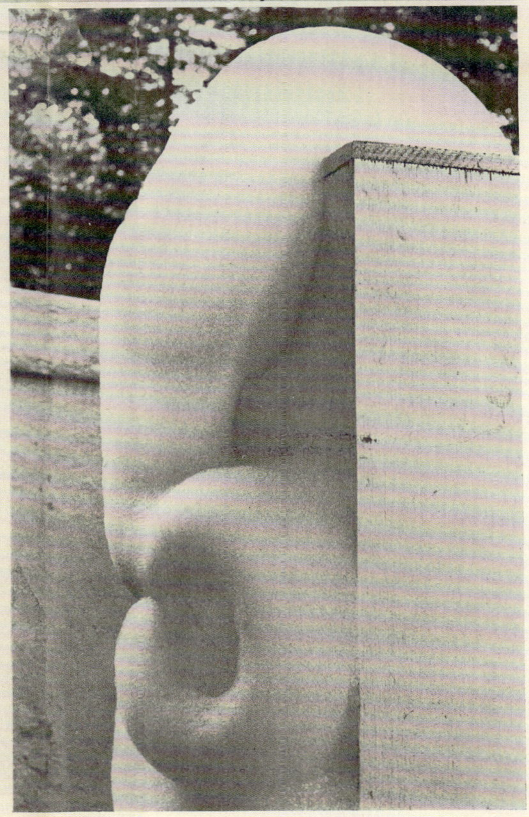

SIGNALS

NEWSBULLETIN OF THE CENTRE FOR ADVANCED CREATIVE STUDY LONDON

DIRECTOR
PAUL KEELER
92 CORNWALL GARDENS
LONDON S.W.7.

VOL 1 NO 2 SEPTEMBER 1964

SIGNALS, the name of our newsbulletin, was inspired by a series of tensile sculptures by **Takis.**
Price per copy of **Signals** is two shillings and sixpence.
Subscription rates: One year (12 issues) thirty shillings for U.K. and Northern Ireland; £3 0s. 0d. sterling for any address abroad, payable in advance by cheque or postal order to **Signals,** 92, Cornwall Gardens, London, S.W.7. *Telephone:* Knightsbridge 0138.
Advertisement rates on request.
Photographs and manuscripts should be submitted with a self-addressed stamped envelope.
The signed statements and articles in this issue do not necessarily reflect the views and policies of **Signals** and of the **Centre for Advanced Creative Study.**

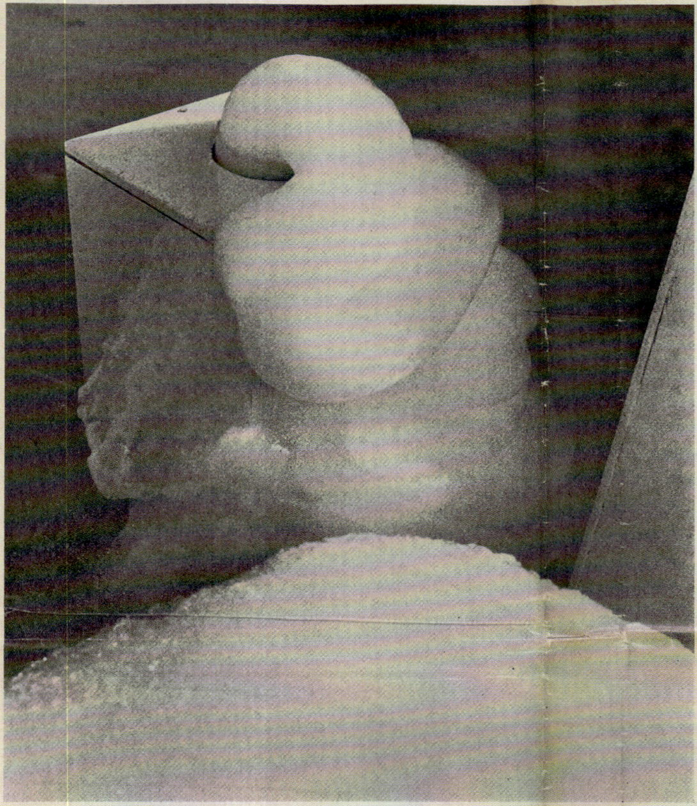

LEFT: DETAIL OF CLOUD CANYONS (BUBBLE MOBILES) 1964 BY DAVID MEDALLA.

Photo by Clay Perry.

Roberto Ganzó was born in Caracas, Venezuela, in 1898. Poet, archeologist, art critic. Spent childhood and youth in Paris where his work, written in French, has received great praise. **Orinoco,** Roberto Ganzó's first poem, was published in 1937 with illustrations by **Fernand Leger** and **Jean Fautrier.** The fragments printed here were included in the catalogue of the exhibition **Venezuela : del paisaje a la expression plastica : 10 artistas contemporaneos** at the *Muséo de Arte Contemporaneo,* Madrid, 17 October 1963. The exhibition was sponsored by the **Fundacion Fina Gómez.**
Other works by **Roberto Ganzó** have been illustrated by **Oscar Dominguez, Gérard Schneider** and **Jacques Villon.** Editions Gallimard published two volumes of Ganzó's poetry, *Poémes* and *Langage.* A collection of poems by Ganzó has also been published by editions Grasset.

ORINOCO

por Roberto Ganzó

fragmentos

Nuestros ojos, nuestras manos de seda
son para tus insectos, Orinoco.
Y vuestros golpes son mortal veneno,
múltiples ramazones elásticas.
Mi sueño ha comenzado en una choza
donde una india acurrucada llora.
Y, el otro está siempre en esta lucha
con su alma ancestral hecha girones.

Buscador de oro, conquistador,
cuanto fango amasado por tus manos!
tus desdeñosos ojos nada ven:
nada del sol y nada del torrente,
nada del hundimiento de las cimas
ni tampoco a esos cóndores voraces
que acechan nuevos muertos en abismos.

Sin embargo que harás tú con ese oro
que encontraste—tal vez—en el crepúsculo?
El último amor está ya muerto y
retrocede la última esperanza.
Conquistador, conquistador dudoso,
sumérgete tú ahora en tu conquista,
Que el otro persigue el sueño lechoso
en donde el hombre celebra una fiesta:

Vosotros, cazadores de cabezas,
Vosotros, embalsamadores de amor
y de imágenes marchitas, cambiásteis
por qué flores los rostros que os sonríen?
Suave alejamiento, dulces cabellos,
serenos ojos, labios que aún se ofrecen,
fuegos tan tibios como ciertas fiebres
y como tus labios, mujer amante,
cuando ya, celosa de mi torpeza,
tú no me ofrecías mas que ternura.
Oro! ha gritado el hombre en su sorpresa.
Pepitas y piraguas que has de perder
a los dados mientras mi sueño boga
entre árboles inundados.

Orinoco, río que arrastras
perfumes y clamores por
paraísos e infiernos,
con tus colores de máscara
y nombre de mujer ebria,
mas, intacto todavía
y muy lejos de vosotros:
India, teatro para locos,
triste Europa, Oriente soso.

Vertedero centelleante
de Los Andes para montes
que, en confundidos rebaños,
heridos bajo la piel,
sangran en ti como carnes.
Mas, cuando la noche sopla
tus bordes, un abanico
se abre, se alumbra y se cierra
y en ese instante es la muerte
bajo los besos de plumas.

Blanda caída de arañas
sobre colibríes frágiles,
tierras móviles preñadas
de vanos sustos y escombros,
sóis de un orden impasible
como toda exaltación
o como el polvo invisible
de un vuelo de mariposas.

Ave fantasma, tus gritos
no revelan tu presencia—
te busqué, te he sorprendido
pero, no eras ni apariencia.
Era el viento entre las cañas,
los juncos de mi nostalgia
lo que mezclaba tu grito de magia
y el fuego de artificio de los pájaros.

Aquí en mis venas os siento,
entrelazados verdores,
silencios y soledades,
plenitud, sombra quemante:
sombra que se desenvuelve
hasta sus sombríos estanques;
ciegos dominios donde oigo
tan solo una melopea
confusa en mi propio fondo
Y, ? Desde cuando?

Bosques de retorcidas raíces y
de tramados impulsos, de combates,
catedrales para los aquelarres,
yo he recorrido vuestras latitudes . . .
He visto los monstruos hechos de arcilla,
los tumultos de deformadas rocas
y, por encima de ellos,
siempre, un mal aliento de ángel.

Y vosotros, aguaceros,
a lo largo de las noches
llenas de niños perdidos,
gota por gota en sofocantes pozos
donde todas las voces se han callado;
y de hoja en hoja, así, sin límite,
gota por gota con color de vino,
igual que un crimen gigantesco y vano,
esas antiguas lluvias suspendidas.

Ser parte de lo que es devorado
por el hambre roja de las hormigas:
campo sonoro, momento de carne
donde la murete hizo un semillero.
Solo, en el corazón de lo que amo
sin que nada hasta hoy me haya salvado,
en una selva, dentro de mí, extinta,
ya la muerte me ha encontrado.

Mi sueño ha perdido sus remeros
mientras la sombra cubre tus espaldas.
Allá, muy lejos, ciudades polares
libran sus ecos en la madrugada.
La noche de las puertas canceladas
lágrimas ha bebido en tu mejilla;
y hé aquí que mi sueño naufraga en
fronteras imaginadas.

Cielo y montes alumbrados,
hierbas de nocturnos aros . . .
En cascadas obstinadas
el río bota sus aguas
para que se las devuelva
el día cuando, a los bordes
del mundo oscilante, se abra
su mano en el océano
en gesto de inmensa ofrenda.

**Versión española
de Reyna Rivas**

previous and above
Signals Newsbulletin 2 (September 1964).

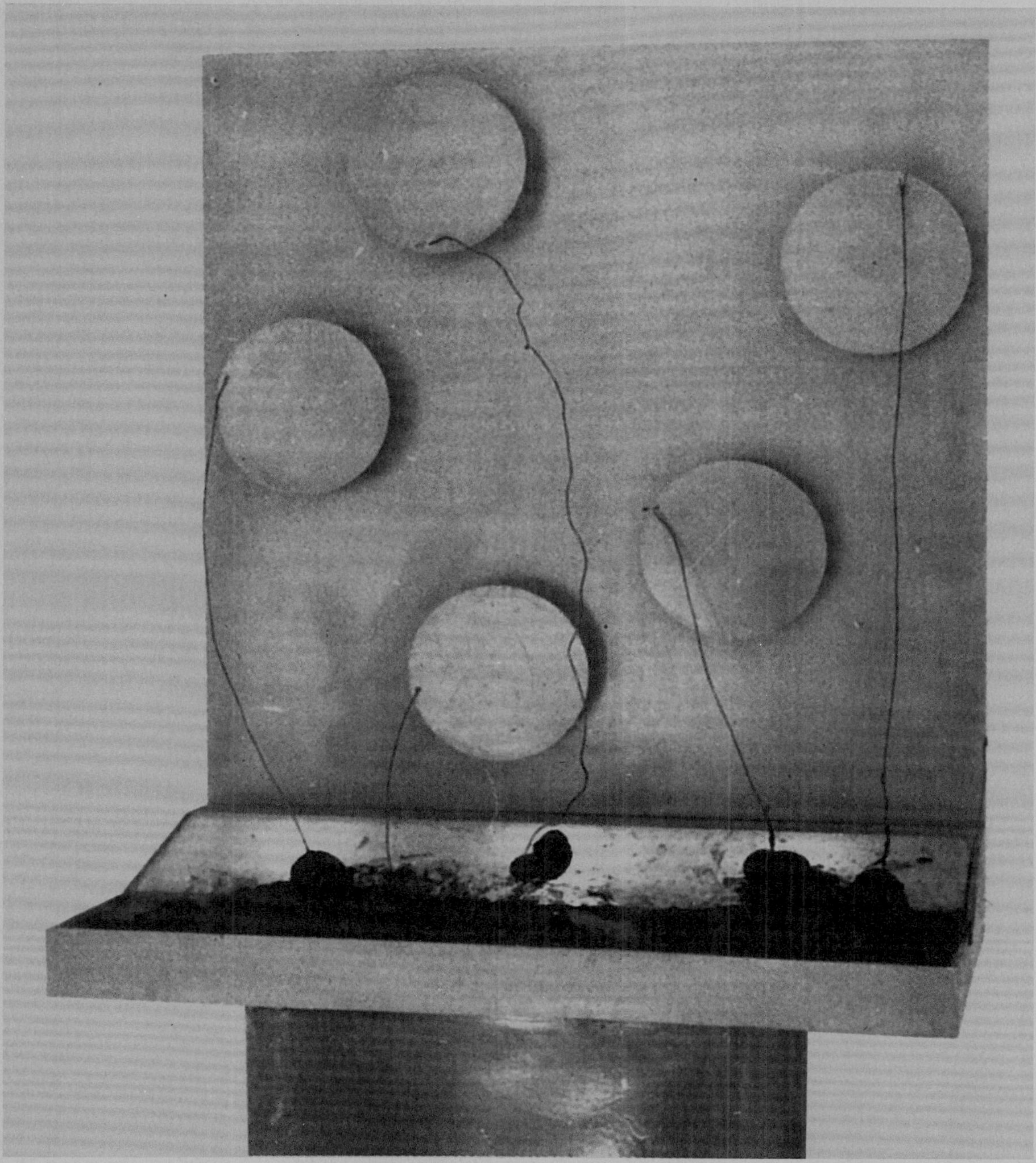

Mud Machine
1964–67

Mud Machine is a biokinetic work that combines science, technology, and art. In this automated sculpture, sponges attached to a motor by wire dip into a pool of oil and mud and smear the concoction onto an electronically lit glass screen. While reminiscent of Jean Tinguely's frantic "painting machines" of the same decade, Medalla's auto-creative works embraced the lull between actions. In an interview with Cid Reyes in *Conversations on Philippine Art*, Medalla states, "In western sculpture, in Baroque art for instance, there is no balance between active and passive. There is pure emphasis on dynamic movement: no point of rest and no point of meditation." In slow grazes across the screen, the mud becomes a type of seismographic record that traces matter reacting to energy. The symbiotic relationship between stillness and movement in Medalla's *Mud Machine* can be seen as a metaphor for competing energies that together produce meaning and forms of knowledge.

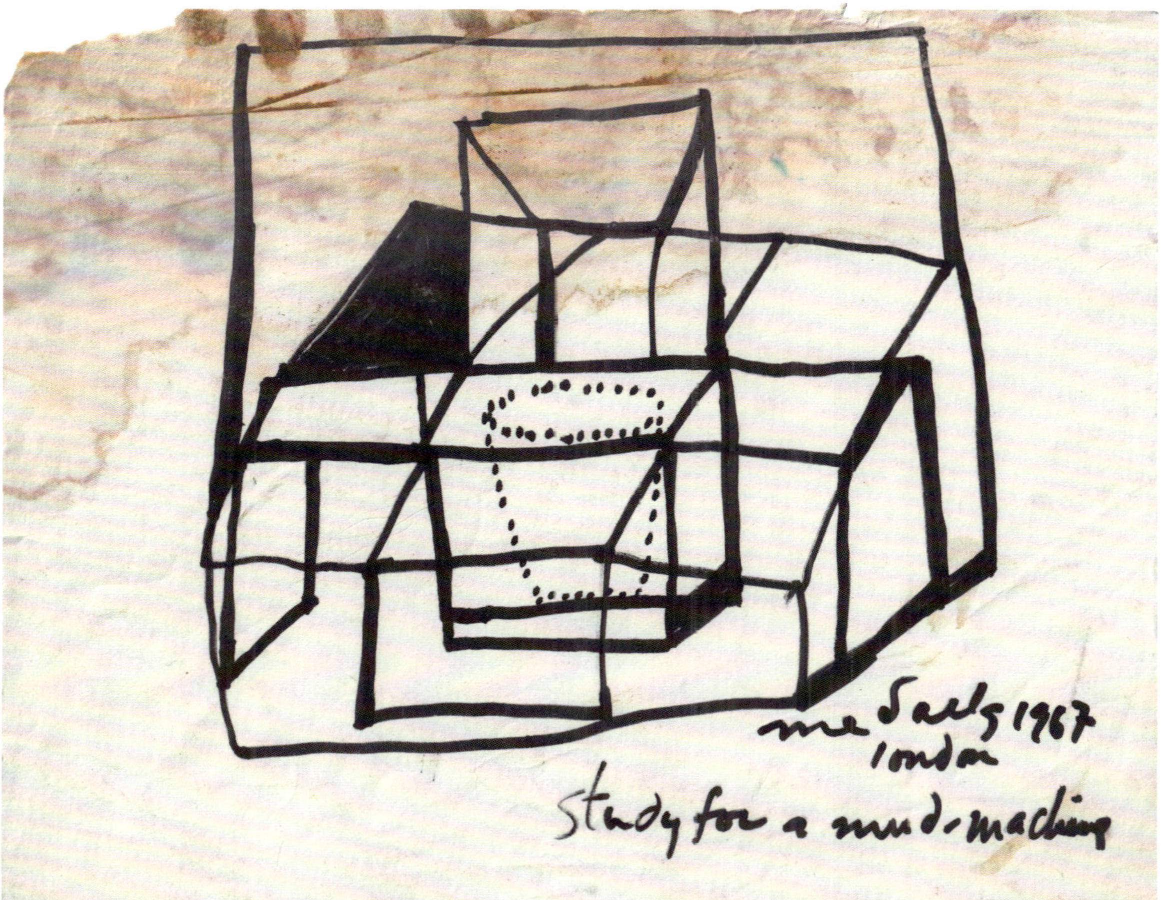

previous
Mud Machine, 1967. Wire, sponge, oil, mud, glass screen. Dimensions unknown.

above
Study for a mud-machine, 1967. China ink on paper. 8 × 9 15⁄16 in. (20.3 × 25.3 cm).

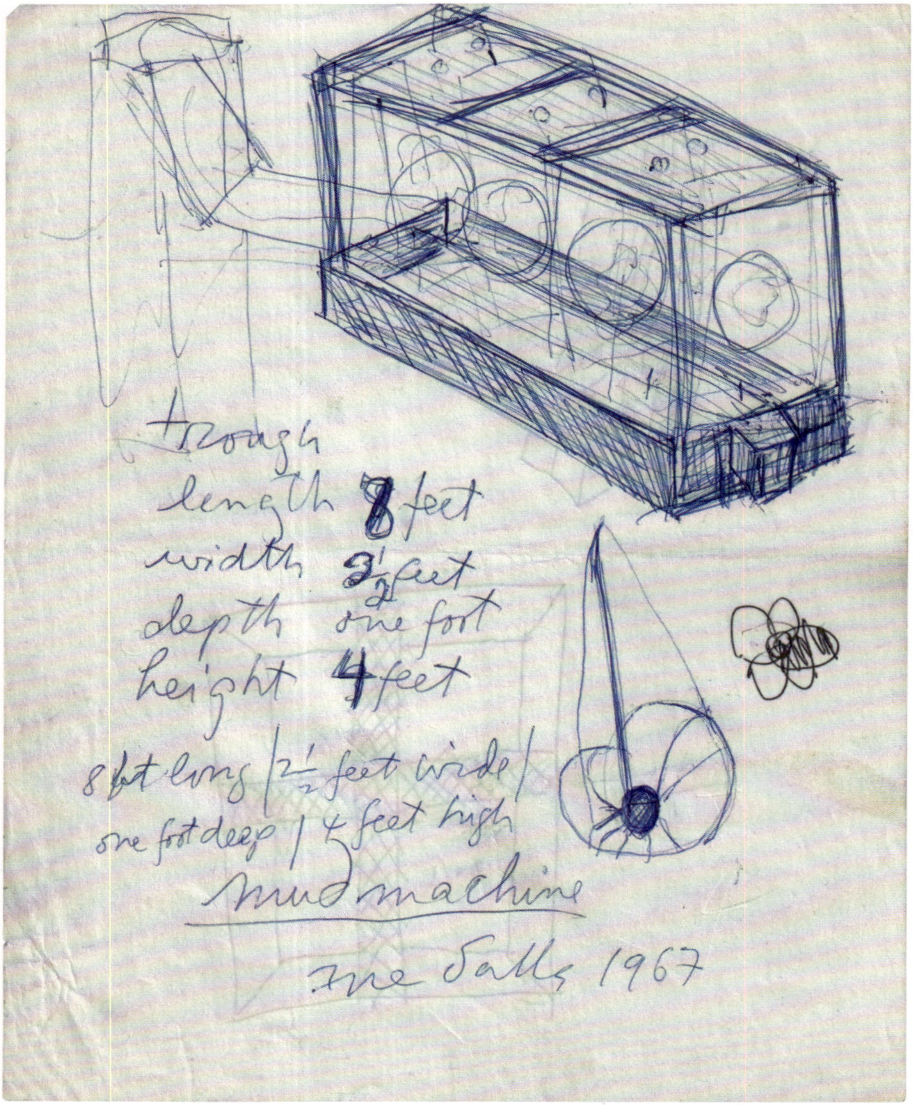

Mud Machine, 1967. Ballpoint pen on paper, recto and verso. 9 15⁄16 × 8 in. (25.3 × 20.3 cm).

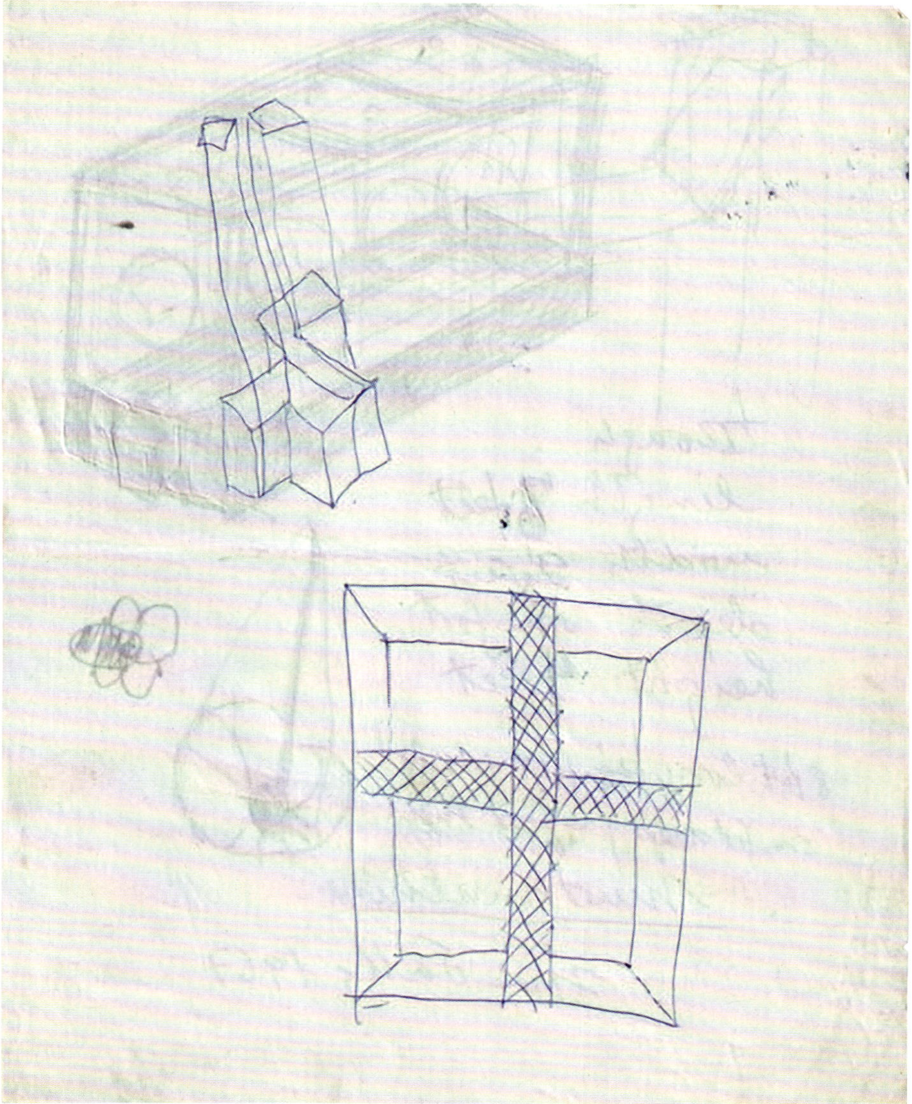

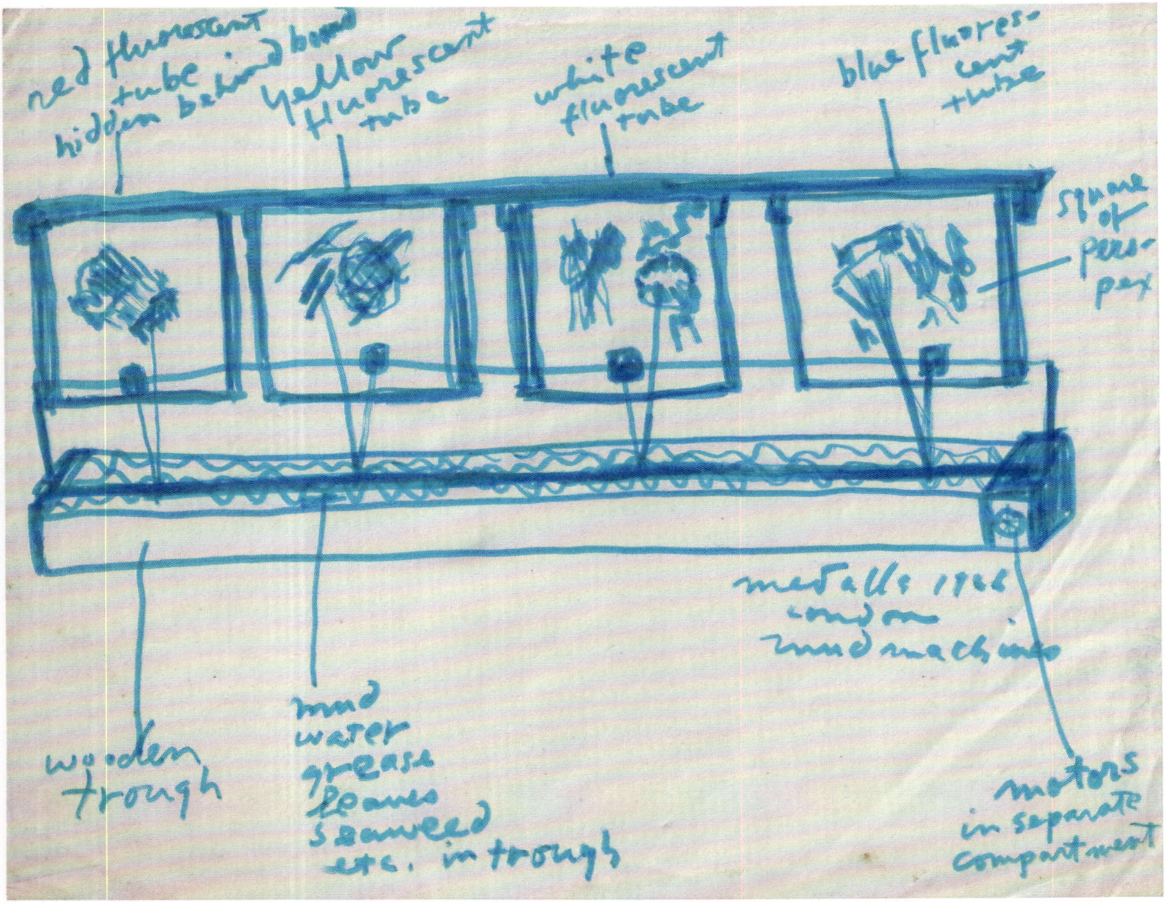

Mud machines, 1966. Felt-tip marker on paper. 8 × 9 15⁄16 in. (20.3 × 25.3 cm).

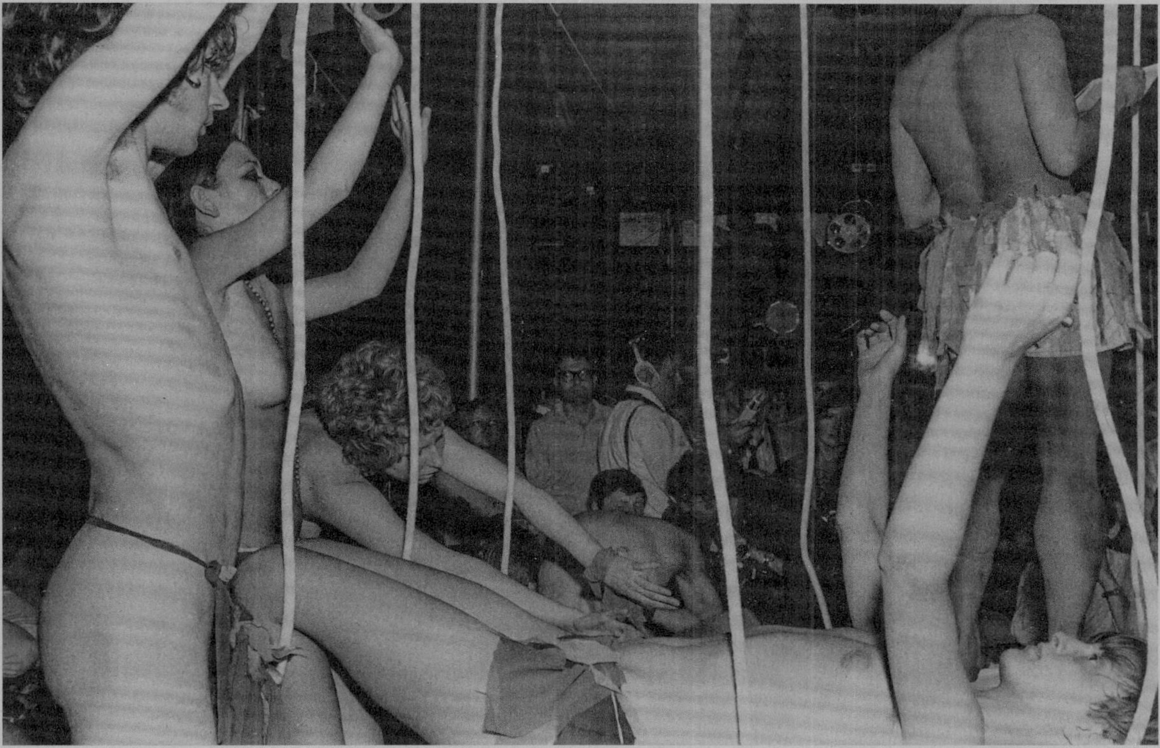

The Exploding Galaxy 1967–68

In 1967, Medalla and Paul Keeler initiated the psychedelic commune known as the Exploding Galaxy at 99 Ball Ponds Road in East London. The group was originally envisioned as an experimental artists' collective inspired by the subversive methods of experimentation promoted by the Dada art movement of the early twentieth century. In 1967, they produced the recurring performances *The Bird Ballet* and *The Buddha Ballet*. With these and other works, Medalla and Keeler imagined forms of theater that rejected hierarchy and blurred the lines between spectator and performer. Their unconventional approach was met with opposition from neighbors, who regularly called the police on the house. One police raid in particular, which occurred while Medalla was out of the country, involved planted drugs and the arrests of members of the commune. Following the dissolution of the Exploding Galaxy in 1968, Medalla and his collaborator John Dugger left for India to study the Kathakali dance-drama of Kerala. In eighteen months, Dugger and Medalla traveled to Italy, Spain, Senegal, South Africa, Kenya, Pakistan, India, Sri Lanka, Nepal, Singapore, Thailand, and the Philippines in order to learn more about the global artistic practices that had influenced their collective experiments with the Exploding Galaxy.

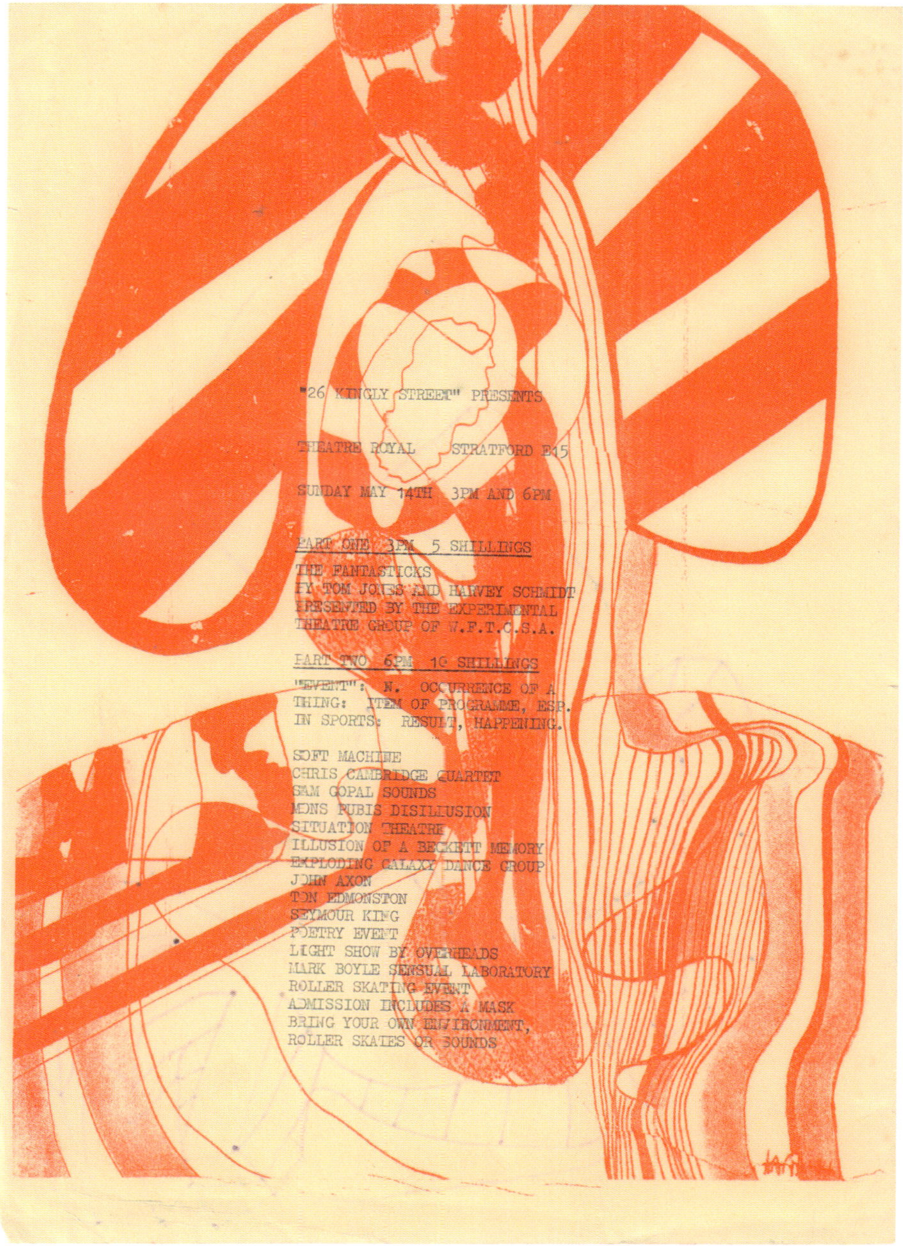

previous
The Exploding Galaxy, 99 Ball Ponds Road, London, 1967.

above
Exhibition announcement including the Exploding Galaxy, Theatre Royal, 26 Kingly Street, London, 1968.

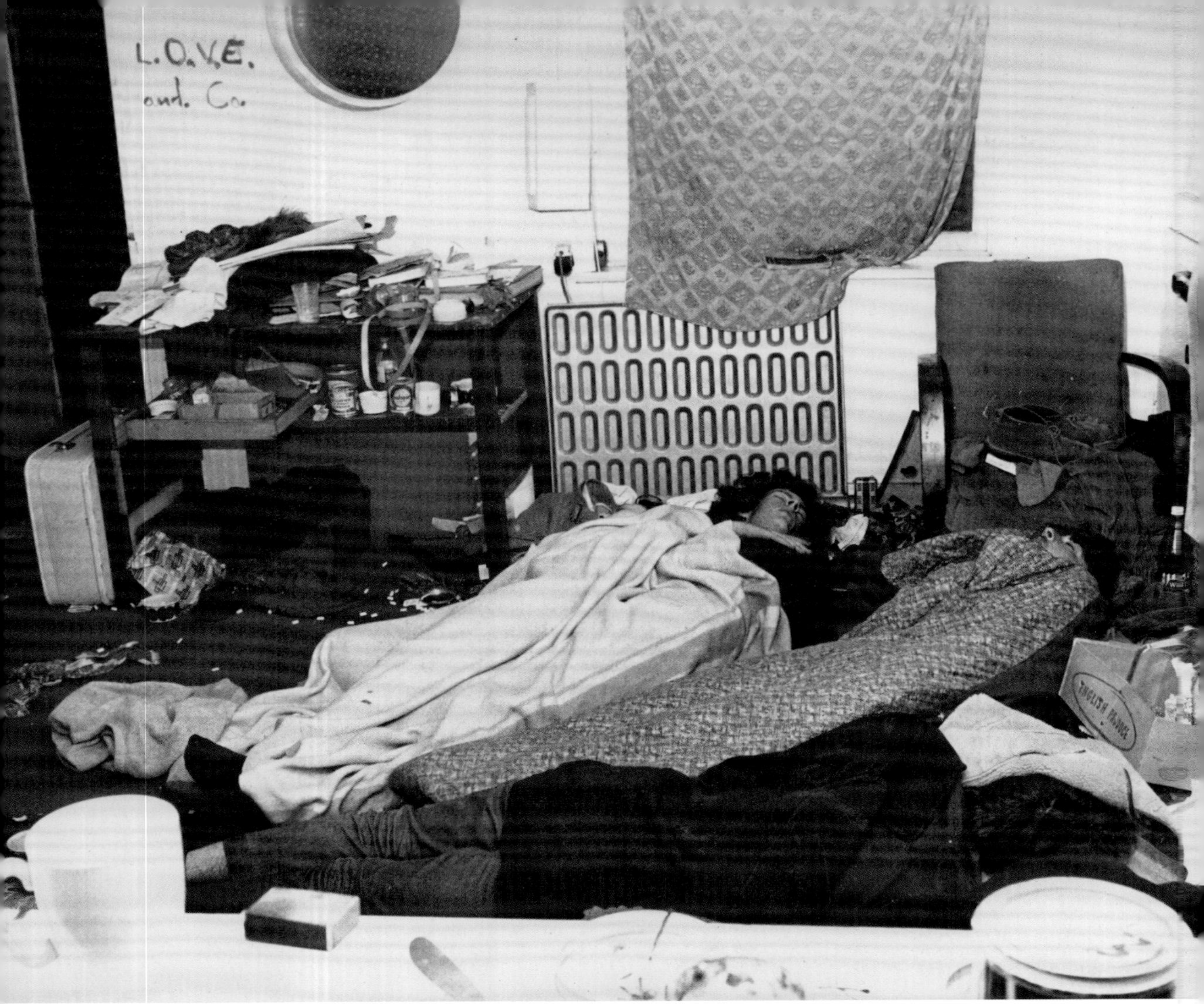

above
The Exploding Galaxy, 99 Ball Ponds Road, London, 1967.

opposite
David Medalla in costume, 99 Ball Ponds Road, London, 1968.

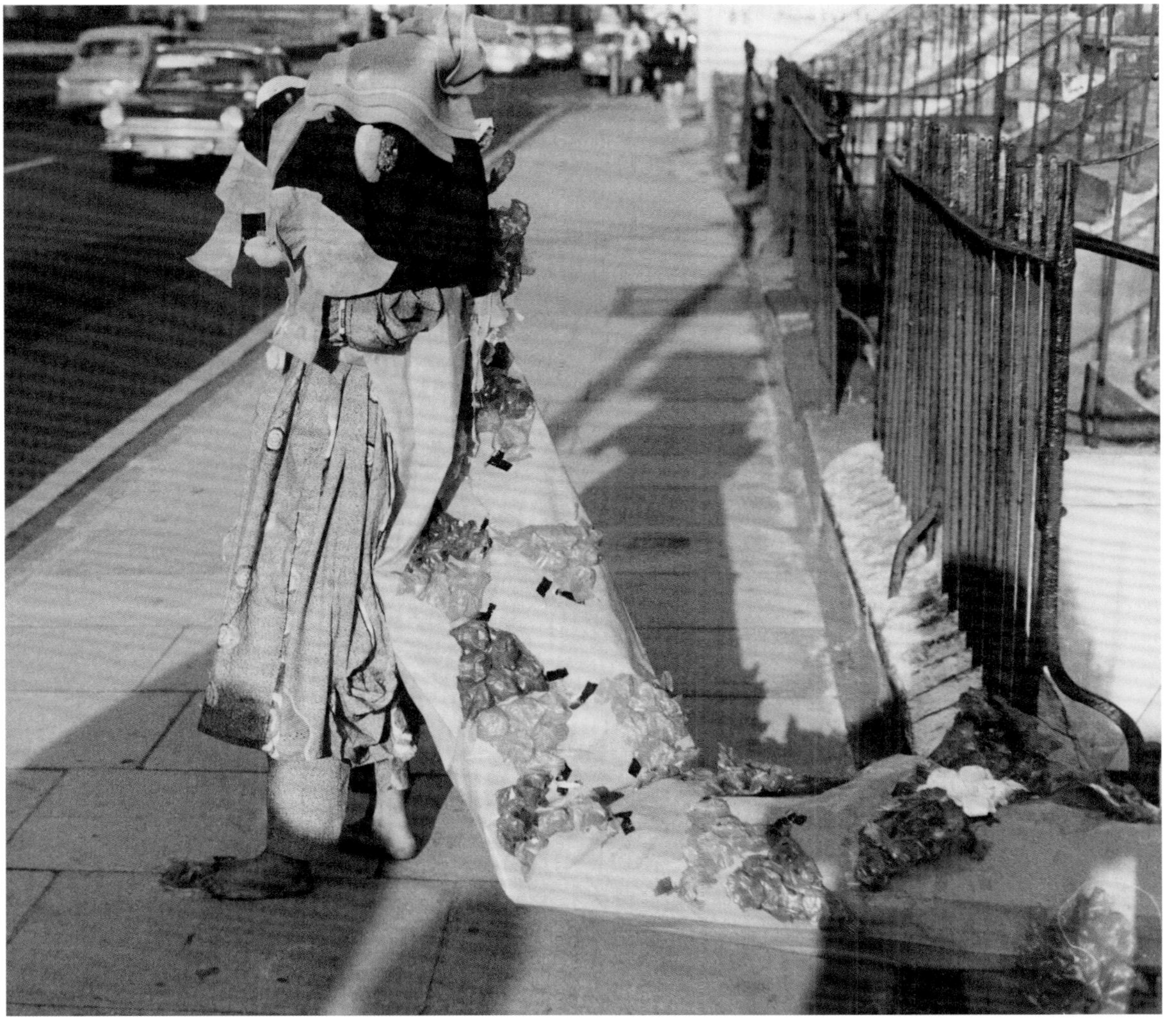

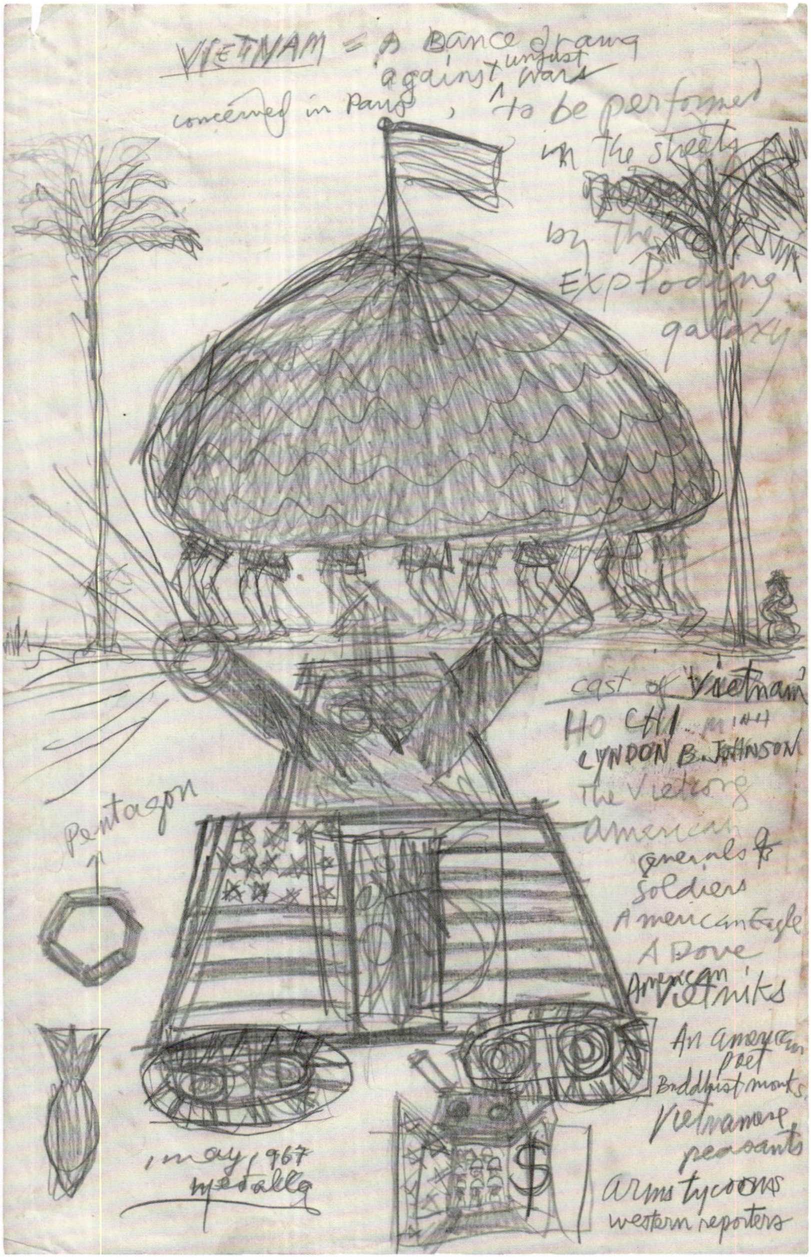

above
Vietnam—A Dance drama against unjust wars, 1967. Graphite on paper. 15 15⁄16 × 10 in. (40.5 × 25.4 cm).

opposite
David Medalla in Hyde Park, London, 1967.

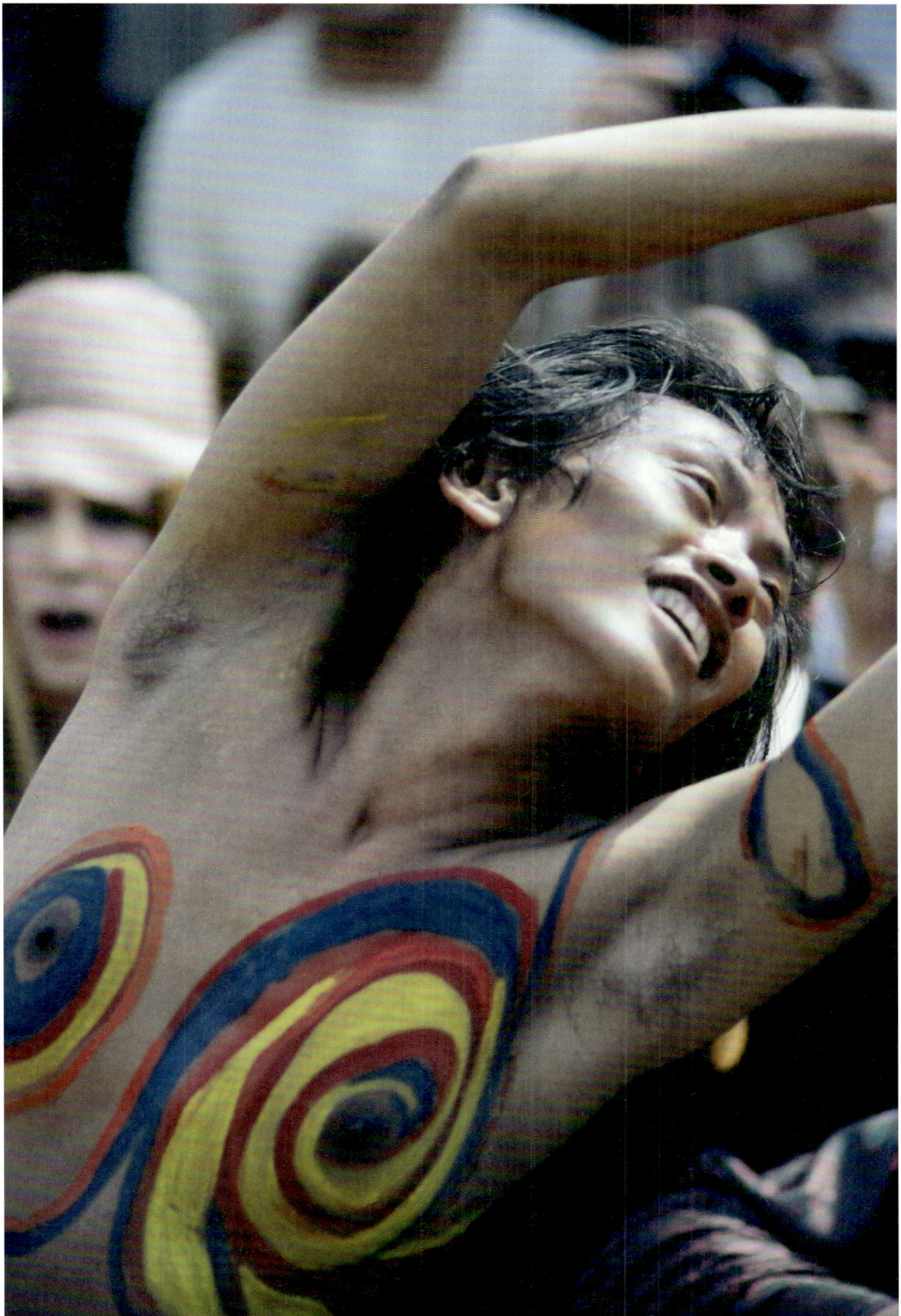

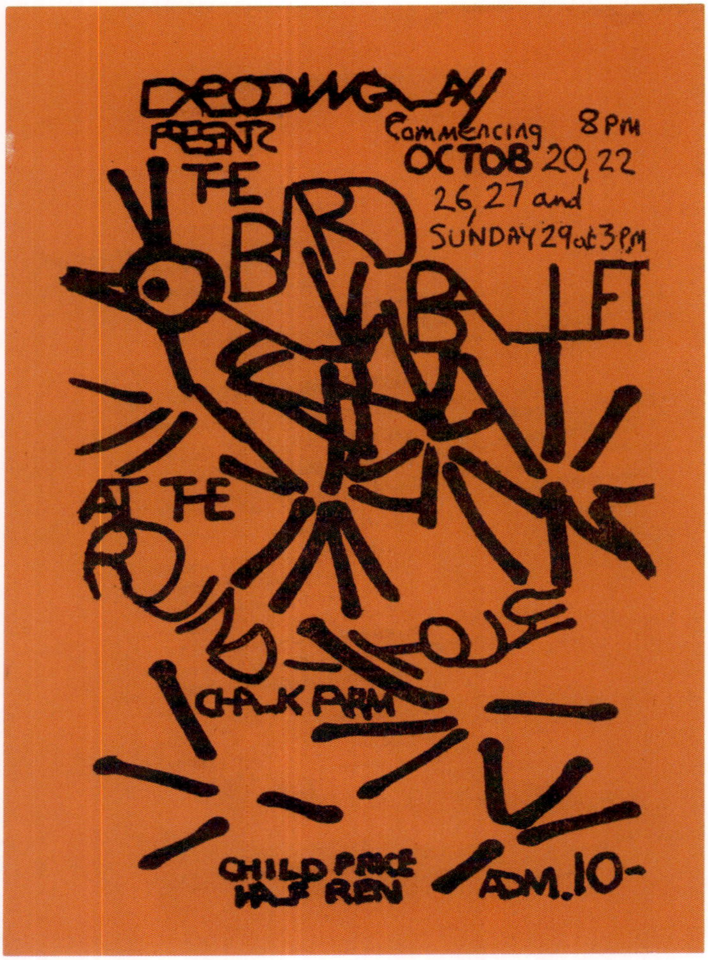

The Buddha Ballet and The Bird Ballet, both 1967

The experimental artist collective the Exploding Galaxy enacted *The Buddha Ballet* at Parliament Hill in London every weekend during the summer of 1967 and into 1968, when the group disbanded. These performances, which were loosely based on Buddhist fables, sought to situate historical forms of knowledge in contemporary contexts. The guide for *The Buddha Ballet* was *Milinda Panha* (*The Questions of King Milinda*), a Buddhist text dating from sometime between 100 BCE and 200 CE. This text, which chronicles a dialogue between Menander I, a Greco-Bactrian king, and Nagasena, a Buddhist sage, highlights the ways in which the spiritual systems of the two cultures complemented one another. In the performance *The Bird Ballet*, which the group organized that same year at Roundhouse in London, participants were encouraged to choose a bird—in existence or of their own creation—and embody it. Around sixty birds took form, with the audience becoming the actors. Throughout his career, Medalla expanded the possibilities for experiencing works of art by encouraging viewers to become participants.

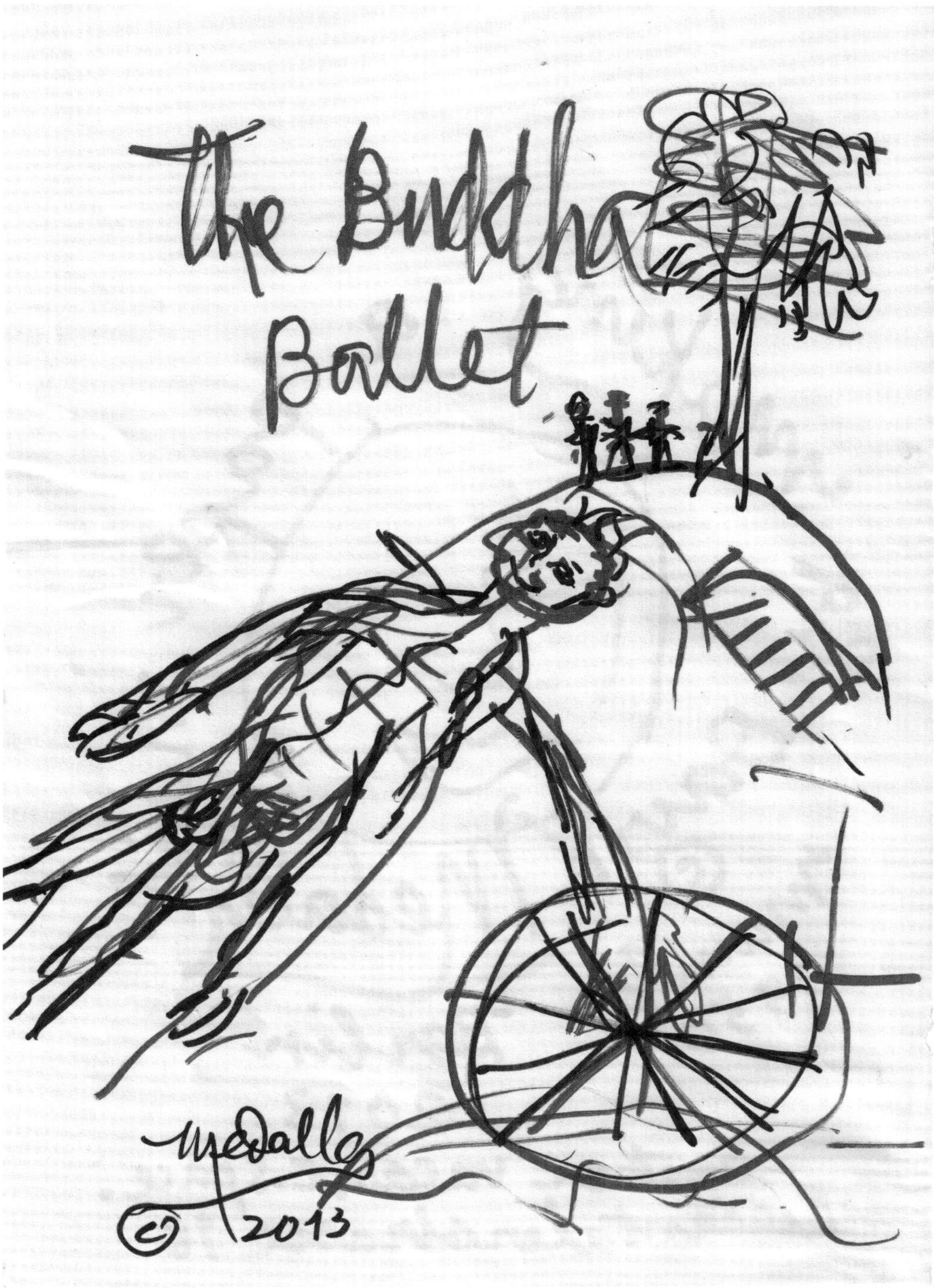

opposite
Announcement for *The Bird Ballet*, 1967.

above
The Buddha Ballet, 2013. Felt-tip marker on paper. One of three gate-folded sheets, 11½ × 8¼ in. (29.3 × 20.7 cm) each.

The Buddha Ballet at Parliament Hill, London, 1968.

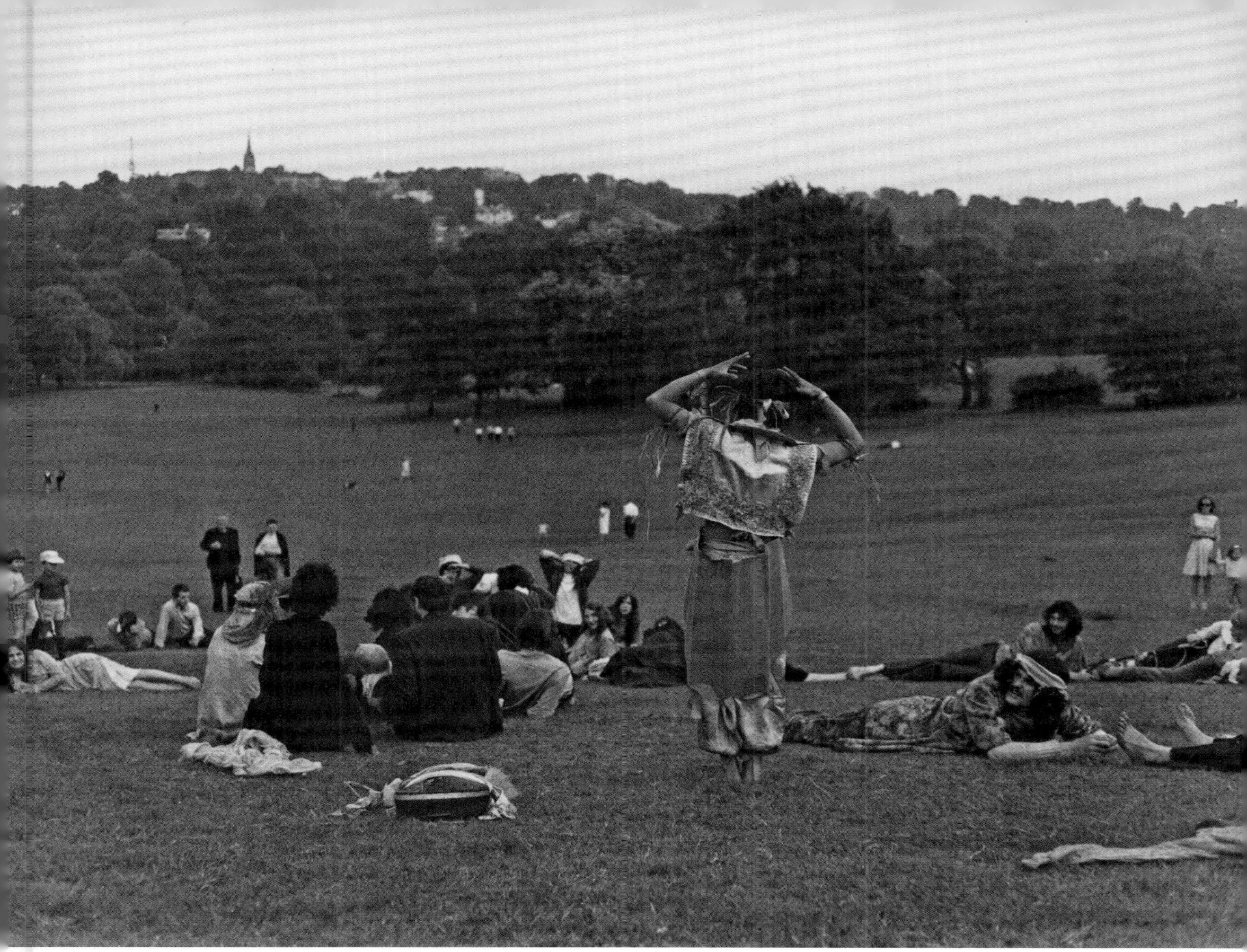

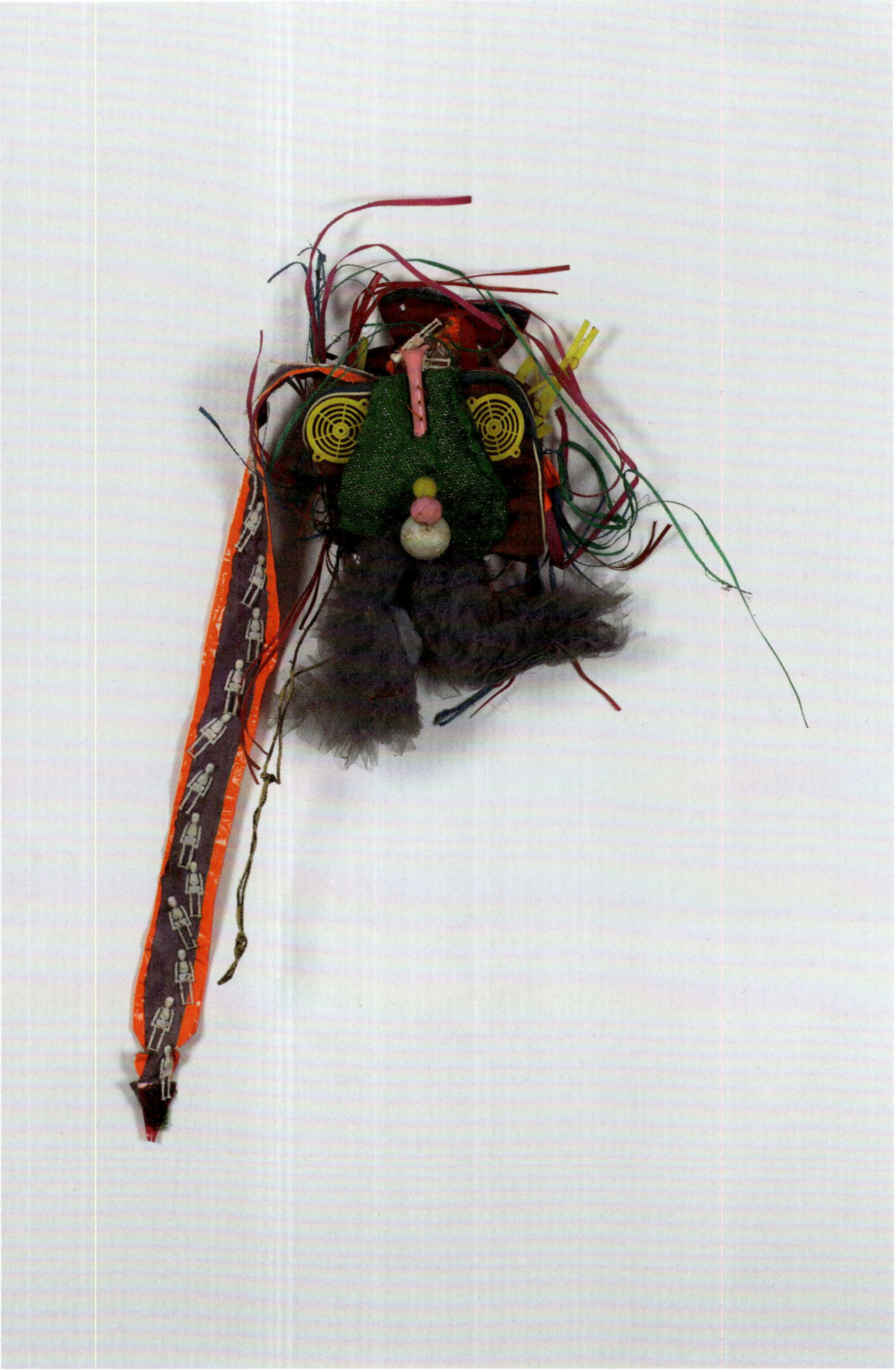

The Bird Ballet Mask, 1967. Plastic, ribbons, artificial leather purse, plastic toys, string, plastic balls, nylon fabric. 24 × 11 13⁄16 × 3 9⁄16 in. (61 × 30 × 9 cm).

SINGING THE BODY ELECTRIC!

by John Dugger

Curved Space Tubes 1969 (orange tubes)

Put the suspended orange tubes to your ears. Listen to the jetsounds of your body and the sounds of inner and outer space.

Body Conductors 1969. (grey tube)

Take the grey tube – put the ends to your ears. Rub the surface of the tube across the surface of your body and across the bodies of other people. Listen to the sonar landscape of the body.

3. Sandals for the Path 1969.

Put the sandals on your feet. Hold the two transparent tubes to your ears and listen to the landscape as you walk.

A Stitch in Time 1972 by David Medalla.

Stitch anything you like (poems, songs, pictures, diagrams, slogans, etc.) on the suspended cotton sheets.

'Hail the Coming of Socialism to Tibet!'

Sonar sand machine by David Medalla (1963-73)

take the small stick. strike gently the suspended Tibetan bell make it ring!

A Stitch in Time
1968–2019

A Stitch in Time was a participatory artwork in which Medalla invited visitors to use needles and thread to sew on a large swath of fabric suspended from the ceiling, resulting in a collaboration that evolved over the course of its display. The sculpture took other forms as part of *People's Participation Pavilion* (1972) at documenta 5 in Kassel, Germany, and at international venues until 2019. *A Stitch in Time* was born when two of Medalla's former lovers (until then unknown to one another) visited him in London. When they departed, the artist gave each a handkerchief embroidered with messages and a needle and thread, encouraging them to sew as a way to pass the time while traveling. Years later, Medalla recognized one of the handkerchiefs—adorned with textiles, beads, and embroidery—on a stranger's backpack at Schiphol Airport in Amsterdam. The themes of love, travel, and chance encounters recur in the artist's work.

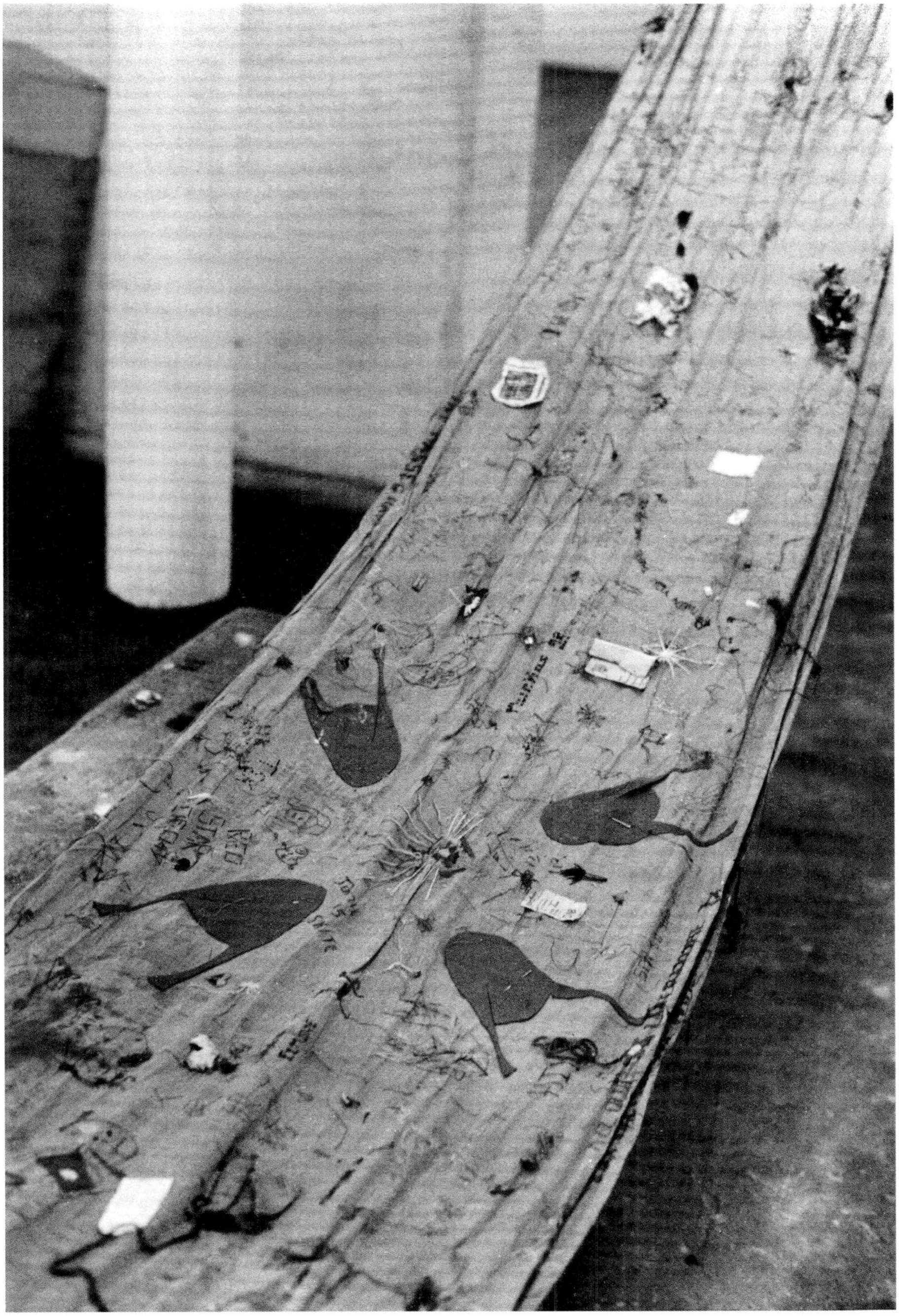

previous
Instructions for *Singing the Body Electric!* by John Dugger and *A Stitch in Time* by David Medalla, n.d. Felt-tip marker on cardstock. $19\frac{11}{16} \times 23\frac{5}{8}$ in. (50 × 60 cm).

above
A Stitch in Time, Art Meeting Place, London, 1974.

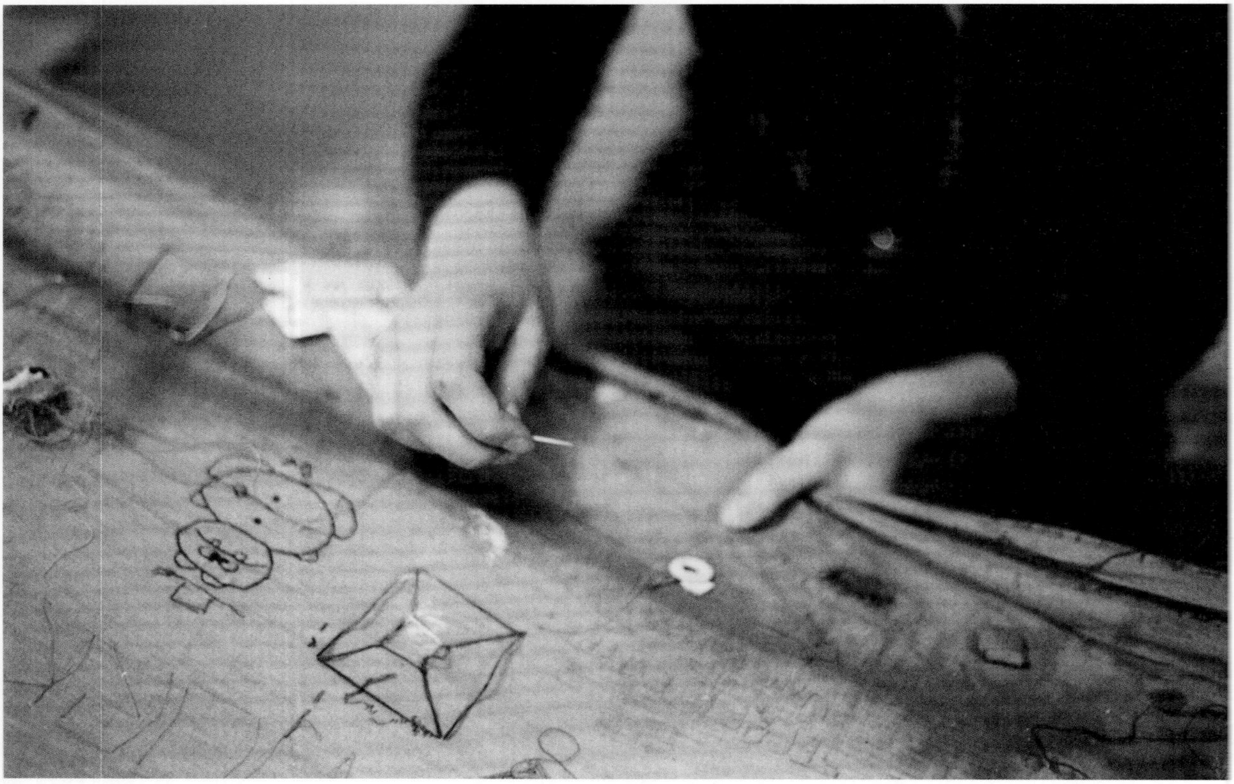

A *Stitch in Time*, Art Meeting Place, London, 1974.

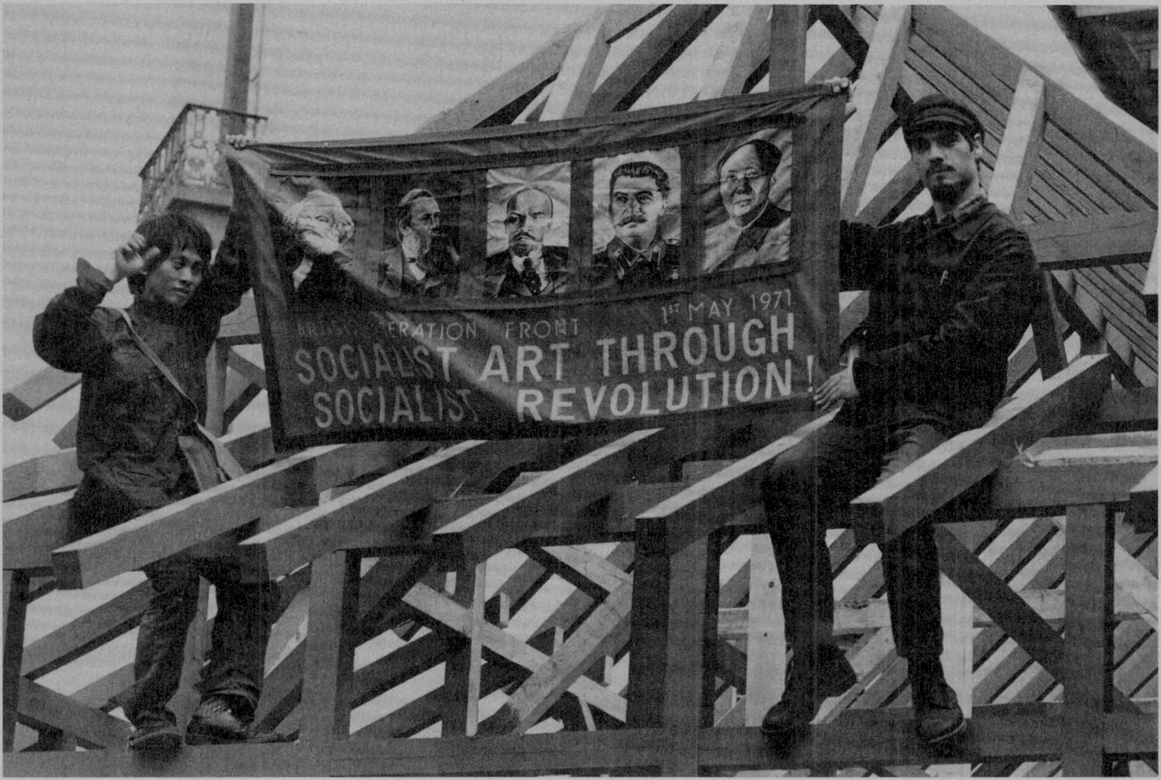
1ST MAY 1971
SOCIALIST ART THROUGH
SOCIALIST REVOLUTION!

Artists' Liberation Front 1970–74

In 1970, Medalla and John Dugger founded the Artists' Liberation Front in response to the global rise in dictatorships that were aided and abetted by US foreign policy. This artists' group explored the potential of political artmaking through participatory works, such as *Down with the Slave Trade!* (1971), *The International Dust Market* (1972), *Games of Sea and Tides* (1972), *People Weave a House!* (1972), and *Porcelain Wedding* (1973–74). They valued the Maoist example of communal labor, as evidenced in *People Weave a House!*, which encouraged visitors to build a house together using materials available in the gallery. The group eventually expanded and was reconstituted as Artists for Democracy.

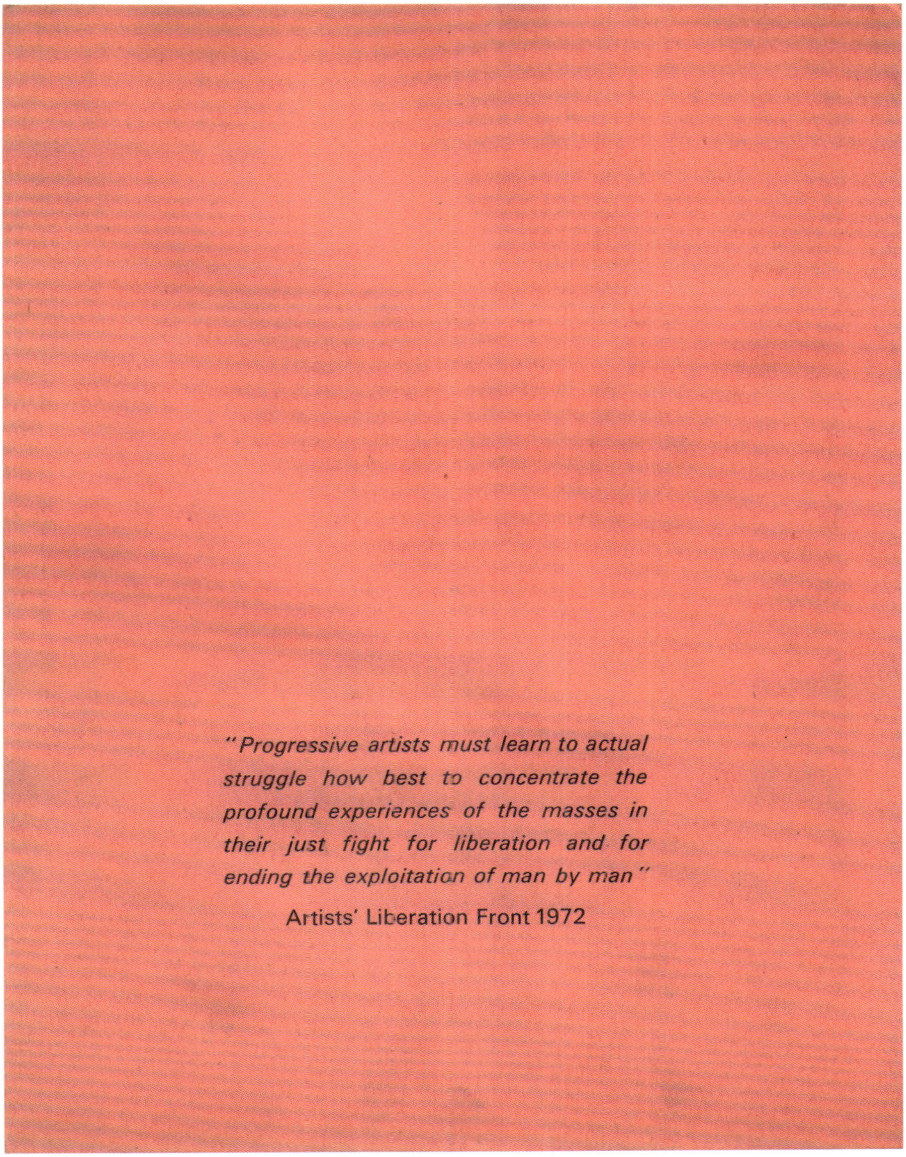

"Progressive artists must learn to actual struggle how best to concentrate the profound experiences of the masses in their just fight for liberation and for ending the exploitation of man by man"

Artists' Liberation Front 1972

previous
John Dugger and David Medalla, *People's Participation Pavilion*, documenta 5, Kassel, Germany, June 30–October 8, 1972.

above
Pamphlet for Artists' Liberation Front, 1972.

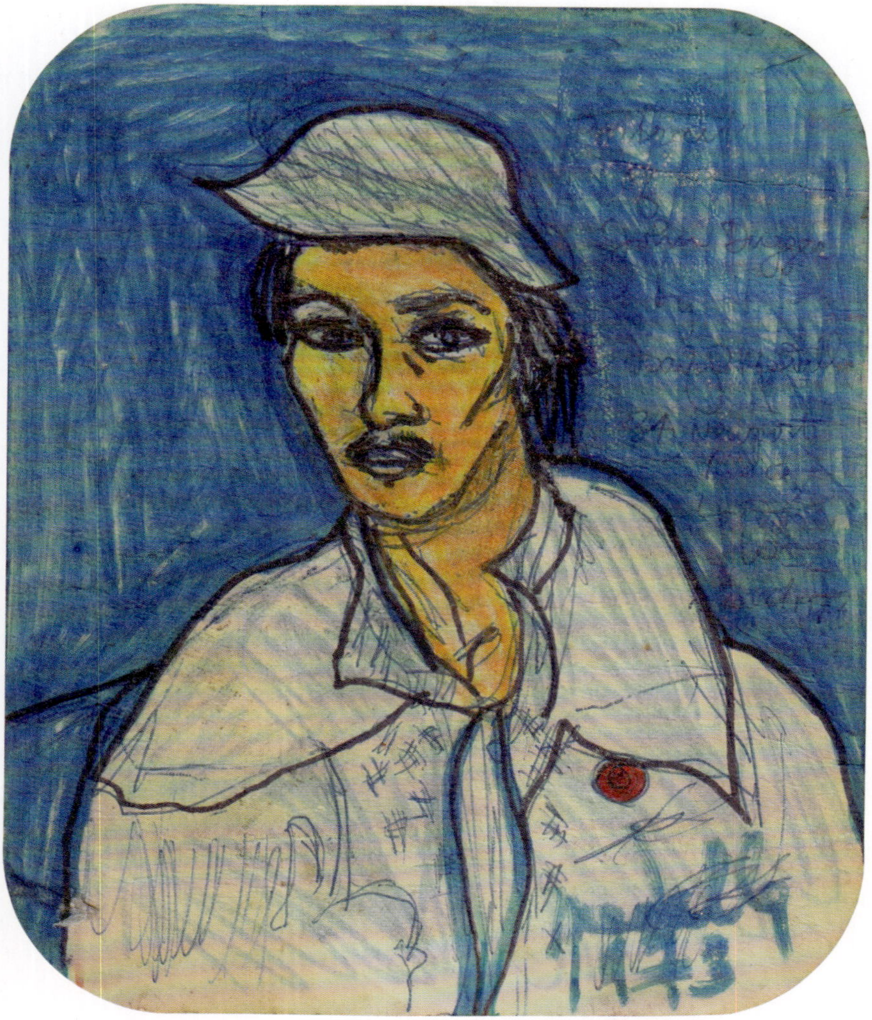

above

Untitled, 1973. Ballpoint pen, colored pencil, felt-tip marker, and watercolor on aluminum-foil-coated board. 5$\frac{7}{16}$ × 4$\frac{1}{2}$ in. (13.8 × 11.5 cm).

opposite

Poster for *listen to the sonar trees*, 1969.

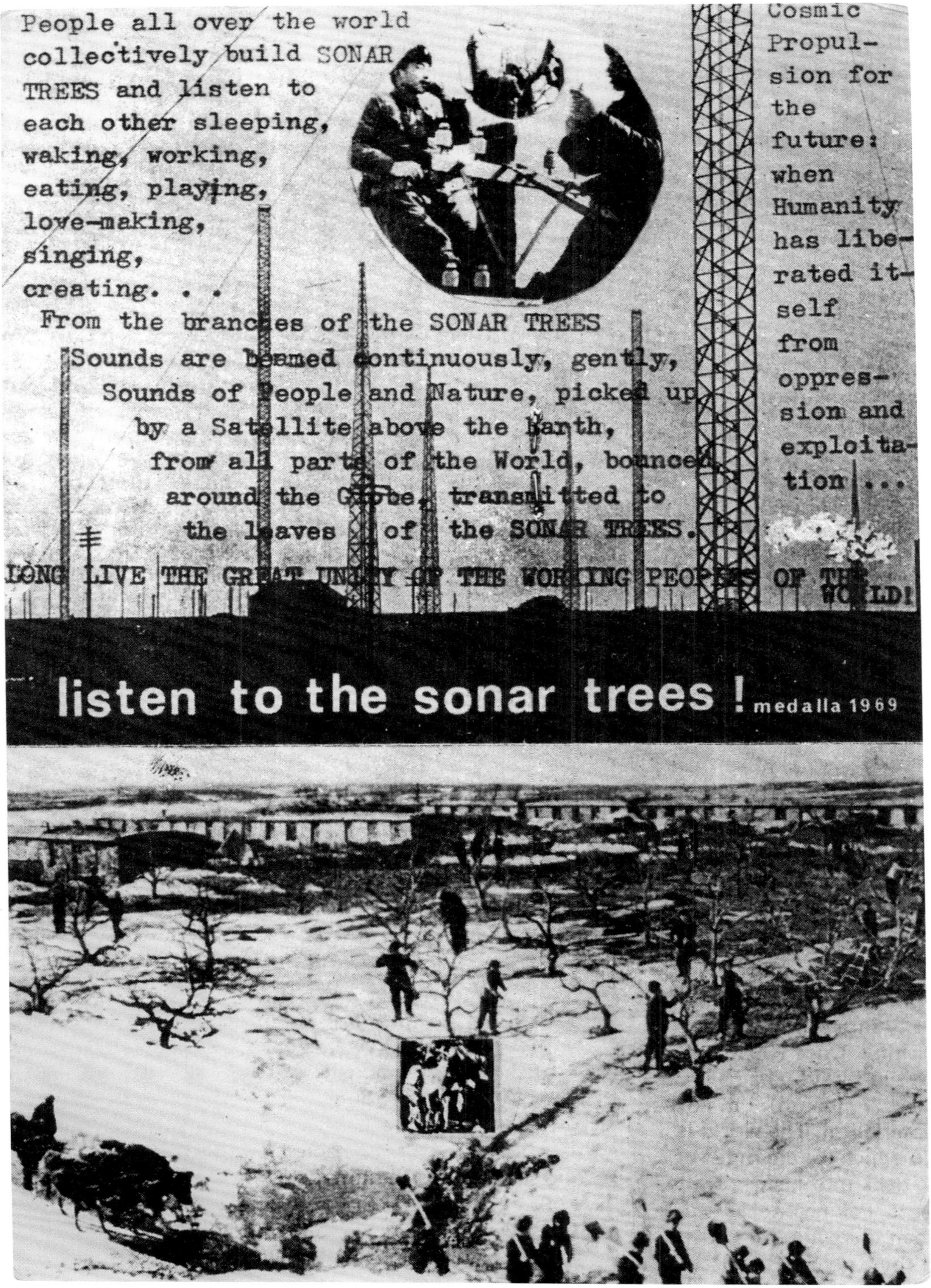
People all over the world
collectively build SONAR
TREES and listen to
each other sleeping,
waking, working,
eating, playing,
love-making,
singing,
creating. . .
From the branches of the SONAR TREES
Sounds are beamed continuously, gently,
Sounds of People and Nature, picked up
by a Satellite above the Earth,
from all parts of the World, bounced
around the Globe, transmitted to
the leaves of the SONAR TREES.
LONG LIVE THE GREAT UNITY OF THE WORKING PEOPLES OF THE WORLD!
Cosmic
Propul-
sion for
the
future:
when
Humanity
has libe-
rated it-
self
from
oppres-
sion and
exploita-
tion ...
listen to the sonar trees !
medalla 1969

People's Participation Pavilion, 1972

In 1972, curator Harald Szeemann invited John Dugger to participate in documenta 5, the fifth iteration of the quinquennial international contemporary art exhibition in Kassel, Germany. Dugger asked Medalla to be his collaborator, and the two artists decided to erect their installation in an area just outside the Fridericianum that was being used as a waste disposal site for the previous iteration of Documenta. Amidst the debris, Dugger and Medalla constructed *People's Participation Pavilion*, with the help of students and workers from Kassel. This large building of red-painted wood was inspired by Asian and Oceanic architecture. The entrance was filled with water, and visitors were required to take off their shoes before entering. In this way, the structure acted as a filter, giving visitors a chance to pause and "cleanse their palates" while taking in the hundreds of artworks in the exhibition. Inside, the pavilion contained straw mats; works by Dugger and Medalla, including an installation by Dugger that featured a live snake in a pit and Medalla's *A Stitch in Time* and Kumbum series; posters that supported liberation struggles around the world; and a letter from Medalla denouncing the Tate's decision not to acquire his Cloud Canyons sculpture. (The museum eventually acquired *Cloud Canyon No. 3* [1963/2004] over thirty years later.) Despite its high attendance, *People's Participation Pavilion* was mostly ignored by the art press.

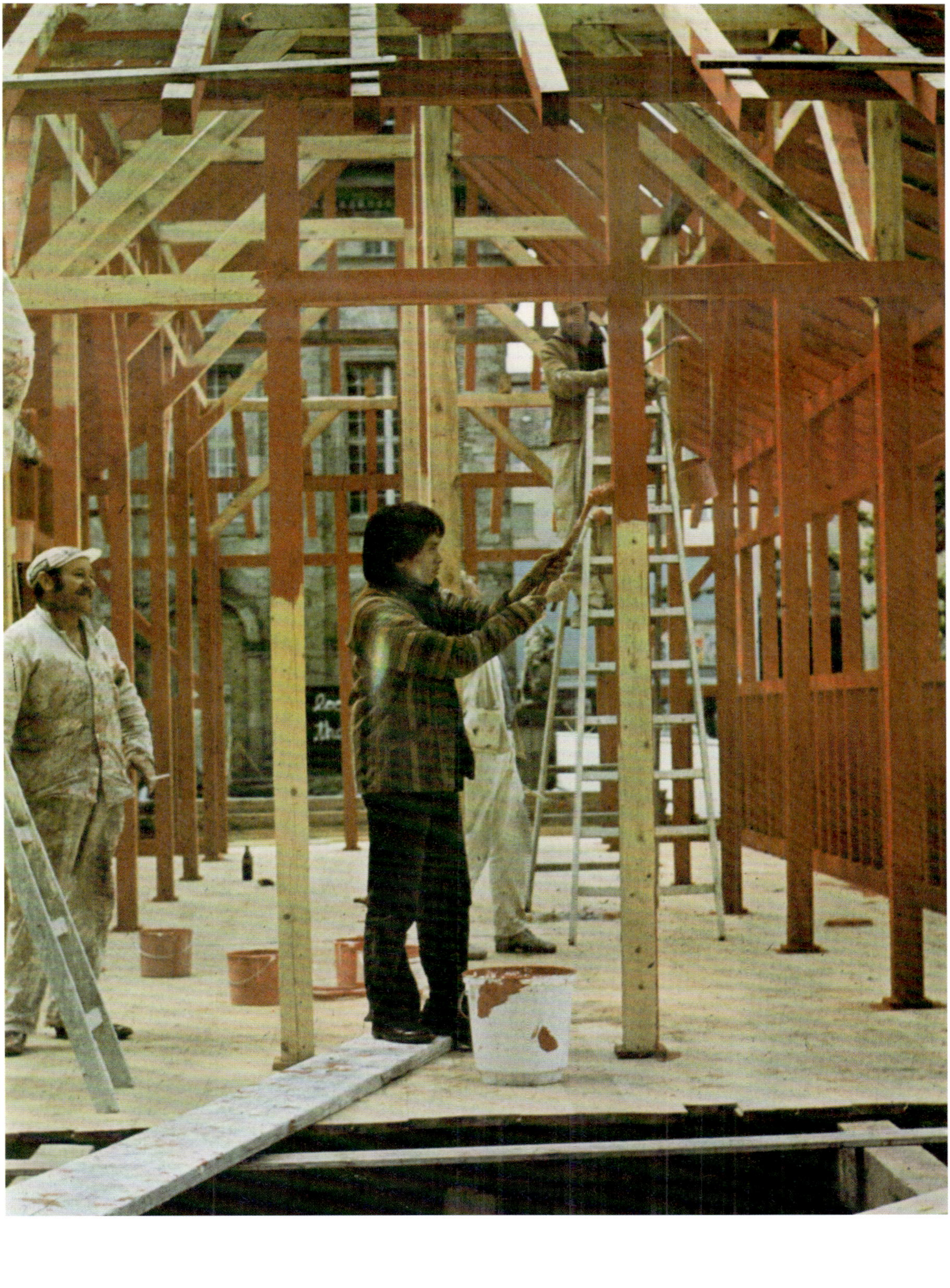

John Dugger and David Medalla, *People's Participation Pavilion*, documenta 5, Kassel, Germany, June 30–October 8, 1972.

_K_O_P_I_E_

David Medalla
chambre 22

Auftrag am 13.5.70
Str. 200.-

Grand Hotel du Midi

22, rue Sommerard/Musée Cluny

Paris 6è

Tel. ODE 1785

Harald Szeemann
Kunsthalle Bern
Suisse

10th may 1970

ar Harald Szeemann,
I am now in Paris with my friend the american sculptor John Scott Dugger. We are poor and we are having a difficult time. Please contribute some money to the MEDALLA RELIEF FUND. Send cash or cheque to me soon c/O the above adress.
In Asia + Africa from 1968 to early 1970 Dugger + I made several wonderful explorations. We swept (balayer en français) (with a sonar broom I constructed) ALL THE SOUNDS of Four seas (the Mediterranean, the Arabian, the China and the Red Sea) and three oceans (the Indian, the Atlantic and the Pacific Oceans) - we collected all the sounds ~~in a container~~ of the four seas and three oceans, sealed the sounds in a container and plunged the container into the depths of the Philippines (the deepest part of the ocean in the world).

In 1969 I made my first HOMMAGE TO TARZAN in MADRAS, INDIA. In Kandy, Ceylon in the same year John Dugger constructed his first set of 'SANDALS FOR THE PATH', multiples in which the spectators carry with them a selection of sandscapes : deserts, arctic scenes, forests, jungles, rivers, lakes, etc..
I threw a ~~bridge of sounds~~ BRIDGE OF SOUNDS ACROSS THE ABYSS in the Himalaya, in the kingdom of Mustang (northern Nepal, south of Tibet).
Kathmander last December 1969, I sent by air my first CARGO NO ONE : DESTINATION : MOEBIUSVILLE, ISLE DE PALINDROME, it is a set of ten sonar constructions including a number of GAMES FOR A LINE AND A CONE.
I have just finished my MICRO HISTOIRE DE L'ART CHINOIS DE LA DYNASTIE TANG-CLUNY JUSQU'AU BOUT DU SOUNG-MIDI - this is illustrated with a million micro-dot photos of Chinese masterpieces which I myself invented.
I am now working on three major projects:
1. THE SECOND HOMAGE TO TARZAN
2. LE BAL CHINOIS (for audiance-paricipation)
3. A prject dedicated to Mao-tse tung for sending the WALL OF CHINA as a satellite around the MOON.

Write me soon, yours DAVID MEDALLA

I stand in France until November 1970

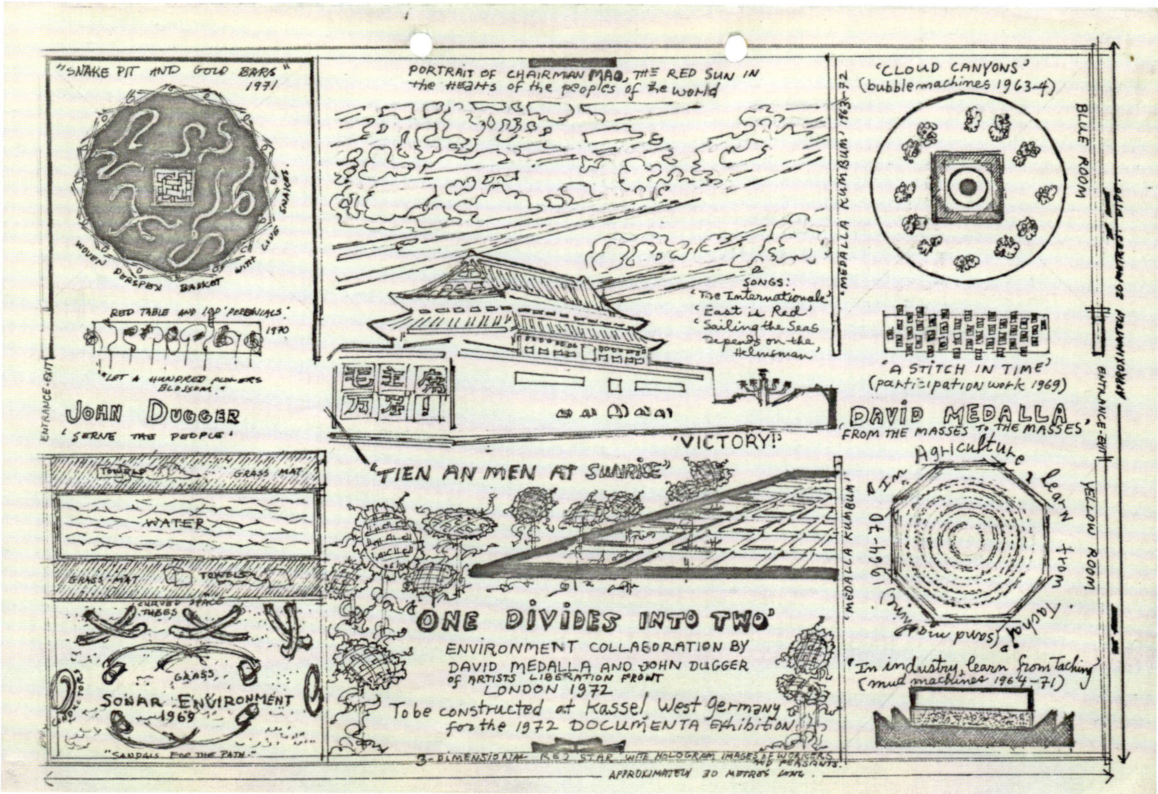

opposite
Letter from David Medalla to Harald Szeemann, May 10, 1970.

above
Proposal for John Dugger and David Medalla's *People's Participation Pavilion*, 1972. Felt-tip marker on paper. 8 1⁄5 × 11 3⁄5 in. (21 × 29.5 cm).

People Weave a House!, 1972

With Medalla's assistance, John Dugger created *People Weave a House!* within the context of the Artists' Liberation Front. This "participation-production," as the artists called it, took place at the Institute of Contemporary Arts in London. Visitors were encouraged to work collectively to weave a house from transparent plastic tubing. This idea of harnessing communal labor stemmed from Dugger's trip to China, which took place right before the exhibition, and his and Medalla's support of Chairman Mao and the Chinese Communist Party (despite the artists' stance as advocates for liberation). In addition to the house, the exhibition featured Dugger's handwritten protest banners, including some that condemned Ferdinand Marcos's establishment of martial law in the Philippines in 1972.

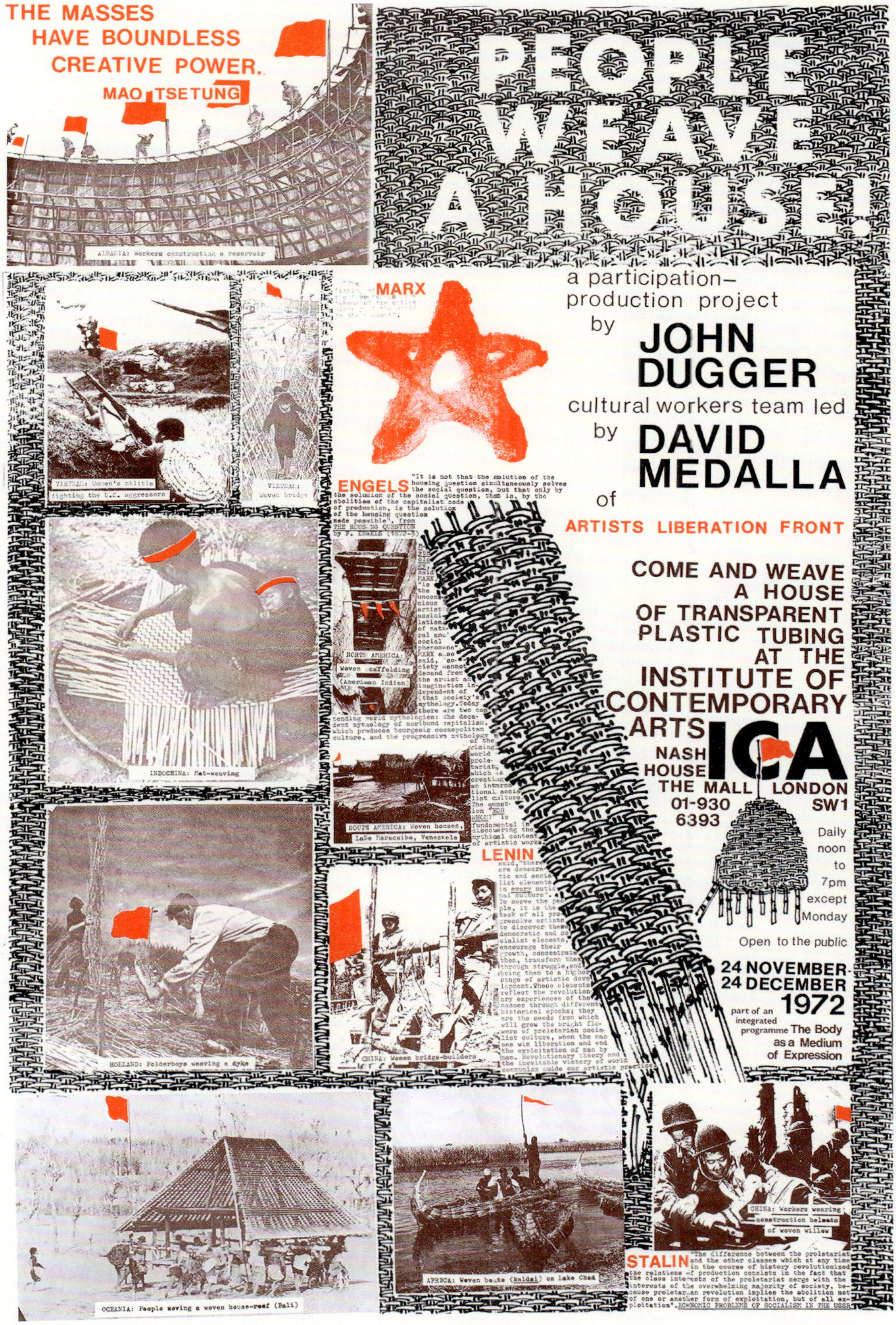

John Dugger, Exhibition poster for *People Weave a House!*, 1972.

Porcelain Wedding, 1973–74

Born out of Medalla's involvement with the Artists' Liberation Front, *Porcelain Wedding* was a "participation propulsion" (or participation-production) that took place on a number of occasions between 1973 and 1974. The original performance occurred at the Edinburgh College of Art in Scotland. Two art-student volunteers served as the work's substrate, which entailed lying naked on a table and being covered in clay by the other participants. The clay was molded to their bodies, cut into small squares, baked in a kiln, then pieced together to form suits. These body coverings mimic the jade burial suits of the Western Han Dynasty, which had been discovered in China in the preceding years. Each time *Porcelain Wedding* was recreated in a new context, different wedding rituals were performed. In Edinburgh, patterns of constellations were carved into the crust of a pie; at the Art Meeting Place in London, visitors were invited to create clay sculptures that alluded to the seven days of creation. In each iteration, *Porcelain Wedding* used clay, one of humankind's most ancient materials, to reflect on ritual in relationship to culture.

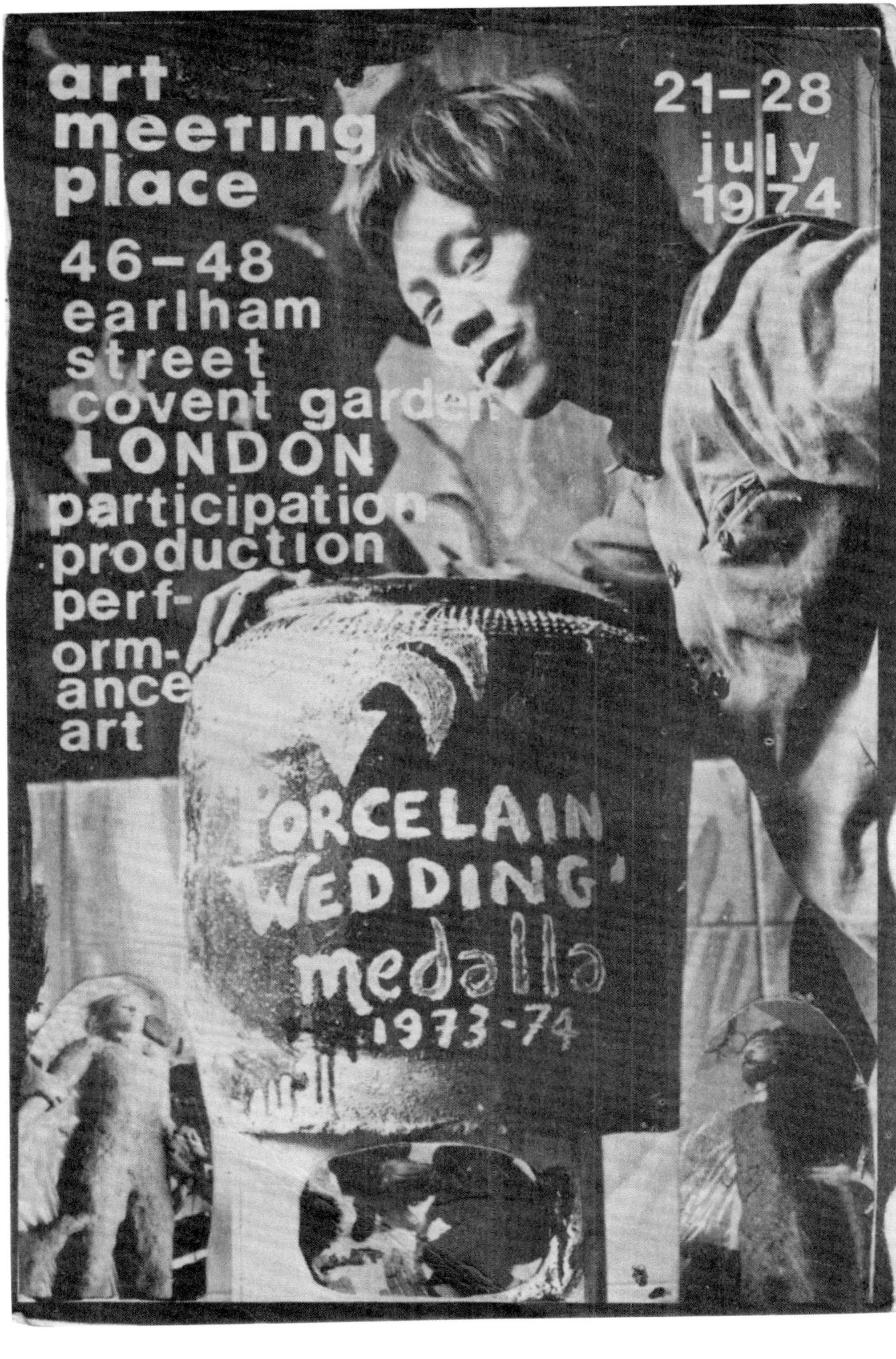

Announcement for *Porcelain Wedding*, Art Meeting Place, London, July 21–28, 1974.

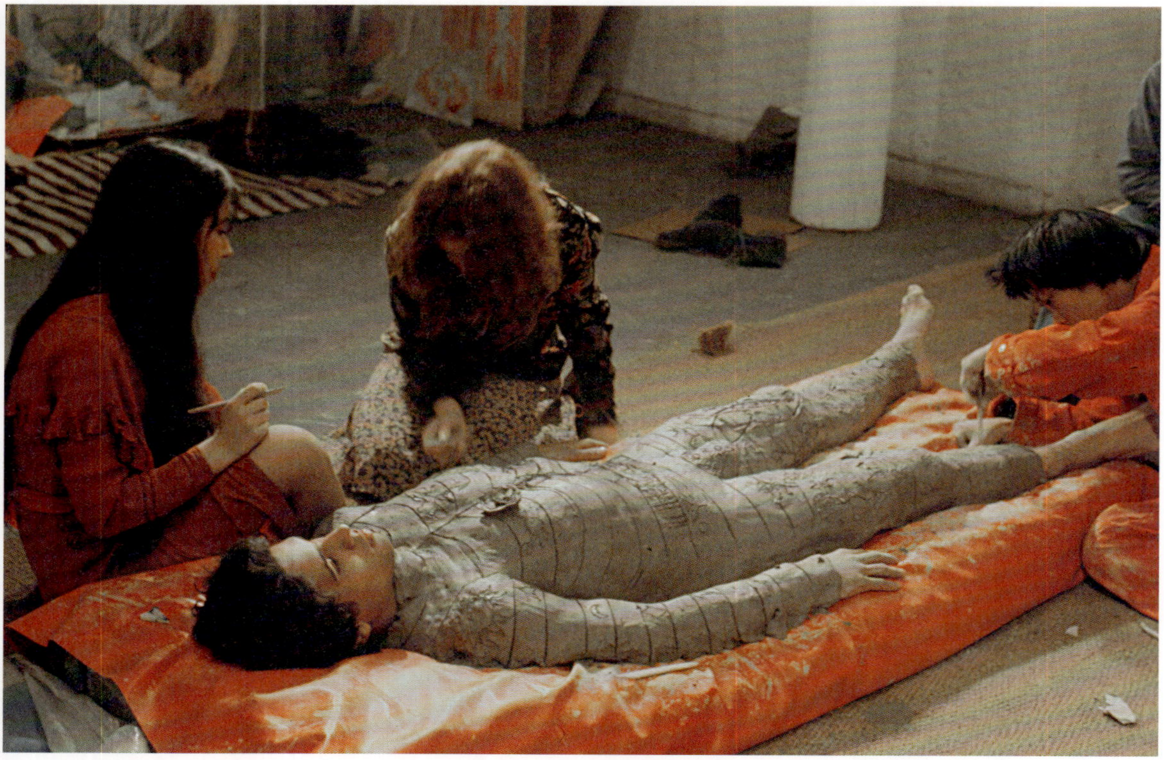

Porcelain Wedding, Art Meeting Place, London, July 21–28, 1974.

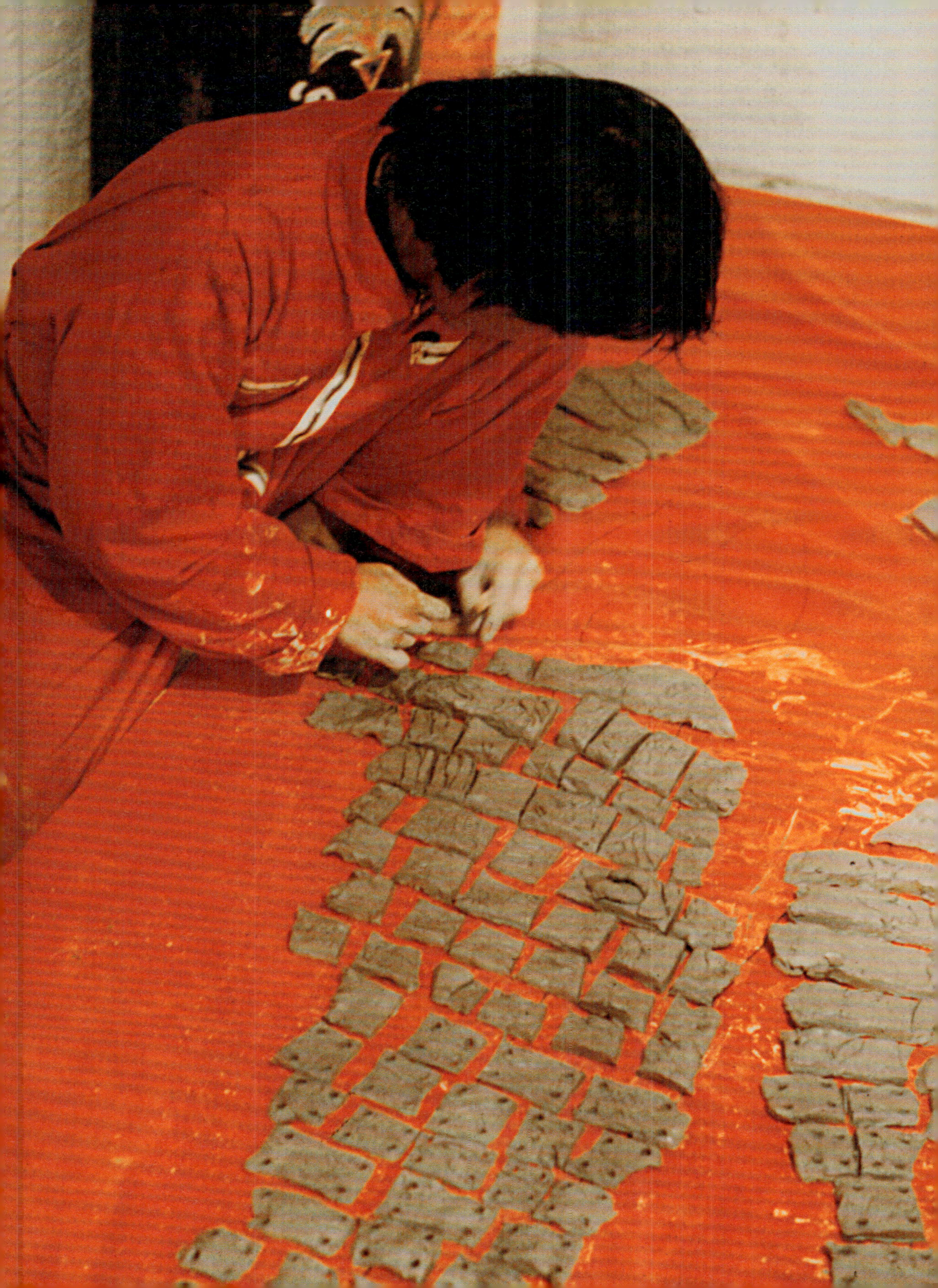

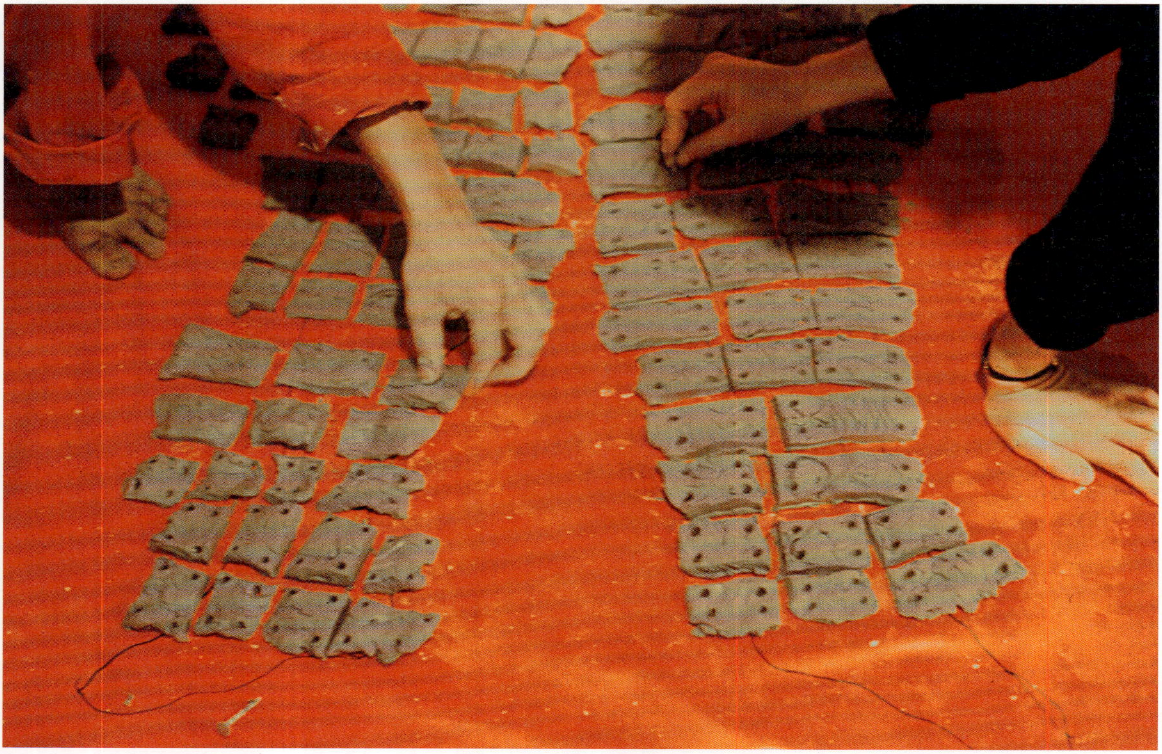

Porcelain Wedding, Art Meeting Place, London, July 21–28, 1974.

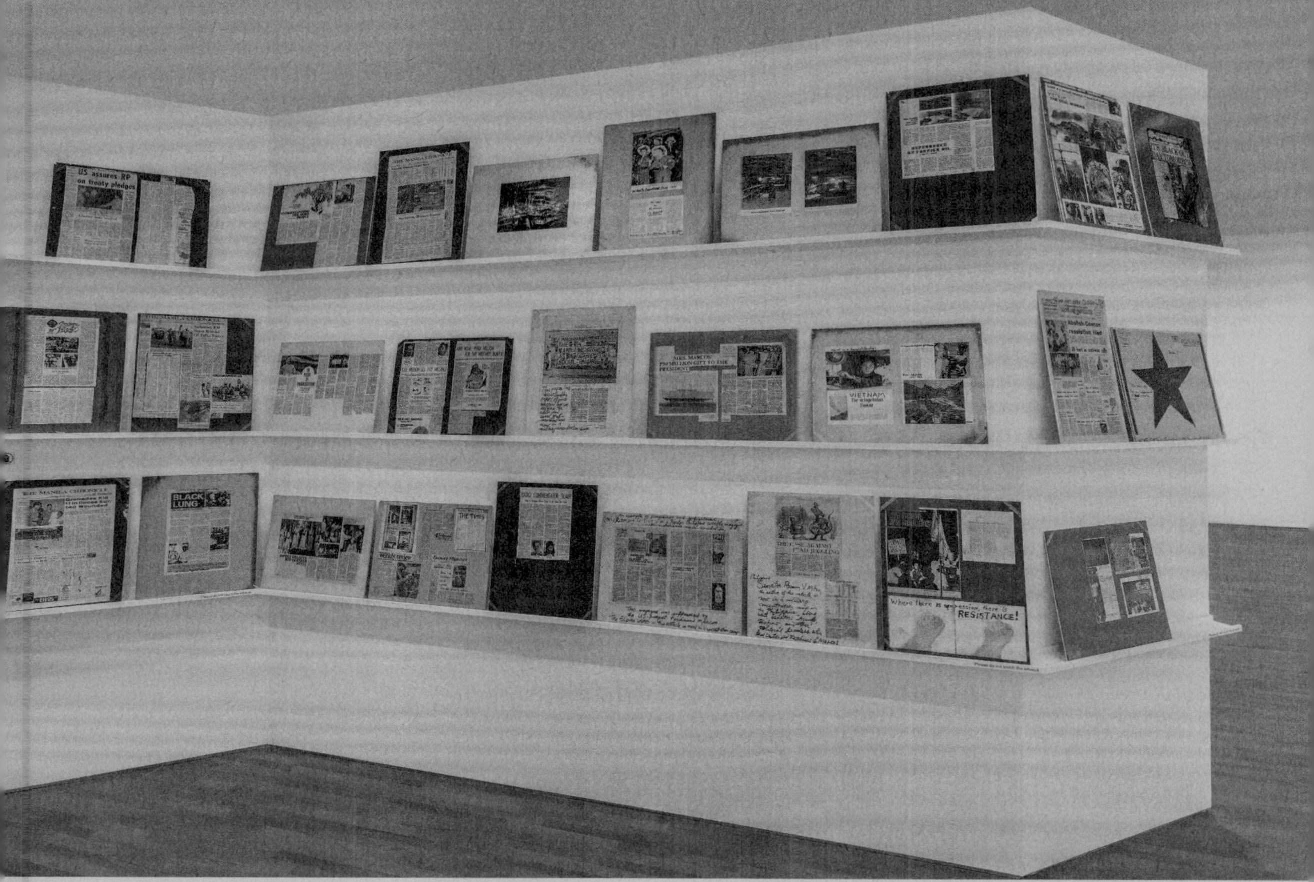
US assures RP on treaty pledges
BLACK LUNG
VIETNAM
RESISTANCE!

Kumbum
1971–72

Medalla named the Kumbum series for the Kumbum Stupa in Tibet, a multistory cluster of chapels designed in the form of a three-dimensional mandala that signifies the Buddhist Cosmos. The Kumbum banners include several bodies of politically engaged work, such as the collages shown at the *People's Participation Pavilion* and the Africa Liberation Drawings. Many of the placards display a mix of news clippings related to the Philippines and images of Medalla's work, all framed by a colorful border. The content of the news clippings, sourced primarily from the *Manila Chronicle*, centers on social injustices and liberation movements. One work in particular details the closure of the *Manila Chronicle* by President Ferdinand Marcos and the consignment of news staff to concentration camps. Like many of the artist's works, the Kumbum collages are a reflection of Medalla's spiritual beliefs and also a call to action.

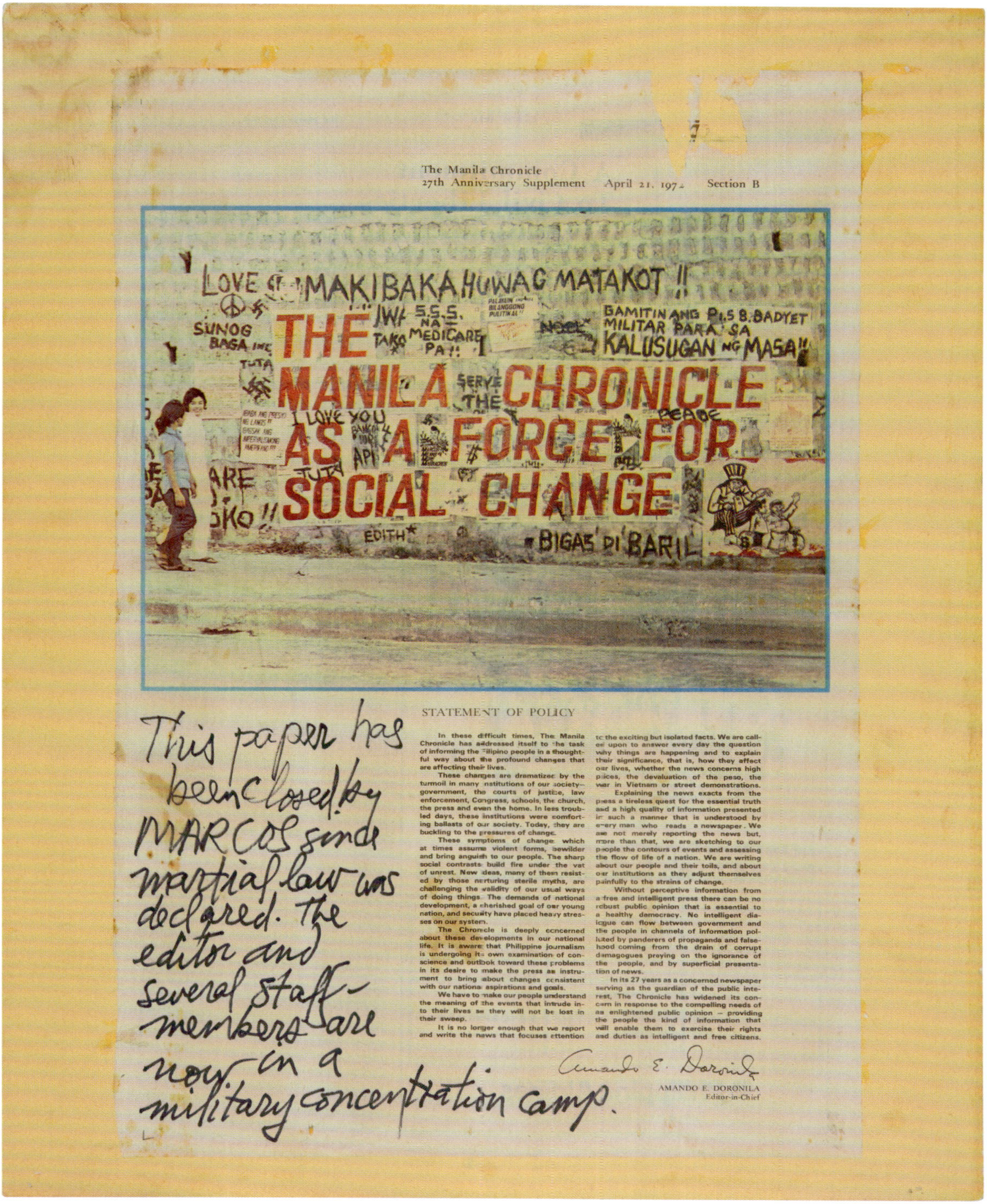

previous
Kumbum, 1971–72. Newspaper clippings and ink on mat boards. Installation view, *Suddenly Turning Visible: Art & Architecture in Southeast Asia (1969–1989)*, National Gallery Singapore, November 19, 2019–November 29, 2020.

above
Kumbum, 1971–72 (detail). Newspaper clippings and ink on mat board. 24 15/16 × 19 15/16 in. (63.3 × 50.6 cm).

There is no con-
troversy abou t
need for a Cult
Center. But the
building itself is
most controversi
in Philippine his

MRS. MARCOS' ₱50 MILLION GIFT TO THE PRESIDENT

By CELSO AL. CARUNUNGAN

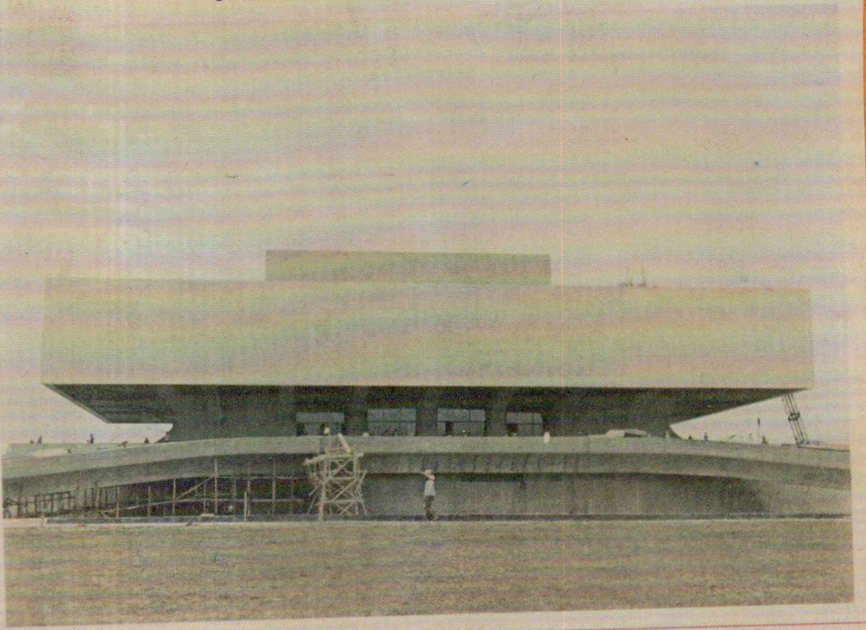

THE *Cultural Center stands on a site that aroused much controversy when American businessman Harry S. Stonehill started his reclamation project there some years ago.*

B RLI

NO other building in Phili
tory has been more controve
the ₱50 million Cultural Cen
formally opened last Septe
This is not surprising, if co
sidering the fact that almo
thing about the Center has
deviled by argument.

Let us start with the
which it now stands. In
land was reclaimed from M
by American businessman
Stonehill, and several hun
ple, from ordinary teacher
government officials, bought
it for possible residential si
the government instituted pr
against Stonehill and he
land was seized, it being
of fraudulent enterprise.
was deported in August 19
buyers were left holding th

"Exciting Drama

The plans for the Cultu
building, made by promin
tect Leandro Locsin, were
intended for the RP-US Cul
ter in 1964. It was to hav
monument to the friendly
tween the Philippines and
States but it was an ab
According to Nimia Arroy
article in the Sunday Ti
series of events to the bas
exciting drama, replete wi
nations, buck-passing f
even news manipulation th
wire services."

One of the trustees o
fated Philippine American
Foundation was Antonio Q
is now the deputy direct
present Cultural Center.

The creation by Execu
No. 30 of the Cultural Cen
Philippines raised another
sy, since a law was pass
the Macapagal administra
ing the National Commissi
ture, the purposes of wh

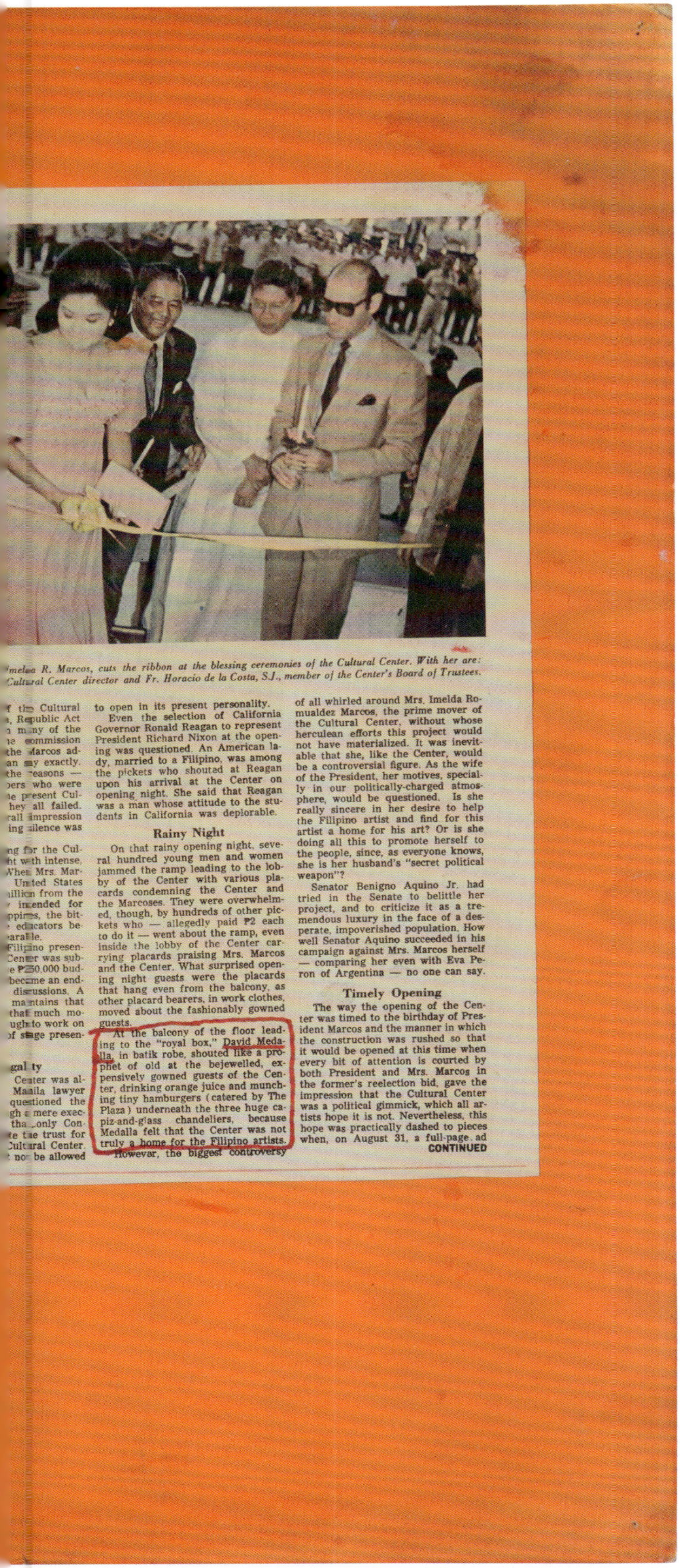

[...]melda R. Marcos, cuts the ribbon at the blessing ceremonies of the Cultural Center. With her are: [...] Cultural Center director and Fr. Horacio de la Costa, S.J., member of the Center's Board of Trustees.

f the Cultural
, Republic Act
many of the
e commission
the Marcos ad-
an say exactly.
the reasons —
bers who were
e present Cul-
hey all failed.
rall impression
ing silence was

ng for the Cul-
ht with intense.
When Mrs. Mar-
United States
illion from the
intended for
ppines, the bit-
educators be-
arable.
Filipino presen-
Center was sub-
e ₱50,000 bud-
became an end-
discussions. A
maintains that
that much mo-
ugh to work on
of stage presen-

gal ty

Center was al-
Manila lawyer
questioned the
gh a mere exec-
tha only Con-
te the trust for
Cultural Center.
not be allowed

to open in its present personality.

Even the selection of California Governor Ronald Reagan to represent President Richard Nixon at the opening was questioned. An American lady, married to a Filipino, was among the pickets who shouted at Reagan upon his arrival at the Center on opening night. She said that Reagan was a man whose attitude to the students in California was deplorable.

Rainy Night

On that rainy opening night, several hundred young men and women jammed the ramp leading to the lobby of the Center with various placards condemning the Center and the Marcoses. They were overwhelmed, though, by hundreds of other pickets who — allegedly paid ₱2 each to do it — went about the ramp, even inside the lobby of the Center carrying placards praising Mrs. Marcos and the Center. What surprised opening night guests were the placards that hang even from the balcony, as other placard bearers, in work clothes, moved about the fashionably gowned guests.

At the balcony of the floor leading to the "royal box," David Medalla, in batik robe, shouted like a prophet of old at the bejewelled, expensively gowned guests of the Center, drinking orange juice and munching tiny hamburgers (catered by The Plaza) underneath the three huge capiz-and-glass chandeliers, because Medalla felt that the Center was not truly a home for the Filipino artists.

However, the biggest controversy of all whirled around Mrs. Imelda Romualdez Marcos, the prime mover of the Cultural Center, without whose herculean efforts this project would not have materialized. It was inevitable that she, like the Center, would be a controversial figure. As the wife of the President, her motives, specially in our politically-charged atmosphere, would be questioned. Is she really sincere in her desire to help the Filipino artist and find for this artist a home for his art? Or is she doing all this to promote herself to the people, since, as everyone knows, she is her husband's "secret political weapon"?

Senator Benigno Aquino Jr. had tried in the Senate to belittle her project, and to criticize it as a tremendous luxury in the face of a desperate, impoverished population. How well Senator Aquino succeeded in his campaign against Mrs. Marcos herself — comparing her even with Eva Peron of Argentina — no one can say.

Timely Opening

The way the opening of the Center was timed to the birthday of President Marcos and the manner in which the construction was rushed so that it would be opened at this time when every bit of attention is courted by both President and Mrs. Marcos in the former's reelection bid, gave the impression that the Cultural Center was a political gimmick, which all artists hope it is not. Nevertheless, this hope was practically dashed to pieces when, on August 31, a full-page ad

CONTINUED

Kumbum, 1971–72 (detail). Newspaper clippings and ink on mat board. 19 15⁄16 × 24 15⁄16 in. (50.6 × 63.3 cm).

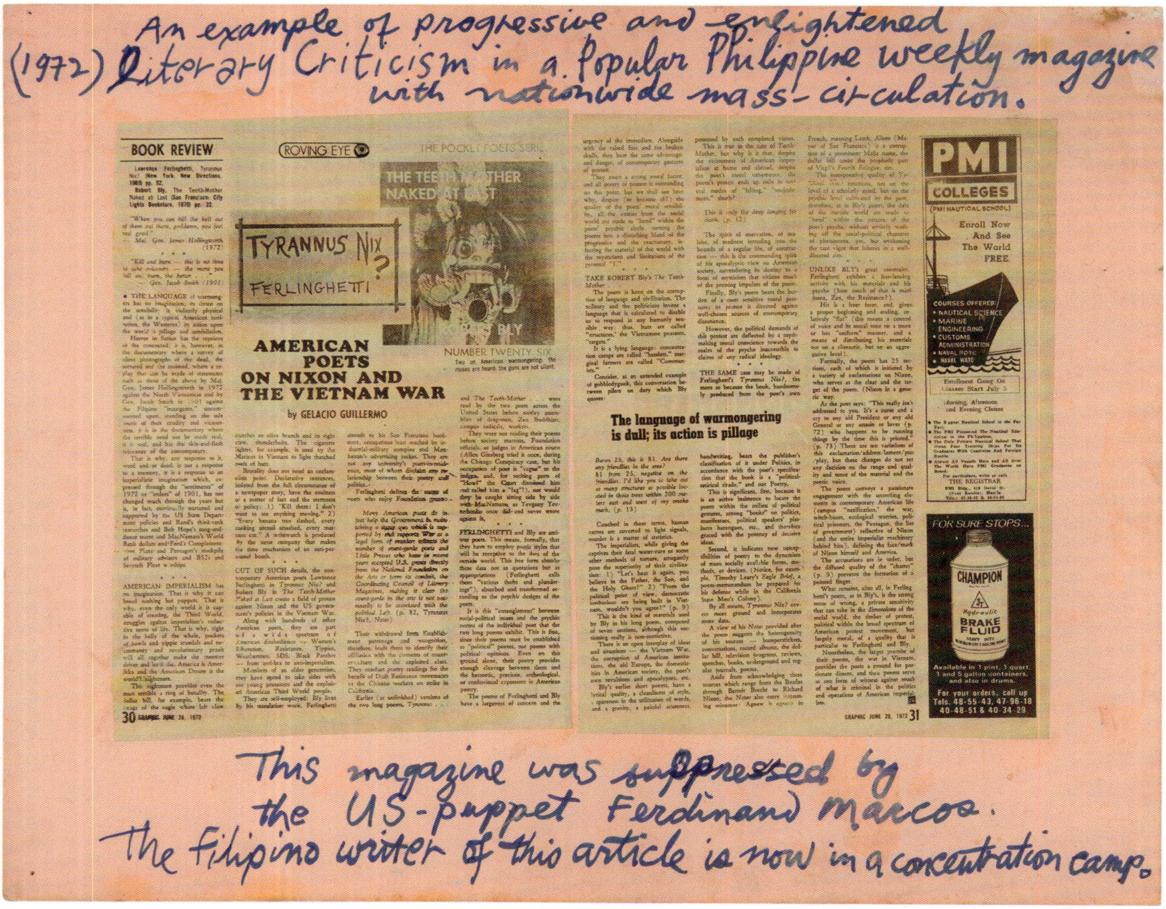

above
Kumbum, 1971–72 (detail). Newspaper clippings and ink on mat board. 19 15⁄16 × 24 15⁄16 in. (50.6 × 63.3 cm).

opposite
Guerilla Fighter of the M.P.L.A. Angola, 1974. Ink on paper mounted on mat board. 24 15⁄16 × 19 15⁄16 in. (63.3 × 50.6 cm).

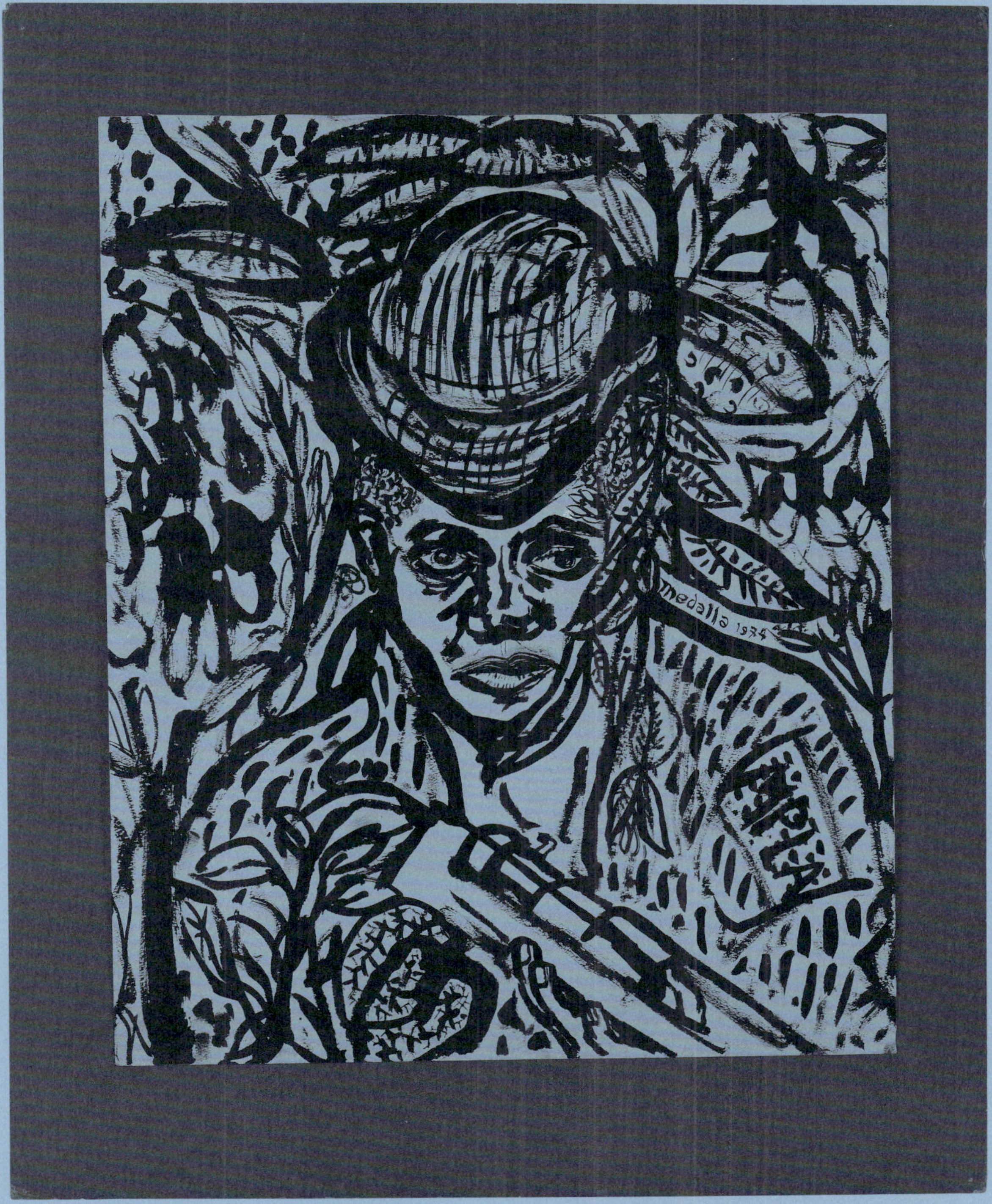
medalla 1974

Africa Liberation Drawings 1974

Medalla became increasingly interested in global politics following his travels to Africa and Asia in 1968. In October 1971, he attended a speech by Amilcar Cabral, leader of the African Party for the Independence of Guinea and Cape Verde (PAIGC), in London with Guy Brett. Medalla and Brett were impressed with Cabral's condemnation of colonialism and his faith in the resilience of those committed to the struggle for independence. Medalla executed the Africa Liberation Drawings within the context of the Artists' Liberation Front and in response to the resistance movements in Angola (the People's Movement for the Liberation of Angola, MPLA), Mozambique (the Mozambique Liberation Front, FRELIMO), Guinea-Bissau, and Cape Verde (PAIGC), as led by Cabral, Agostinho Neto, Eduardo Mondlane, and others. Interwoven with fragments of poetry, songs, and political speeches, the drawings also recreated photographs attributed to solidarity organizations in London. With these works, Medalla strove to contribute to the struggles for independence in Africa by amplifying their messages in the British context.

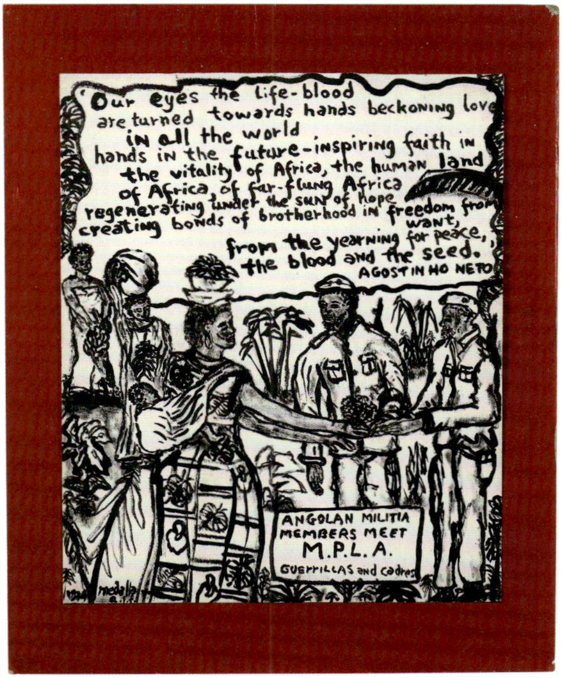

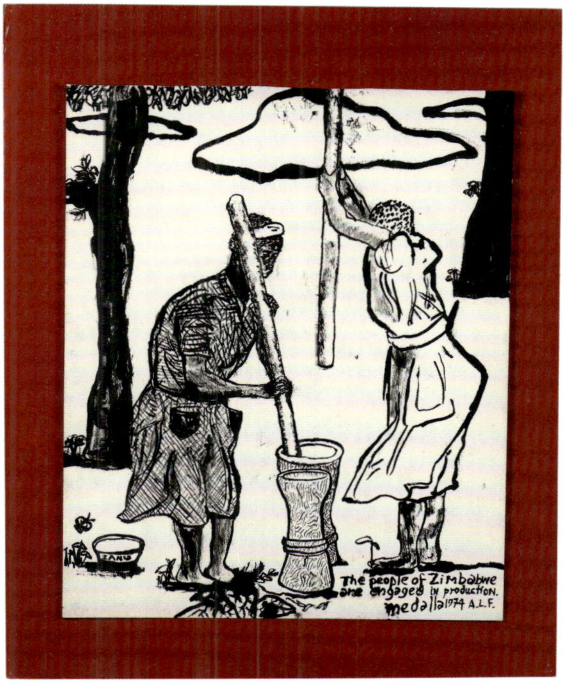

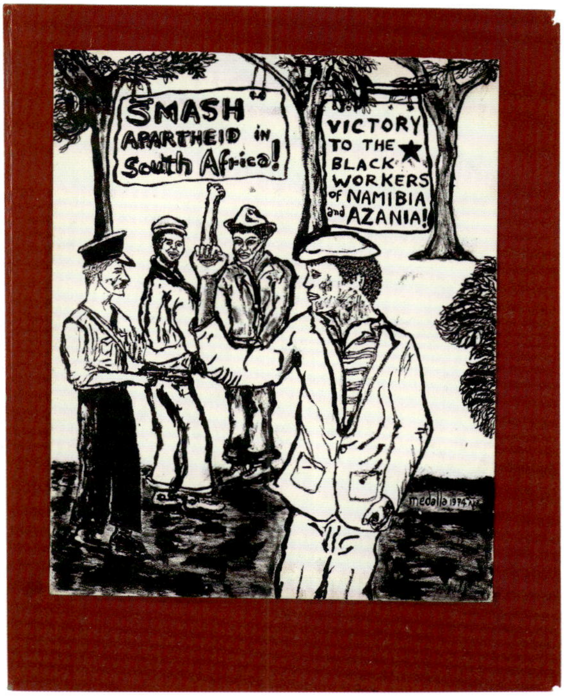

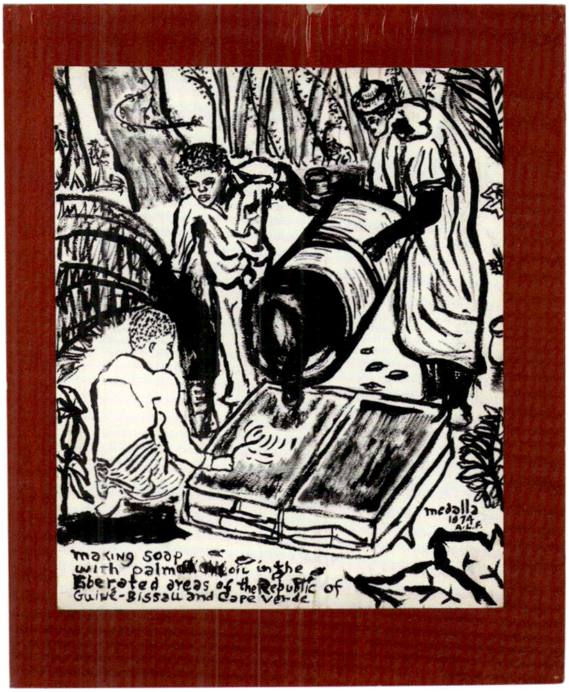

top left
Angolan Militia Members Meet M.P.L.A. Guerillas and Cadres, 1974. China ink on paper mounted on mat board. 24 15⁄16 × 19 15⁄16 in. (63.3 × 50.6 cm).

top right
The People of Zimbabwe Are Engaged in Production, 1974. China ink on paper mounted on mat board. 24 15⁄16 × 19 15⁄16 in. (63.3 × 50.6 cm).

bottom left
Smash Apartheid in South Africa! Victory to the Black workers of Namibia and Azania!, 1974. Ink on paper mounted on mat board. 24 15⁄16 × 19 15⁄16 in. (63.3 × 50.6 cm).

bottom right
Making soap with palm oil in the liberated areas of the Republic of Guiné-Bissau and Cape Verde, 1974. Ink on paper mounted on mat board. 24 15⁄16 × 19 15⁄16 in. (63.3 × 50.6 cm).

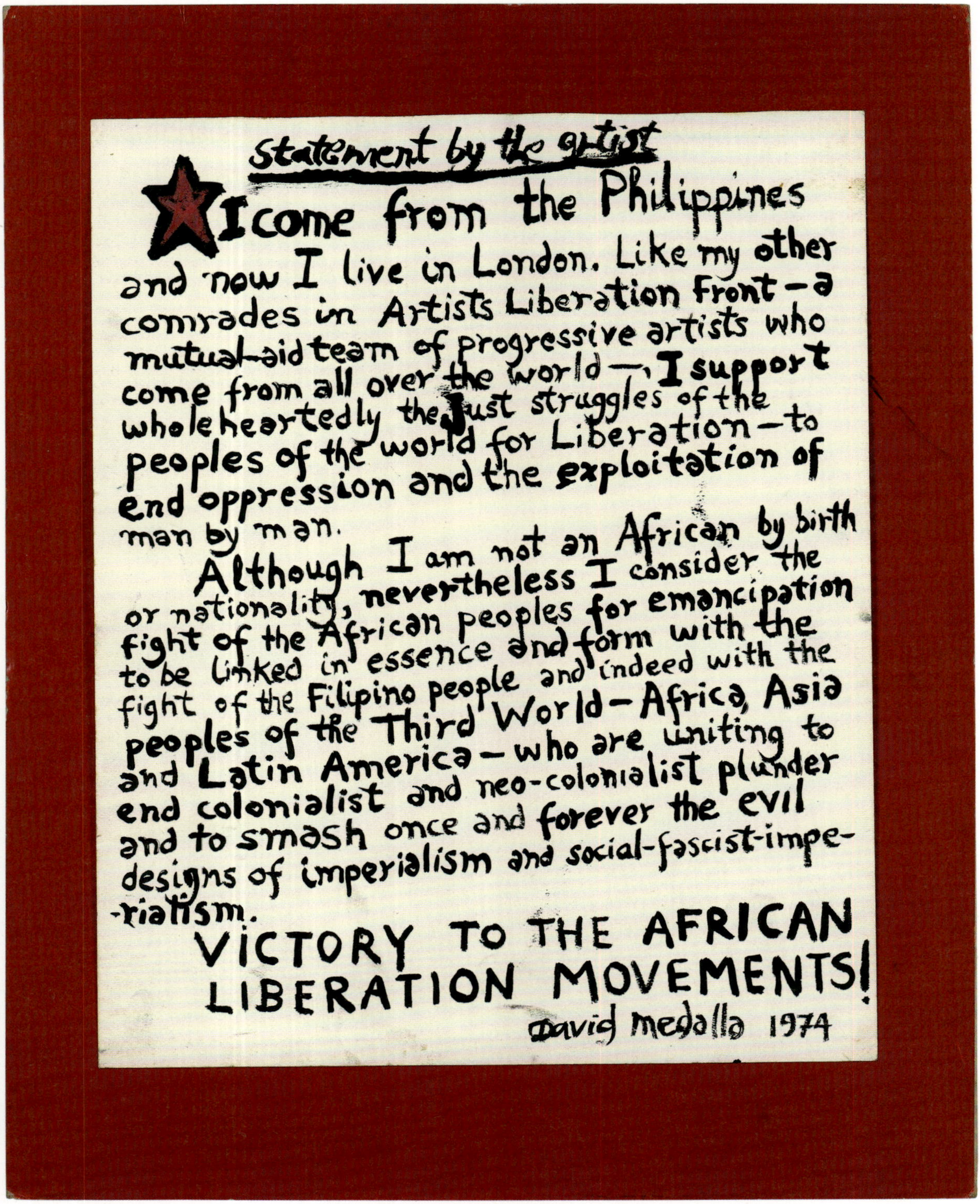

Statement by the artist

I come from the Philippines and now I live in London. Like my other comrades in Artists Liberation Front — a mutual-aid team of progressive artists who come from all over the world —, I support wholeheartedly the just struggles of the peoples of the world for Liberation — to end oppression and the exploitation of man by man.

Although I am not an African by birth or nationality, nevertheless I consider the fight of the African peoples for emancipation to be linked in essence and form with the fight of the Filipino people and indeed with the peoples of the Third World — Africa, Asia and Latin America — who are uniting to end colonialist and neo-colonialist plunder and to smash once and forever the evil designs of imperialism and social-fascist-impe-rialism.

VICTORY TO THE AFRICAN LIBERATION MOVEMENTS!

David Medalla 1974

Statement by the artist, 1974. Ink on paper mounted on mat board. 24 15⁄16 × 19 15⁄16 in. (63.3 × 50.6 cm).

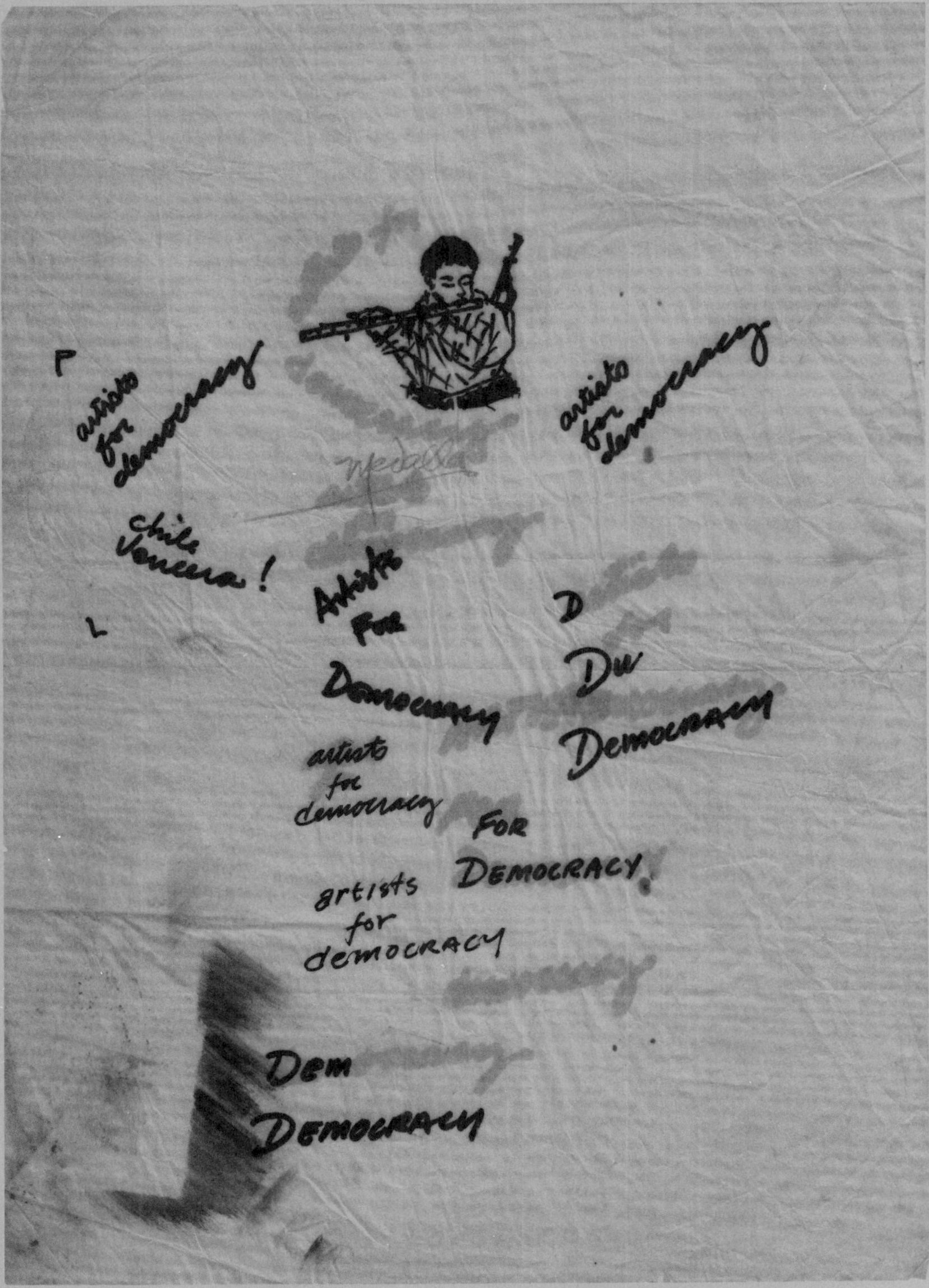
artists for democracy
artists for democracy
Chile Vencera!
Artists FOR Democracy
Democracy
artists for democracy
FOR DEMOCRACY
artists for democracy
Dem
DEMOCRACY

Artists for Democracy 1974–77

During a conversation in 1974, John Dugger, Guy Brett, Cecilia Vicuña, and Medalla discussed expanding opportunities for artists to engage with political movements. In this conversation, Vicuña brought up the Chilean military coup of September 1973, which overthrew the socialist government of Salvador Allende. To show support for the resistance in Chile, they formed the group Artists for Democracy and mobilized artists to create works in the service of political change. In September 1974, they organized the Arts Festival for Democracy in Chile at the Royal College of Art in London. Dugger constructed a banner that hung behind the festival's speakers; it read "Chile Vencera" (Chile will overcome). Following this festival, the artists' group opened the Fitzrovia Cultural Center at 143 Whitfield Street, London, which remained active until 1977. During this period, Medalla created several politically motivated works, including *Tatlin at the Funeral of Malevich* (1976) and *Eskimo Carver* (1977).

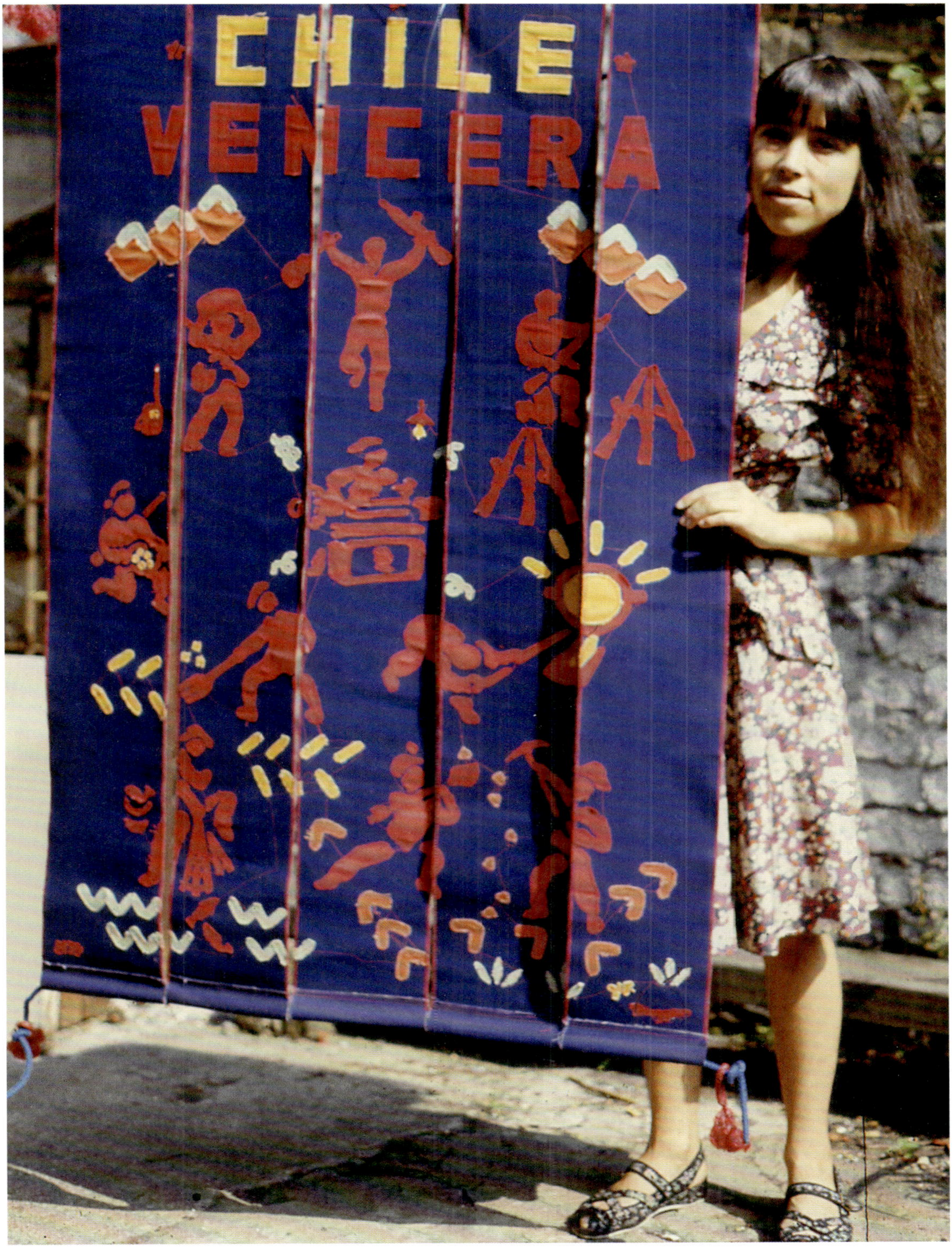

previous

Artists for democracy—Chile vencera!, 1975. Felt-tip marker on rice paper. 11 5/8 × 8 3/16 in. (29.6 × 20.8 cm).

above

Cecilia Vicuña with John Dugger's prototype for *Chile Vencera* banner, 1974.

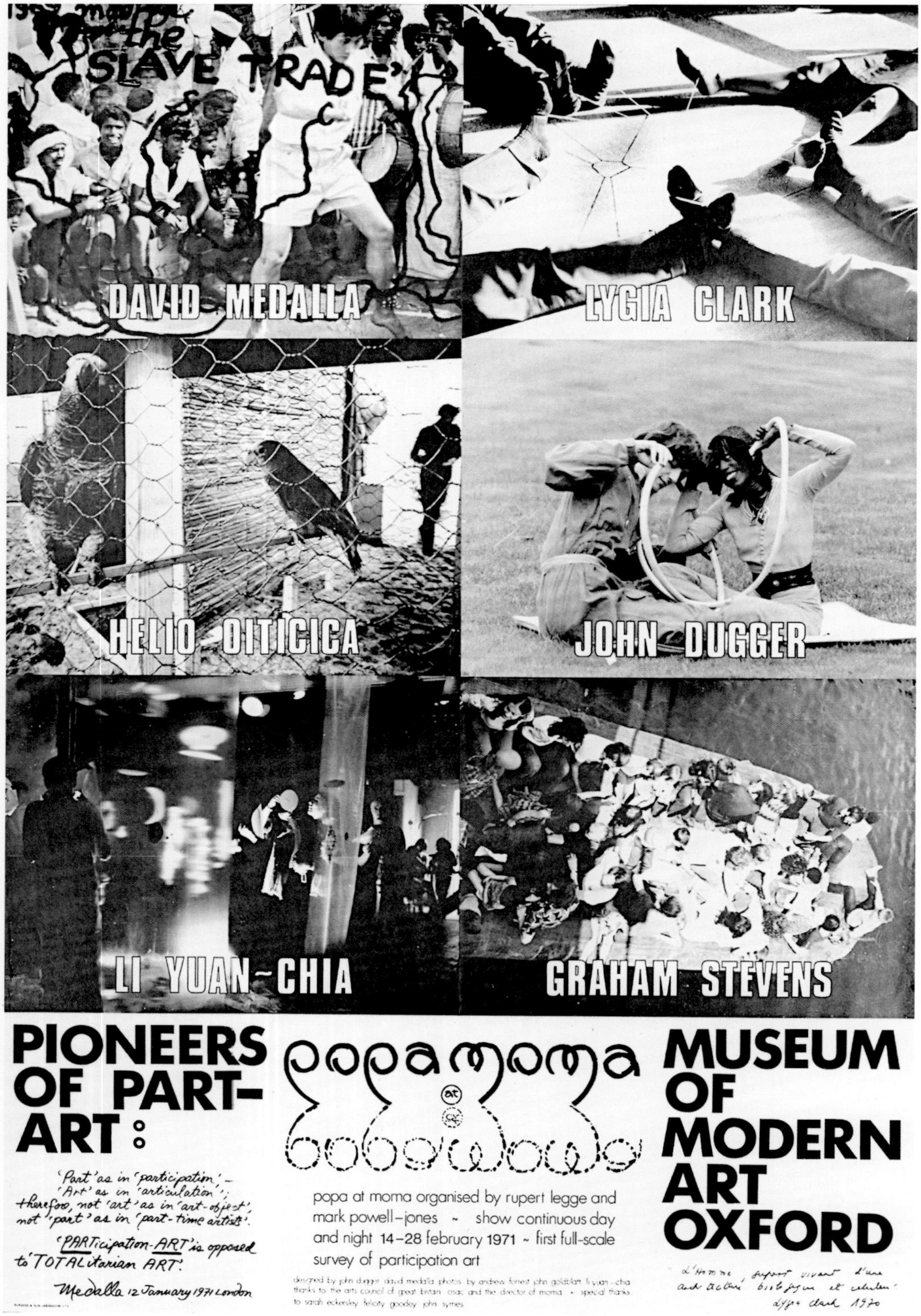

SLAVE TRADE
DAVID MEDALLA
LYGIA CLARK
HELIO OITICICA
JOHN DUGGER
LI YUAN-CHIA
GRAHAM STEVENS
PIONEERS OF PART-ART:
'Part' as in 'participation' – 'Art' as in 'articulation'; therefore, not 'art' as in 'art-object', not 'part' as in 'part-time artists'.
'PARTicipation-ART' is opposed to 'TOTALitarian ART'.
Medalla 12 January 1971 London
popamoma
art
popa at moma organised by rupert legge and mark powell-jones ~ show continuous day and night 14–28 february 1971 ~ first full-scale survey of participation art
designed by john dugger david medalla photos by andrew forrest john goldblatt li yuan-chia thanks to the arts council of great britain osac and the director of moma • special thanks to sarah eckersley felicity goodey john symes
MUSEUM OF MODERN ART OXFORD

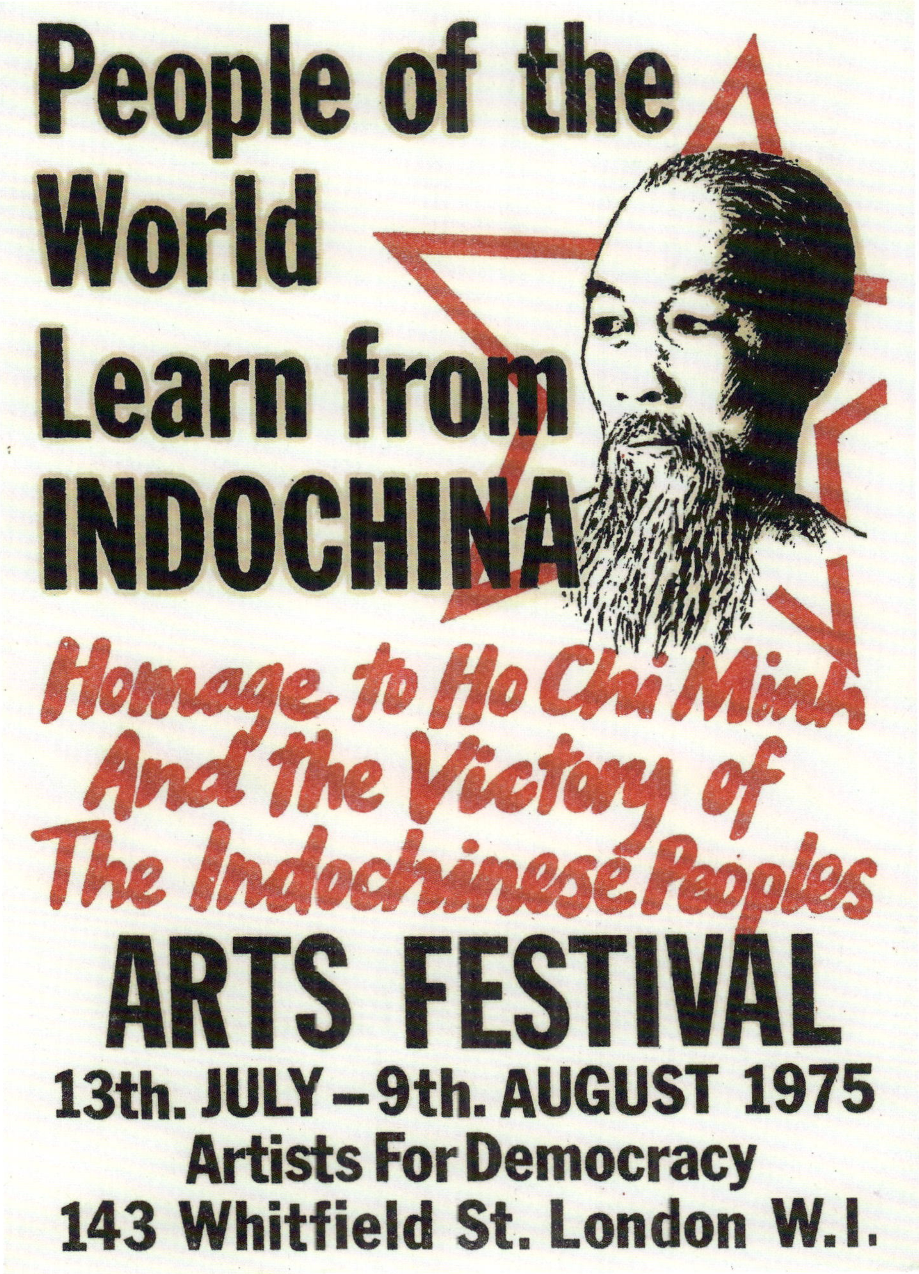

opposite
John Dugger, Exhibition poster for *Pioneers of Part-Art*, February 14–28, 1971.

above
Lynn MacRitchie and David Turner, Announcement for Artists for Democracy Vietnam Arts Festival, July 13–August 9, 1975.

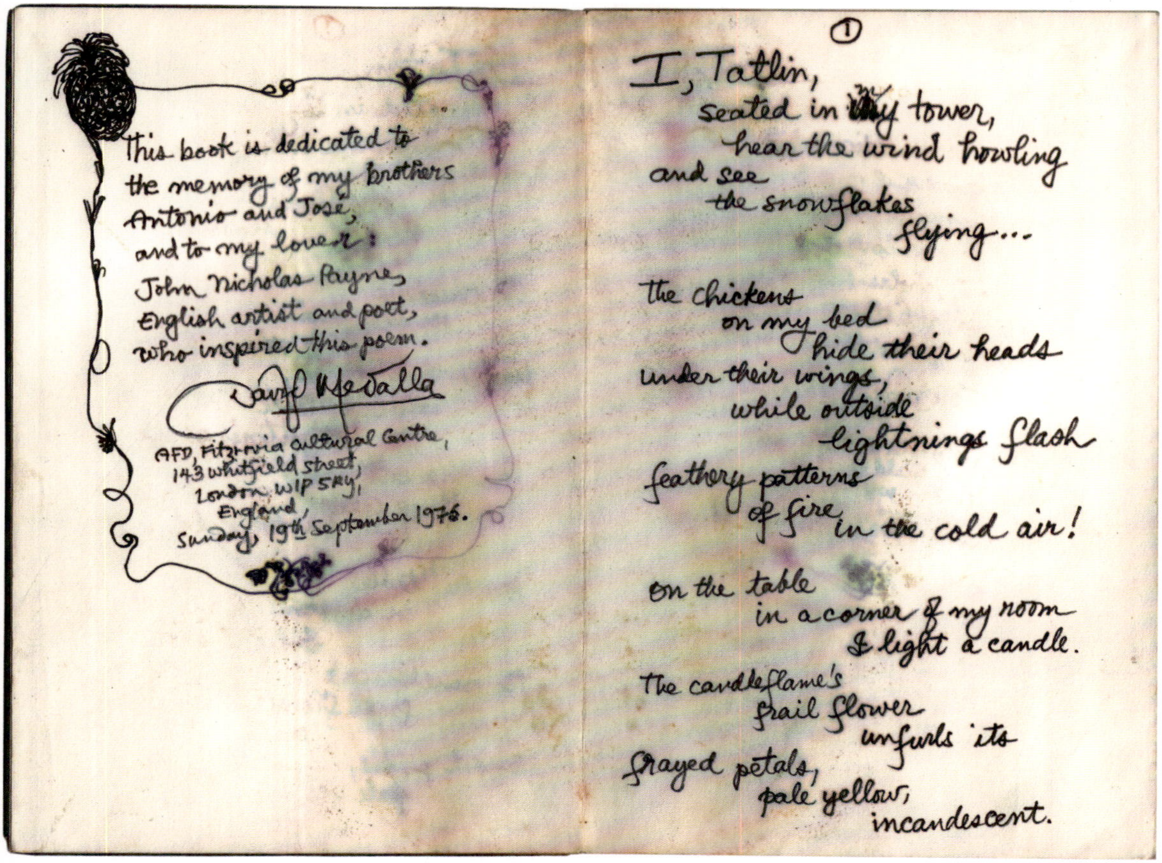

Tatlin at the Funeral of Malevich, 1976

Tatlin at the Funeral of Malevich was conceived under the umbrella of Artists for Democracy as a tribute, in the form of poems and drawings, to the Russian artists Kazimir Malevich and Vladimir Tatlin. These two artists envisioned their respective contributions to the twentieth-century art movements of Suprematism and Constructivism in the service of the Russian Revolution. The elegies and performances in *Tatlin at the Funeral of Malevich* were accompanied by songs written by Medalla. In one iteration, Medalla portrays Tatlin eating a fish, a motif repeated throughout the poem and performance. In this and other works, Medalla uses biographical details of artists from the historical avant-garde to link himself with their works and ideologies.

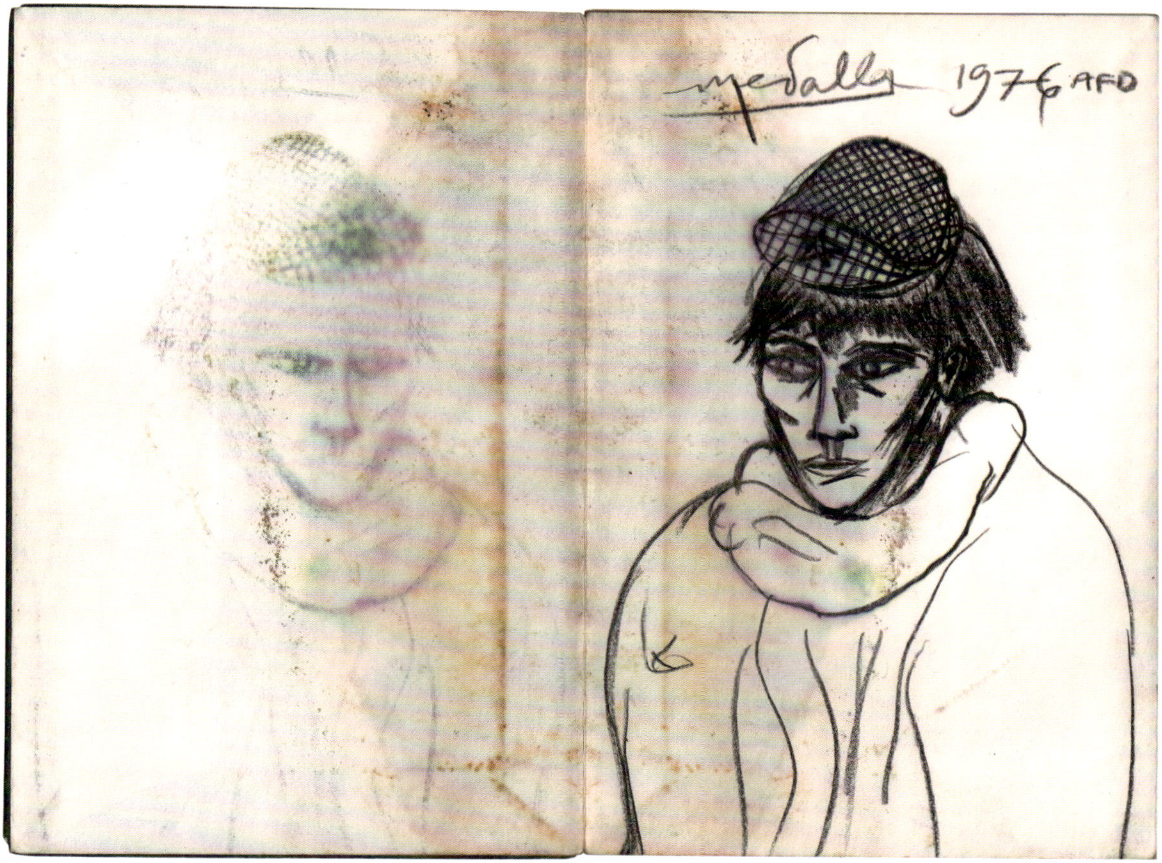

Interior spreads of *Tatlin at the Funeral of Malevich*, 1976. Ink and colored pencil on paper in linen-bound, accordion-folded notebook. 10 × 13 × ⅛ in. (25.4 × 33.02 × 0.3 cm).

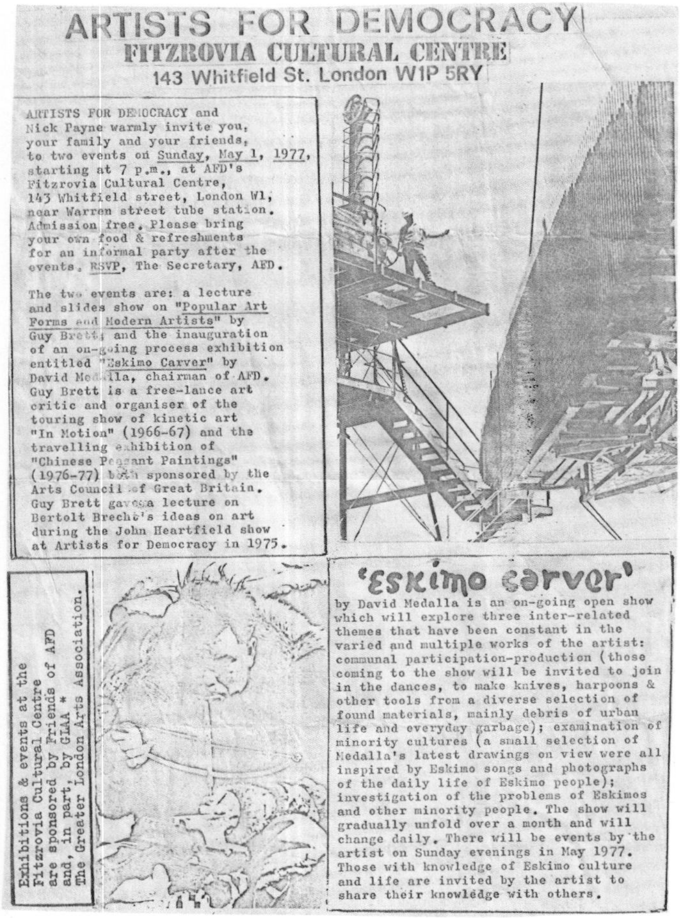

ARTISTS FOR DEMOCRACY
FITZROVIA CULTURAL CENTRE
143 Whitfield St. London W1P 5RY

ARTISTS FOR DEMOCRACY and Nick Payne warmly invite you, your family and your friends, to two events on Sunday, May 1, 1977, starting at 7 p.m., at AFD's Fitzrovia Cultural Centre, 143 Whitfield street, London W1, near Warren street tube station. Admission free. Please bring your own food & refreshments for an informal party after the events. RSVP, The Secretary, AFD.

The two events are: a lecture and slides show on "Popular Art Forms and Modern Artists" by Guy Brett, and the inauguration of an on-going process exhibition entitled "Eskimo Carver" by David Medalla, chairman of AFD. Guy Brett is a free-lance art critic and organiser of the touring show of kinetic art "In Motion" (1966-67) and the travelling exhibition of "Chinese Peasant Paintings" (1976-77) both sponsored by the Arts Council of Great Britain. Guy Brett gave a lecture on Bertolt Brecht's ideas on art during the John Heartfield show at Artists for Democracy in 1975.

Exhibitions & events at the Fitzrovia Cultural Centre are sponsored by Friends of AFD and, in part, by GLAA * The Greater London Arts Association.

'Eskimo Carver'

by David Medalla is an on-going open show which will explore three inter-related themes that have been constant in the varied and multiple works of the artist: communal participation-production (those coming to the show will be invited to join in the dances, to make knives, harpoons & other tools from a diverse selection of found materials, mainly debris of urban life and everyday garbage); examination of minority cultures (a small selection of Medalla's latest drawings on view were all inspired by Eskimo songs and photographs of the daily life of Eskimo people); investigation of the problems of Eskimos and other minority people. The show will gradually unfold over a month and will change daily. There will be events by the artist on Sunday evenings in May 1977. Those with knowledge of Eskimo culture and life are invited by the artist to share their knowledge with others.

Eskimo Carver, 1977

In 1977, Medalla organized *Eskimo Carver* at the Fitzrovia Cultural Center in London; it was the last exhibition within the framework of Artists for Democracy. The exhibition consisted of three interrelated parts that were inspired by Inuit culture and highlighted some of the ways in which Inuit communities have historically been misrepresented and mistreated. First was a selection of Medalla's drawings and transcriptions of Inuit oral poetry, which is unique in that community members rarely sing or perform the songs of others; instead, each person creates their own song or poem to recite. The second aspect of the exhibition was a performance, entitled *Alaska Pipeline*, that Medalla created in response to the media's blatantly biased portrayals of Inuit communities during the construction of the Trans-Alaska Pipeline System between 1974 and 1977. For *Eskimo Carver*'s third element, Medalla encouraged visitors to create knives out of nonperishable garbage collected in the surrounding neighborhood. The results were displayed on the wall in the gallery. Some makers labeled their knives, for example as "love knives" or "invisible knives." The themes of the exhibition were influenced in part by an experience Medalla had while walking near the Centre Pompidou in Paris. He noticed a tourist throwing away a pamphlet that contained an image of an Inuit man carving a small ivory statuette. Medalla was reminded of Robert Flaherty's 1922 documentary (much of which is known to have been staged), *Nanook of the North*, in which Allakariallak (called Nanook in the film) carves blocks of snow and builds an igloo by hand.

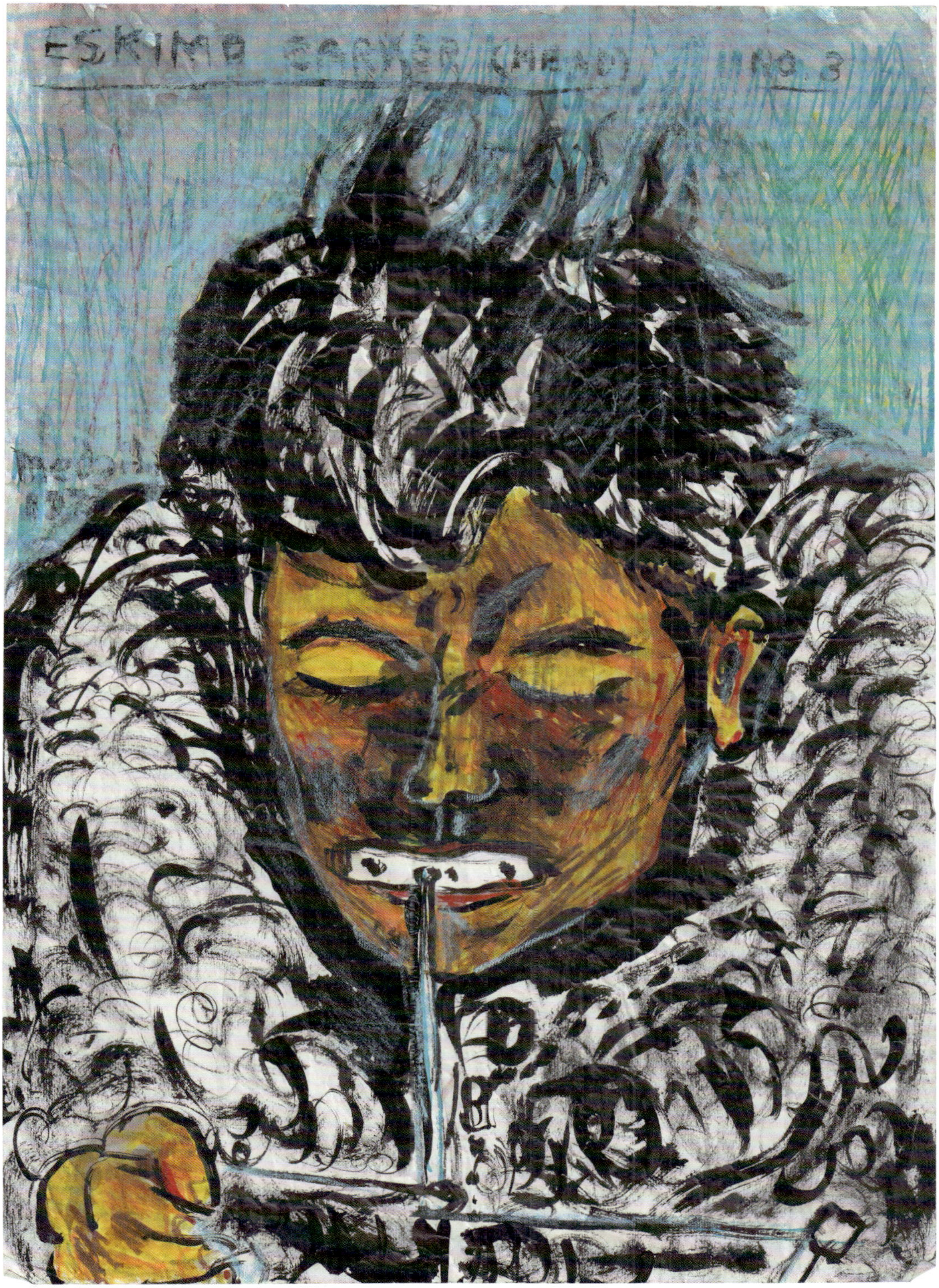

opposite
Announcement for *Eskimo Carver*, Fitzrovia Cultural Centre, London, 1977.

above
Eskimo Carver No. 3, 1977. Watercolor, China ink, and crayon on paper. 11 ½ × 8 ⅛ in. (29.2 × 20.7 cm).

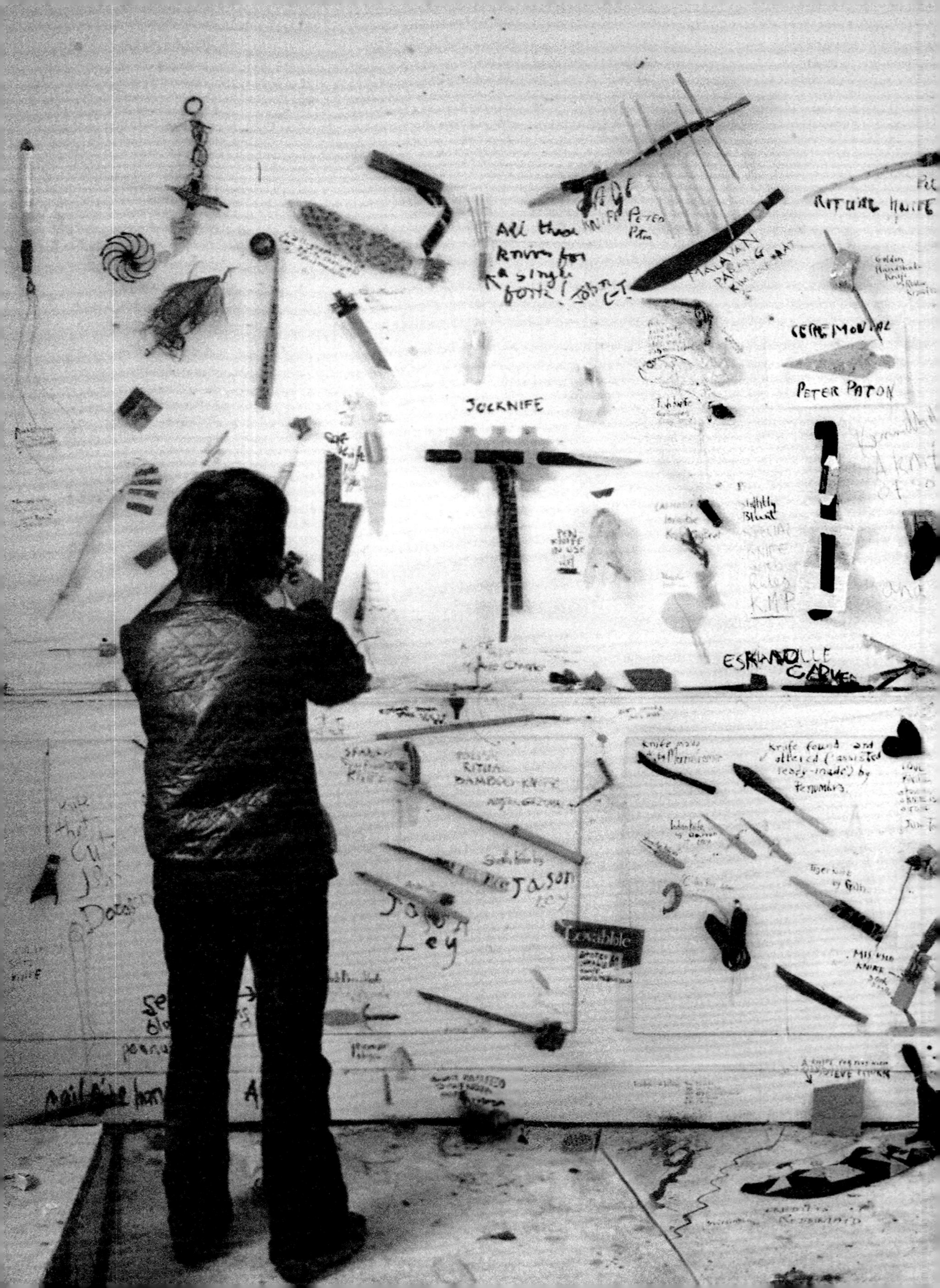

All these knives for a single bottle!
RITUAL KNIFE
CEREMONIAL
PETER PATON
JOCKNIFE
Jason
Ley
Lovable

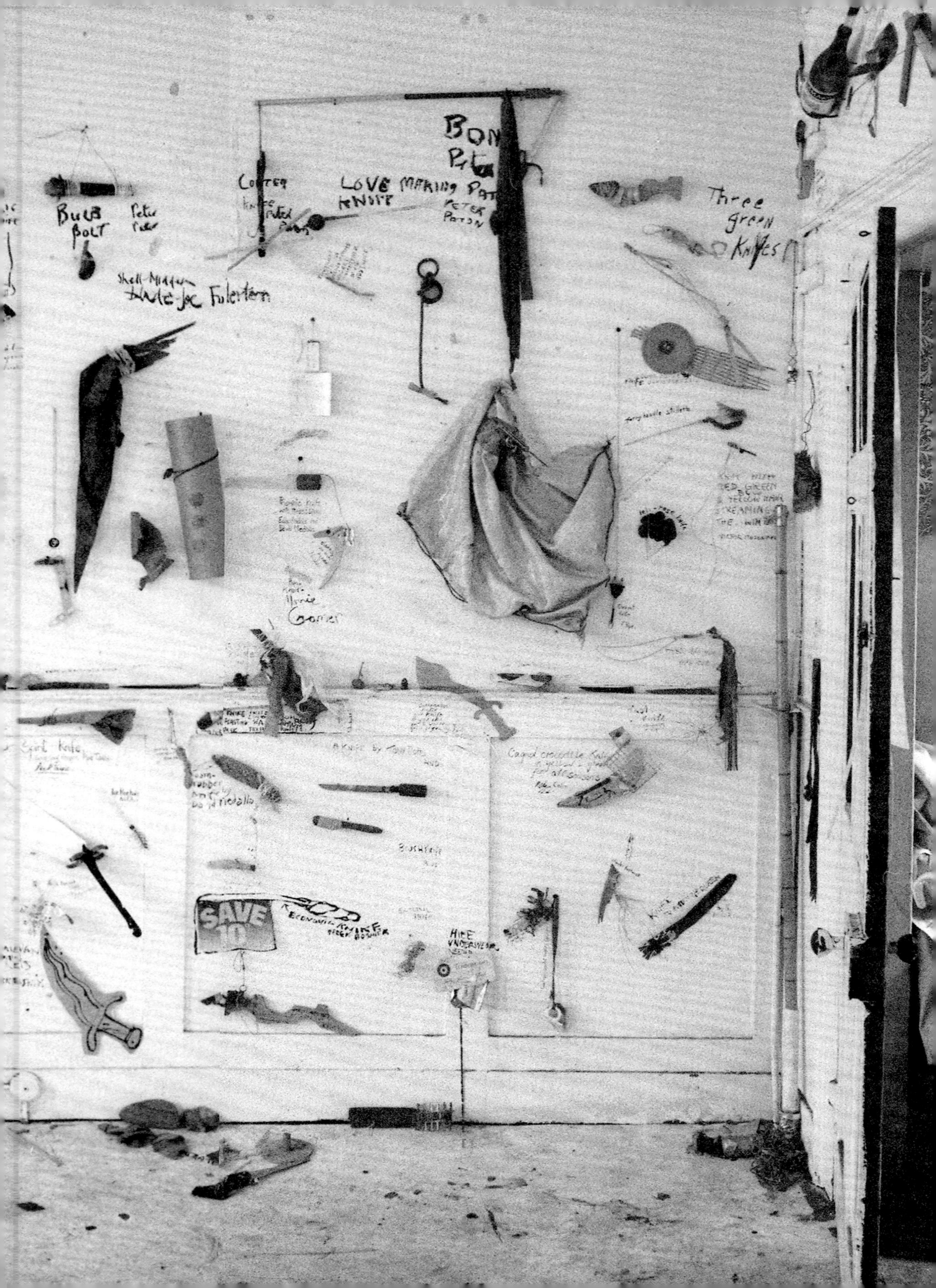

Bulb Bolt
LOVE MAKING
KNIFE
PETER PATON
Three green Knifes
Shell-Midden
Caged crocodile Knife
SAVE 10
BUSHKNIFE

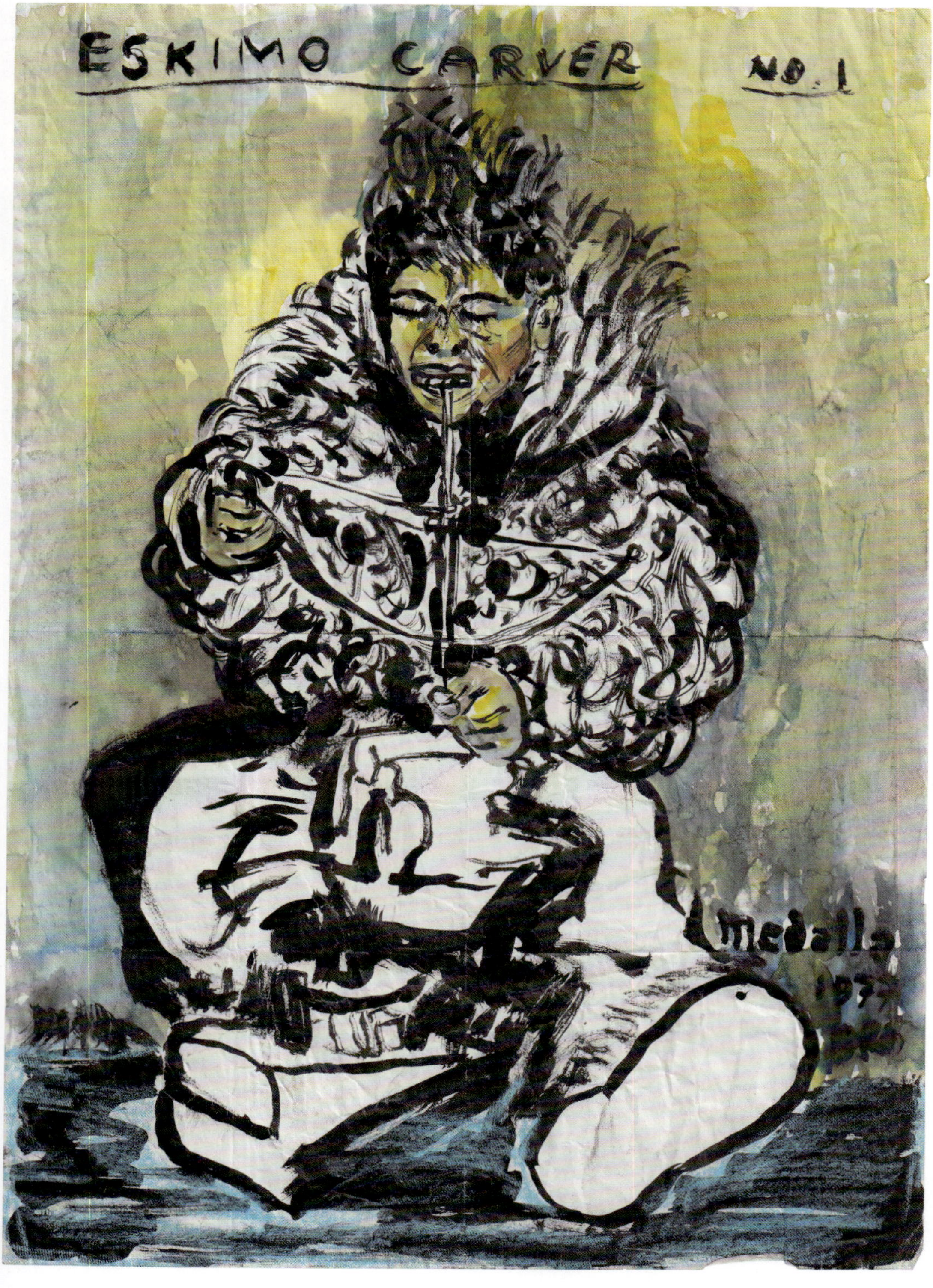

previous
David Medalla installing *Eskimo Carver*, Fitzrovia Cultural Centre, London, 1977.

above
Eskimo Carver No. 1, 1977. Watercolor and China ink on paper. 11½ × 8⅛ in. (29.2 × 20.7 cm).

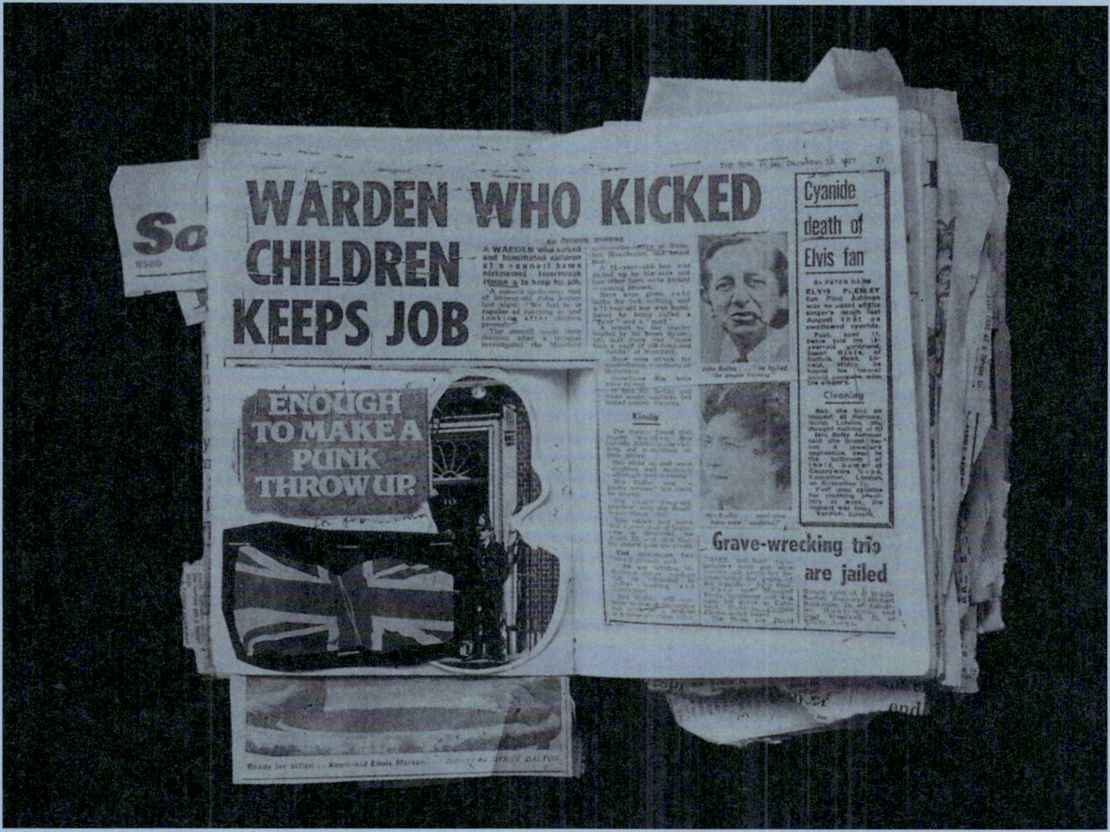
WARDEN WHO KICKED CHILDREN KEEPS JOB
Cyanide death of Elvis fan
ENOUGH TO MAKE A PUNK THROW UP.
Grave-wrecking trio are jailed

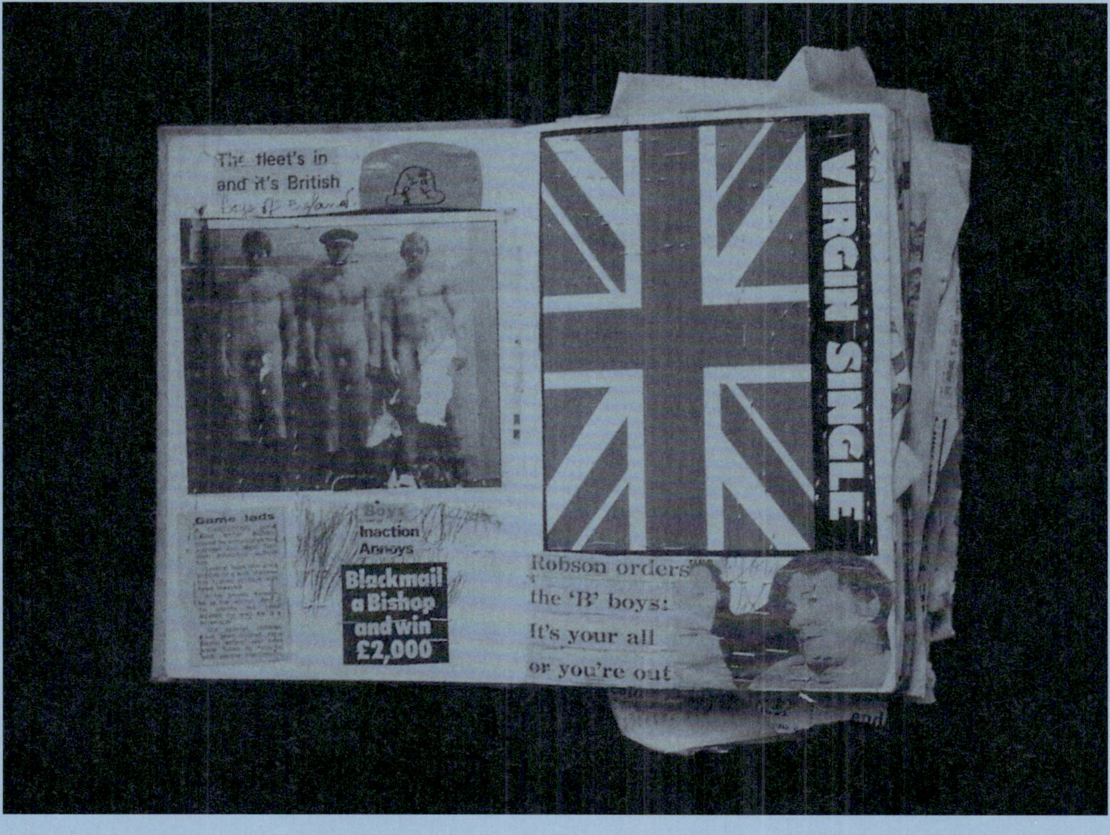
The fleet's in and it's British
VIRGIN SINGLE
Boys Inaction Annoys
Blackmail a Bishop and Win £2,000
Robson orders the 'B' boys: It's your all or you're out

Rhapsody of the Dagger and Ammonia Boy
1979–81

Rhapsody of the Dagger and Ammonia Boy is a series of paintings on wood. The works are accompanied by a poem that reads: "Armed with ammonia bottle and a dagger / I stalk the streets of Kennington / A stalk of sorrow in a dismal town / A sullen dancer with an angry frown." The paintings riff on *Boys of England*, a popular periodical of the nineteenth century that detailed activities and advice for youth. In an episodic format, Medalla's paintings depict contemporary newspaper accounts of a boy stalking the streets of South London, throwing ammonia in the faces of passersby and lunging at them with a knife. Clippings of articles about this story and others from the South London Press comprise Medalla's book of collages, *Boys of England: A Feverish Triumph* (1977–78). In the 1970s, Medalla experienced similar encounters while living in South London, in which xenophobic young men harassed him and ultimately compelled him to move away from the neighborhood.

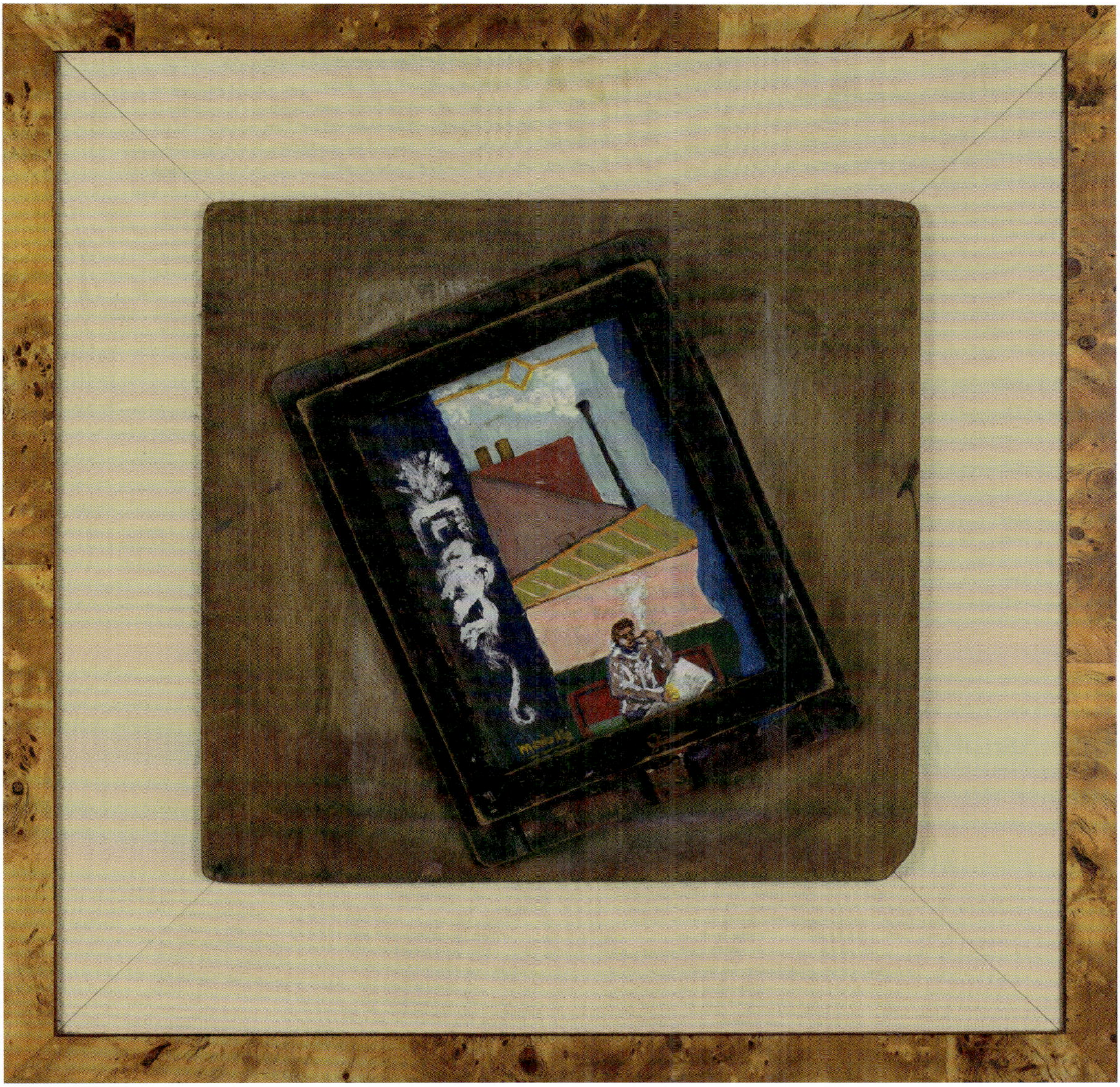

previous
Interior spreads of *Boys of England: A Feverish Triumph*, 1977–78. Collage in notebook. Dimensions unknown.

above
Rhapsody of the Dagger and Ammonia Boy, 1979. Wooden objects and acrylic on wood panel in decorative frame. 26 3⁄16 × 25 7⁄8 × 1 in. (66.5 × 65.7 × 2.5 cm).

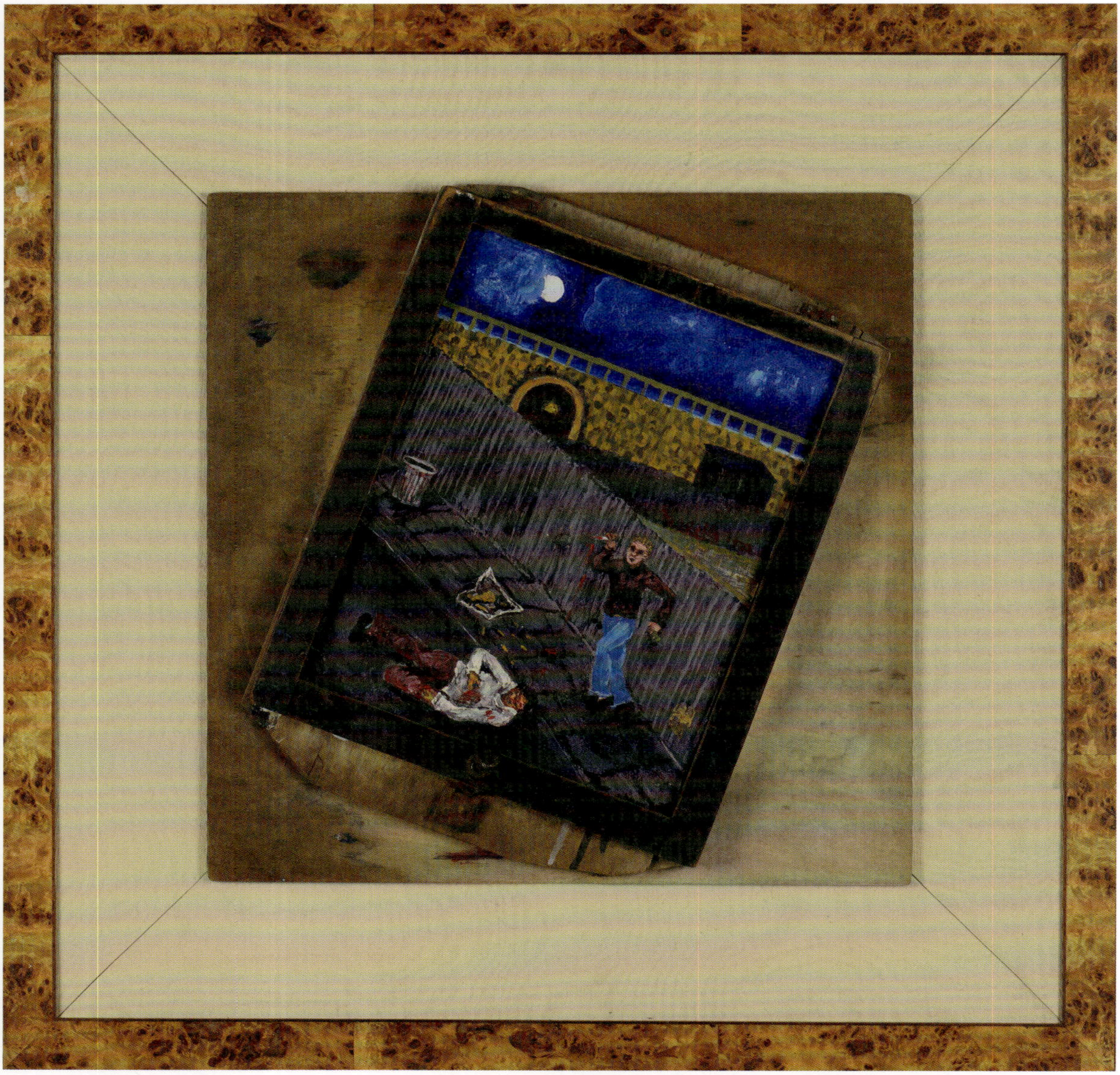

Rhapsody of the Dagger and Ammonia Boy: MOON-LIGHT, 1979. Wooden objects and acrylic on wood panel in decorative frame. 26 3⁄16 × 25 7⁄8 × 1 in. (66.5 × 65.7 × 2.5 cm).

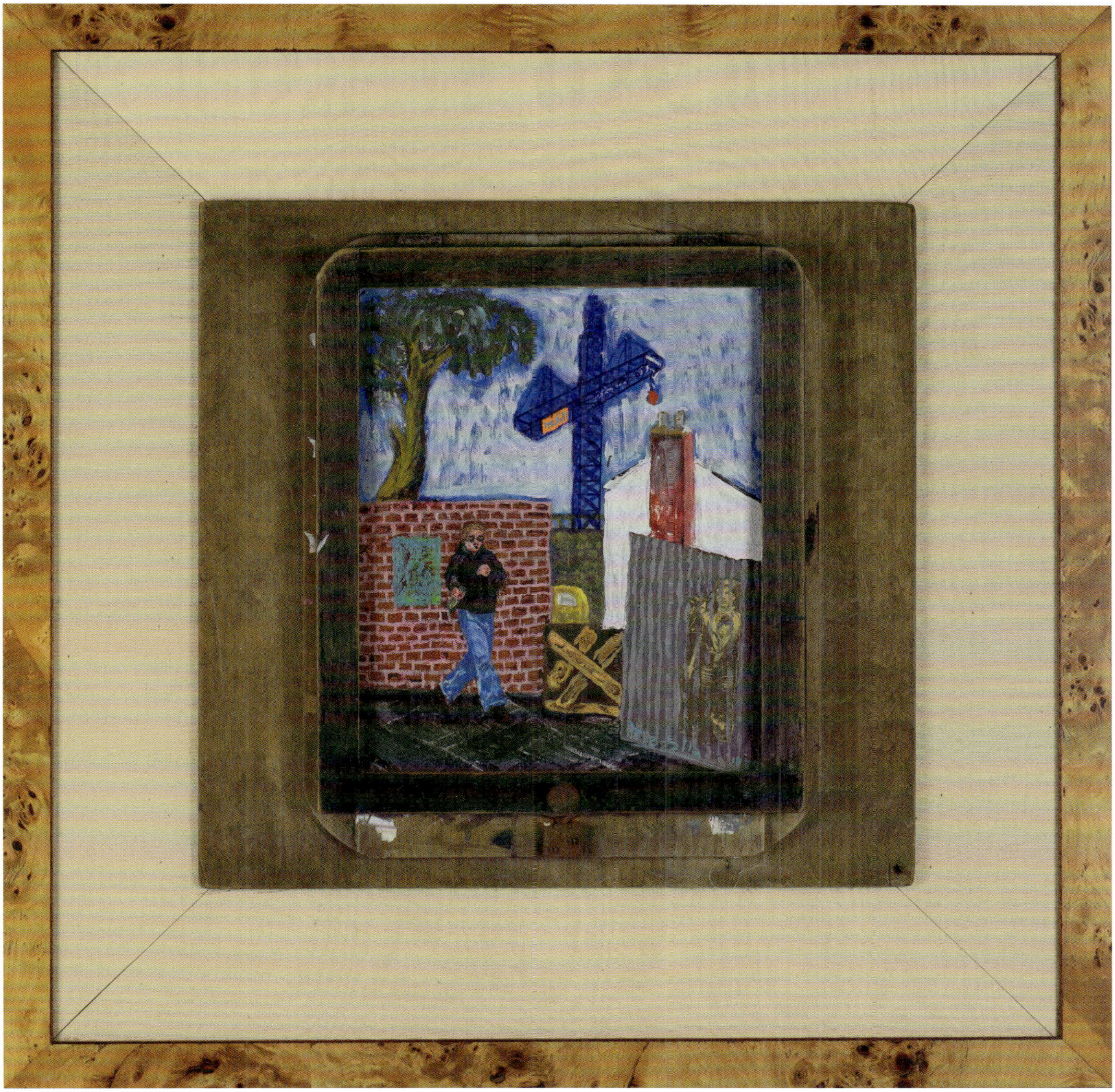

Rhapsody of the Dagger and Ammonia Boy, 1979. Wooden objects and acrylic on wood panel in decorative frame. 26 3⁄16 × 25 7⁄8 × 1 in. (66.5 × 65.7 × 2.5 cm).

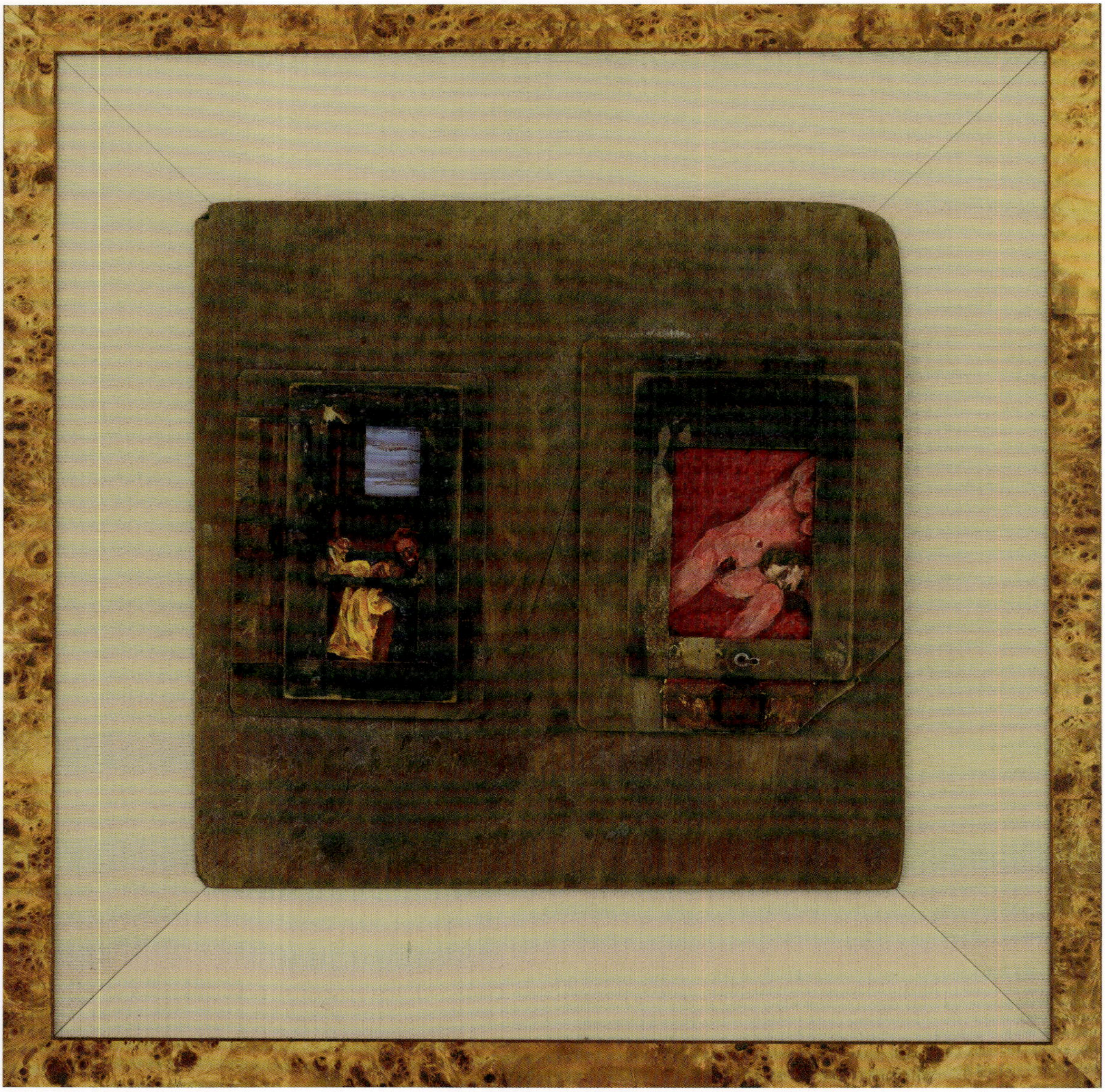

Rhapsody of the Dagger and Ammonia Boy (Interior Scene), 1979. Wooden objects and acrylic on wood panel in decorative frame. 26 3⁄16 × 25 7⁄8 × 1 in. (66.5 × 65.7 × 2.5 cm).

SHP from David Cortés de Medalla ~~artist in residence at~~
South ~~Hill Park Arts Centre~~, Bracknell, ~~Berkshire~~. Tel 0344,
~~Bracknell (0344) 27272~~. 123 Brook Drive, London SE11

replies by DAVID MEDALLA to the Performance Art Survey (1985) of PERFORMANCE magazine

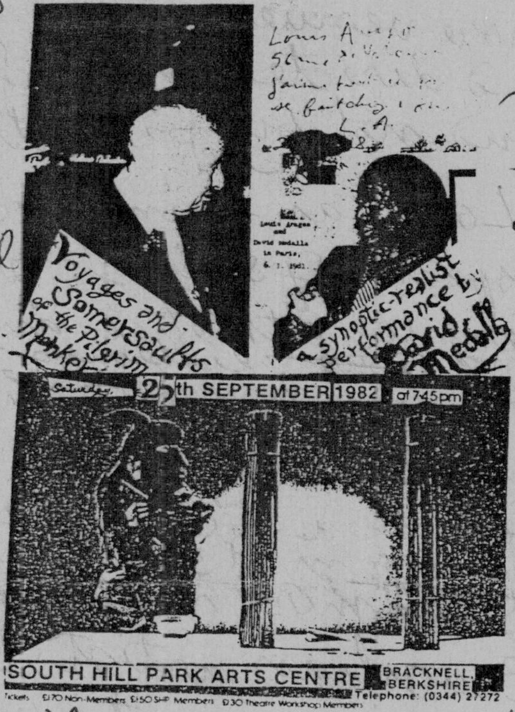

LOUIS ARAGON and DAVID MEDALLA

I call my performance style 'synoptic-realist' (a phrase I invented in 1977, in London) because all my performances and ~~in~~ impromptus are synoptic realisations of all the different levels of reality: optical sensations as well as paravisual phenomena, historical reality as well as visionary states, the reality of everyday existence (which I often experience ironically) and the hidden reality of my as well as other people's dream-lives.

) Freedom, of all peoples and of the individual. No one yet on our planet is, alas, completely free. Freedom means, ultimately, the transcending of all closed systems and ~~circuito~~ circuitous ideologies (religious as well as political). Corrollary to this freedom are ~~the~~ constrained physical movement and psychical growth of every individual, ~~etc~~ an the solution to erotic fulfillment

PTO

Synoptic-Realism 1979–2020

Medalla's work often disrupts linear depictions of time and space in order to reframe and reimagine past and present realities. In an essay outlining his philosophy of artmaking, he wrote, "I invented the term 'synoptic-realism' to signify the synthesis of the methods (languages) available to the artist which will enable him/her to articulate in coherent, vibrant, imaginative and organic ways his multiple experiences of reality, and to construct the forms most appropriate to these experiences of reality." Medalla first coined the term *synoptic-realism* in 1979, and it represented for him an artist's lexicon that included performances, impromptu events and occurrences, paintings, and poetry.

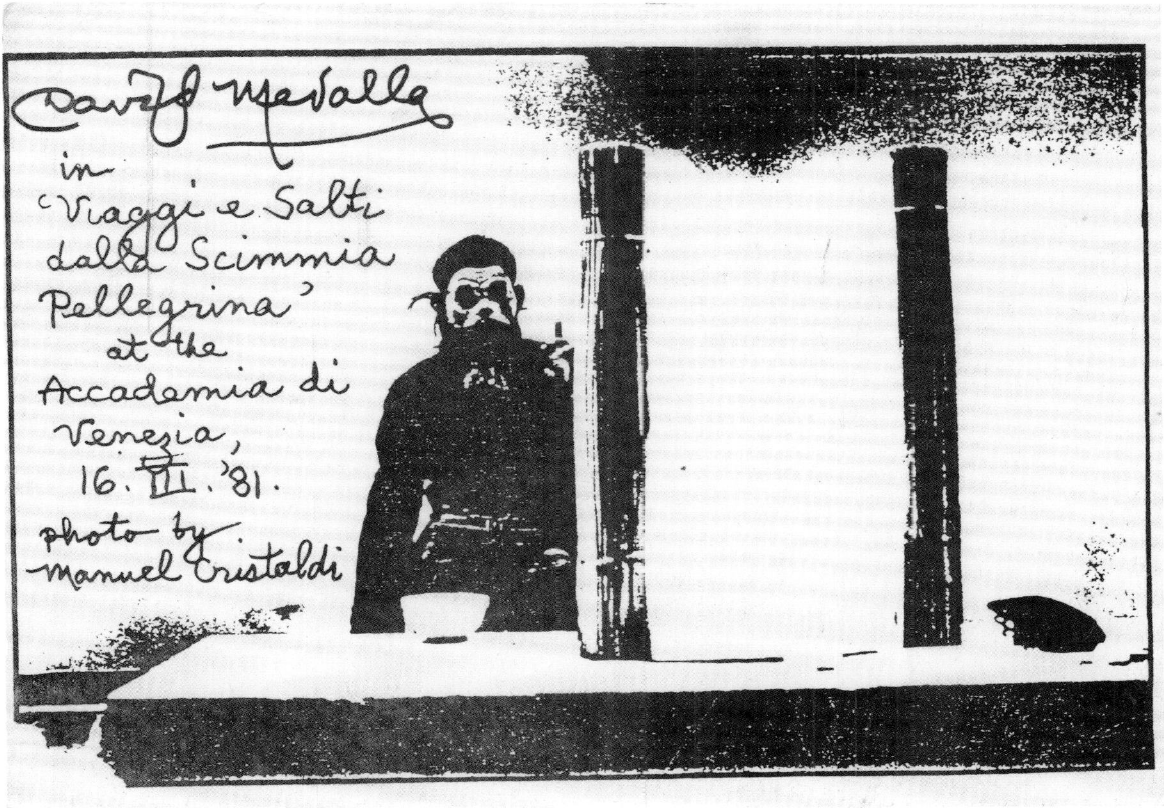

previous
Replies by David Medalla to the Performance Art Survey of Performance Magazine, 1985. Ballpoint pen on photocopy. 11⅝ × 8¼ in. (29.6 × 21.0 cm).

above
Announcement for Synoptic-Realism performance, Accademia di Venezia, Venice, 1981.

Proust Tropicale et Marcel Maritime, 1979.
Crayon and ballpoint pen on photocopy.
11 11⁄16 × 8 1⁄4 in. (29.7 × 21.0 cm).

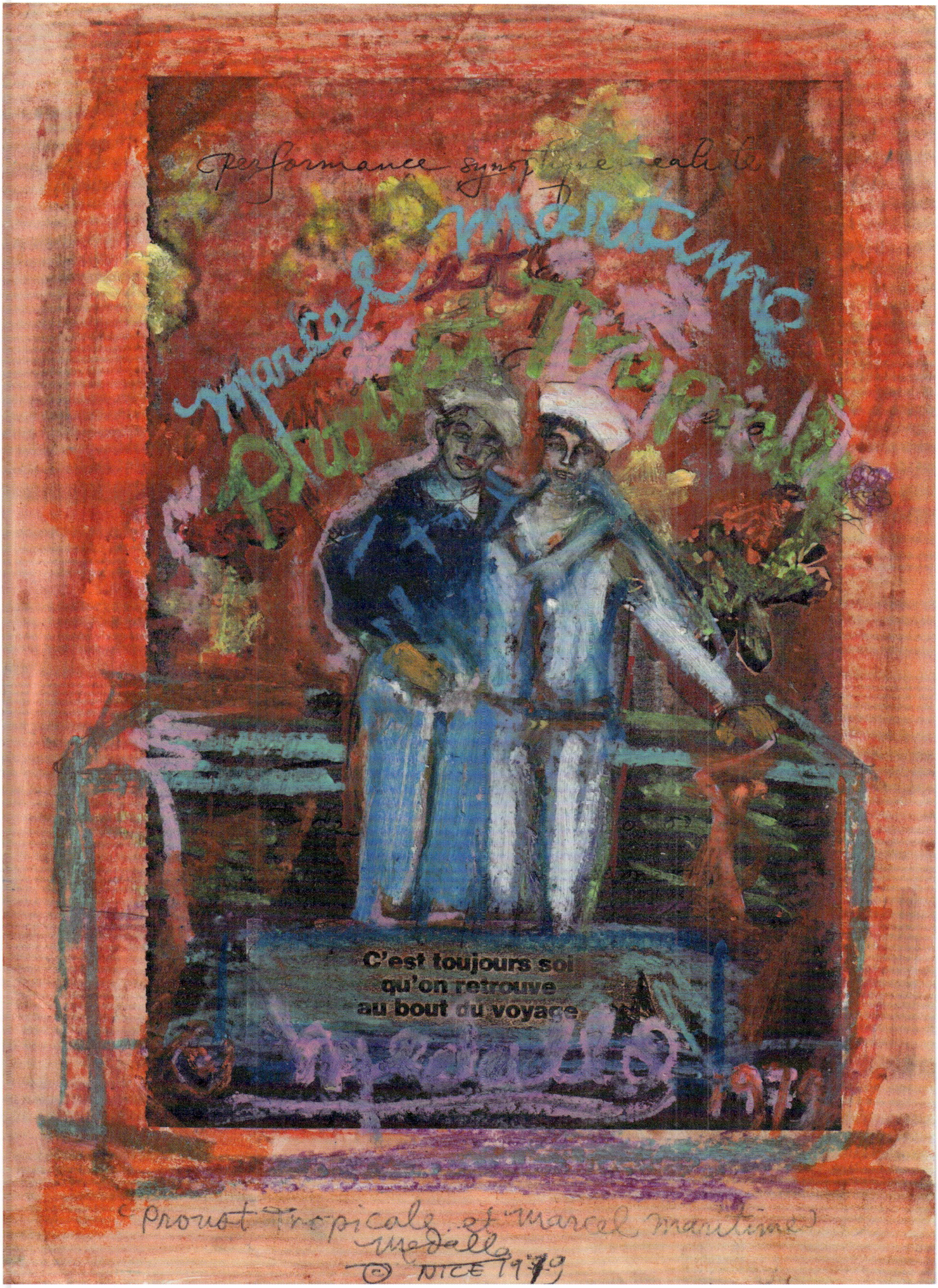
C'est toujours soi
qu'on retrouve
au bout du voyage

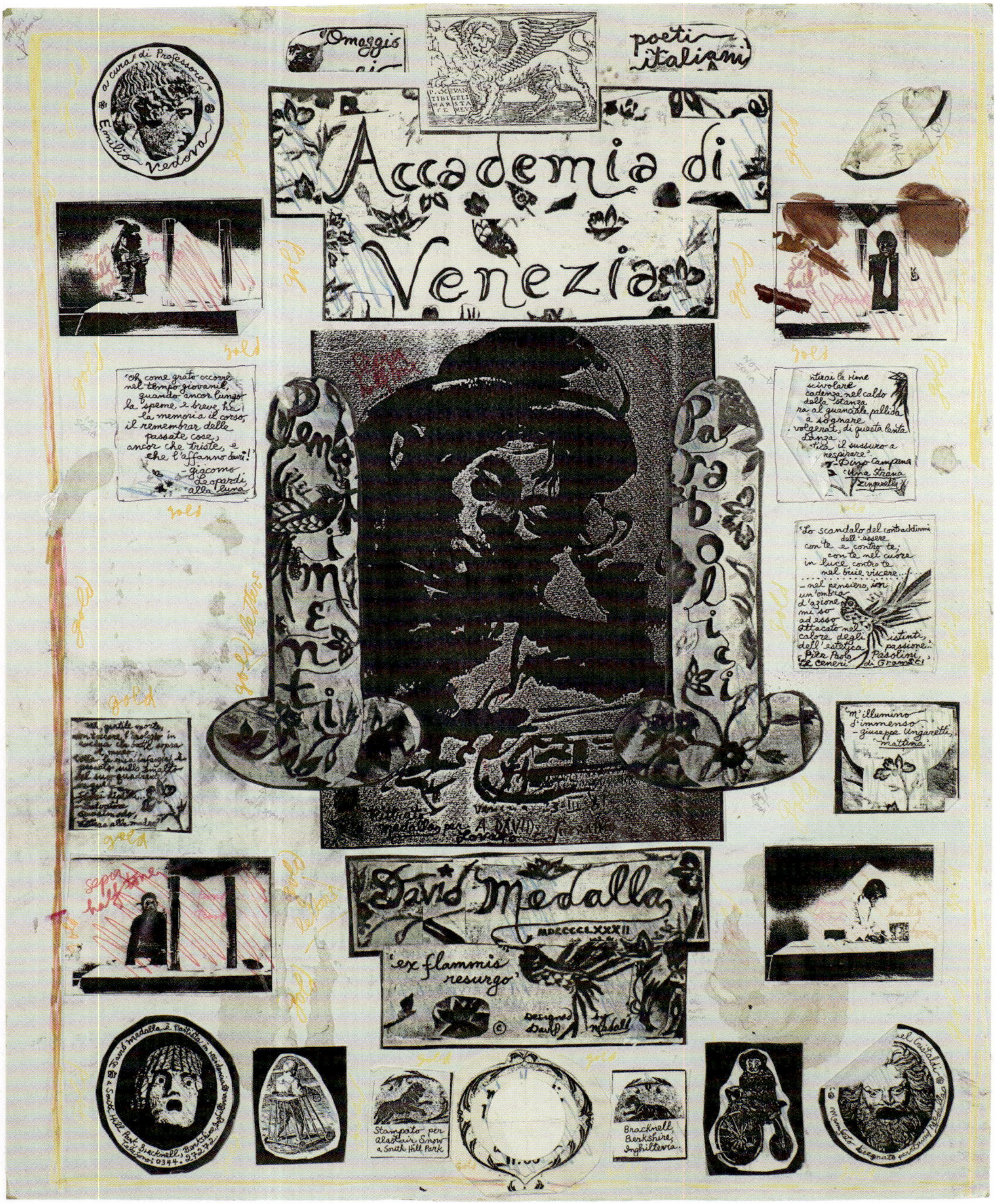

Untitled, 1982. Photocopies and felt-tip marker on cardstock. 24 7⁄8 × 19 15⁄16 in. (63.2 × 50.7 cm).

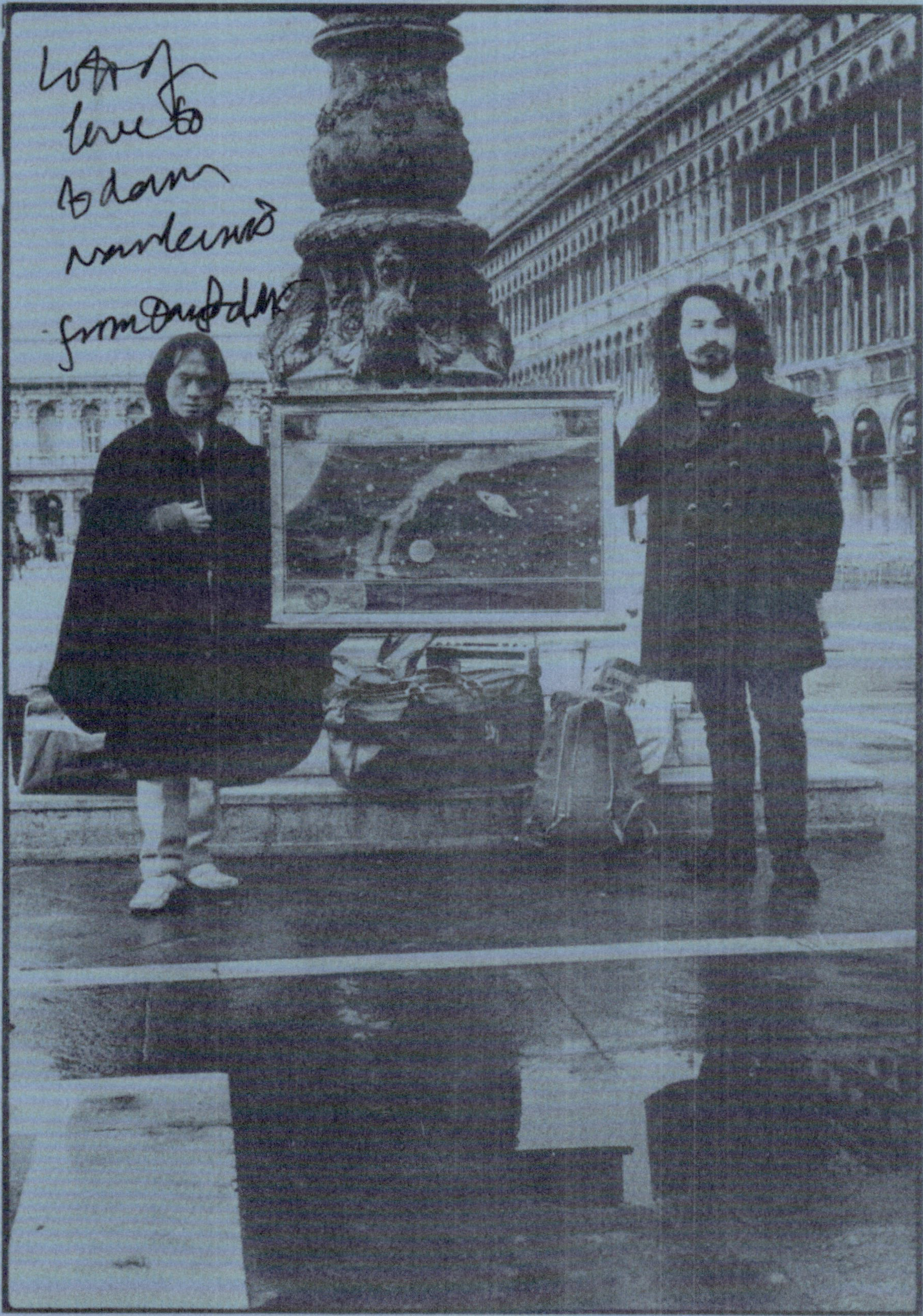
love to
adam

Impromptus
1980–2019

Throughout his life, Medalla imagined and executed spontaneous works of art that required no formal planning, approval, or outside funding. In 1980, he designated these fleeting ventures—which took the form of short performances and interventions that were sometimes documented by a camera—Impromptus. In many of these works, the artist wears a paper mask, which enabled him to step into a variety of identities. In the Impromptu *Psychic Self-Defense* (1983), Medalla stands in front of Westminster's stately clock tower, Big Ben, which is clad in scaffolding. In either hand, the artist holds statues of Beethoven and Mozart; a sprig of leaves adorns the top of his head, and he wears a mask torn from the cover of the eponymous book. For nearly forty years, Medalla was an itinerant shapeshifter, interacting with the forms he encountered around the world. As his longtime collaborator and dear friend Guy Brett observes in his book *Exploding Galaxies: The Art of David Medalla*, "For Medalla, identity is kinetic, shared, a complex amalgam."

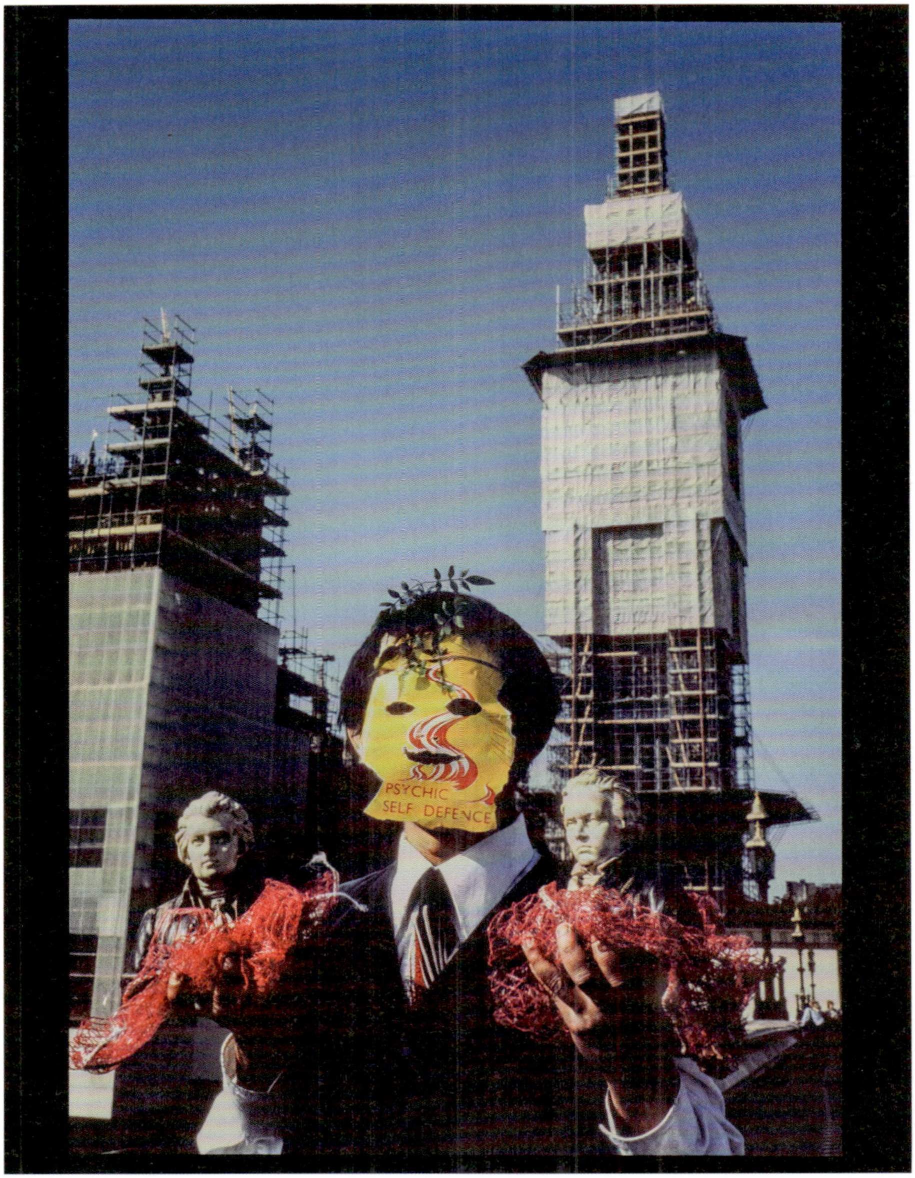

previous
Postcard for David Medalla and Lovato Guerrino, *Qui posano insieme / Here They Pose*, 1981. Offset. 5 15⁄16 × 3 15⁄16 in. (15.2 × 10.1 cm).

above
Psychic Self-Defense, 1983. C-print. 15 15⁄16 × 12 3⁄16 in. (40.5 × 31 cm).

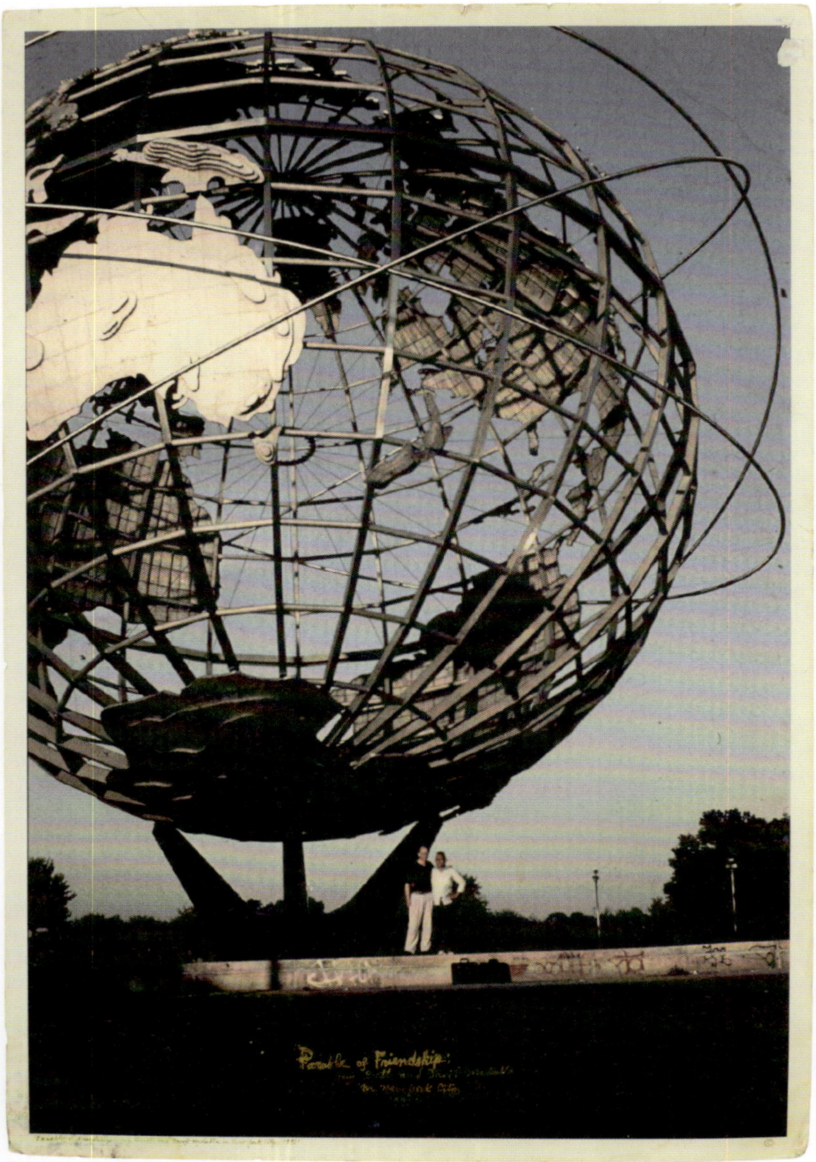

above
Parable of Friendship: Guy Brett and David Medalla in New York City, 1991. Inkjet on archival paper and marker on foamboard. 31 13⁄16 × 42 15⁄16 in. (80.8 × 109 cm).

opposite
MEDALLA SALUTA ROMA, 1980. Offset. 10 1⁄16 × 7 7⁄8 in. (25.5 × 20.3 cm).

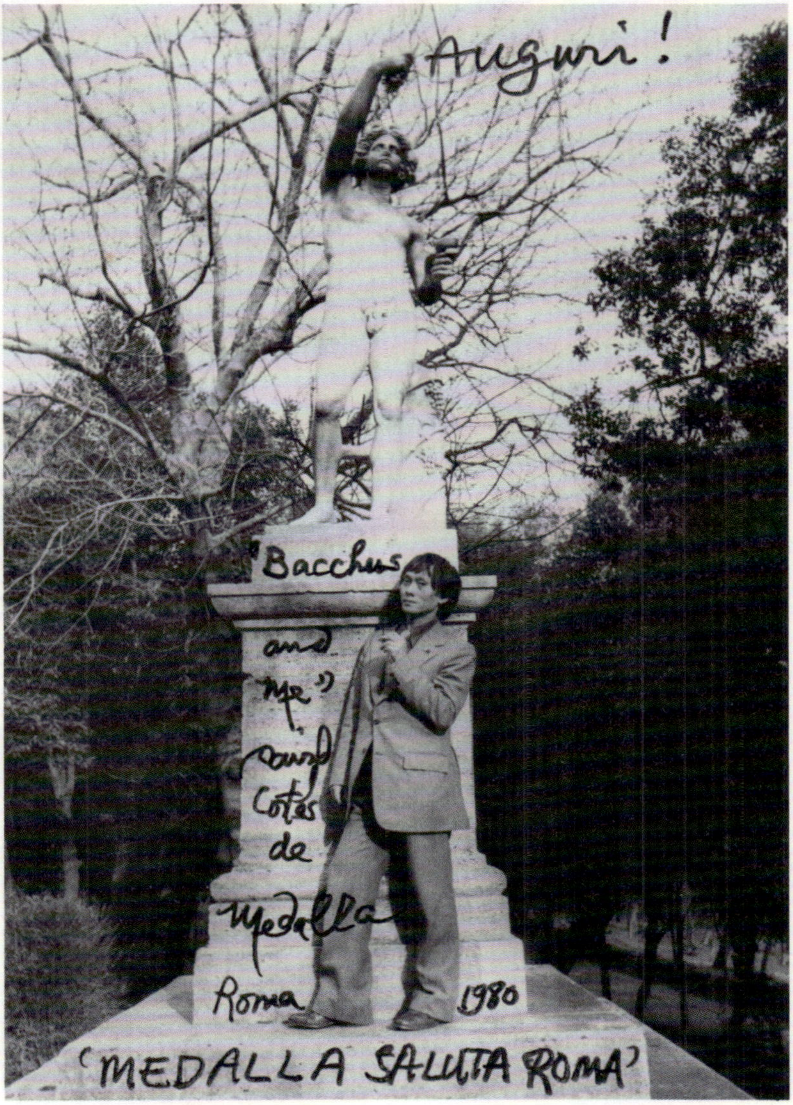
Auguri!
"Bacchus
and
me"
cours
Cotes
de
Medalla
Roma 1980
'MEDALLA SALUTA ROMA'

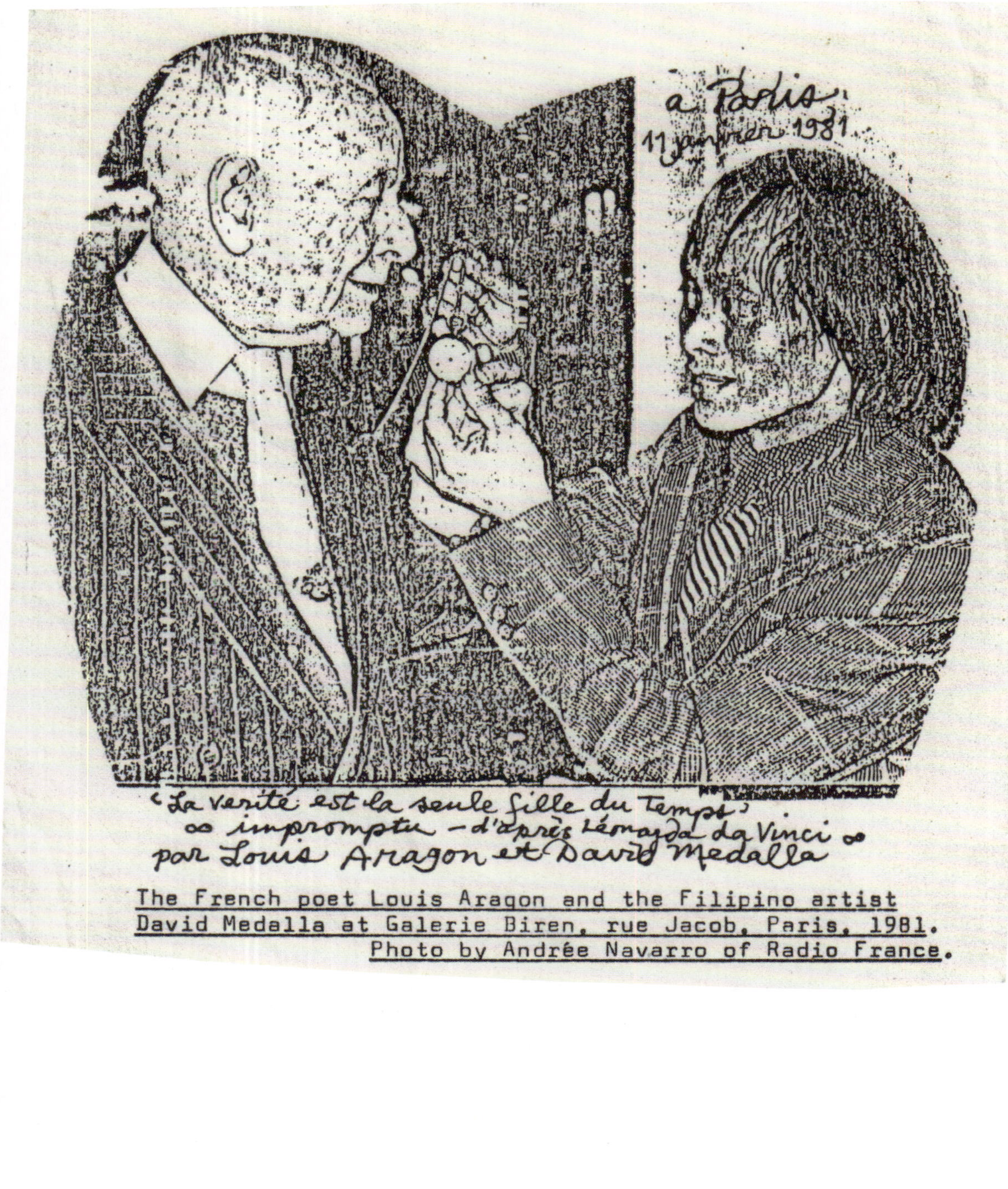

David Medalla with Louis Aragon: An Impromptu in Paris, 1981. Photocopy. 6 ⅞ × 6 ⅞ in. (17.5 × 17.5 cm).

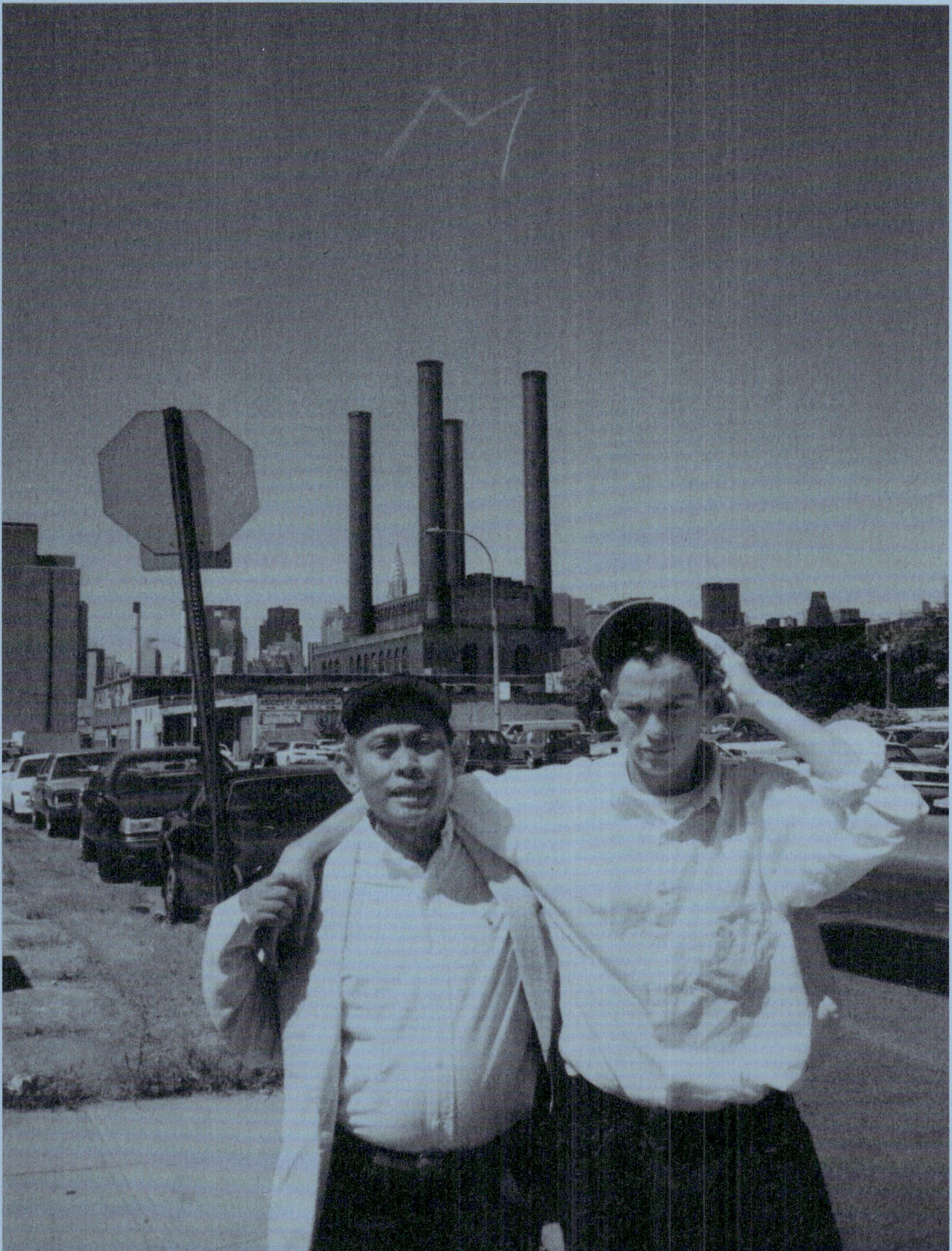

Mondrian Fan Club 1991–2018

The Mondrian Fan Club was born in 1991 of Adam Nankervis and Medalla's shared admiration of the Dutch painter Piet Mondrian. The artists believed that the time Mondrian spent in London, from 1938 to 1940, had produced a shift in the imagination and representation of spatial organization in British art. The pair also appreciated Mondrian because his work was overlooked during his lifetime, as was theirs. Together, they made the Mondrian Fan Club works, which Nankervis described as "ethereal airborne global graffiti." The two met up at various junctures around the world—from Waikiki to Paris—and performed fleeting tableaux. In each iteration, the artists held up a constructed letter; taken together, the letters spelled out the phrase "The Secret History of the Mondrian Fan Club." Rather than quoting specific works of art in homage, as many artists do, Medalla situated himself in the lived experiences of other artists. For example, to honor Mondrian's documented passion for dance, Medalla and artist Tina Keane created the film *David Teaching Guy and Rose the Boogie Woogie* (1994), with curator and writer Guy Brett in the role of Mondrian. *Mondrian in Excelsis* (1993) ruminates on the late artist's obsession with vertical and horizontal tension by picturing a sidelong erection—presumably that of Nankervis—inside a pair of customized Mondrian-themed swim trunks. The two artists even found inspiration in the painter's death. Their performance *Mondrian in Extremis* (1992) commemorated Mondrian's final illness and delirium by placing chrysanthemums on his grave.

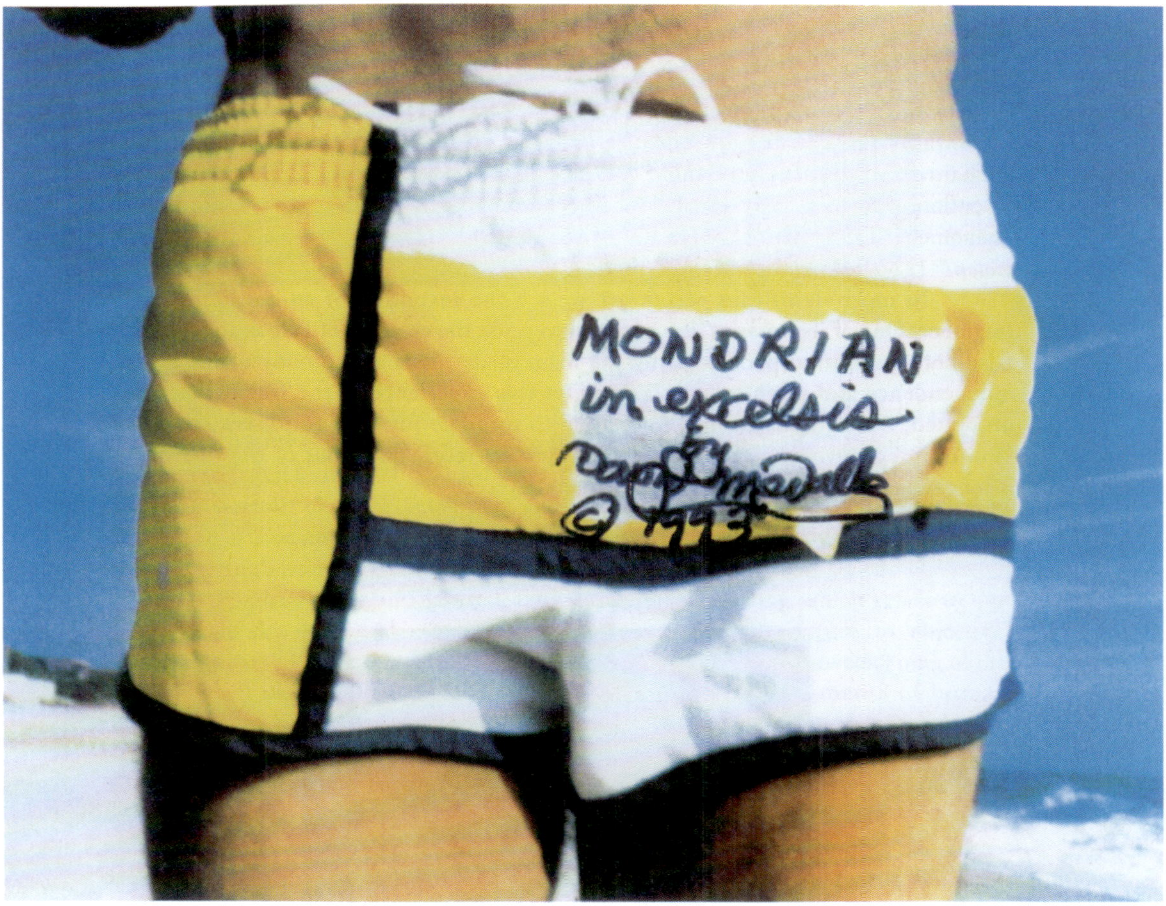

previous
Mondrian Fan Club, *The Letter "M" Over Manhattan*, 1995. C-print. 12 1/16 × 10 3/16 in. (30.7 × 25.8 cm).

above
Mondrian Fan Club, *Mondrian in Excelsis*, 1993. Inkjet on archival paper. 12 5/8 × 18 1/2 in. (32 × 47 cm).

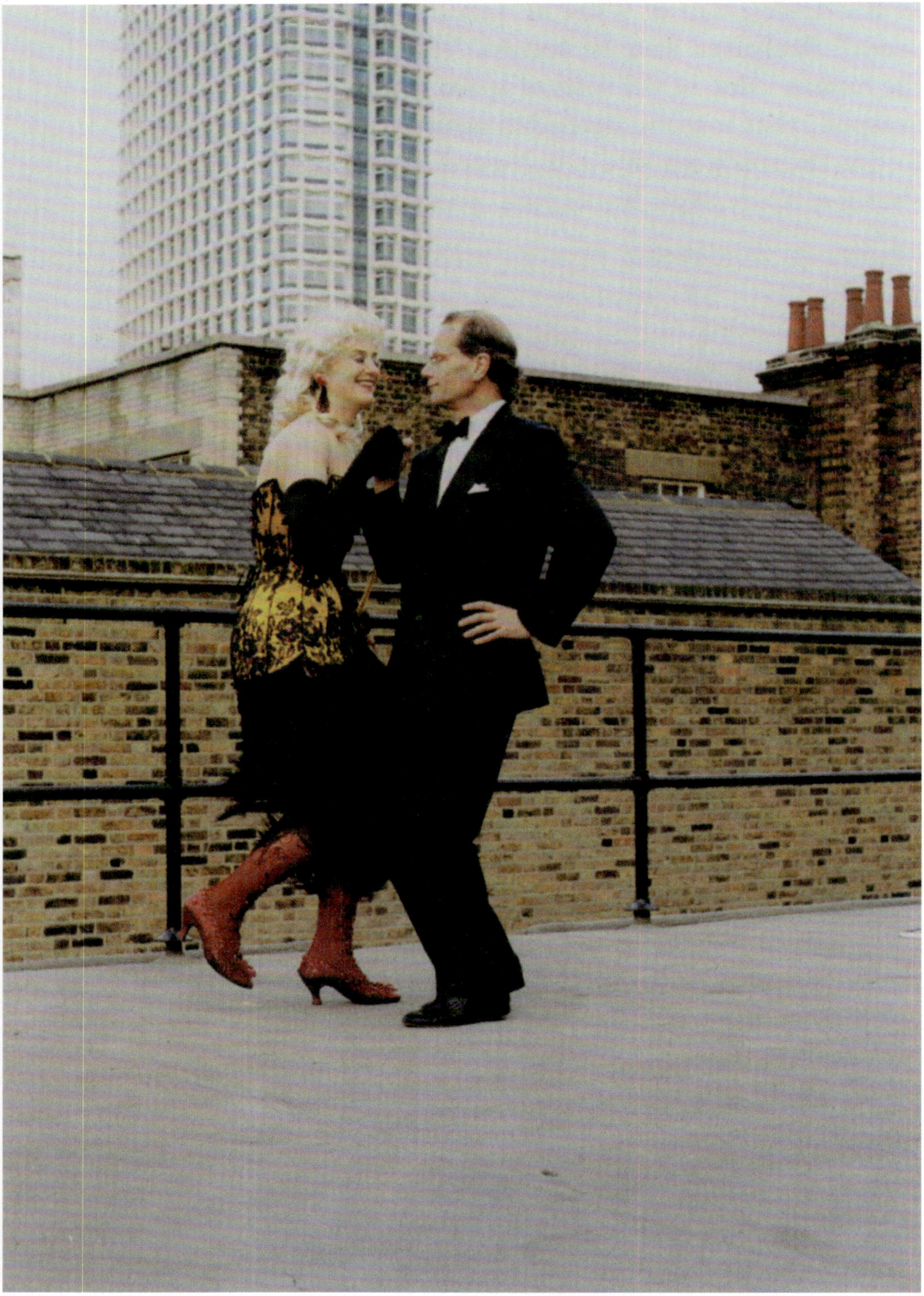

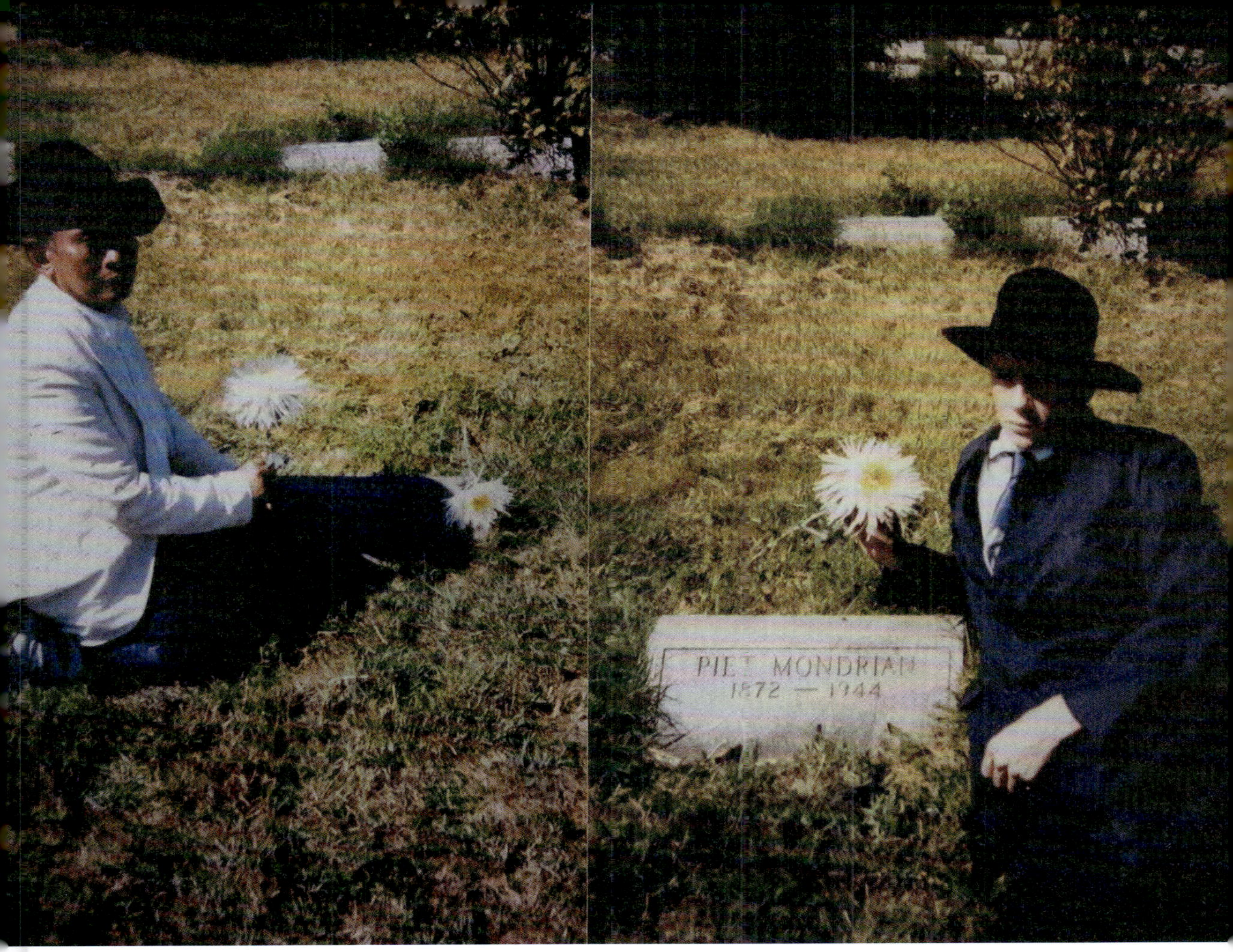

opposite
Rose English with Guy Brett (as Piet Mondrian) being directed by David Medalla in Tina Keane's video *David Teaching Guy and Rose the Boogie Woogie*, 1994.

above
Mondrian Fan Club, *Cypress Hills Cemetery*, 1994. 12 5/8 × 18 1/2 in. (32 × 47 cm).

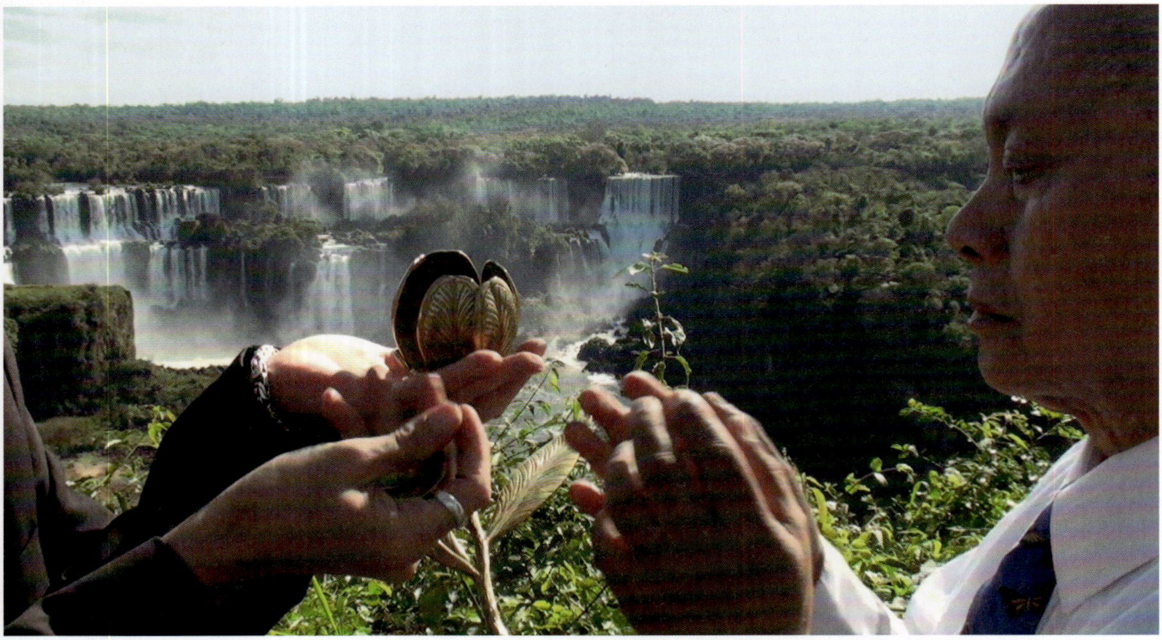

Renata Padovan, *Tulips for Iguazu*, 2010.
Still from digital video, color, sound, 7:35 min.

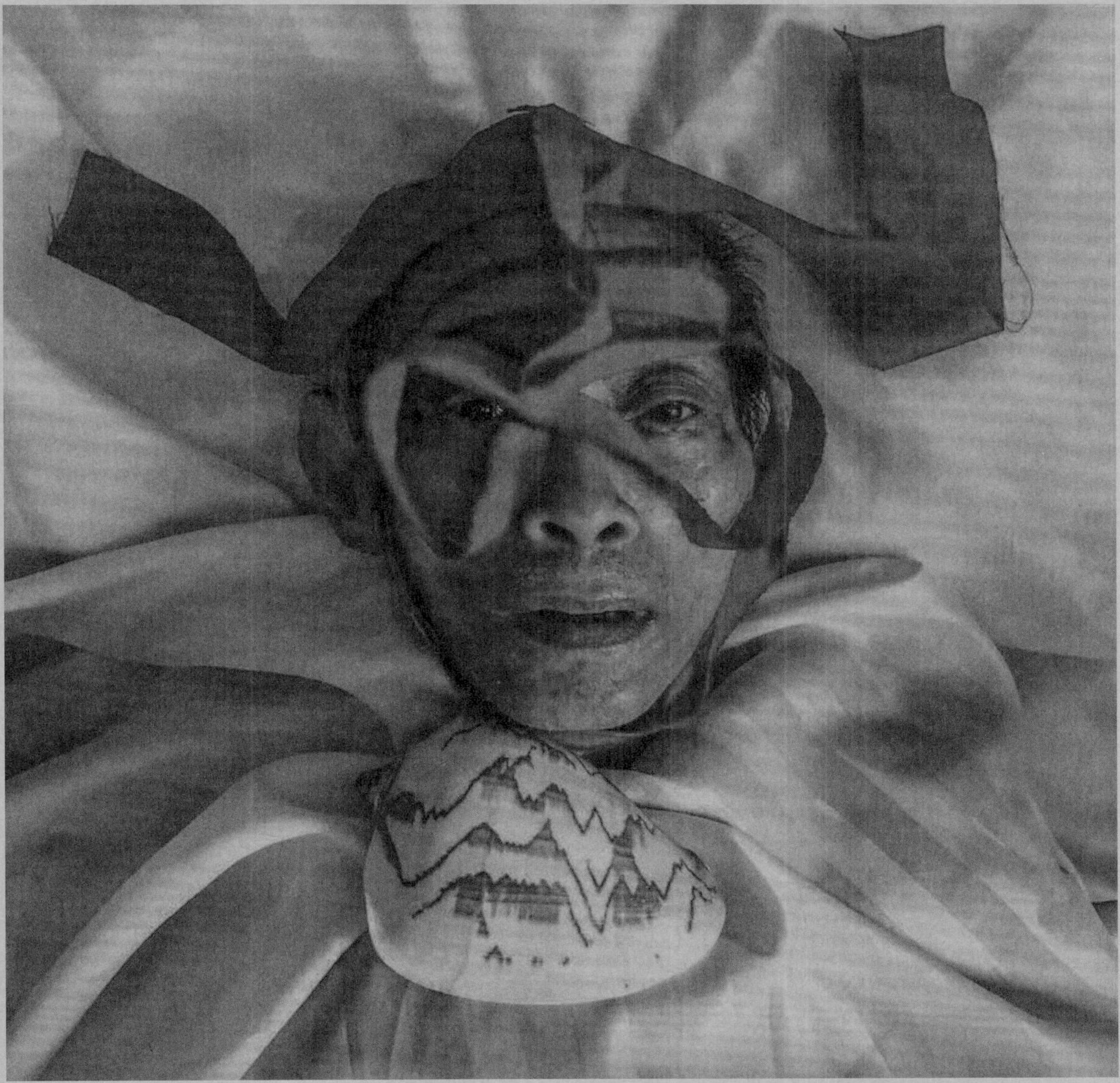

Sirens
2017–19

Adam Nankervis's photographs of Medalla in the Sirens series are the final works in their decades-long artistic collaboration. Medalla suffered a stroke in 2016 that left him partially paralyzed. After being released from the hospital, the pair continued to travel, with Nankervis acting as Medalla's caretaker. When Medalla's illness caused him to be unable to feel sensation in the majority of his body, Nankervis created masks on his face, offering one of the only sensory experiences Medalla could receive. The masks recorded in the Sirens series pay homage to various cultural figures, including the artists Marcel Duchamp and Man Ray, Chinese opera star Mei Lanfang, Russian poet Vladimir Mayakovsky, and even Medalla himself, whose artistic life had always involved pseudonyms, masquerade, and role play. In Nankervis's words, they made these masks as a way of "using beauty as a tool to trick the eclipse."

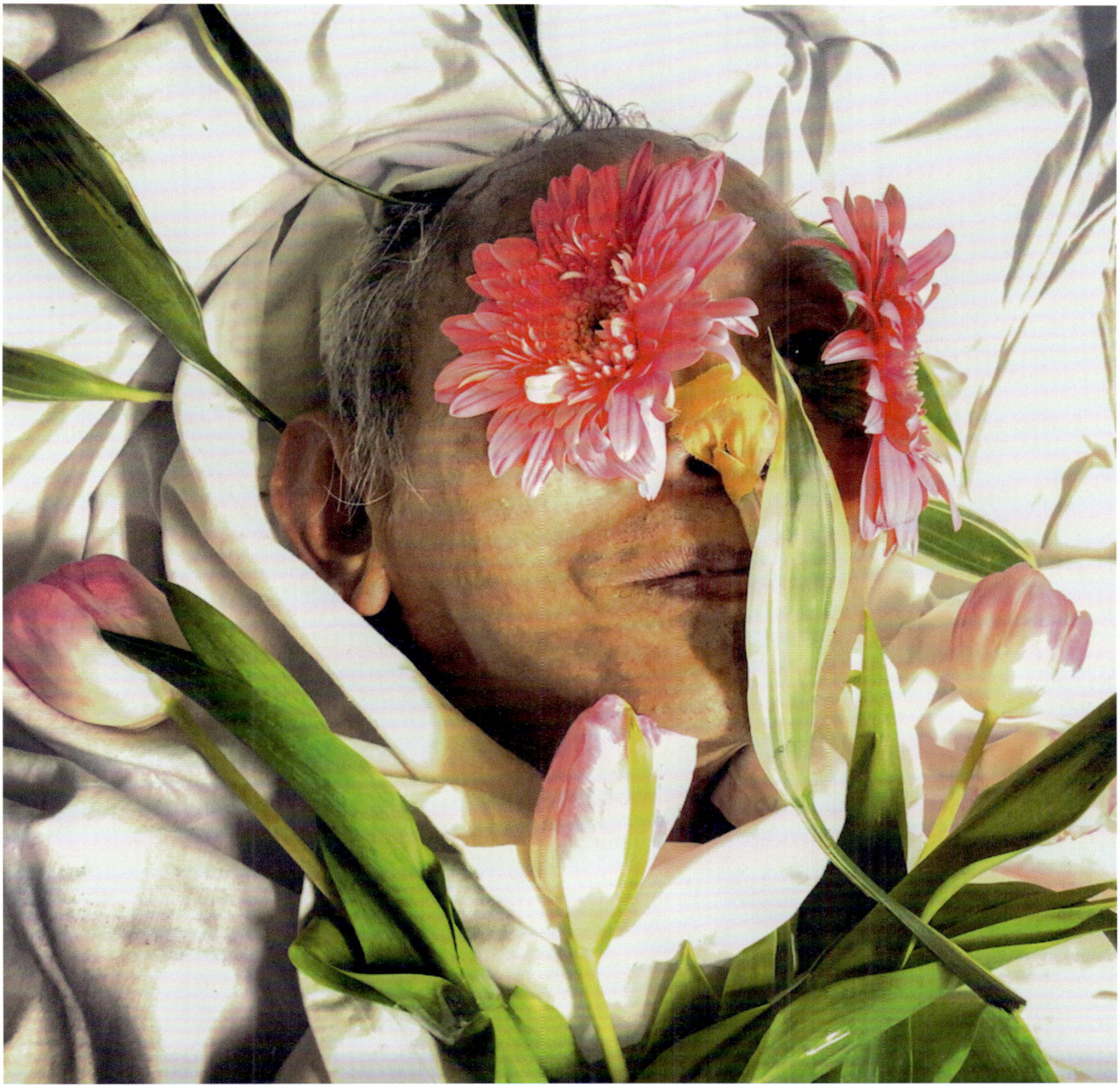

previous
Adam Nankervis, *David Medalla, The Fairy Mountain, a homage to Mei Lan Fang*, 2017. C-print. 31 7⁄16 × 23 5⁄8 in. (79.8 × 60 cm).

above
Adam Nankervis, *David Medalla, mondrian in excelsis*, 2018. C-print. 31 7⁄16 × 23 5⁄8 in. (79.8 × 60 cm).

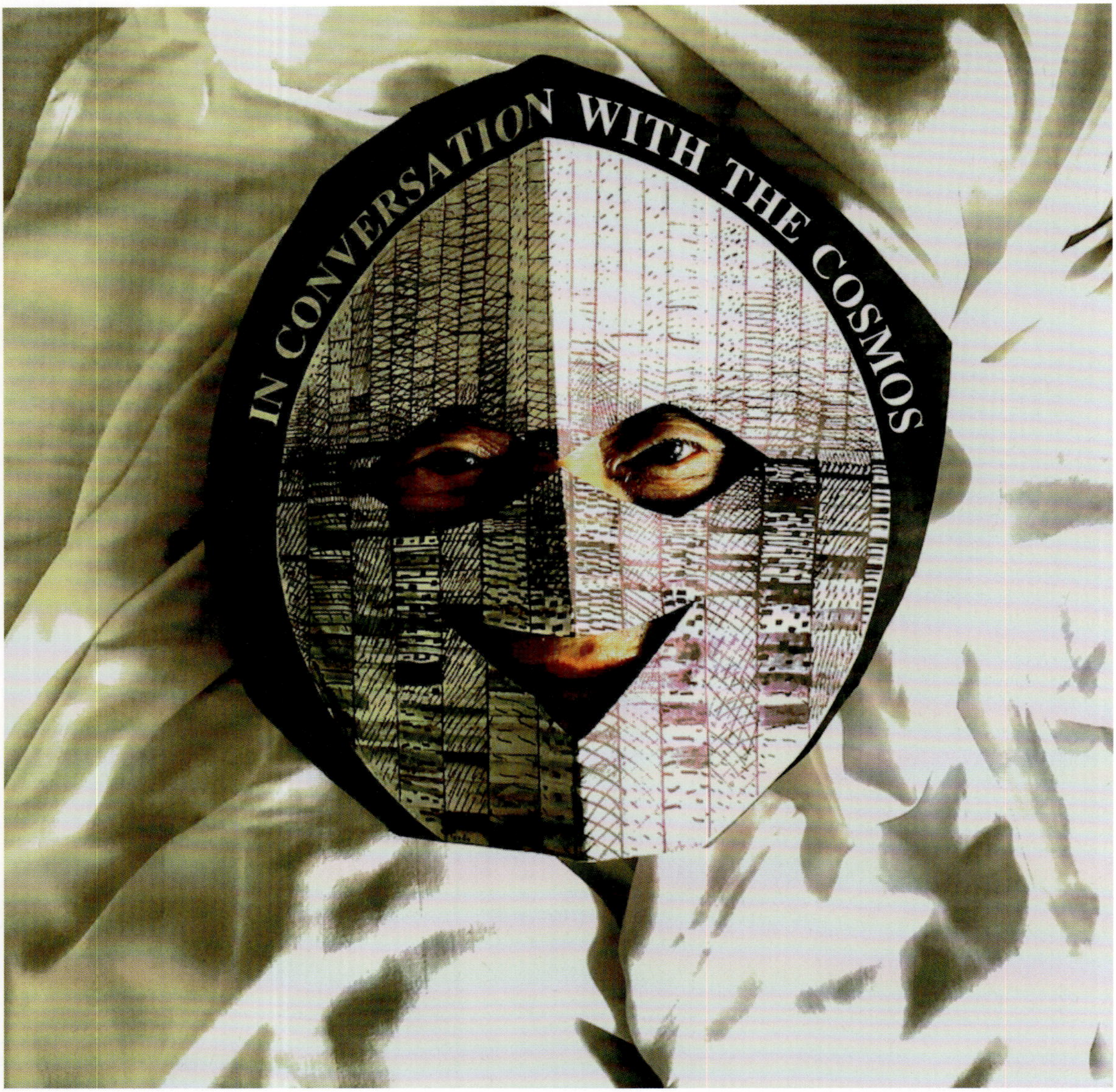

Adam Nankervis, *David Medalla in conversation with the cosmos*, 2017. C-print. 31 7⁄16 × 23 5⁄8 in. (79.8 × 60 cm).

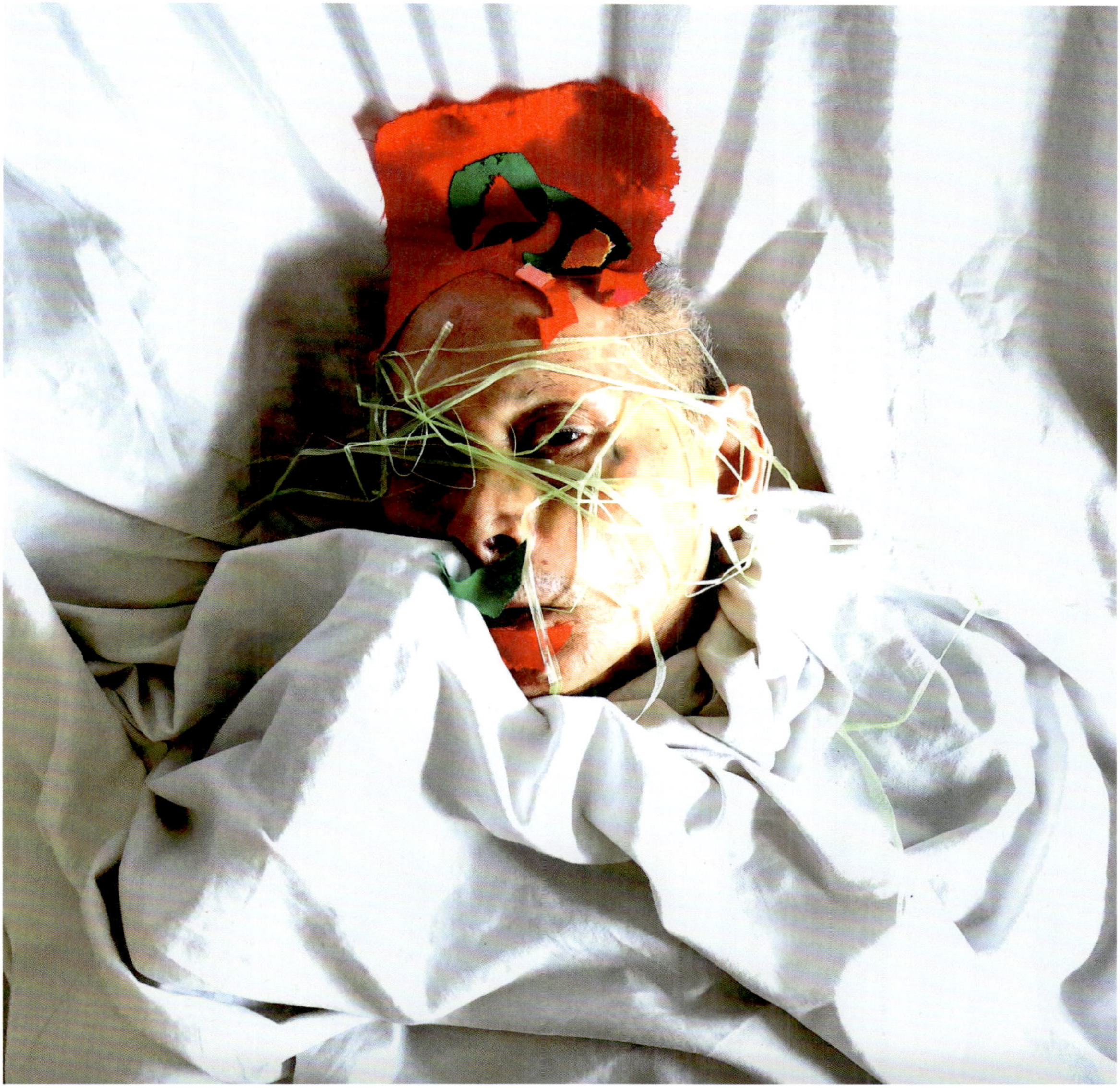

Adam Nankervis, *David Medalla, hunaman weaving rainbows*, 2018. C-print. 31 7⁄16 × 23 5⁄8 in. (79.8 × 60 cm).

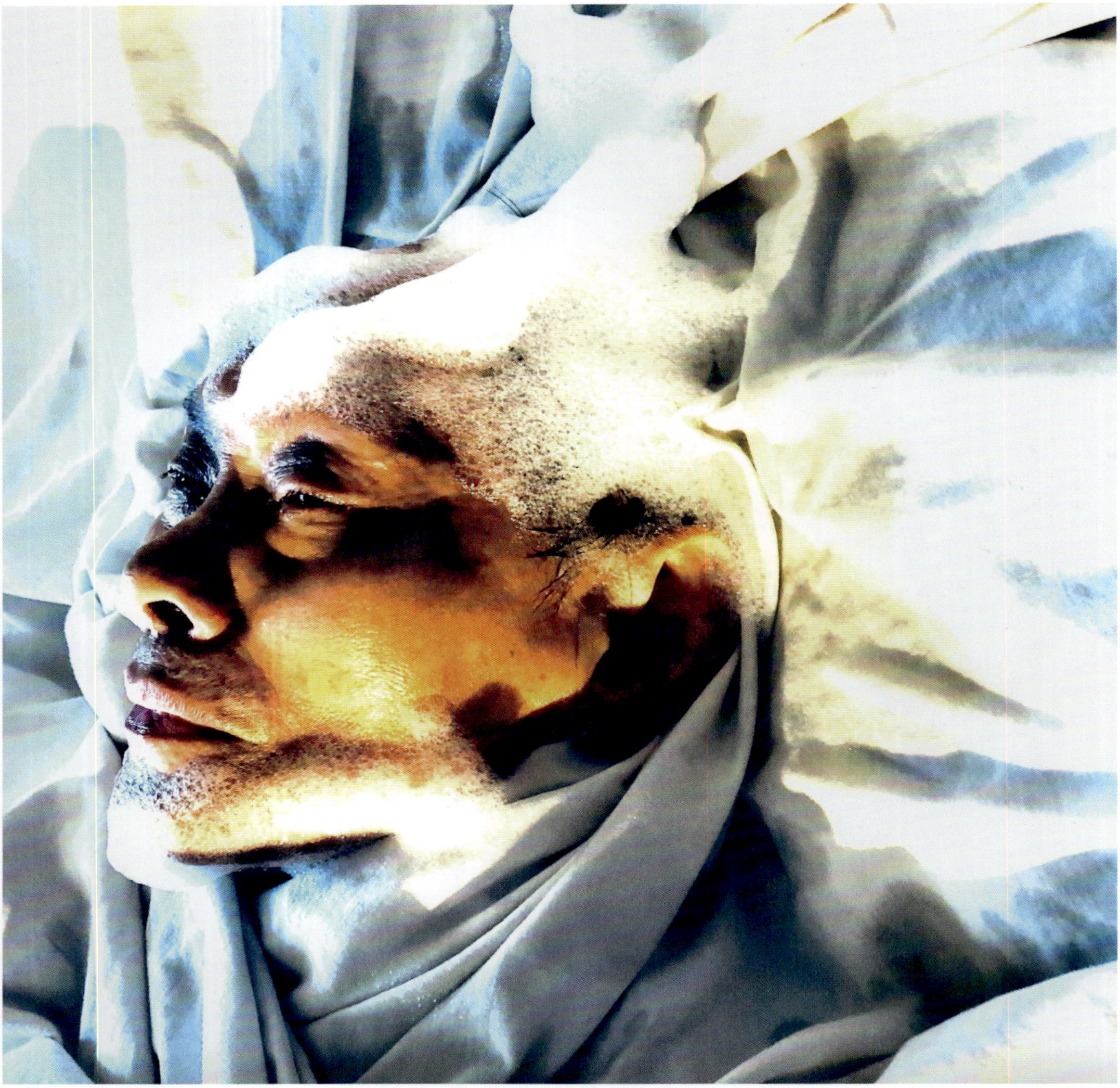

Adam Nankervis, *David Medalla a cloud in trousers homage to mayakovsky duchamp and man ray manila*, 2019. C-print. 31 7/16 × 23 5/8 in. (79.8 × 60 cm).

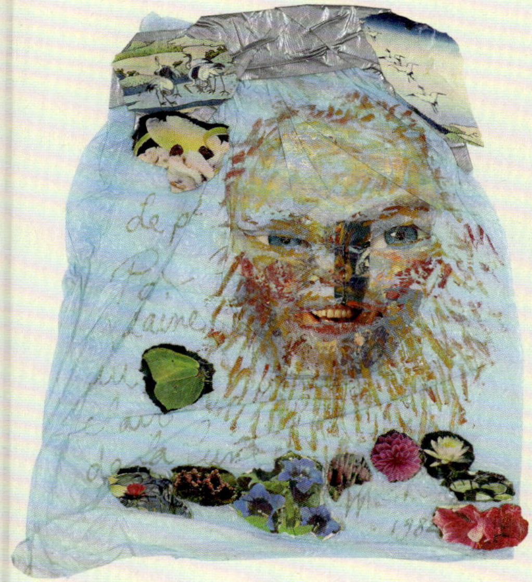

14

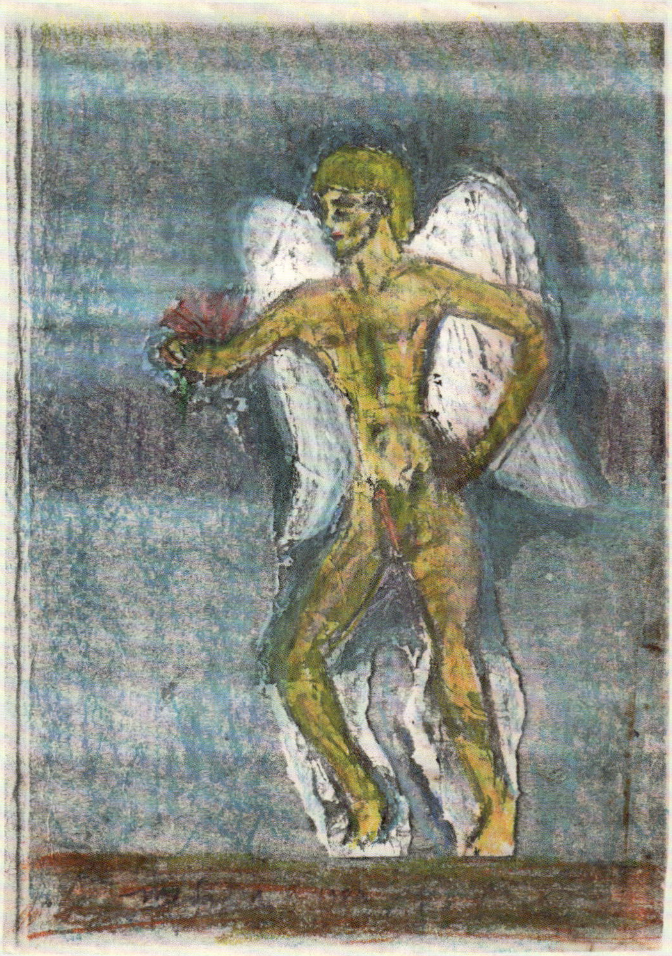

15

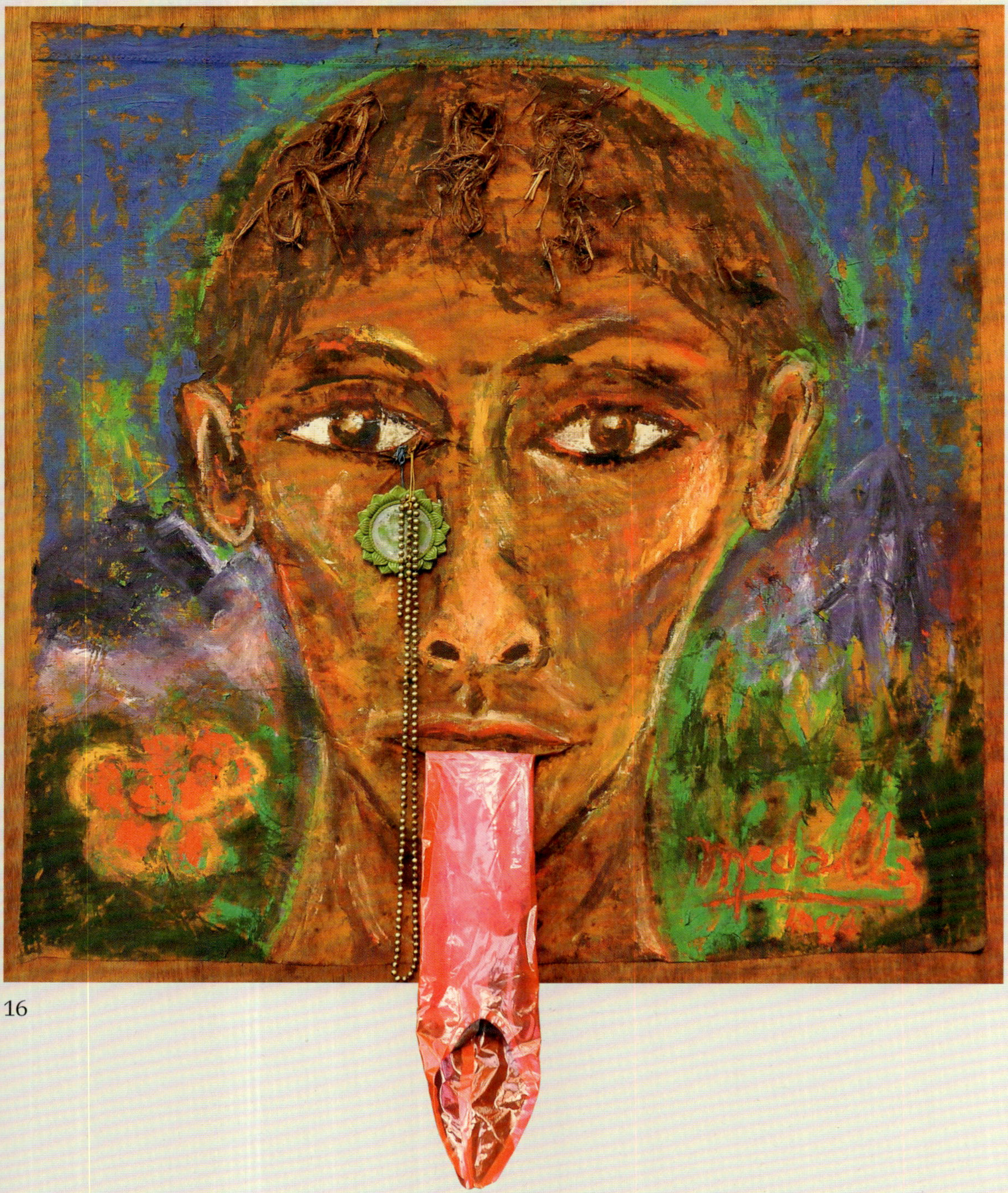

16

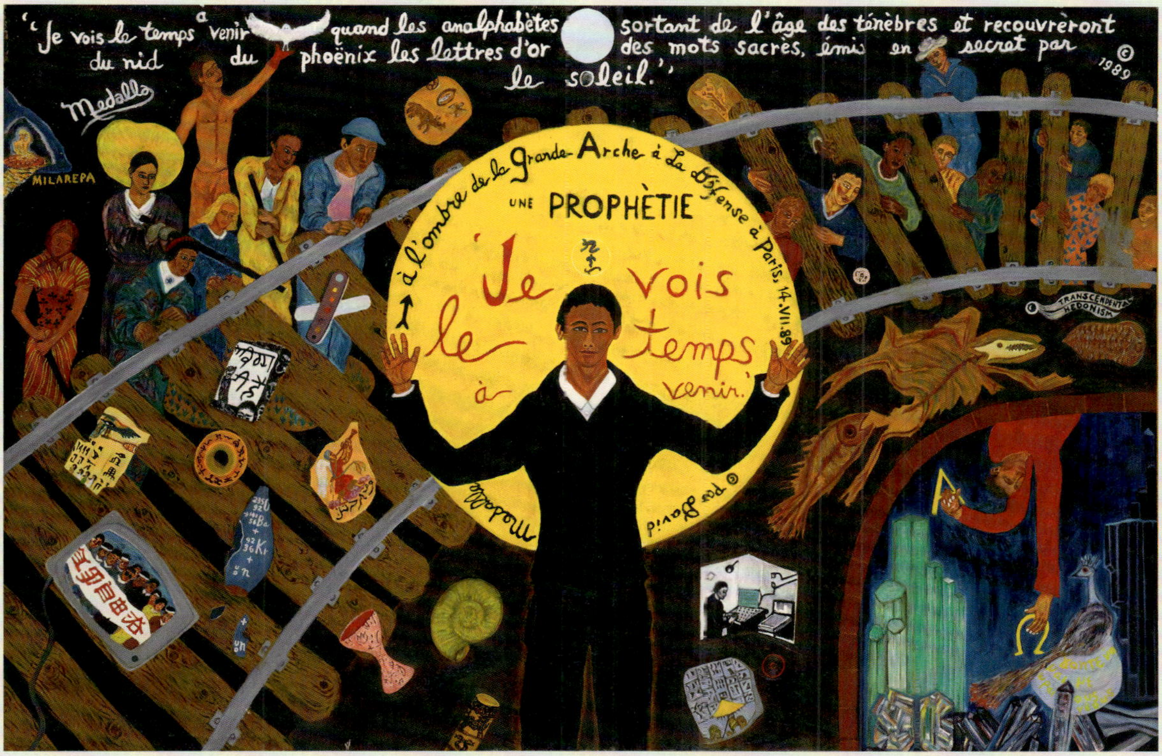
'Je vois le temps à venir quand les analphabètes sortant de l'âge des ténèbres et recouvrèront du nid du phoenix les lettres d'or des mots sacrés, émis en secret par le soleil.'
© 1989
Medalla
MILAREPA
à l'ombre de la Grande Arche à La Défense à Paris, 14.VII.89
UNE PROPHÈTIE
Je vois le temps à venir.
Medalla

17

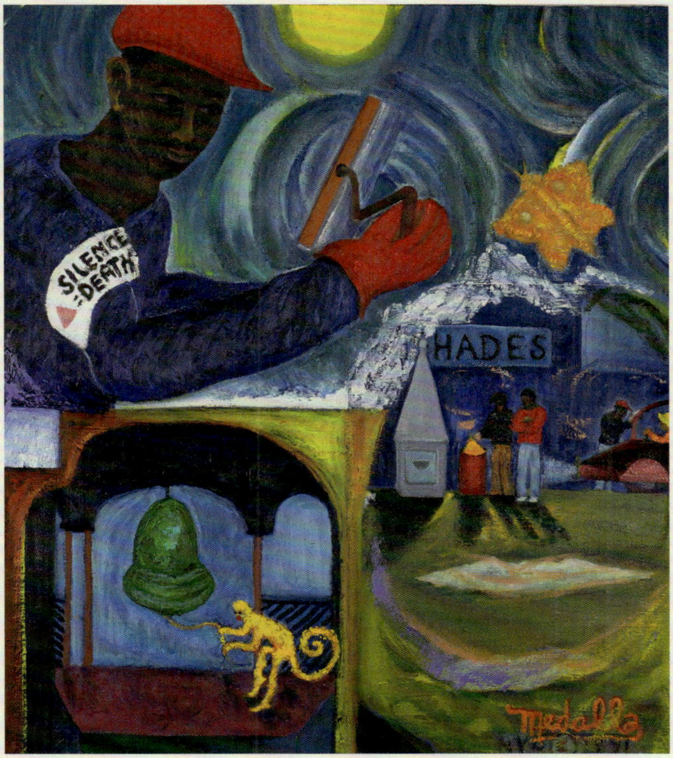
SILENCE = DEATH
HADES
Medalla

18

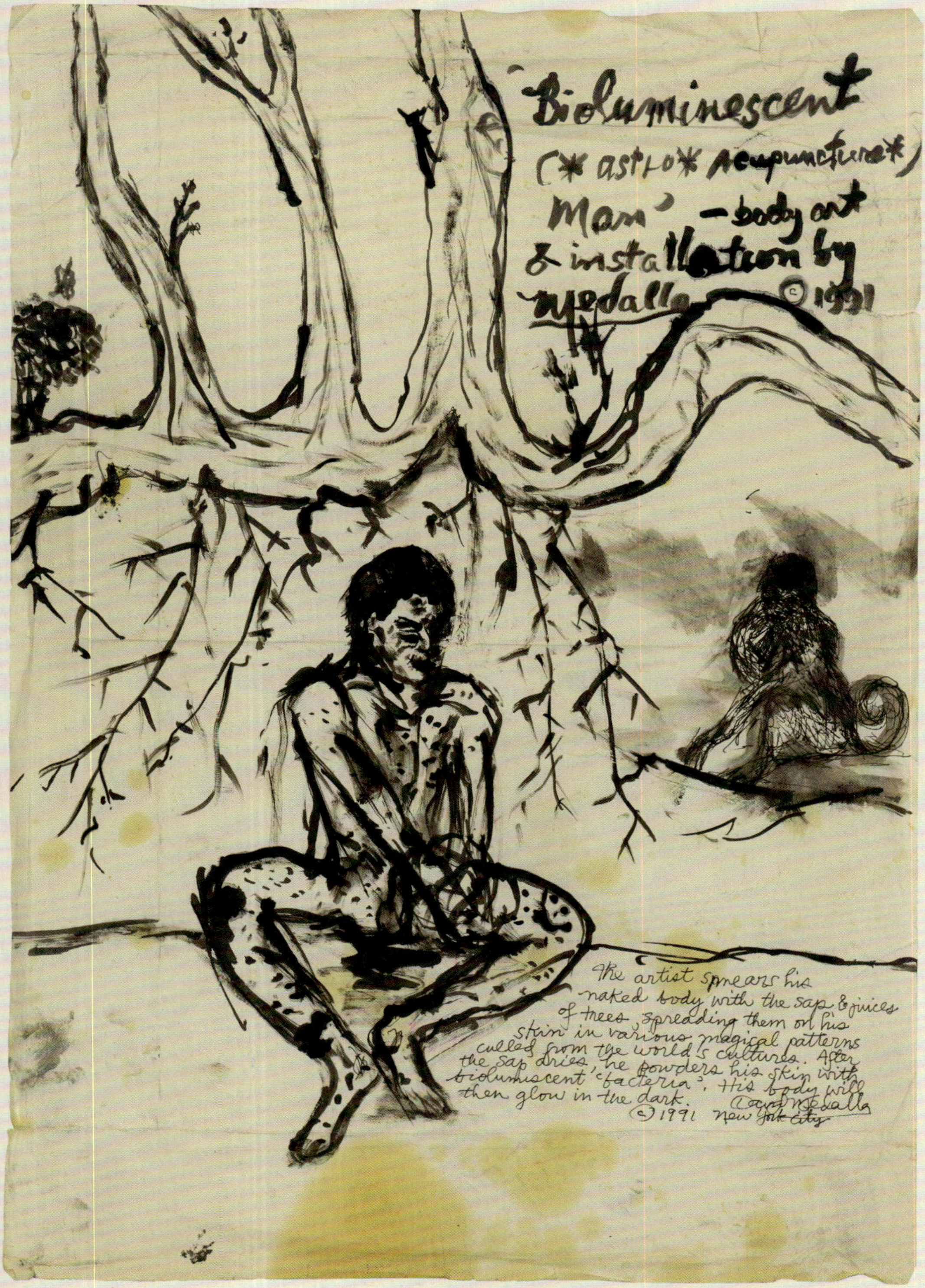
"Bioluminescent
(* astro* acupuncture*)
Man" – body art
& installation by
Medalla © 1991
The artist smears his
naked body with the sap & juices
of trees, spreading them on his
skin in various magical patterns
culled from the world's cultures. After
the sap dries, he powders his skin with
bioluminescent 'bacteria'. His body will
then glow in the dark.
David Medalla
© 1991 New York City

19

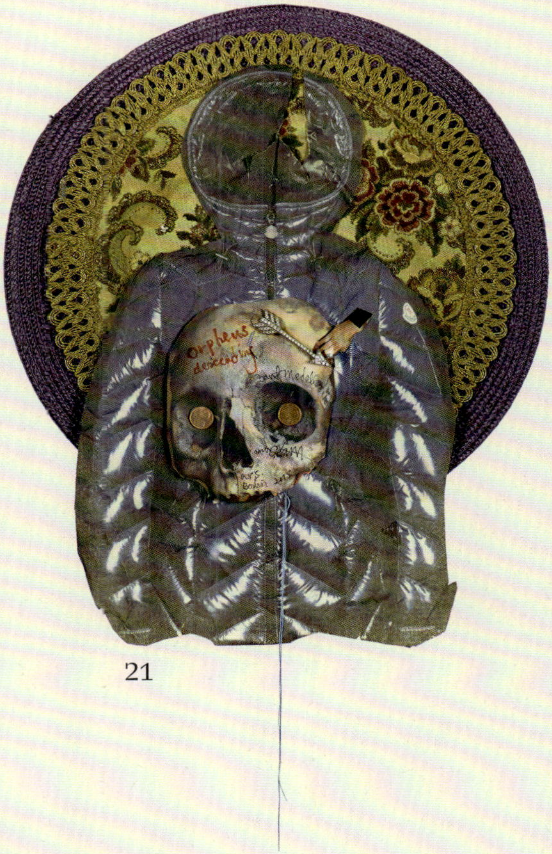

21

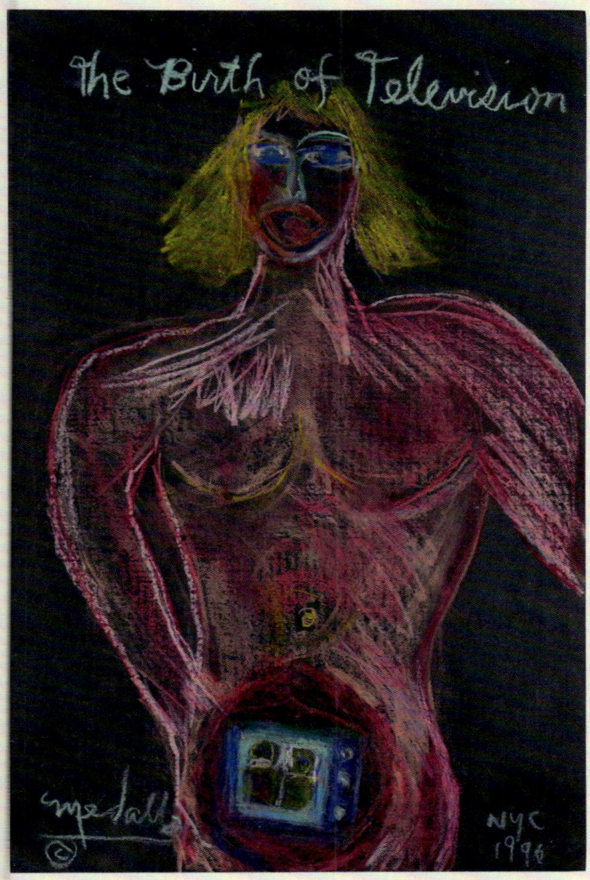

20

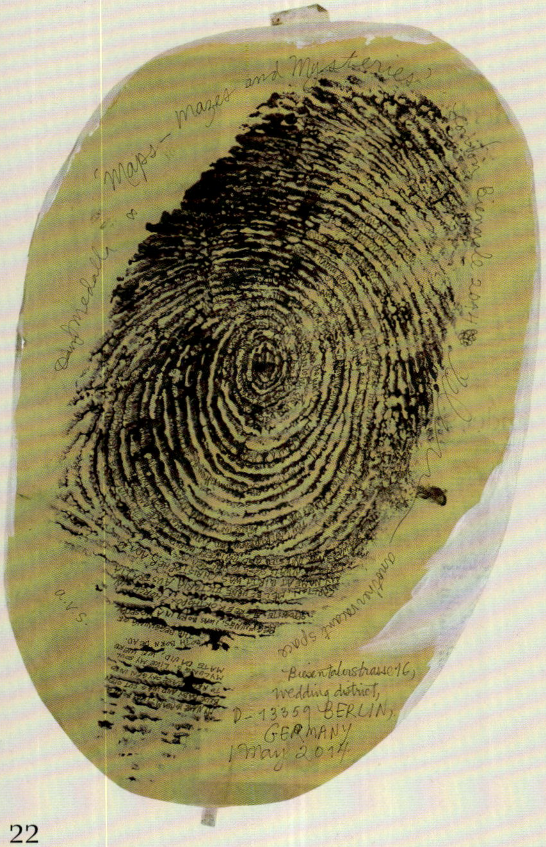
Maps – Mazes and Mysteries
Biesentalerstrasse 16,
Wedding district,
D-13359 BERLIN,
GERMANY
1 May 2014

22

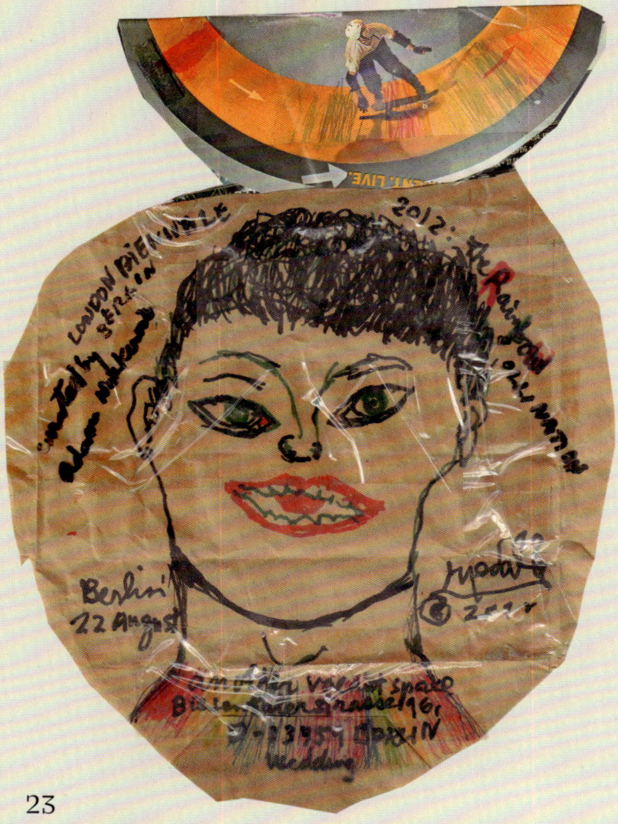
2012:
LONDON BIENNALE
Berlin
22 August
D-13359 BERLIN
Wedding

23

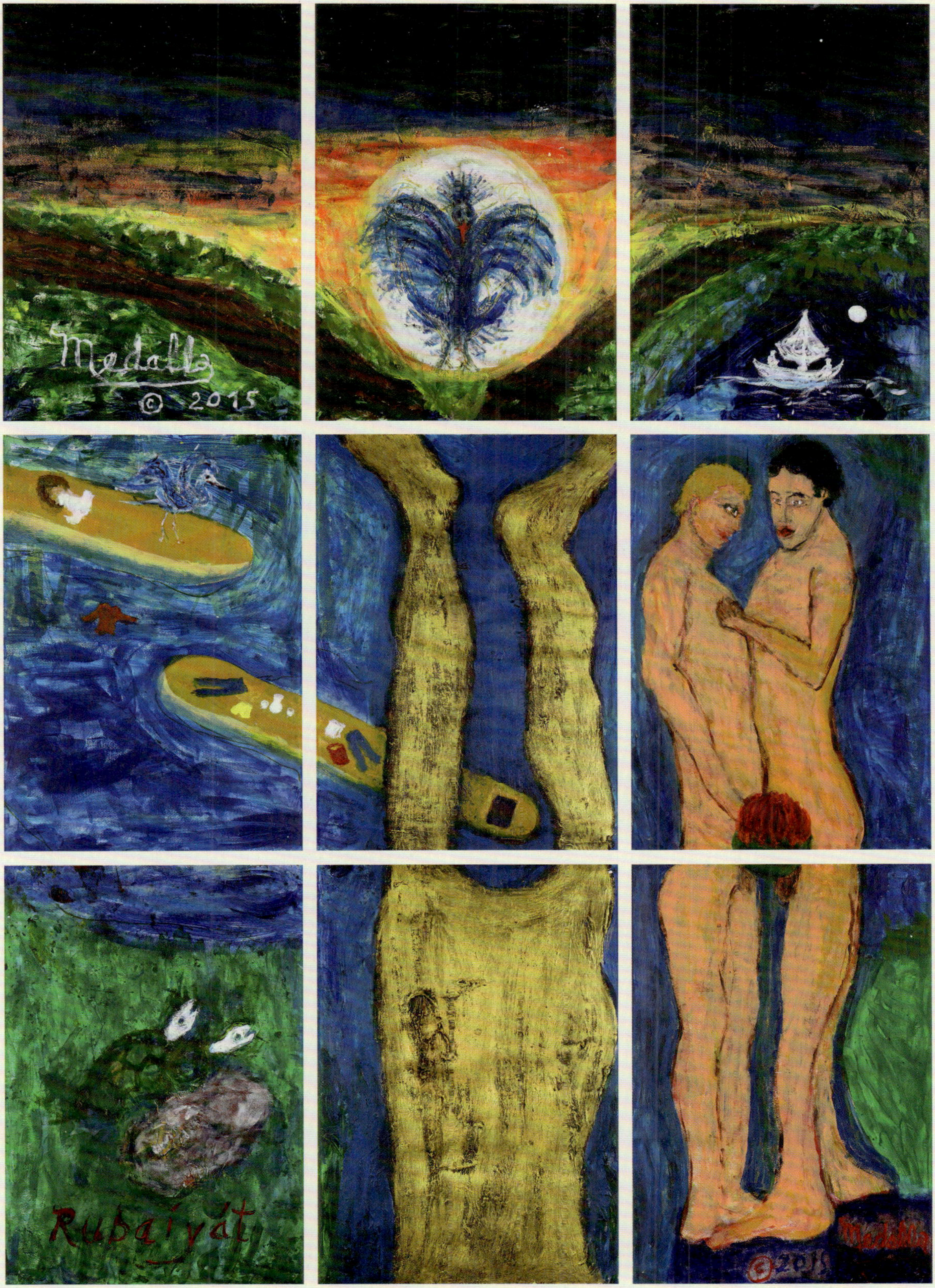

24

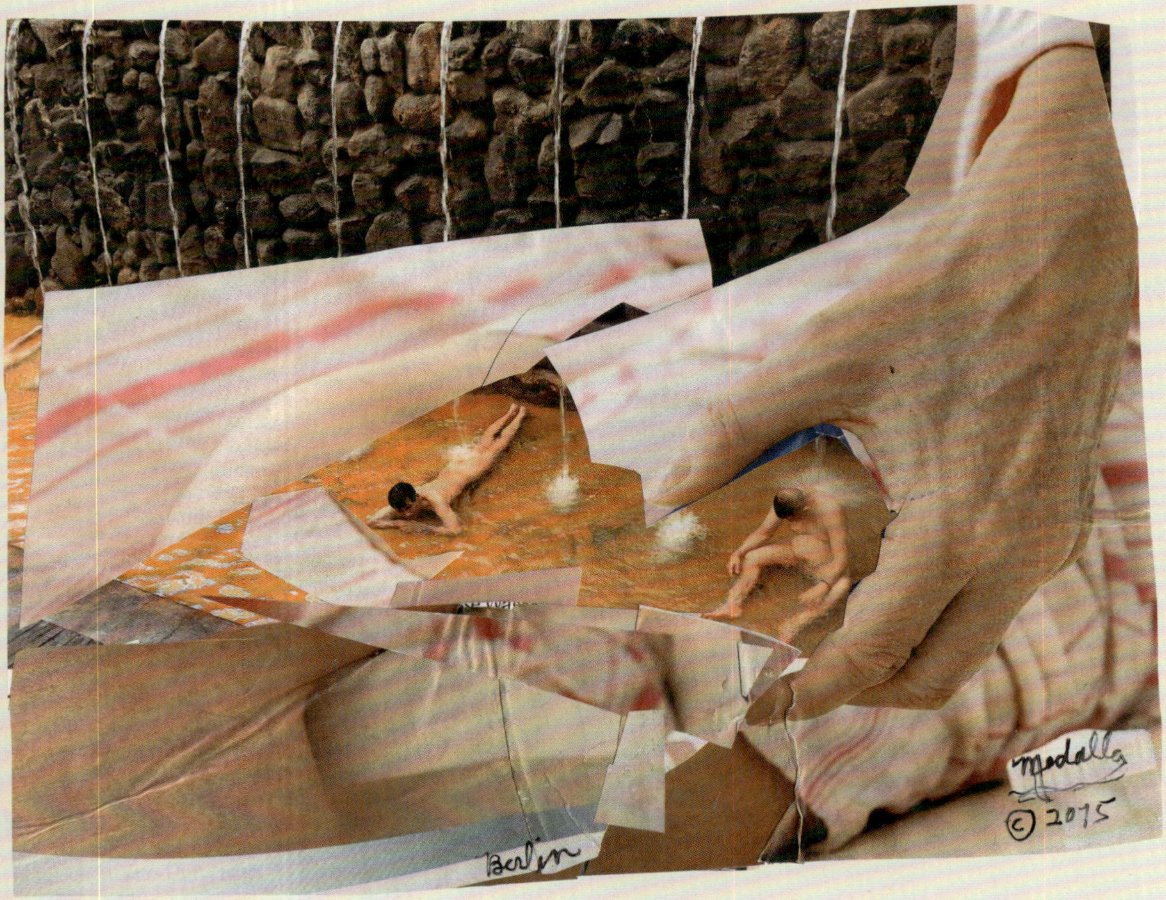

25

Chronology

Nyah Ginwright

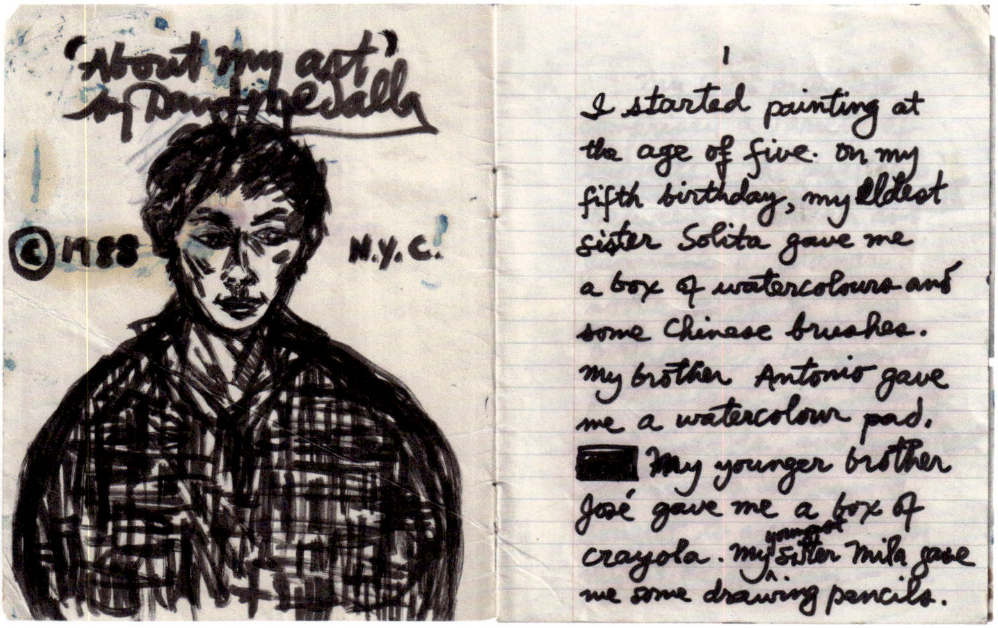

1938
David Cortez Medalla is born on March 23, in Manila, Philippines. (Some sources indicate a birth year of 1942.)

1940
At the age of three, Medalla witnesses, right outside of his home, a young guerilla soldier frothing from the mouth after being shot by a Japanese Kempeitai.

1942
Japanese military forces occupy Manila.

1947
While on holiday in Cebu City, Philippines, Medalla initiates what he calls his first sculpture in the coastal town of Dalaguete. With family members and local inhabitants, he transforms a small coral island off the coast into a large sculpture shaped like a tortoise.

1949
Completes elementary school at the Philippine Normal School and learns English with Americans in a nearby camp at Wallace Field.

1951
Begins first year of high school at the University of the Philippines, where he studies for five months.

1952
Attends Saint Mary's University Senior High School in Bayombong, Nueva Vizcaya, Philippines, for one year. He meets American anthropologist Henry Otley Beyer, PhD, who is studying the Igorots, an Indigenous mountain tribe. Medalla begins learning epic songs from the Igorots and transcribes the songs into English.

Attends two days of high school at the University of San Carlos in Cebu City and spends the next four months reading at a library on Colon Street.

Goes missing for three weeks after falling asleep on the Hong Kong–bound *SS President Wilson*.

1953
Is featured in the *Campus Journal* and the *Philippine Collegian* at the University of the Philippines.

1954
Francisco Arcellana, a professor at the University of the Philippines, interviews Medalla for *Saturday Morning Magazine*, on the recommendation of fellow University of the Philippines professor Wilfrido Guerrero. The article is entitled "A Boy With Feelings for Words."

Invited to give special lectures at the University of the Philippines by university president Vidal Tan, who later allows Medalla to enroll in the College of Liberal Arts without a high school diploma.

Attends Louis August Jonas Foundation's Camp Rising Sun for gifted young writers in Rhinebeck, New York, on the

Interior spread of *About my Art*, 1988. Felt-tip marker and acrylic on ruled notebook paper. Closed: 8 3⁄16 × 6 1⁄2 × 1⁄8 in. (20.8 × 16.5 × 0.3 cm).

recommendation of President Tan, Dr. Pura Santillan Castrence of the Department of Foreign Affairs cultural office, and University of the Philippines English professor Josefina Constantino.

Begins studying at Columbia University, New York, as a special student by recommendation of poet and faculty member Mark Van Doren. He focuses on Greek drama under Moses Hadas, modern philosophy under John Randall, classical literature under Lionel Trilling, and poetry under Léonie Adams.

Meets New York–based Filipino writers and artists, including José Garcia Villa and Alfonso Ossorio.

1955

Returns to Manila.

Attends painting classes taught by Fernando Zóbel de Ayala.

Hosts a symposium on art and pornography at his family home, which he converted into an art studio and salon named La Cave D'Angely.

1956

Meets Jaime Gil de Biedma, an important figure of postwar Spanish literature.

Holds first solo exhibition of paintings, drawings, and sculptures at La Cave D'Angely. Signs his work "Gaybriel."

Completes the painting *My Sister at the Sewing Machine*, which is later exhibited at Ateneo Art Gallery at Ateneo de Manila University.

1957

Attends protest at the United States embassy after the Philippine government remains silent when a US serviceman (George E. Roe) who has injured a Filipino is sent home to the United States in order to escape the Philippine legal system. Mecalla and writers Adrian Cristobal, Andres Cristobal Cruz, and Danny Villanueva are subsequently arrested, then released shortly thereafter.

Founds both the Poetry Club of Manila and the Blue Bamboo Studio, where he hosts poetry readings and performances.

Selected as the youngest artist in the 500-year survey of Philippine art organized by UNESCO, which is shown in the Social Hall of the Department of Foreign Affairs of the Philippines, Pasay City, Philippines.

Paints *Self-Portrait*, now in the collection of the National Museum of the Philippines.

1958

Cofounds a literary journal titled *Prufrock* with Filipino art critic Petronilo Daroy and poets Epifanio "Sunny" San Juan Jr. and Jun Lansang.

1959

Opens second solo exhibition, titled *Homage to Apollo* and featuring studies of the male nude, at 2250 F. B. Harrison, Pasay City, Philippines.

1960

Arrives in Marseilles, France by ship via Indochina, Singapore, Sri Lanka, India, Pakistan, East Africa, and Egypt.

Gives his first performance, entitled *The Poet in Abyssinia*, at the Academy Raymond Duncan, Paris.

Meets many artists and writers, including Guy and Sebastian Brett, Man Ray, Walt Disney, Yves Klein, Takis, Jean Tinguely, and Lucio Fontana.

Spends a month writing and painting in Charleville, France, before settling in London.

1961

Returns to Paris and reconnects with Filipino poet José Garcia Villa.

Meets philosopher Gaston Bachelard at the José Corti bookstore; together they visit museums and the Chartres Cathedral.

1962

Presents a solo exhibit at the Mayflower Bar at Jordans in Buckinghamshire, England, organized by Paul Keeler and Guy Brett.

1963

Organizes, with Paul Keeler, *Soundings One*, an international art exhibition held at the Ashmolean Museum, Oxford, England.

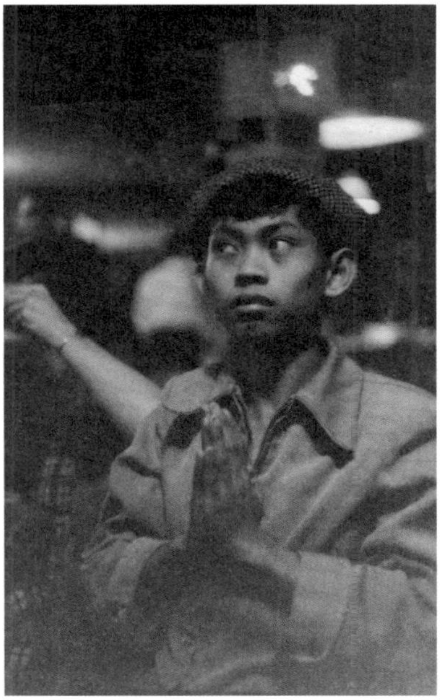

Untitled, 2011 (detail). Photo album. 8 7/8 × 13 × 1 in. (22.5 × 33 × 2.5 cm).

Begins developing his first kinetic works while traveling regularly between Paris, London, and Amsterdam.

Paul Keeler organizes a group exhibition at Villa Foscari (La Malcontenta, by Italian architect Andrea Palladio), near Venice. The exhibition includes Medalla's Sand Machine, part of a series the artist describes as "a metaphor for the future, when technology will be able to use solar power to help irrigate the world's deserts."

1964

Cofounds the Centre for Advanced Creative Study with Paul Keeler. Shortly thereafter, it reopens as Signals London at 92 Cornwall Gardens, London, with additional cofounders Christopher Walker, Gustav Metzger, Guy Brett, and Marcello Salvadori.

Signals features artists Alejandro Otero, Antonio Calderara, Dom Sylvester Houédard, Gerhard von Graevenitz, Hélio Oiticica, Liliane Lijn, Li Yuan-Chia, Lygia Clark, Mary and Kenneth Martin, Mathias Goeritz, Naum Gabo, Sérgio de Camargo, Soto, and Takis, among others.

Presents a work from his Cloud Canyons series, also known as "bubble machines," in the first exhibition of kinetic art in Britain, *Structures Vivantes: Mobiles/Images*, at the Redfern Gallery, London, curated by Paul Keeler.

Begins Mohole Flower, a conceptual project that proposes to retrieve a core sample from the Earth's crust.

1965

Ferdinand Marcos becomes president of the Philippines and establishes an authoritarian regime shortly thereafter.

Medalla's "MMMMMMM . . . Manifesto (a fragment)" is published in the *Signals Newsbulletin*.

Mounts a solo exhibition at the Mercury Gallery, London, where he presents paintings inspired by the voyage of Ulysses.

1966

Organizes *Soundings Three*, a survey of British art at Signals.

Alongside Paul Keeler and Guy Brett, Medalla curates *Towards the Invisible*, featuring artists from the United Kingdom, at Signals.

Exhibits one of his Cloud Canyons in the exhibition *Weiss auf Weiss*, curated by Harald Szeemann, at the Kunsthalle Bern, Switzerland.

Shows kinetic works in *Art and Movement*, curated by William Buchanan, at the Royal Scottish Academy, Edinburgh, Scotland.

Signals' main financial contributor—Paul Keeler's father, Charles Keeler—withdraws his support, and the gallery closes soon after. Edits the last issue of Signals Newsbulletin.

1967

Cofounds the Exploding Galaxy artists' collective with John Dugger and moves into a communal house co-owned with Paul Keeler at 99 Ball Ponds Road, London.

Presents a solo exhibition of kinetic works at Indica Gallery, London.

Writes and directs the performance *Fuzz Death* at the old Alexandra Palace, as part of a fourteen-hour show to fundraise for the *International Times*.

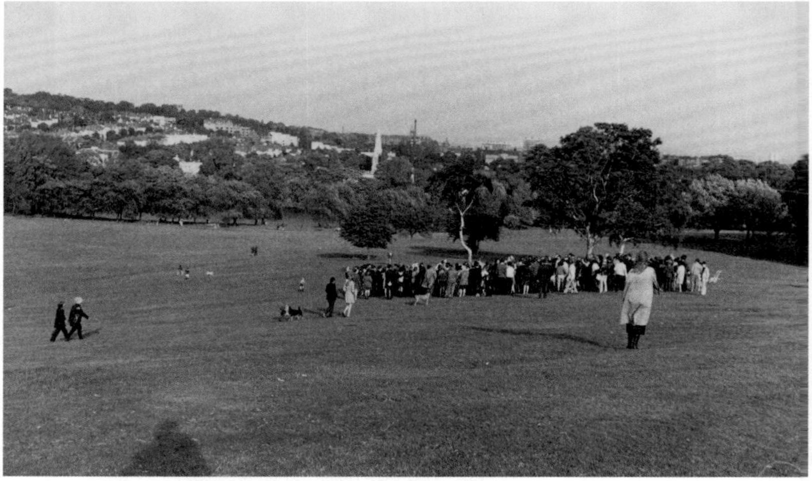

above

The Buddha Ballet at Parliament Hill, London, 1968.

opposite, top

Announcement for *June Exhibition*, Lisson Gallery, London, June 1–July 1, 1967.

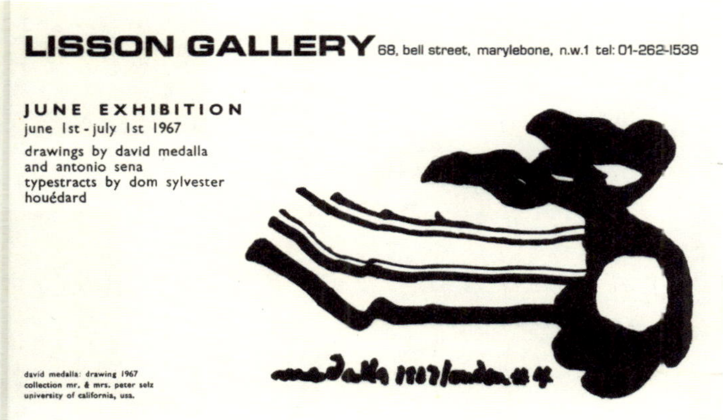

Creates *The Buddha Ballet* and *The Bird Ballet* with John Dugger.

1968

Police raid the house at 99 Ball Ponds Road while Medalla is in the Netherlands; three members of the group are charged with illegal drug possession, including John Dugger. Paul Keeler publishes *Planted!*, a record of the event that alleges that police planted drugs in the house.

After the Exploding Galaxy's dissolution, Medalla travels with John Dugger and others to Spain, Italy, France, South Africa, Senegal, Kenya, Pakistan, Sri Lanka, Singapore, Thailand, Philippines, Nepal, and eventually India, where they study Indian dance with Kathakali dancers.

Presents a work from his Cloud Canyons series in the exhibition *Air Art*, curated by Willoughby Sharp at the University of California Berkeley Art Museum.

Marcel Duchamp produces *Bouche-évier (Sink Stopper)*, also known as *Medallic Sculpture*, as an ode to Medalla's Cloud Canyons series.

Initiates the participatory work *A Stitch in Time.*

1969

Participates in Harald Szeemann's *Live in Your Head: When Attitudes Become Form* at Kunsthalle Bern.

Exhibits work in *Earth Art* at the Herbert F. Johnson Museum of Art, Ithaca, New York.

While in the Philippines, begins Gentle Genticles. The series is based on garments he observed during the time he spent with Indigenous tribes while assisting anthropologist Henry Otley Beyer, PhD, in the north of Luzon, Philippines, and in the southern Philippines.

Protests the opening of the Cultural Center of the Philippines in Manila, a nationalist institution envisioned by First Lady Imelda Marcos, and subsequently leaves the country.

1970

In Paris, makes a down payment on a boathouse, naming it *Bateau Mayflower II*.

Has a solo exhibition at the Camden Arts Festival, where his work combines Marxism with Buddhist ideology inspired by early Ming pottery.

1971

Participates in, then withdraws from *Popa at Moma: Pioneers of Part-Art*, Museum of Modern Art, Oxford, England.

In London, becomes a staff student advisor at the Slade School of Fine Art and lecturer on Asian culture at Saint Martin's School of Art.

Cofounds the Artists' Liberation Front with John Dugger in London.

Creates Kumbum, a series of collages now held in the collection of the National Gallery Singapore.

While in Kathmandu, Nepal, with John Dugger, Medalla builds a collection of Tibetan *thangkas* that are later featured in an exhibition of tantric art curated by Philip Rawson and Hugh Shaw for the Arts Council of Great Britain, held at the Hayward Gallery, London.

In a participatory event, *Down with the Slave Trade!*, Medalla invites the public to insert themselves into a system of linkages he proposes "would never become entangled."

1972

Exhibits *A Stitch in Time* at the Rijksuniversiteit, Utrecht, the Netherlands, and in *Survey of the Avant Garde in Britain* at Gallery House, London, curated by Sigi Krauss and Rosetta Brooks.

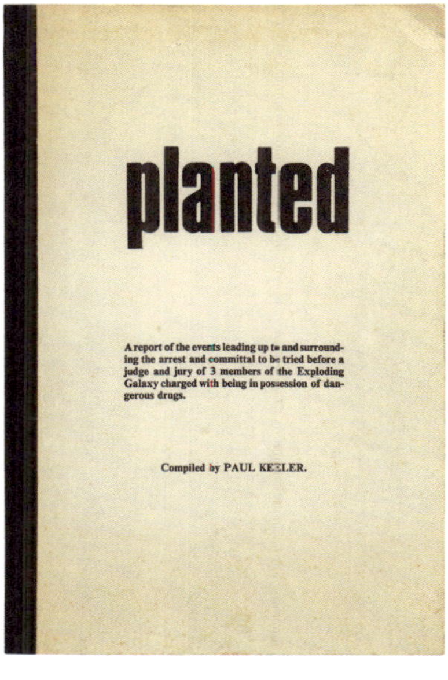

right
Paul Keeler, *Planted* (London: Stanhope Press and the Exploding Galaxy, 1968).

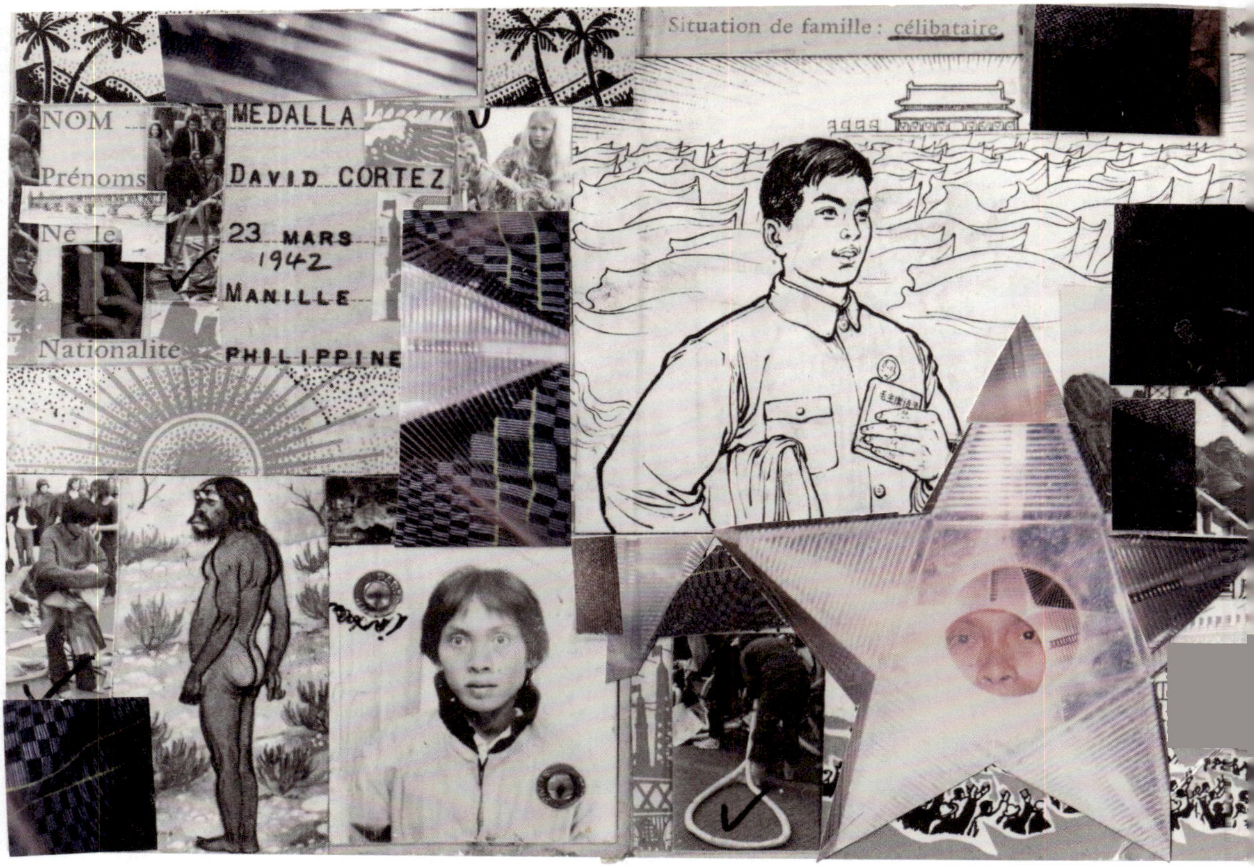

With John Dugger, Medalla exhibits *People's Participation Pavilion* at documenta 5, curated by Harald Szeemann, in Kassel, Germany.

Exhibits *International Dust Market* and *A Stitch in Time* at the Ikon Gallery, Birmingham, England.

Presents another collaboration with John Dugger, *People Weave a House!*, at the Institute of Contemporary Arts, London.

Installs the poster *Dazibao*, denouncing the dictatorship of President Marcos in the Philippines, at the Institute of Contemporary Arts, London.

In response to growing public opposition, President Marcos implements martial law in the Philippines.

1973

Enacts *Porcelain Wedding*, a participation performance at Edinburgh College of Art, Scotland, curated by Lynn MacRitchie.

Participates in Peter Kennedy's video *Other than Art's Sake* with six other artists and art groups in London and New York that are committed to social change.

Begins lecturing on general studies at the Chelsea School of Art, London, and Chinese culture at the University of South Hampton, England.

1974

Expands Artists' Liberation Front into Artists for Democracy (AFD) with Cecilia Vicuña, John Dugger, and Guy Brett. The group organizes the Arts Festival for Democracy in Chile at the Royal College of Art, London.

Jane England, gallery director and Medalla's close friend, photographs the 1974 iteration of *Porcelain Wedding* at Art Meeting Place, London.

Completes Africa Liberation Drawings, a series of works on paper that portray the daily life of revolutionaries with photographs sourced from solidarity organizations in London.

Carte d'Identite, 1972. Photo collage. 7 × 10 ⅜ in. (17.8 × 26.3 cm).

1975

Alongside artists Rasheed Araeen and Tina Keane, Medalla is included in the AFD-organized exhibition *New Art Works*, dedicated to the Indochinese struggle.

Organizes a performance cycle titled *Tatlin at the Funeral of Malevich* at the Serpentine Gallery, London.

AFD opens the Fitzrovia Cultural Centre at 143 Whitfield Street, London. Medalla is the director and Nick Payne is the manager. The center displays text and art by artists of Indigenous nations.

Participates in the *International Video Encounter*, curated by Jorge Glusberg, at Espace Cardin, Paris.

Medalla is interviewed by the Filipino writer Cid Reyes for the book *Conversations on Philippine Art*.

In response to Lea Lublin's video *Is Art an Enigma?*, Medalla performs *Johannes Vermeer of Delft* with AFD members Sylvia Stevens and Steve Oxley at the Serpentine Gallery, London.

1976

Receives the Visual Arts Award from the Greater London Arts Association.

Stages *Thunderous Applause,* a survey of three years of work, at Acme Gallery, London, curated by John Sharkey.

1977

AFD's last event, *Eskimo Carver*, appears at the Fitzrovia Cultural Centre, London.

Performs *The Dialogue between Tatlin and Malevich* with Catalan artist Oriol de Quadras at Acme Gallery, London.

Completes the painting *James Dean and David Medalla*.

1978

Begins Reciprocal Didacticks, a series of twelve performances with Oriol de Quadras.

Conducts a series of five performances with Oriol de Quadras, titled *A la recherché des cinq inconnus (In search of the five strangers)*, at various locations throughout Paris.

1979

Organizes *Mayfair Illuminations 1 & 2*, with Oriol de Quadras and Rino Telaro, and invites artists to hold exhibitions and events in Hill House, an empty mansion on Berkeley Square, London.

Reciprocal Didacticks series continues as *Circumnavigation of the World* at the Institute of Contemporary Arts, London, and *Beachcombers Dream Tree* at Hill House, London.

Exhibits Rhapsody of the Dagger and Ammonia Boy at Chenil Gallery, London.

Leaves London and embarks on a five-year trip, performing in Italy, Germany, the Netherlands, Belgium, France, and Spain.

Black Phoenix publishes a conversation between Medalla and Rasheed Araeen about the relationship between art and politics.

1980

Reconstructs a story on the building of the Boudhanath stupa in Kathmandu, Nepal, and creates a dance-drama entitled *The First Mirror in China*, based on a story told to him by Brazilian artist Lygia Clark.

Performs *Truth Is the Only Daughter of Time* at the Stedelijk Museum, Amsterdam.

Invited by artist William Xerra to participate in the Vive festival, Pavia, Italy.

1981

Performs *Equatorial Sybil*, a "synoptic-realist" performance, at the East-West Festival of the Guild of Transcultural Studies, London.

Presents *Voyages and Somersaults of the Pilgrim Monkey*, a synoptic-realist performance, at the Accademia di Belle Arti di Venezia, Venice, Italy, and the Accademia di Belle Arti di Brera, Milan.

1983

Awarded Artist in Residence at South Hill Park Art Centre in Bracknell, England, where he organizes the First International Festival of Performance Art with Gavin Henderson, Alistair Snow, and Jeni Walwin.

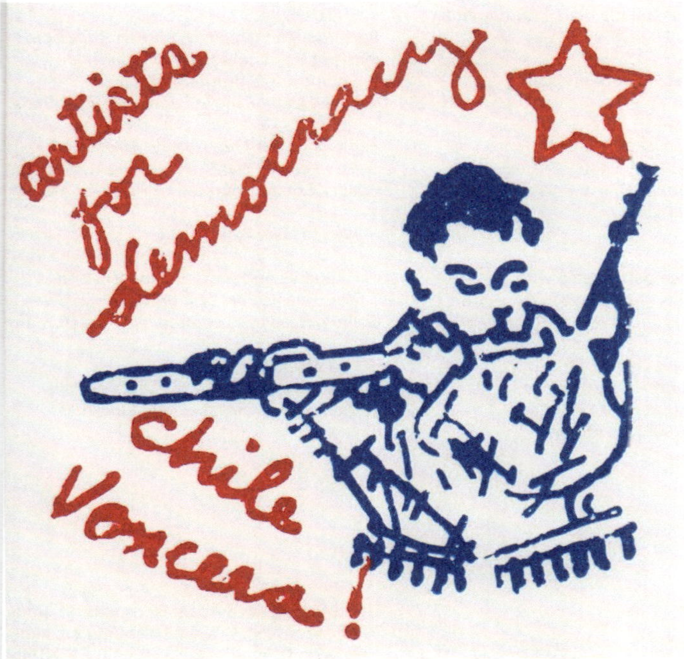

Sticker for Arts Festival for Democracy in Chile, London, 1974.

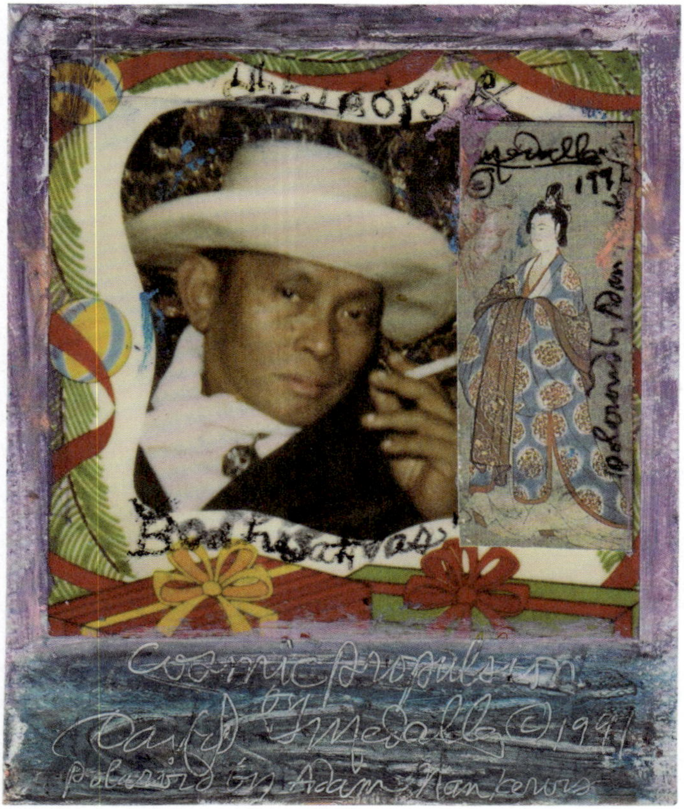

Performs *The Hand of Marie Curie* in the Perfortijd festival at the Theatre de Lantaren in Rotterdam, the Netherlands, curated by Wink van Kempen. Later, he writes and codirects the film version of *The Hand of Marie Curie* with Mark Greaves.

Performs *Bonjour Beau, Bonsoir Brummel* and *Bongo Ba, Bonsai, Brahma*, two related performances, at Galeria d'Art Contemporain des Musées de Nice, France.

Begins his Parables of Friendship painting series.

Organizes the artist group Octetto Ironico with James Acheson, Lesley Butler, Kevin Goss, Sonia Knox, Roberta Kravitz, Alistair Snow, and Anna Threw.

1984

Begins a creative partnership with German artist Kai Hilgemann in the work *The Signs and Wonders of David and Kai*.

Co-organizes and participates in the Second International Festival of Performance Art at South Hill Park Art Centre in Bracknell, England.

Participates in Perfotijd 2 in Rotterdam, the Netherlands.

Performs *Metamorphosis of an Enigma* at Cirque Divers, Liege, Belgium.

1985

Visits the Philippines with Kai Hilgemann and they participate in a joint exhibition entitled *Signs and Wonders of David and Kai* at Pinaglabanan Gallery, Manila.

1986

Ferdinand Marcos commits electoral fraud, which leads to increased anti-Marcos demonstrations and, ultimately, his exile in Hawaii with his wife, Imelda.

Begins the painting series Luz. Vi. Minda. (Filipiniana) in Coron, Palawan, central Philippines.

The Auckland City Art Gallery in New Zealand commissions one of Medalla's Cloud Canyons for the exhibition *Chance and Change: A Century of the Avant-Garde*, curated by Andrew Bogle.

1987

Begins Shot in the Dark, a new performance series in partnership with Brian Morgan.

Begins work on his painting *A Memory of Mr. Morley's Harp-Shop in South Kensington*

1988

Presents *A Celebration of World Mythologies*, one of many works he designates as "Impromptus," at the flea market in Rotterdam, the Netherlands. Guy Brett photographs the performance.

Performs an Impromptu with Brian Morgan in the Indian Army Memorial Room at the Royal Military Academy Sandhurst, Berkshire, England. Guy Brett photographs the performance.

1989

Performs *The Dream of Andres Bonafacio*, marking the bicentenary of the French Revolution, in a program organized by Hermine Demoriane at Espace Donguy, Paris.

Exhibits in *The Other Story: Afro-Asian Artists in Post-War Britain* at the Hayward Gallery, London, curated by Rasheed Araeen.

Moves to New York.

Participates and performs in *Here and There: Travels Part Two* at the Clocktower Gallery, New York, curated by Chris Dercon.

1990

Writes a weekly column, titled "Medalla in Manhattan," for the *Filipino Express* newspaper.

David Medalla and Adam Nankervis, *Cosmic Propulsion*, 1991. Crayon, ballpoint pen, and collage on Polaroid. 4¼ × 3½ in. (10.8 × 8.9 cm).

Exhibits in *Public Mirrors: Artists Against Racial Prejudice*, curated by Tom Finkelpearl, Rebecca Quaytman, and Ken Chu at Clocktower Gallery, New York.

1991

Awarded an Artist Fellowship from the New York Foundation for the Arts.

Exhibits in *Shocks to the System: Works from the Arts Council Collection*, curated by Isobel Johnston at the Royal Festival Hall, London, and the City Art Gallery Manchester, England.

Initiates collaboration with Adam Nankervis on a series of timed and site-specific performances in New York dedicated to Piet Mondrian, under the name Mondrian Fan Club.

1992

Performs *Five Immortals at Drop-Dead Prices* at the Great Hall of Cooper Union, New York, organized by Franklin Furnace.

Exhibits in *FluxAttitudes* at the New Museum, New York, curated by Cornelia Lauf and Susan Hapgood.

Presents *New York Epiphanies* in a solo exhibition at the Philippines Center, New York, curated by Eva Florentino.

Awarded a second Artist Fellowship from the New York Foundation for the Arts.

Awarded a fellowship from the Jerome Foundation.

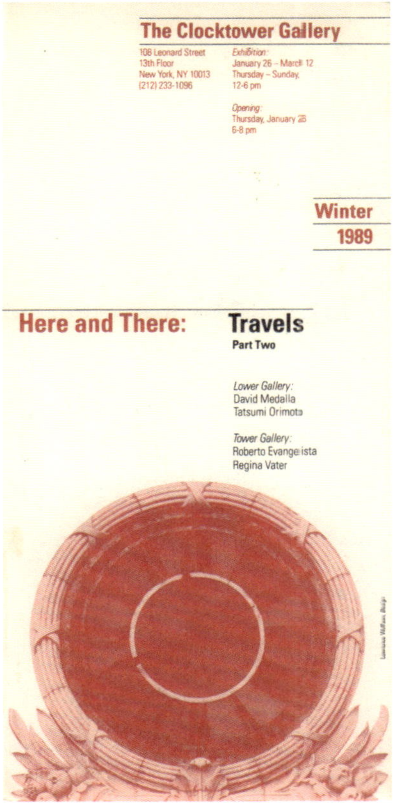

1993

Lectures on transcendental art at the mid-Manhattan branch of the New York Public Library.

Presents a solo exhibition at the Empire Gallery, New York, with a collection called *Dream of Shamans in Manhattan.*

1994

Presents a major exhibition of new works, titled *The Secret History of the Mondrian Fan Club Part II*, at 55 Gee Street in Clerkenwell, London. He later opens up the venue to artists, dancers, filmmakers, architects, and writers to exhibit their work and perform.

Travels with Guy Brett and Adam Nankervis to Buckinghamshire, England, for Nankervis's Impromptu in front of the Mayflower Barn.

1995

Presents a solo exhibition, *The Secret History of the Mondrian Fan Club Part II*, at the Institute of International Visual Arts, London.

1996

Performs an Impromptu titled *Homage to José Rizal*, where he poses with a full-size statue of the Filipino writer. He later makes a collage based on the work.

On Waikiki Beach, Medalla and Nankervis create one of their Cosmic Graffiti series of Impromptus of the Mondrian Fan Club. A circle of red hibiscus flowers forms the letter *O*. A photograph of the work is exhibited at the *Live/Life* show at the Musée d'Art Moderne de Paris, curated by Hans Ulrich Obrist, and at Cafe Einstein, Berlin.

Presents Cloud Canyons in the exhibition *L'Informe*, curated by Yve-Alain Bois and Rosalind Krauss, at the Centre Pompidou, Paris.

1997

Participates in *A Quality of Light*, an international visual arts event in St. Ives, Cornwall, England.

Participates in the 2nd Johannesburg Biennale, curated by Okwui Enwezor, and completes two installations for the Johannesburg Art Gallery in an exhibition curated by Gerardo Mosquera.

1998

As an artist in residence, Medalla exhibits with Adam Nankervis in *Art Lifts Berlin*, curated by Friedrich Meschede, at daadgalerie, Berlin.

Participates in *Arte y Acción* at Museu d'Art Contemporani, Barcelona.

Announcement for *Here and There: Travels Part Two*, The Clocktower Gallery, New York, January 26–March 12, 1989.

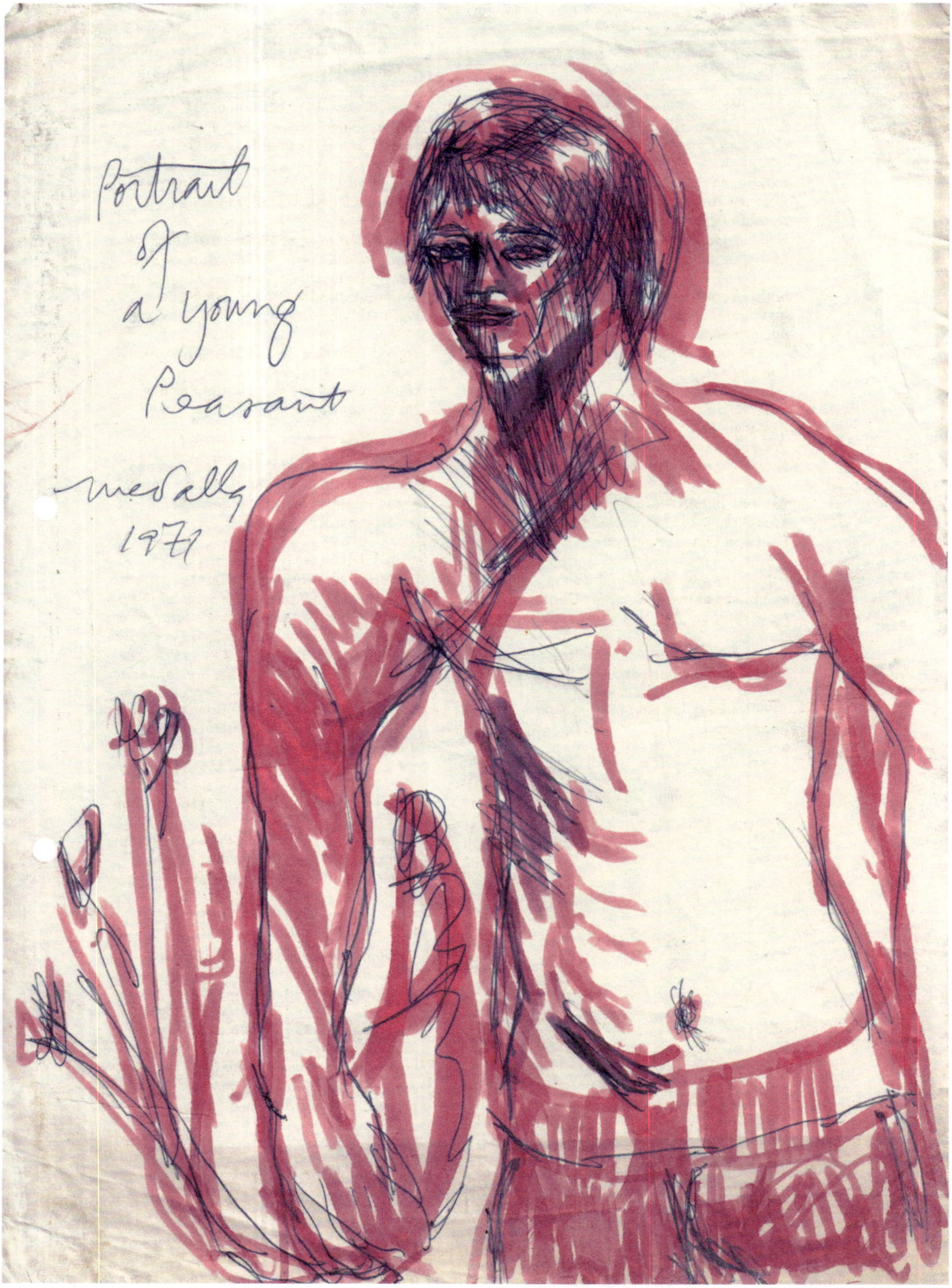

Portrait of a Young Peasant, 1971. Felt-tip marker and ballpoint pen on paper. 11 3⁄4 × 8 7⁄16 in. (29.8 × 21.5 cm).

Participates in *Out of Action: Between Performance and the Object, 1949–1979*, curated by Paul Schimmel at the Museum of Contemporary Art, Los Angeles, which travels to Museum Angewandte Kunst, Vienna; Museu d'Art Contemporani, Barcelona; and Museum of Contemporary Art, Tokyo.

1999

Creates an Impromptu entitled *The Songs of Songs.*

2000

Installs *Cloud Canyons no. 12* in the Plaza Central del Raval in Barcelona.

Organizes the London Biennale and opens it to all international artists.

Participates in *Rio Trajetorias* with a poem written on a star-shaped balloon filled with the breath of the artists in the London Biennale. He releases the balloon, and it floats above Rio de Janeiro.

Participates in *Force Fields: Phases of the Kinetic*, curated by Guy Brett at the Hayward Gallery, London.

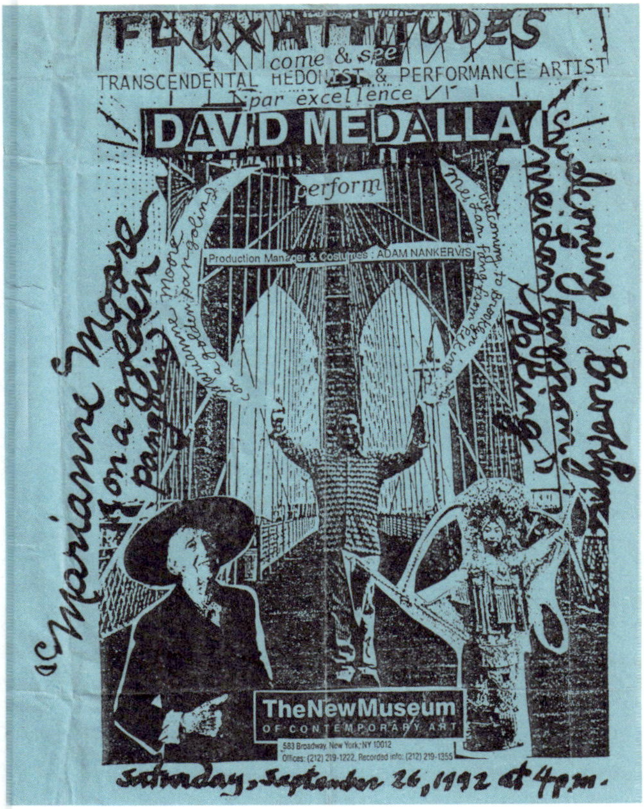

2003

Participates in *Pulse: Art, Healing, and Transformation* at the Institute of Contemporary Art, Boston.

2004

Gilane Tawadros edits the anthology *Changing States: Contemporary Art and Ideas in an Era of Globalisation* (Institute of International Visual Arts, London, 2004), which features *A Stitch in Time* and *Signals Newsbulletin*.

2005

Guy Brett curates Medalla's solo show *Anywhere in the World* at the Institute of Contemporary Arts London.

2006

Participates in *Metropolis Rise: New Art from London* at the Temporary Contemporary, London, curated by Jen Wu and Anthony Gross.

Participates in Dashanzi International Arts Festival (DIAF) at the 798 Space, Beijing, curated by Jen Wu and Anthony Gross.

Invites participating artists from the 2006 London Biennale to write messages on balloons, which are then released above Alexandra Palace at Hornsey, north London, for the finale of the exhibition.

Tate Modern acquires its first work by Medalla: *Cloud Canyons No. 3: An Ensemble of Bubble Machines (Auto Creative Sculptures)* (1964/2004).

2007

Performs *Four Aces* with what he describes as "sixteen handsome young men of different nationalities" at the Swiss Institute in New York as part of Performa 07.

Participates in Deformes performance art festival, Chile, curated by Gonzales Rabanal.

2008

Presents a talk at the Accademia di Belle Arti, Florence, upon the invitation of Vittoria Biasi.

Holds an Impromptu at the beginning of the London Biennale on the wooden esplanade of the Bibliothèque nationale, Paris.

Presents *Urbi et orbis* (The city and the world) to honor Rome at *La notte bianca*, an exhibition and performance festival co-curated by Raffaella Losapio and Vincenzo Ceccato.

Exhibits *Night Fishing on Manila Bay* and performs *Homage to the Venus de Milo* at the Royal Academy of Arts, London, as part of the exhibition *Event Horizon*, curated by Jen Wu and Anthony Gross.

Invitation for *Fluxxattitudes* performance, New Museum, New York, September 26, 1992.

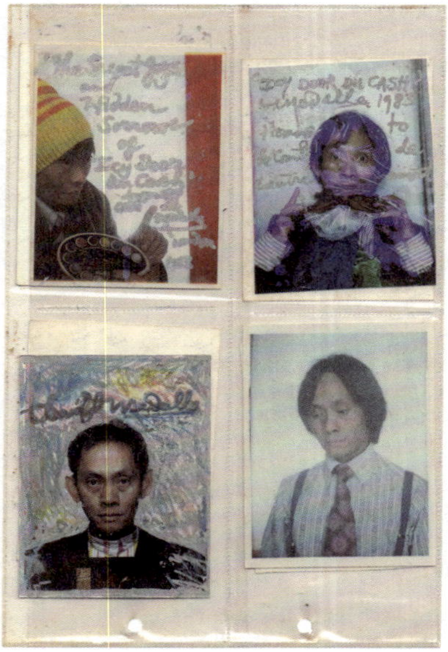

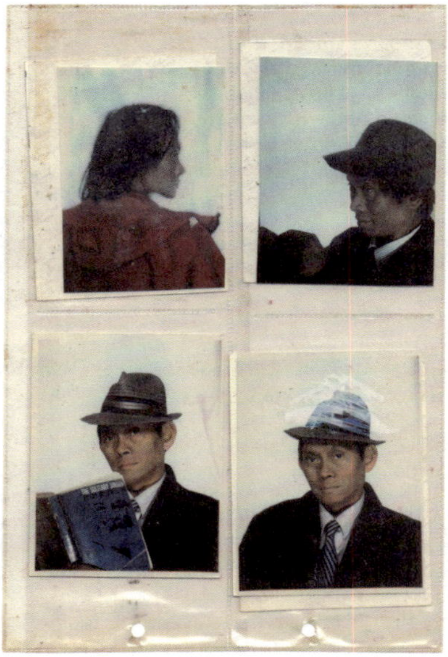

Participates in the 16th Biennale of Sydney: *Revolution—Forms That Turn*, curated by Carolyn Christov-Bakargiev at the Museum of Contemporary Art Australia.

2009

Writes a dedication on a green balloon and releases it in the courtyard of St. James Church in Piccadilly, London, in memory of Willoughby Sharp, artist, art entrepreneur, editor, and publisher of the art magazine *Avalanche*.

Included in *The Death of the Audience*, curated by Pierre Bal-Blanc at Secession, Vienna.

2010

Participates in *This Could Happen to You: Ikon in the 1970s* at the Ikon Gallery, Birmingham, England.

Performs an homage, *Arco/Iris: Rainbow Samba for Hélio Oiticica*, with Adam Nankervis at the Casa França-Brasil, Rio de Janeiro.

Exhibits *So Pulo: The Secret History of the Mondrian Fan Club: Part 3* with Adam Nankervis at Baró Galeria, São Paulo.

Creates Cosmic Pandora Micro-Box out of found objects he collected during a four-month stay in Brazil. This piece is later published in the book *Flying Too Close to the Sun: Myths in Art from Classical to Contemporary*, written by James Cahill (Phaidon, 2018).

2011

Participates alongside Adam Nankervis and Jevijoe Vitug in the exhibition *Overflow* at the More Space Gallery, Las Vegas.

Participates in conversation with art historian Axel Wielder, *Live Archive: David Medalla*, at Archive Kabinett, Berlin, with support from Archive Kabinett, Iniva, General Public, Galleria Duemila, and Purissima "Petty" Benitez-Johannot, and organized by Lian Ladia and Jerlyn Jareunpoon.

Mounts solo exhibition *Cloud Canyons: Kinetic Works and Cosmic Propulsions (1964–2011)*, curated by Adam Nankervis, at another vacant space, Berlin.

The New Museum organizes *David Medalla: Cloud Canyon no. 14*, curated by Gary Carrion-Murayari as part of the museum's Stowaways series.

Conducts an interview with Adam Nankervis for *Mousse Magazine*, titled "A Stitch in Time: David Medalla."

Participates in *A Wake: Still Lives and Moving Images* at MOMENTUM, Berlin, curated by Leo Kuelbs, Rachel Rits-Volloch, and Adam Nankervis.

2012

Exhibits works from his series Cloud Canyons in *Migrations*, Tate Britain's contribution to the Summer Olympics celebrations in London.

Presents a talk at Tate Britain and launches the publication *The Life and Art of David Medalla*, edited by Purissima "Petty" Benitez-Johannot (Vibal Foundation and Arte Filipino, 2012).

Organizes the London Biennale, titled *The Rainbow*, in which he invites artists to dress in colors corresponding to the rainbow and meet at specific locations throughout London during the last week of July and first week of August.

Mounts solo exhibition *Tuloy Po Kayo* at the Ateneo Art Gallery at Ateneo de Manila University and receives the Tanglaw ng Lahi Award from the university.

2013

Exhibits in *Reflections from Damaged Life: An Exhibition on Psychedelia* at Raven Row, London, curated by Lars Bang Larsen, and *Art Turning Left: How Values Changed Making 1789–2013*, at Tate Liverpool, England.

2014

Presents the Impromptu *Mirages* on Staten Island, New York.

2015

Participates in the 8th Asia Pacific Triennial of Contemporary Art (APT8), Queensland, Australia, curated by Yason Banal and Khaled Sabsabi.

above
Untitled, 2011 (details). Photo album. 8⅞ × 13 × 1 in. (22.5 × 33 × 2.5 cm).

opposite
Interior spread of *I am an enigma even to myself—An Artist's Archives*, 2009. Ink, ballpoint pen, and collage in notebook. Closed: 6⅛ × 4 5⁄16 × ½ in. (15.5 × 11 × 1.3 cm).

Performs the Impromptu *Mirages II* at another vacant space, Berlin.

2016

Paints *Tongues Talk—(Synchronisations)* and *M'illumino d'Immenso (Giuseppe Ungaretti)* for the exhibition *66/16* at the Galleria Enrico Astuni, Bologna, Italy.

Nominated for the Hepworth Prize for Sculpture.

Suffers a stroke.

2017

Showcases drawings, paintings, and kinetic works in the exhibition *Locus Solo, Homage to Arthur Rimbaud*, curated by Lorenzo Bruni at the Galleria Enrico Astuni, Bologna, Italy.

Creates a neon sculpture entitled *Self Portrait with Dinosaur-Dante*, which is based on his painting series Hello-Buon giorno da Bologna.

Participates in *Kunst in Europa 1945–1968* at ZKM Center for Art and Media, Karlsruhe, Germany.

Presents *A Stitch in Time* and *The Mondrian Fan Club* (with Adam Nankervis) in *Viva Arte Viva*, the 57th International Art Exhibition of the Venice Biennale, curated by Christine Macel.

2020

A film by Live Art Development Agency (LADA), titled *Documenting Live*, details Medalla's performance *Passato, Presente, Futuro*.

Medalla passes away at the age of 82 in Manila.

2022

Ferdinand "Bongbong" Marcos Jr., son of former president Ferdinand Marcos, is sworn into presidency in the Philippines.

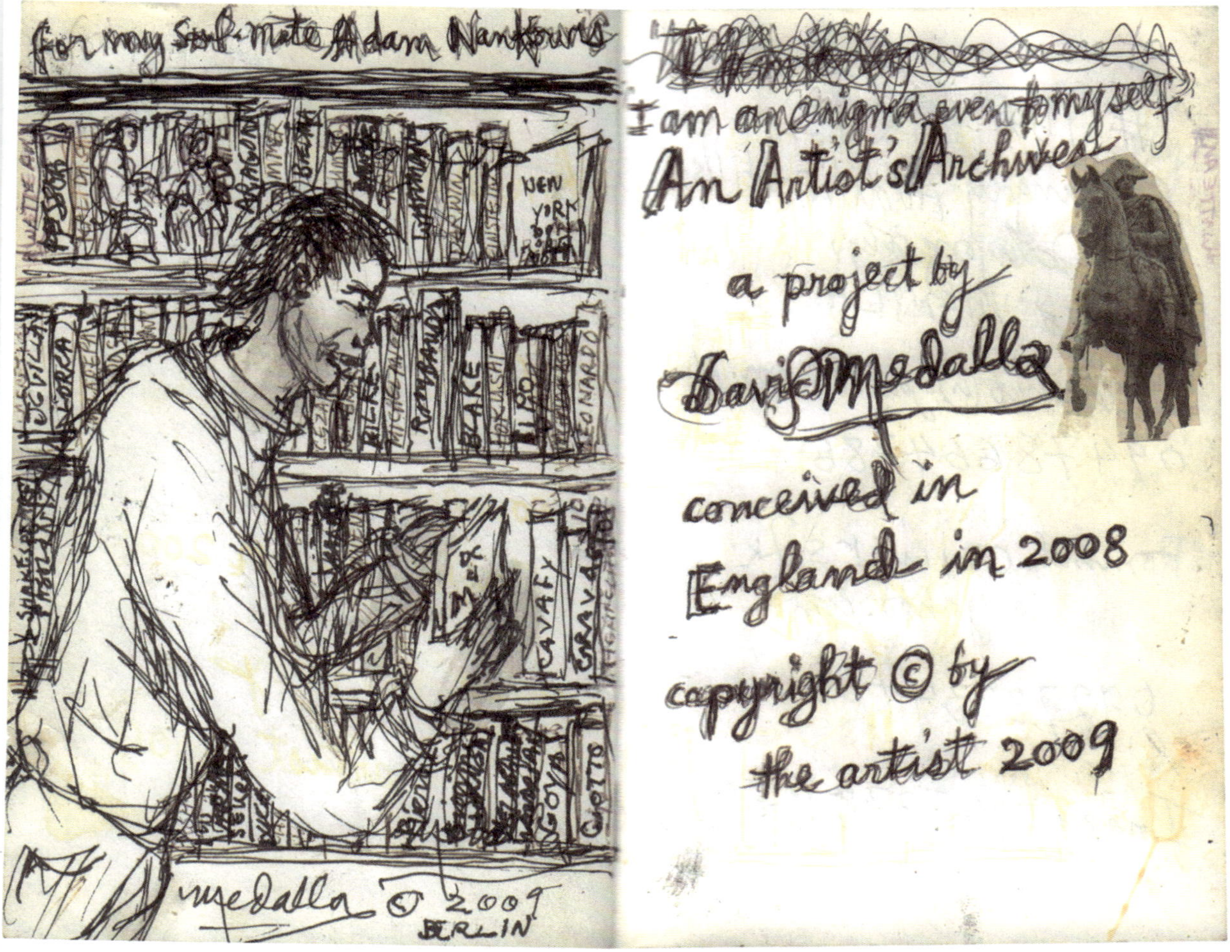

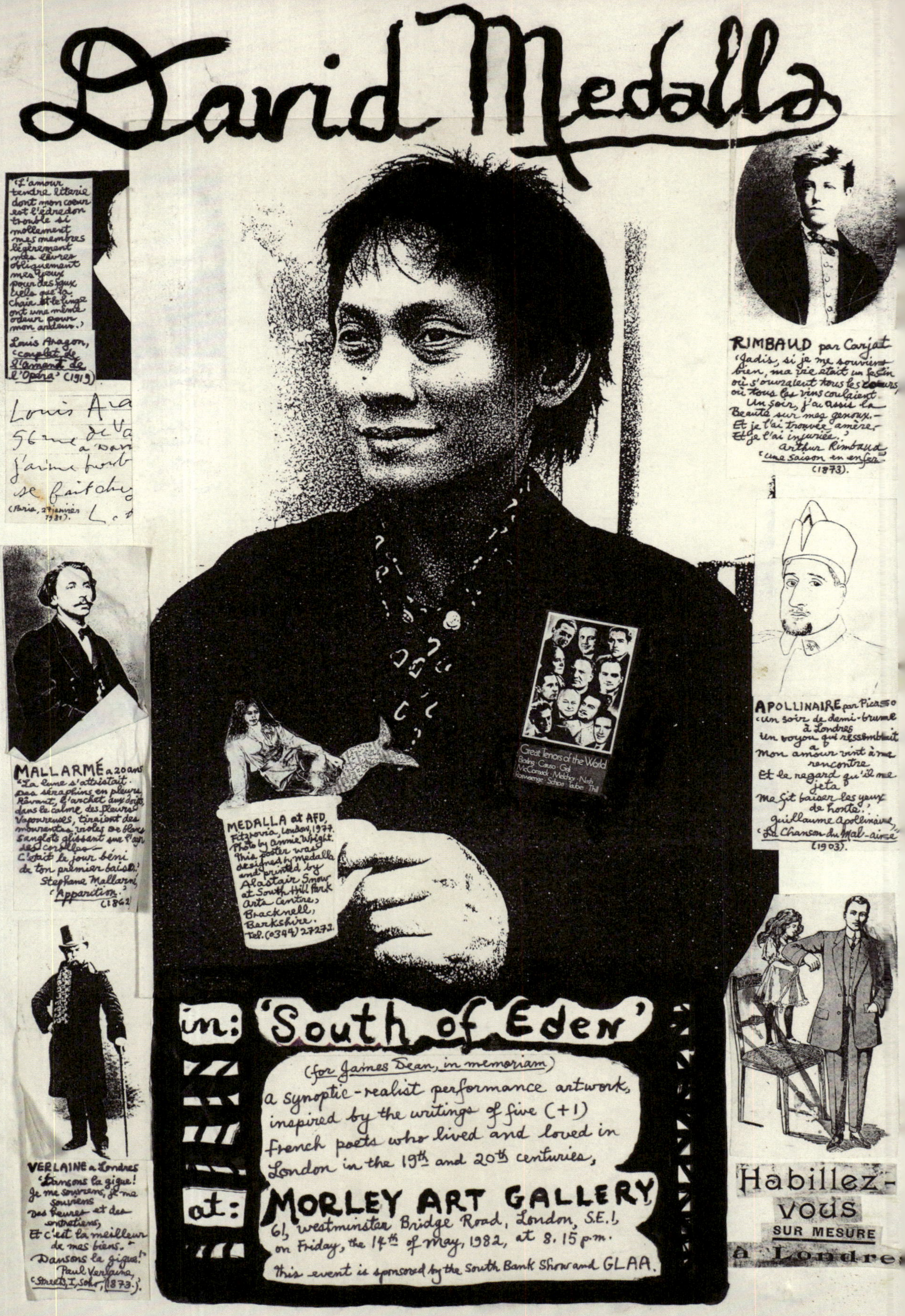
David Medalla
'L'amour tendre litière dont mon coeur est l'édredon trouble si mollement mes membres légèrement mes lèvres obliquement mes yeux pour des yeux tels que la chair et le linge ont une même odeur pour mon ardeur.'
Louis Aragon, 'couplet de l'amant de l'Opéra' (1919)
Louis Ara
(Paris, 27 janvier 1981).
RIMBAUD par Carjat
'Jadis, si je me souviens bien, ma vie était un festin où s'ouvraient tous les coeurs, où tous les vins coulaient.
Un soir, j'ai assis la Beauté sur mes genoux.– Et je l'ai trouvée amère.– Et je l'ai injuriée.'
Arthur Rimbaud
"une saison en enfer"
(1873).
MALLARMÉ a 20 ans
'La lune s'attristait.
C'était le jour béni de ton premier baiser.'
Stephane Mallarmé,
'Apparition.'
(1862)
APOLLINAIRE par Picasso
'Un soir de demi-brume à Londres
Un voyou qui ressemblait à
Mon amour vint à ma rencontre
Et le regard qu'il me jeta
me fit baiser les yeux de honte.'
Guillaume Apollinaire,
'La Chanson du Mal-aimé'
(1903).
Great Tenors of the World
MEDALLA at AFD, Fitzrovia, London, 1977. Photo by Annie Wright. This poster was designed by Medalla and printed by Alastair Snow at South Hill Park Arts Centre, Bracknell, Berkshire. Tel. (0344) 27272.
VERLAINE a Londres
'Dansons la gigue!
Je me souviens, je me souviens
Des heures et des entretiens,
Et c'est le meilleur de mes biens.
Dansons la gigue!'
Paul Verlaine,
'Streets, I, Soho', (1873).
in: 'South of Eden'
(for James Dean, in memoriam)
a synoptic-realist performance artwork, inspired by the writings of five (+1) French poets who lived and loved in London in the 19th and 20th centuries,
at: MORLEY ART GALLERY,
61, Westminster Bridge Road, London, S.E.1, on Friday, the 14th of May, 1982, at 8.15 p.m.
This event is sponsored by the South Bank Show and GLAA.
Habillez-vous
SUR MESURE
à Londres

Acknowledgments

Aram Moshayedi

Since the passing of David Medalla in December 2020, numerous individuals have taken on the task of recounting his artistic life. This publication and exhibition aim to be part of that ongoing conversation, rather than a comprehensive picture of the elusive artist and his multifarious body of work. The conflicting accounts of his myriad personae from those who knew him contribute to a palimpsest of his life. The artist's apparent fondness for self-mythologizing and subtle disdain for the tidiness of historical memory do not make it easy to narrate a story using his material remnants. He was concrete about certain facts along the timeline of his life and would recount select biographical data and origin stories time and again in his notebooks and the margins of his readymade books. But the more paths we followed and interlocutors we engaged, the more impish the inconsistencies became. From the historical distance we now occupy, Medalla coheres and disintegrates in equal measure. Nevertheless, an assembly of varied and often contradictory voices has helped us to sift through the fragments the artist left behind.

Medalla's partner Adam Nankervis's commitment to this history is especially heartfelt and stirring. Without Adam's support and collaboration, it is an understatement to say that this project could not have happened. He has devoted an astounding amount of time and energy to cataloging and preserving the archive and material accumulations amassed by Medalla over the course of his peripatetic life. Those efforts formed the basis of our initial research; without them, it is impossible to imagine an exhibition or publication that might start to convey a sense of Medalla's artistic thinking. Adam has lovingly managed the operations of this task from the modest confines of his ongoing project in Berlin, another vacant space, and he has been generous and open in allowing us into that shared environment as *David Medalla: In Conversation with the Cosmos* took form. Early on in this process, we were aided by Elmar Kaiser; more recently, Daniel Kupferberg has assisted in the bulk of the coordination, tirelessly acting as an unofficial representative of the Medalla archive. Daniel's is truly a labor of love, and there is no amount of appreciation that could adequately express the degree to which he has committed himself to this project and fielded our many requests, which became even more difficult after Medalla's death.

I am grateful to the David Medalla Archive and another vacant space for facilitating a large percentage of the exhibition's loans. I'm also appreciative of the staff from the galleries and institutions that assisted with additional loans and image requests, as well as the private lenders who kindly agreed to part with their works for the duration of the exhibition. A full list of lenders is included elsewhere in the publication, but it would be an oversight not to acknowledge them here as well.

The contents of this publication were molded during a rigorous and thoughtful exchange with the designers at A Practice for Everyday Life. Organizing a catalogue of this scale, with an

previous
Untitled, 1982. Photocopies and felt-tip marker on cardstock. 24 13⁄16 × 19 7⁄8 in. (63 × 50.5 cm).

opposite
Arthur & Co., Impromptu, Notting Hill Gate, London, 1993.

emphasis on new scholarship and the inclusion of previously unpublished material, is never easy, and I am indebted to the team for the patience and care they have dedicated to this process. They have been inspiring thought partners, and our conversations about the various artworks and materials are reflected in the organizational approach to the exhibition. Mary DelMonico of DelMonico Books has remained committed to the project from the start, and I cannot thank her enough for the unwavering support that she has repeatedly extended toward projects of this sort, no matter how nebulous and challenging.

Essays by Magalí Arriola and CJ Salapare offer imaginative scholarly approaches to Medalla's artistic legacy. I am appreciative that both have taken the time to develop innovative research at a moment of renewed interest in the artist's broader output. Magalí has also been instrumental in seeing the exhibition travel to the Museo Tamayo Arte Contemporáneo in Mexico City, and I couldn't be more honored to have her thoughts on Medalla's practice reflected here. CJ worked for a brief period as a curatorial intern at the Hammer Museum before going on to complete his PhD with a dissertation on the work of Medalla and Pacita Abad. Having CJ represented here, as a fresh voice in the art history of the Philippines and beyond, is meaningful for the overall project. The words of Magalí, CJ, and myself have been carefully edited by Elizabeth Pulsinelli, who remains precise and caring in her approach. I am ever grateful for her clarifying efforts. Others who have contributed with the logistical dimensions of this publication include Anne Koch, Susanne Rübsam, and Natalie Schmidt of the documenta archiv, Kassel, Germany; Jennifer Belt of Art Resource, Inc, New York; Alejandra Altamirano, Guy Brett Archive; Leah Saltoun, Richard Saltoun, and Sonja Teszler of Richard Saltoun Gallery, London; and Valentina Bandelloni of Scala Archives, Bagno a Ripoli, Italy. Helping to ensure the quality of the

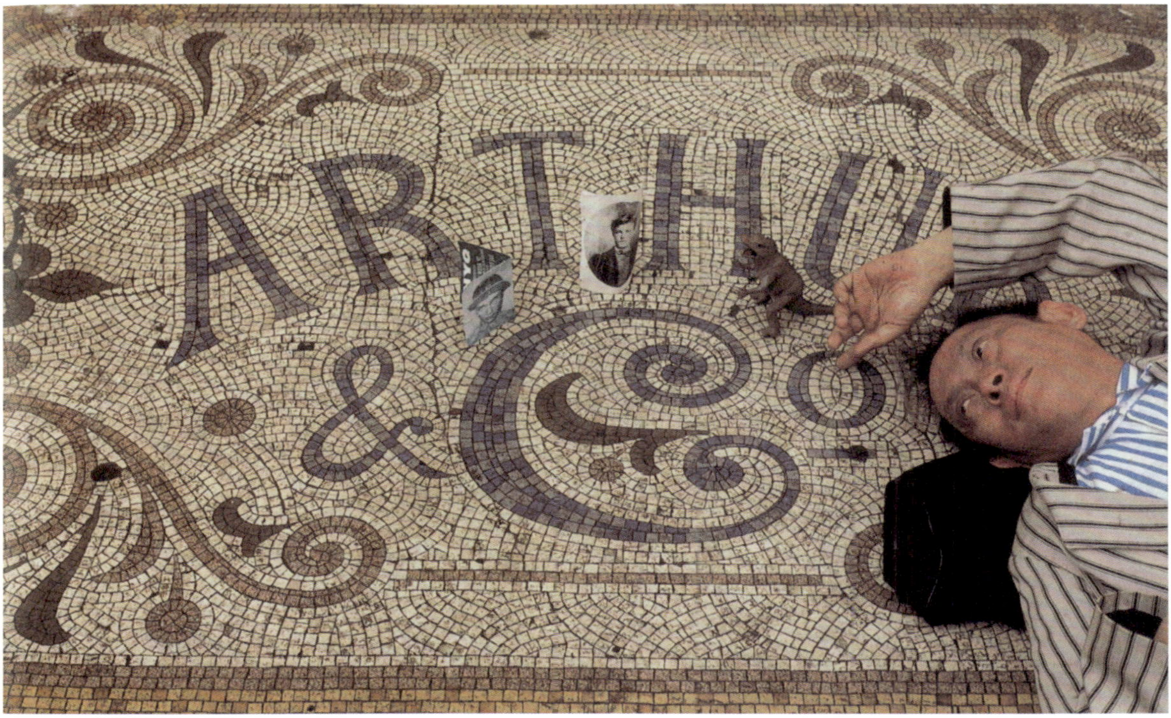

publication, Rachel Walther provided additional proofreading and Tony Manzella and his team at Echelon Color, Santa Monica, finessed the color separations.

The dedication of the Hammer Museum's staff brought this publication and exhibition to fruition. Director Ann Philbin has led the museum's orchestration of this exhibition and many others that have preceded it under her stewardship. I am grateful for the trust and encouragement she has provided me throughout our time together at the Hammer. The disparate voices of the museum's curatorial department past and present—Connie Butler, Erin Christovale, Pablo José Ramírez, and Ali Subotnick—have been invaluable to me as the project has taken shape. Cynthia Burlingham, deputy director of curatorial affairs, has been particularly patient as the project has evolved and changed since its inception. Esther Zeilig's administrative dexterity has kept the department intact while many projects are being organized concurrently. Michael Nock, director of exhibitions and publication management, has helped to oversee all practical aspects of the planning process, and I am grateful for his wisdom and willingness to accommodate changes as the exhibition unfolded. Adam Peña and his team of exhibition designers, including Emilio Bustos and Yeganeh Malouhi, have deftly assembled the many different types of materials that comprise this survey. Angelica Perez-Aguirre, Jason Pugh, Michael Terzano, and Chris Zickefoose have assisted with the safe handling of artworks and objects in the exhibition; I am appreciative of their collective efforts and those of the parttime members of the installation crew. Portland McCormick, director of registration

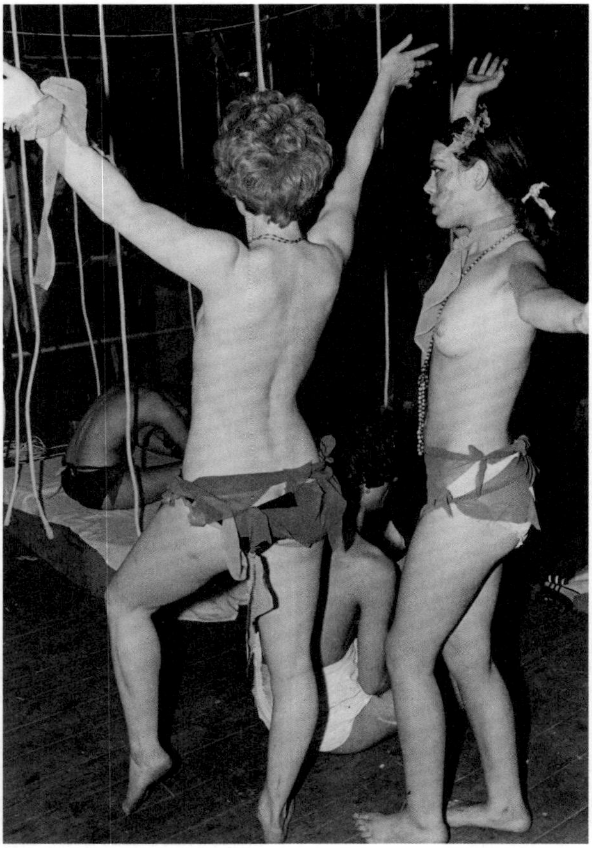

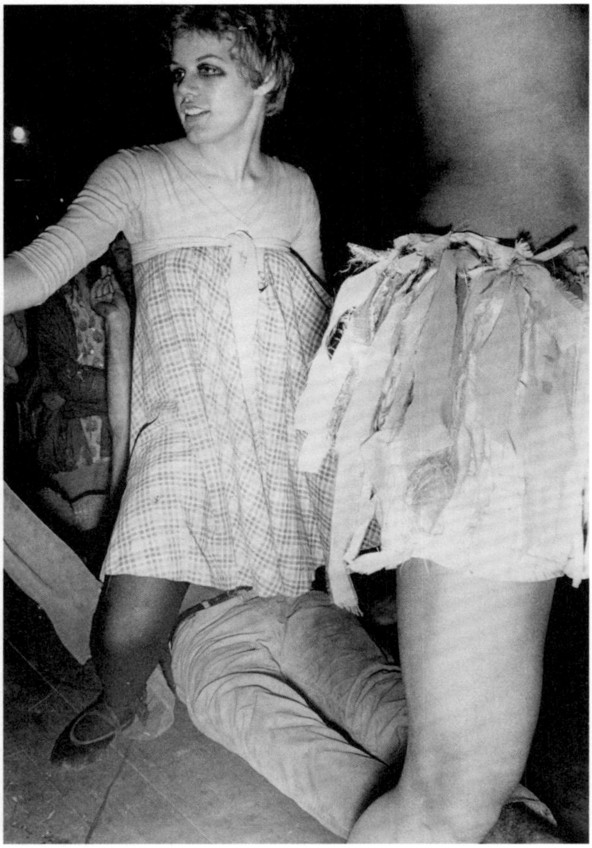

and collections management, skillfully oversaw the installation, with registrar Emma Rudman coordinating shipments and taking on the bulk of the exhibition's coordination in the galleries. The efforts of other registrars in the department—Shira Abramsohn, Susan Hersey, and Linda Yun—are always valued and appreciated.

Other key members of the museum staff who were instrumental in coordinating *In Conversation with the Cosmos* include Michael Harrison, deputy director, finance, operations, and administration; Fred Yeries, deputy director, external affairs; Reshma Bishnoi, director, legal affairs; Belén Pena, director of development, individual giving; Courtney Raterman Casal, director of foundations and special projects; Beth Harker, grant writer; Dylan King, manager, annual giving; Jessica Vrazilek, manager, individual giving; Scott Tennent, chief communications officer; Lisa Davis, associate director, communications and marketing; Santiago Pazos, senior manager, public relations; Philip Leers, associate director, digital initiatives; Tara Morris, senior graphic designer; Lauren Graycar, graphic designer; Ramonchito Espinosa, design and production specialist; Gabriel Noguez Ibarra, senior media producer; Ashley Kruythoff, digital communications manager; Jim Fetterley, museum and technical director; Tim Ferris, theater production supervisor; Michael Monahan, associate director, technology; Elizabeth Powers Marks, manager, director's office; Cheyenne Assil, assistant, director's office; Claudia Bestor, director, public programs; and Shannon Cynowa, associate director, academic programs.

In addition to the other museum staff from the departments of Academic Programs, Communications, Curatorial, Development, Public Programs, Exhibition Registration and Preparation, Finance, the Hammer Store, Operations and Facilities, Public Programs, Security, Technology, and Visitor Experience, I would like to extend a heartfelt appreciation for the commitment that Nyah Ginwright has made to this project and, by extension, to the legacy of David Medalla. Nyah inherited the responsibilities of curatorial assistant from Nicholas Barlow, who worked diligently in the early stages of the project's inception. Nyah's involvement has extended beyond serving as an organizational lead and carefully crafting the explanatory texts and thorough chronology included here. She also has been a valued confidant, and she now ranks as a specialist on the evasive artist this exhibition is dedicated to better understanding. I would also like to thank Jessi DiTillio for her detailed attention to the publication. Jessi arrived at a crucial moment, taking on the mantle of project manager of exhibitions and publications from Emma Vale, who was unexpectedly pulled away from the museum. Emma and Jessi have played a crucial role in producing this substantive document.

Many others contributed to this venture in ways that were essential, including those who offered advice, suggestions, and leads for contacts. Those people include Ria T. Aguilar and Boots Herrera, Ateneo Art Gallery at Ateneo de Manila University; Malik Al-Mahrouky, José Kuri, Monica Manzutto, Mario Navarro,

The Exploding Galaxy, 99 Ball Ponds Road, London, 1967.

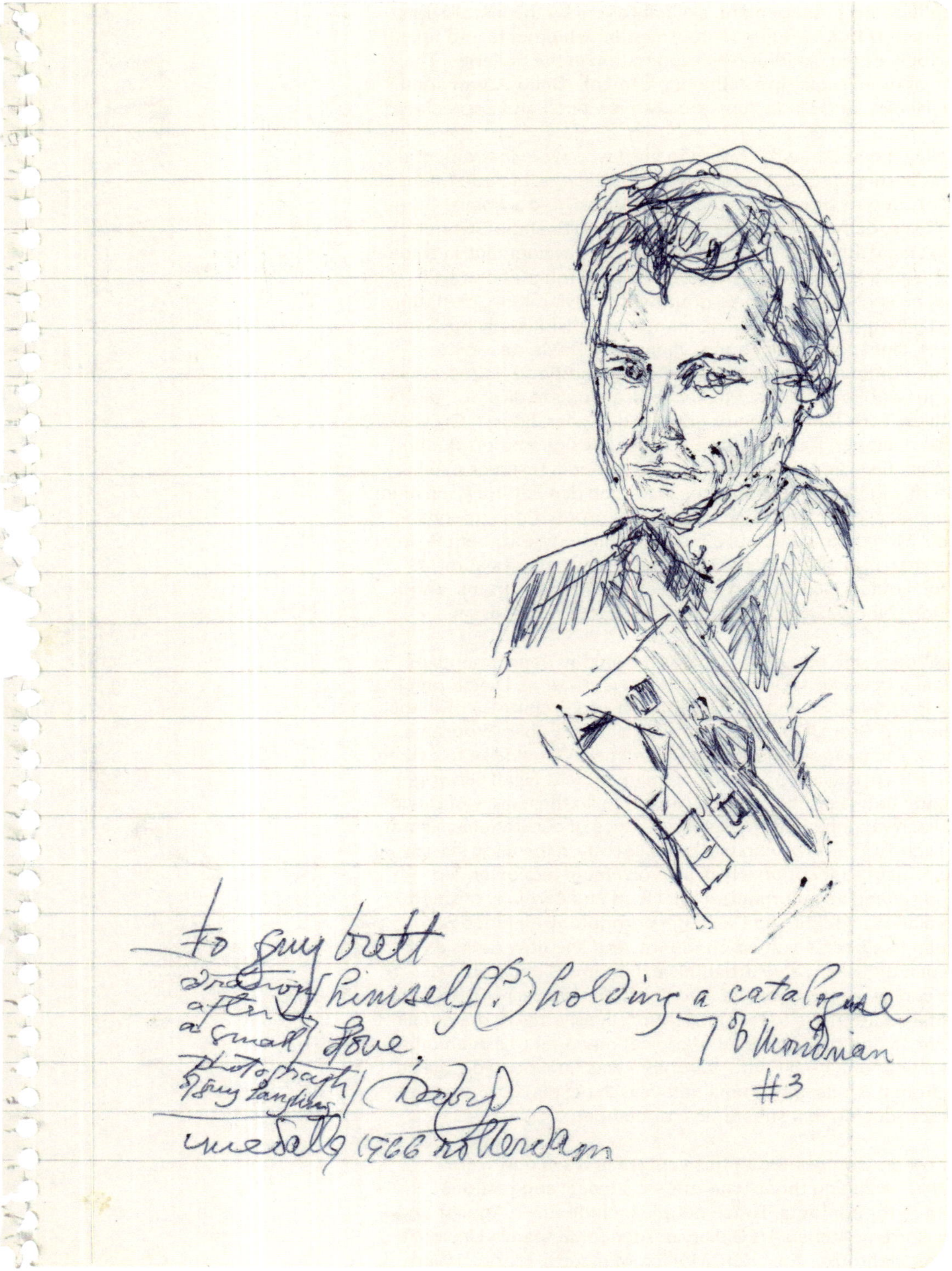
to guy brett
himself (?) holding a catalogue
of Mondrian
love,
#3
1966 rotterdam

Martha Reta, Karime Sierra, and Julia Villaseñor, kurimanzutto, Mexico City/New York; John Auerbach and Edward Tang; Heidrun Bachmaier; Ben Barcelona; Jeremy Barns, Anne Rosette Crelencia, Caroline Marie D. Duque, Verna Joson, Jorell M. Legaspi, and Danelyn Sumaylo, National Museum of the Philippines, Manila; Christine Meleo Bernstein and Armyan Bernstein; Lucy Biddle, Chloe Page, and Alex Sainsbury, Raven Row, London; José Luis Blondet, Museum of Contemporary Art, Los Angeles; Steven Cairns, Institute of Contemporary Arts, London; Aimee Calfin, Evan Dresman, Ann Harezlak, Aliya Kalla, Theresa Marino, Virginia Mokslaveskas, Glenn Phillips, Tracey Schuster, Getty Research Institute, Los Angeles; Kim and Lito Camacho; Simon Castets and Fabian Gröning, LUMA Arles; Wing Chan and David Morris, Afterall Research Centre, London; Michael Chapman; Johnny Chen, Joleen Loh, Shabbir Hussain Mustafa, Dr. Eugene Tan, Jia Yun, and Arabelle Zhuang, National Gallery Singapore; Christophe Cherix and River Bullock, The Museum of Modern Art, New York; Niamh Coghlan and Richard Saltoun, Richard Saltoun Gallery, London; Tina Colayco, Metropolitan Museum of Manila; Trickie Colayco-Lopa, Art Fair Philippines; Elena Crippa and Michael Wellen, Tate Britain, London; Joselina Cruz, Museum of Contemporary Art and Design, Manila; Thomas Dane, Olivia Rawnsley, and Hannah Wright, Thomas Dane Gallery, London/Naples; Ursula Davila; Jill Drower; the E. Rhodes and Leona B. Carpenter Foundation; Jane England and Peter Gordon Stables, England & Co. Gallery, London; Rose English; Flávia França, Galeria Luisa Strina, São Paulo; Patrick D. Flores; Anna Furney and Marie-Capucine Pineau-Valencienne, Venus Over Manhattan, New York; Adrian Glew, Tate Archive, London; Brian Guerin; Bruce Hainley; Karen Hillenburg; Hannah Hoffman; Charles Hustwick; Beth and Ken Karmin; Bo Kim; Kelly Kivland, Wexner Center for the Arts, Columbus, Ohio; Edward Lee; Marta Lusena; Lynn MacRitchie; Karen Marta; Courtney J. Martin, Yale Center for British Art, New Haven, Connecticut; Miranda Massie; Brooke Matzek; Micki Meng; Sohrab Mohebbi; Isabel Moseley, Francesca Nugent, and Laura Peterle, Arts Council Collection, London; Jill Mulleady; Shahryar Nashat; Hans Ulrich Obrist, Serpentine Galleries, London; Melanie Ouyang Lum; Renata Padovan; Clay Perry; Emma Poveda; Paulino and Hetty Que; David Regan and Edgar Cervantes; K.J. Relth-Miller, the Academy Museum of Motion Pictures; Fabio Rossi and Karen Wong, Rossi & Rossi, Hong Kong; Miljohn Ruperto; Ana Sampietro, Museo Tamayo Arte Contemporáneo, Mexico City; Gabriel Sims; Sally Tallant, Queens Museum, New York; Maria Taniguchi; Cecilia Vicuña; Michael Waldrep; and The Andy Warhol Foundation for the Visual Arts.

In immeasurable ways, the people and organizations listed here have facilitated and helped to shape the project, including many who have provided access to the multitudinous selves and worlds that David Medalla inhabited in his lifetime and beyond. Above all, I am grateful to the artist for leaving behind a rich body of biokinetic, cosmic, and synoptic art. My only regret is that he is not here to share in this moment.

to guy brett #3, 1966. Ballpoint pen on ruled paper. 8 1/16 × 5 7/8 in. (20.5 × 15 cm).

Endnotes

A Love That Leaves No Traces

Aram Moshayedi

1
David Medalla, "MMMMMMM ... Manifesto (a fragment)," first published in *Signals Newsbulletin* 8 (June 1965).

2
Gregor Quack, "David Medalla Bonner Kunstverein," *Artforum* 60, no. 6 (February 2022): 153.

3
David Medalla, "Interview with Rasheed Araeen and David Medalla," *Black Phoenix* 3 (1979): 14.

4
Medalla, "Interview with Rasheed Araeen," 14.

5
Guy Brett, *Exploding Galaxies: The Art of David Medalla* (London: Kala Press, 1995), 63.

And then, and then, and then ... David Medalla: A short tale about a flower, a letter, an egg, a monkey, and an artist

Magalí Arriola

1
David Medalla, "MMMMMMM ... Manifesto (a fragment)," first published in *Signals Newsbulletin* 8 (June 1965). Medalla was editor of *Signals Newsbulletin*, an international journal that incorporated critical essays, poetry, and scientific studies, and documented much of the experimental art that was exhibited at Signals London, the space he founded with the members of the Centre for Advanced Creative Study. Medalla cofounded the center in 1964 with fellow artists Gustav Metzger and Marcello Salvadori, curators Guy Brett and Paul Keeler, and the art critic Christopher Walker.

2
Medalla, "MMMMMMM ... Manifesto (a fragment)."

3
David Medalla, "Interview with Rasheed Araeen and David Medalla," *Black Phoenix* 3 (1979): 11.

4
David Medalla, quoted in Chanon Kenji Praepipatmongkol, "David Medalla: Dreams of Sculpture," *Oxford Art Journal* 43, no. 3 (December 2020): 342–43.

5
Medalla, "Interview with Rasheed Araeen," 11.

6
The original Mohole Flower sculpture was destroyed by a fire in the artist's studio. Medalla produced a new version to be exhibited in *What Do You Dream Of? The Mohole Flower and Other Tales*, which I curated at Galeria Luisa Strina, São Paulo, in 2018.

7
These words are from an inscription on the base of the original sculpture.

8
David Medalla, quoted in Guy Brett, *Exploding Galaxies: The Art of David Medalla* (London: Kala Press, 1995), 62. "My sculptures breathe and perspire, grow and decay. They correspond to my view of external and internal reality. Naturally I do not see any demarcation between internal and external 'reality.' For me interior space and exterior space are mutually interchangeable." In this context, the concepts of interior and exterior spaces should be understood simultaneously as the artist's inner life and as contextual exploration.

9
Brett, *Exploding Galaxies*, 63.

10
Medalla, quoted in Praepipatmongkol, "Dreams of Sculpture," 13.

11
Medalla, quoted in Brett, *Exploding Galaxies*, 68.

12
Medalla, quoted in Brett, *Exploding Galaxies*, 93. "By a method of freely linking one person with another, and by linking people together to form a united and mobile whole I seek to increase the awareness of voluntary cooperation between one person and another, and cooperation between the individual and the group, without either the individual or the group dominating.... It is a collective expression of variable, random and volitional movement initiated by the individual participants acting as a whole; the work exists only as a living complex of these instantaneous and momentary movements, and therefore cannot be consumed in isolation (by a solitary individual) or exploited and speculated upon like the majority of art objects." Medalla was clearly also expressing a political critique aimed at the art market and its forms of consumption.

13
Brett, *Exploding Galaxies*, 93.

14
Medalla, quoted in Brett, *Exploding Galaxies*, 95.

15
Letter to Michael Adams, October 22, 1985, in Brett, *Exploding Galaxies*, 292. Medalla started early on his career as a painter and never abandoned the discipline. He claimed that everything he had ever done, including his performances (some of which staged *tableaux vivants*), were paintings.

16
David Medalla's notes on *Parables of Friendship: Myself and Lovato Guerrino at Castello in Venice*, in Brett, *Exploding Galaxies*, 206.

17
Brett, *Exploding Galaxies*, 132. Medalla used the term *synoptic-realism* for the first time in 1979, in relation to Rhapsody of the Dagger and Ammonia Boy (1979–81), a series of works that dealt with *fait divers* about a young man who attacked people in the streets of Kensington with a knife and threw ammonia in their faces, a story that evoked for Medalla the misery and violence of urban life in London at the time.

18
Of the references, Medalla writes, "Incidentally, in the title sequence of the film *Rebel Without a Cause*, the actor James Dean (whom I knew in New York, in the early 1950s) is seen winding a toy monkey, similar to one in my painting [*Parables of Friendship: Myself and*

Lovato Guerrino at Castello in Venice].... The sequence of Jimmy and the toy monkey which moved me deeply when I first saw the film must have lodged in the inner recesses of my memory; it surfaced again, in a metamorphosed way, in my own performance of *Voyages and Somersaults of the Pilgrim Monkey*, which in some ways was an oblique homage to James Dean and other friends in my past." Medalla's notes on *Parables of Friendship: Myself and Lovato Guerrino at Castello in Venice*, in Brett, *Exploding Galaxies*, 205.

19
Medalla, quoted in Brett, *Exploding Galaxies*, 147.

20
Yve-Alain Bois, "Virtual," in Brett, *Exploding Galaxies*, 213. The artist's candid form of expressiveness seems to echo his delicate and childlike appearance.

21
Brett, speaking of the vision of Guerrino holding the egg under the moonlight, in *Exploding Galaxies*, 173.

What the Wind Carries

CJ Salapare

1
For their lights and insights on David Medalla, I thank Gregg Bordowitz, Kim Conaty, Christie Costello, Gabriella Daris, Adrienne Edwards, Zanna Gilbert, Sofia Gotti, Every Ocean Hughes, Lumen Iglesia, Min Sun Jeon, Colton Klein, Matthew Villar Miranda, David Morris, Carol Ockman, Sarah Shi, Elisabeth Sussman, Amy Tobin, Julie Tolentino, and Lauren Young. I am especially grateful to Nyah Ginwright, Aram Moshayedi, and Elizabeth Pulsinelli for their clarity of eye and mind throughout the editing process.

2
This idea came to Medalla and Nankervis on their first visit to São Paulo in 2007. They later reworked and transfigured the concept in a recorded performance (*Tulips for Iguazu*) and related exhibition (*The Secret History of the Mondrian Fan Club—Part 3: So Pulo*) at Baró Galeria in 2010. "I have often wondered why Mondrian dropped one of the letter 'A's in his surname.... Was it because Mondrian wanted to say goodbye to his ethnic origin and become a full-pledged [*sic*] member of the world of avant-garde artists, which he became when he moved to France?" Medalla continues, "When Adam Nankervis and I first visited São Paulo in 2007, we thought of Mondrian, whose life and ideas inspired several Brazilian artists, including Lygia Clark, Lygia Pape and Hélio Oiticica. We thought we could emulate Mondrian by 'dropping' the letter 'A' from São Paulo." See David Medalla, *David Medalla and Adam Nankervis: The Secret History of the Mondrian Fanclub—Part 3: So Pulo* (September 18–November 20, 2010), artists' statement, Baró Galeria, São Paulo, https://www.1fmediaproject.net/2010/09/18/david-medalla-e-adam-nankervis-baro-galeria-sao-paulo-brazil/.

3
Per Adam Nankervis's website, another vacant space: "Medalla and Nankervis created the individual letters pertaining to the names or specific locales within different cities where they would and do meet, to create a letter, an airborne piece global graffiti, which will eventually complete the sentence Medalla and Nankervis have started to formulate since the exhibition, *The Secret History of the Mondrian Fan Club*, Gee Street London 1994." See Adam Nankervis, "Mondrian Fan Club," another vacant space, www.anothervacantspace.com/Mondrian-Fan-Club-David-Medalla-Adam-Nankervis.

4
Dore Ashton, "An Impromptu for David Medalla and Guy Brett," in Guy Brett, *Exploding Galaxies: The Art of David Medalla* (London: Kala Press, 1995), 8.

5
Ashton, "An Impromptu," 8.

6
David Medalla, "Synoptic-Realism" (1981), 1, Guy Brett Collection, Tate Archive.

7
Adam Nankervis, "A Stitch in Time: David Medalla," *Mousse Magazine* (June 2011), https://www.moussemagazine.it/magazine/david-medalla-adam-nankervis-2011/.

8
Nankervis, "A Stitch in Time." Medalla stated, "The thing I like best about this work is that whenever anyone is involved in the act of stitching, he or she is inside his or her own private space, even though the act of stitching might occur in a public place."

9
Art historian Chanon Kenji Praepipatmongkol refers to "the possibility of haphazard connections and revelations" in "David Medalla: Dreams of Sculpture," *Oxford Art Journal* 43, no. 3 (December 2020): 359. Artist Sonia Boyce and art historian Dorothy Price describe the work's origin story and its originary handkerchief as "an uncanny loop of affections and estrangement," in "Dearly Beloved or Unrequited? To Be 'Black' in Art's Histories," *Art History* 44, no. 3 (2021): 469.

10
In Medalla's words: "All my work is informed by personal experience. It is the seed to which I apply a transcendent dialogue." Nankervis, "A Stitch in Time."

11
This is a reference to Italo Calvino, *Baron in the Trees* (Turin, Italy: Giulio Einaudi Editore, 1957).

12
Parables of Friendship is the title of a 1983 artwork by Medalla. It is also the name of a 2022 publication that accompanied his survey exhibition at Bonner Kunstverein in Bonn, Germany, and Museion in Bolzano, Italy.

13
Yve-Alain Bois, "Virtual," in Brett, *Exploding Galaxies*, 213.

14
Yve-Alain Bois, "Angels with Guns: A Memoir on Guy Brett (and David Medalla)," *October* 179 (2022): 28.

15
Medalla, "Synoptic-Realism," 1.

16
Rasheed Araeen, *The Other Story* (London: Hayward Gallery/Southbank Centre, 1989), 56

17
Sharon Marcus, Heather Love, and Stephen Best, "Building a Better Description," *Representations* 135 (Summer 2016): 10. In discussing the aesthetic, political, and ethical imperatives of description, the three authors note, "A better description would faithfully capture—this is its robust realism—the world's messy profusion of stray details that cannot be assimilated to an already existing theory and that sometimes might not even precipitate a new one."

18
In an undated work, Medalla wrote: "The sensitive stranger is the person I address in my art. Strangers from all over the world eventually become my dear friends." See Steven Cairns and Fatima Hellberg, eds., *David Medalla: Parables of Friendship* (Bonn, Germany, and Bolzano, Italy: Bonner Kunstverein and Museion, 2022), 217.

19
For a selection of writings and research on Signals, see the *Signals Newsbulletin*, 1964–66; Pamela Lee, *Chronophobia: On Time in the Art of the 1960s* (Cambridge, MA: MIT Press, 2004); John A. Tyson, "Signals Crossing Borders: Cybernetic Words and Images and 1960s Avant-Garde Art," *Interfaces* 38 (2017); and Isobel Whitelegg's 2018 exhibition *Signals: If You Like I Shall Grow*.

20
Brett kept these drawings in his writing desk until 2020, when he gifted them back to Medalla after the artist had returned to Manila. Soon after, the works found their way into an online exhibition in memory of their friendship.

21
David Medalla, *Some Reflections on the Random in Life and Art*, 1985. Ink on paper, 11¾ × 8¼ in. (29.8 × 21 cm). The Museum of Modern Art, Gift of the Gilbert B. and Lila Silverman Instruction Drawing Collection, Detroit. © another vacant space, Berlin.

22
See Medalla, *David Medalla and Adam Nankervis: The Secret History of the Mondrian Fan Club—Part 3: So Pulo*, artists' statement.

23
André Kertész, *Chez Mondrian, Paris*, 1926. Gelatin silver print, image: 4 5/16 × 3 1/8 in. (10.9 × 7.9 cm). Getty Museum, © Estate of André Kertész.

24
Medalla, *David Medalla and Adam Nankervis: The Secret History.*

25
See Nankervis, "Mondrian Fan Club," another vacant space.

26
Brett, *Exploding Galaxies*, 187. For more information on Mondrian's posthumous reception, see Nancy Troy, *The Afterlife of Piet Mondrian* (Chicago: University of Chicago Press, 2014), specifically the chapter titled "The Mondrian Brand." For more information on Medalla's fascination with Mondrian, see Jun Terra, "David Medalla in London," *Third Text* 9, no. 30 (1995): 93–100. According to Terra, Medalla's first encounter with Mondrian took place in the 1950s at the Museum of Modern Art, New York, during the time he was enrolled at Columbia University as a special student at the age of fourteen.

27
Nankervis, "Mondrian Fan Club," another vacant space. Sameer Reddy refers to "Adam Nankervis's nomadic Another Vacant Space, which Nankervis … founded to 'exhibit art or projects that may not find a home in the commercial sector of the art world, nor be ripe enough for museums.'" Sameer Reddy, "Now Showing: Paul Thek in Theory and Practice," *New York Times*, July 20, 2011.

28
Mondrian Fan Club (David Medalla and Adam Nankervis), *Mondrian Pavilion*, at the preview of the 57th International Art Exhibition, Venice, Giardini, May 10, 2017, "Biennale Arte 2017 – Mondrian Fan Club (performance)," BiennaleChannel, YouTube video, 15:00, www.youtube.com/watch?v=spCX7wCrp-E.

Additional Captions

1
Self Portrait, 1957. Oil on canvas. 42 1/16 × 24 1/8 in. (106.8 × 61.2 cm).

2
Untitled, ca. 1959. China ink on paper. 35 13/16 × 24 in. (91 × 61 cm).

3
Portrait of Kent Smith no I, 1959. Ballpoint pen on paper. 12 15/16 × 7 15/16 in. (32.8 × 20.2 cm).

4
Rimbaud, 1962. Graphite on paper. 9 15/16 × 7 7/8 in. (25.3 × 20 cm).

5
Portrait of Bing Kutay, 1959. China ink on paper. 19 5/16 × 14 5/8 in. (49 × 37.2 cm).

6
Study for Luz. Vi. Minda., 1962. Graphite and China ink on paper. 13 5/8 × 9 13/16 in. (34.6 × 25 cm).

7
Study for a monumental peelable sculpture, 1967. Colored pencil on mat board. 12 5/8 × 7 5/8 in. (32.1 × 19.4 cm).

8
Untitled, 1962. Graphite on paper. 9 15/16 × 8 in. (25.3 × 20.3 cm).

9
Untitled, 1965. Felt-tip marker and ballpoint pen on paper. 19 3/4 × 14 in. (50.1 × 35.5 cm).

10
Marcos and His Handful of Hoodlums, 1972. Acrylic on cardstock. 19 3/8 × 29 3/8 in. (49.2 × 74.5 cm).

11
Untitled, 1972. Acrylic on cardstock. 29 5/16 × 19 3/8 in. (74.5 × 49.2 cm).

12
Conversation with Jean-Paul Sartre, 1980. Acrylic and mixed media on mat board mounted on canvas. 24 × 30 × 1 in. (60.9 × 76.2 × 2.5 cm).

13
Found Poem with a Drawing, 1976–78. Collage, felt-tip marker, ballpoint pen, graphite, and white marker on cardboard with elastic bands. 9 15/16 × 7 7/8 in. (25.3 × 20 cm).

14
Le pete Paul Verlaine claire au clair de la Lune, 1982. Oil and collage on plastic. 16 9/16 × 14 9/16 in. (42 × 37 cm).

15
The Naked Angel with a Bouquet of Flowers, 1983. Wax crayon and colored ink on photocopy. 11 3/4 × 8 1/16 in. (29.8 × 20.4 cm).

16
Self Portrait, 1984. Mixed media on paper mounted on wood. 57 × 45 in. (144.8 × 114.3 cm).

17
A Prophecy, 1989. Oil on canvas. 82 11/16 × 122 1/16 in. (210 × 310 cm).

18
New York Footprints No. 1, 1989–91. Oil on canvas. 30 1/4 × 26 1/16 in. (76.8 × 66.2 cm).

19
*Bioluminescent (*astro* Acupuncture*) Man—body art & installation by Medalla*, 1991. China ink and ink pen on paper. 19 1/2 × 13 5/8 in. (49.6 × 34.6 cm).

20
The Birth of Television, 1996. Crayon on drawing board. 19 × 12 1/2 in. (48.2 × 31.7 cm).

21
Orpheus descending, 2015. Newspaper, nylon tapestry, strings, coins, arrow pin. 18 3/16 × 14 3/4 × 1/2 in. (46.2 × 37.4 × 1.3 cm).

22
Maps—Mazes and Mysteries, London Biennale 2014, 2014. Ink pen and acrylic on newspaper. 21 15/16 × 13 11/16 in. (55.7 × 34.8 cm).

23
London Biennale 2012: The Rainbow, 2012. Paper collage, colored pencil, felt-tip marker and clear tape on paper. 13 1/4 × 9 15/16 in. (33.6 × 25.2 cm).

24
Rubaiyat, 2015. Acrylic on paper. Nine parts, 24 × 16 3/4 in. (61 × 42.5 cm) each.

25
Untitled, 2015. Collage. 8 7/8 × 11 15/16 in. (22.6 × 30.4 cm).

Exhibition Checklist*

Unless otherwise noted, all works by David Medalla and courtesy of the David Medalla Archive

Untitled I, 1956
Watercolor on paper
22 1/16 × 16 9/16 in. (56 × 42 cm)
Courtesy of Ateneo Art Gallery, Ateneo de Manila University

David Medalla & friends, 1956
Watercolor on photocopy
13 × 16 9/16 in. (33 × 42 cm)

Self Portrait, 1957
Oil on canvas
42 1/16 × 24 1/8 in. (106.8 × 61.2 cm)
National Fine Arts Collection of the National Museum of the Philippines

Untitled, ca. 1957
Graphite and China ink on paper
11 × 8 7/16 in. (28 × 21.5 cm)

Nude 1958, Paris, 1958
Ballpoint pen and ink on paper
11 15/16 × 5 7/8 in. (30.4 × 15 cm)

Untitled II, 1958
Watercolor on paper
12 5/8 × 7 7/8 in. (32 × 20 cm)
Courtesy of Ateneo Art Gallery, Ateneo de Manila University

Untitled III, 1958
Watercolor on paper
12 5/8 × 7 7/8 in. (32 × 20 cm)
Courtesy of Ateneo Art Gallery, Ateneo de Manila University

Untitled IV, 1958
Watercolor on paper
12 5/8 × 7 7/8 in. (32 × 20 cm)
Courtesy of Ateneo Art Gallery, Ateneo de Manila University

Doveglion—The Poet Jose Garcia Villa (Filipino poet)—Cafe Renzi Greenwich Village NYC, 1959
Ballpoint pen on paper
8 1/16 × 5 7/8 in. (20.5 × 14.9 cm)

Portrait of Geert Jameeris, 1959
Lithograph
8 5/16 × 5 5/16 in. (21.1 × 13.5 cm)

Monchu by Medalla, 1959
China ink, graphite, and watercolor on paper
10 15/16 × 8 3/8 in. (27.8 × 21.3 cm)

Portrait of Kent Smith no 1, 1959
Ballpoint pen on paper
12 15/16 × 7 15/16 in. (32.8 × 20.2 cm)

Portrait of Bing Kutay, 1959
China ink on paper
19 5/16 × 14 5/8 in. (49 × 37.2 cm)

Untitled, ca. 1959
China ink on paper
35 13/16 × 24 in. (91 × 61 cm)

The Caucasian Chalk Circle, 1960
Felt-tip marker, China ink, and watercolor on paper
11 5/16 × 7 3/4 in. (28.8 × 19.7 cm)

Aboard the SS Vietnam on the way to Colombo, 1960
Graphite on paper
10 × 8 in. (25.4 × 20.3 cm)

Study of a Poet, 1961
China ink on paper
11 3/4 × 7 1/2 in. (29.9 × 19 cm)

Autobildnis, 1961
Ballpoint pen on paper with window mat
13 3/4 × 10 1/4 in. (35 × 26 cm)

Untitled, 1962
Graphite on paper
9 15/16 × 8 in. (25.3 × 20.3 cm)

Study for Luz. Vi. Minda. 1962
Graphite and China ink on paper
13 5/8 × 9 13/16 in. (34.6 × 25 cm)

Rimbaud, 1962
Graphite on paper
9 15/16 × 7 7/8 in. (25.3 × 20 cm)

Lava Machine, 1962
Acrylic on paper
19 11/16 × 12 13/16 in. (50 × 32.5 cm)

Rosa Luxemberg, 1962
China ink and ballpoint pen on paper
10 11/16 × 8 1/2 in. (27.1 × 21.6 cm)

Ako Usá, 1962
Watercolor and China ink on paper
20 × 14 in. (50.8 × 35.5 cm)

The Dream Machine, 1963
Mechanical device, mixed media, oil crayon
10 13/16 × 11 × 8 3/8 in. (27.5 × 28 × 21.2 cm)

Charleville, Home of Arthur Rimbaud, 1963
Pastel and colored pencil on paper
16 × 12 in. (40.7 × 30.5 cm)

CUMA—Studies for Lava Machine, 1963
China ink, graphite, and felt-tip marker on paper
19 5/8 × 12 13/16 in. (49.9 × 32.5 cm)

CUMA—study for Lava Machines, 1963
Watercolor on paper
18 15/16 × 12 5/8 in. (48 × 32 cm)
Courtesy of Thomas Dane, London

Study for the mohole flower, 1963
Ballpoint pen on paper
7 × 5 7/16 in. (17.8 × 13.8 cm)

Study of a Poet, 1963
Ballpoint pen on paper
10 × 8 in. (25.4 × 20.3 cm)

Mr. Morley's Harp Shop I, 1963
Ballpoint pen on paper
7 5/8 × 5 5/16 in. (19.4 × 13.5 cm)

mohole flower, 1964
Colored pencil on paper napkin
6 1/2 × 6 1/2 in. (16.5 × 16.5 cm)

Sand Machine, 1963
Wood, brass, sand, bamboo, acrylic sheet, glass beads and other materials
27 5/8 × 23 5/8 × 23 5/8 in. (70.1 × 60 × 60 cm)

Drawing for Smoke Machine, 1964
Ballpoint pen on paper
10 × 7 in. (25.4 × 17.8 cm)

Annotated poem from 1961 by David Medalla to Takis, 1964
Ink pen on photocopy
4 13/16 × 7 1/4 in. (12.2 × 18.4 cm)

Clay Perry
David Medalla's Cloud Canyons 1964
Gelatin silver print
Courtesy of the artist and England & Co Gallery, London

Clay Perry
David Medalla's Cloud Canyons, 1964
Gelatin silver print
Courtesy of the artist and England & Co Gallery, London

Mohole Flower, 1964–72
Mixed media
16 1/8 × 19 11/16 × 3 15/16 in. (41 × 50 × 10 cm)

My Prick, 1965
Marker and pen on paper
7 11/16 × 6 1/16 in. (19.5 × 15.4 cm)

Portrait of Guy Brett, 1965
Ballpoint pen and China ink on paper napkin
7 × 6 15/16 in. (17.8 × 17.6 cm)

Untitled, 1965
Felt-tip marker and ballpoint pen on paper
19 7/8 × 14 in. (50.5 × 35.5 cm)

Untitled, 1965
Felt-tip marker and ballpoint pen on paper
19 3/4 × 14 in. (50.1 × 35.5 cm)

Mud machines, 1966
Felt-tip marker on paper
8 × 9 15/16 in. (20.3 × 25.3 cm)

for guy—love, david #1, 1966
Ballpoint pen on ruled paper
5 7/8 × 8 1/16 in. (15 × 20.5 cm)

To guy, love, (david) #2, 1966
Ballpoint pen on ruled paper
8 1/16 × 5 7/8 in. (20.5 × 15 cm)

To guy, himself in bed #IV, 1966
Ballpoint pen on ruled paper
8 1/16 × 5 7/8 in. (20.5 × 15 cm)

To guy, himself again, washing #VI, 1966
Ballpoint pen on ruled paper
8 1/16 × 5 7/8 in. (20.5 × 15 cm)

For guy brett #V, 1966
Ballpoint pen on ruled paper
8 1/16 × 5 7/8 in. (20.5 × 15 cm)

Guy Brett reading a mondrian catalogue #VII, 1966
Ballpoint pen on ruled paper
8 1/16 × 5 7/8 in. (20.5 × 15 cm)

guy brett at amsterdam airport (after buying tulip seeds) #VIII, 1966
Ballpoint pen on ruled paper
8 1/16 × 5 7/8 in. (20.5 × 15 cm)

Five minutes before departure for london, for guy brett, #IX, 1966
Ballpoint pen on ruled paper
8 1/16 × 5 7/8 in. (20.5 × 15 cm)

One minute after ascent aboard the plane from amsterdam to london, 1966
Ballpoint pen on ruled paper
5 7/8 × 8 1/16 in. (15 × 20.5 cm)

A boy's prayer to the fire god (for guy brett), 1966
Ballpoint pen on ruled paper
5 7/8 × 8 1/16 in. (15 × 20.5 cm)

Guy Brett
Mud Machine, 1967
Gelatin silver print
The Getty Research Institute, Los Angeles (2011.M.30)

Anonymous
The Exploding Galaxy, 1967
Gelatin silver prints
Seven parts, 8 1/8 × 5 15/16 in. (20.6 × 15.1 cm); 6 1/8 × 8 in. (15.5 × 20.3 cm); 10 1/4 × 6 11/16 in. (26 × 17 cm); 6 3/4 × 10 3/16 in. (17.2 × 25.9 cm); 10 3/16 × 7 3/8 in. (25.8 × 18.7 cm); 11 3/4 × 8 1/4 in. (29.9 × 20.9 cm); 8 1/16 × 9 15/16 in. (20.5 × 25.3 cm)

Study for peelable sculpture, 1967
Graphite and colored pencil on paper napkin
6 7/8 × 6 15/16 in. (17.5 × 17.6 cm)

Study for a monumental peelable sculpture, 1967
Colored pencil on mat board
12 5/8 × 7 5/8 in. (32.1 × 19.4 cm)

Study for a monumental peelable sculpture, 1967
Ballpoint pen, colored pencil, and ink pen on paper
10 × 7 15/16 in. (25.4 × 20.3 cm)

Vietnam—A Dance drama against unjust wars, 1967
Graphite and ballpoint pen on paper
15 15/16 × 10 in. (40.5 × 25.4 cm)

mudmachine, 1967
Ballpoint pen on paper
9 15/16 × 8 in. (25.3 × 20.3 cm)

Study for a monumental peelable sculpture, 1967
Graphite on paper
8 1/4 × 5 7/8 in. (21 × 15 cm)

Study for a mud-machine, 1967
China ink on paper
8 × 9 15/16 in. (20.3 × 25.3 cm)

Study for the Mohole Flower, 1967
Felt-tip marker on paper
8 1/4 × 5 11/16 in. (21 × 14.5 cm)

The Bird Ballet Mask, 1967
Plastic, ribbon, tinsel, plastic figurines, glue
13 7/16 × 8 1/4 × 6 11/16 in. (34.2 × 21 × 17 cm)

The Bird Ballet Mask, 1967
Ballpoint pen, crayon, and collage in notebook
24 × 11 13/16 × 3 9/16 in. (61 × 30 × 9 cm)

The Bird Ballet, 1967
Ballpoint pen, crayon, and collaged paper on notebook paper
10 1/16 × 8 × 3/8 in. (25.6 × 20.3 × 0.9 cm)

Untitled, 1967
Ink on paper
7 7/8 × 5 5/16 in. (20 × 13.5 cm)
Courtesy of kurimanzutto, Mexico City/New York

The Exploding Galaxy, 1967
Collaged paper on mat board
5 13/16 × 5 7/16 in. (14.7 × 13.8 cm)

Mohole flower no. 20, 1968
Graphite and ballpoint pen on paper
10 1/4 × 7 7/8 in. (26 × 20 cm)

Guy Brett
The Exploding Galaxy, 1968
Gelatin silver print
The Getty Research Institute, Los Angeles (2011.M.30)

Guy Brett
Ball Ponds Road London, 1968
Gelatin silver print
Two parts, 7 1/2 × 8 7/16 in. (19.1 × 21.5 cm) each
The Getty Research Institute, Los Angeles (2011.M.30)

Paul Overy
The Buddha Ballet, 1968
Gelatin silver print
The Getty Research Institute, Los Angeles (2011.M.30)

Michael Chapman
Exploding Galaxy, 1968
Digitized Super 8 film, color, silent
60:06 min.
Courtesy of Michael Chapman

Paul Keeler, *Planted* (Stanhope Press and the Exploding Galaxy, 1968)
Illustrations and facsimiles in book
15 1/16 × 10 × 1 in. (38.3 × 25.4 × 2.5 cm)
The Getty Research Institute, Los Angeles (2011.M.30)

Cloud Cliffs bubble mobiles, 1968
Felt-tip marker on paper
8 × 9 15/16 in. (20.3 × 25.3 cm)

Mohole Sculpture, 1968
Ink on paper
12 5/8 × 8 1/16 in. (32 × 20.5 cm)

Drawing for a monumental peelable sculpture with fragrant odors, 1968
Ink pen and colored pencil on paper
12 1/8 × 9 3/8 in. (30.8 × 23.8 cm)

Floating stone poem with peelable elements, 1968
Ink pen on paper
10 9/16 × 8 1/4 in. (26.9 × 21 cm)

Mohole flower, 1969
Ballpoint pen and crayon on paper
13 3/16 × 9 5/16 in. (33.5 × 23.7 cm)

Untitled, 1969
Charcoal and gold paint on paper
13 3/4 × 9 7/8 in. (35 × 25.1 cm)

Games of the sea & tides—mass participation propulsion, 1969/71
Crayon or colored pencil on gelatin silver print
6 × 9 7/16 in. (15.3 × 23.9 cm)

Wind, Sea + Stars Game, 1970
China ink on paper
8 1/4 × 11 3/4 in. (21 × 29.8 cm)

Portrait of a Young Peasant, 1971
Felt-tip marker and ballpoint pen on the back side of photocopy
11 3/4 × 8 7/16 in. (29.8 × 21.5 cm)

WORKERS ORGANISE!!! SMASH GROWING FASCISM!!!, 1971
Colored pencil, crayon, graphite, and ink on paper
9 15/16 × 7 15/16 in. (25.2 × 20.2 cm)

Kumbum, 1971–72
Newspaper clippings and ink on mat board
Twenty-eight parts, 24 15/16 × 19 15/16 in. (63.3 × 50.6 cm) each
Gift of David Medalla and Adam Nankervis. Collection of National Gallery Singapore

WE FILIPINOS LIVING ABROAD CONDEMN THE FASCIST REGIME OF MARCOS AND HIS GANG OF HOODLUMS, 1972
Felt-tip marker and typed text on paper
10 1/16 × 8 1/16 in. (25.5 × 20.5 cm)

Untitled, 1972
Acrylic on mat board
29 5/16 × 19 3/8 in. (74.5 × 49.2 cm)

Erhard Wehrmann
documenta 5, 1972
Gelatin silver print
The Getty Research Institute, Los Angeles (2011.M.30)

Balthasar Burkhard
Social Revolution, 1972
Gelatin silver print
The Getty Research Institute, Los Angeles (2011.M.30)

Marcos and His Handful of Hoodlums, 1972
Acrylic on cardstock
19 3/8 × 29 3/8 in. (49.2 × 74.5 cm)

Withdraw All Gestapo, 1972
Acrylic on mat board
29 7/16 × 19 3/8 in. (74.8 × 49.2 cm)

Carte d'Identite, 1972
Photo collage
7 × 10 3/8 in. (17.8 × 26.3 cm)

Untitled, 1973
Ballpoint pen, colored pencil, felt-tip marker, and watercolor on aluminum-foil-coated board
5 7/16 × 4 1/2 in. (13.8 × 11.5 cm)

Angolan Militia Members Meet M.P.L.A. Guerillas and Cadres, 1974
China ink on paper mounted on mat board
24 15/16 × 19 15/16 in. (63.3 × 50.6 cm)

The People of Zimbabwe Are Engaged in Production, 1974
China ink on paper mounted on mat board
24 15/16 × 19 15/16 in. (63.3 × 50.6 cm)

Smash Apartheid in South Africa! Victory to the Black workers of Namibia and Azania!, 1974
Ink on paper mounted on mat board
24 15/16 × 19 15/16 in. (63.3 × 50.6 cm)

Making soap with palm oil in the liberated areas of the Republic of Guiné-Bissau and Cape Verde, 1974
Ink on paper mounted on mat board
24 15/16 × 19 15/16 in. (63.3 × 50.6 cm)

Alfabetizaçao, 1974
Ink on paper mounted on mat board
24 15/16 × 19 15/16 in. (63.3 × 50.6 cm)

Statement by the artist, 1974
Ink on paper mounted on mat board
24 15/16 × 19 15/16 in. (63.3 × 50.6 cm)

FRELIMO freedom-fighters engage in the struggle for production, 1974
Ink on paper mounted on mat board
24 15/16 × 19 15/16 in. (63.3 × 50.6 cm)

"In FRELIMO we always emphasise the importance / of production . . .", 1974
Ink on paper mounted on mat board, tape
24 15/16 × 19 15/16 in. (63.3 × 50.6 cm)

P.A.I.G.C. Cadres Playing Draughts, 1974
Ink on paper mounted on mat board
24 15/16 × 19 15/16 in. (63.3 × 50.6 cm)

Angolan Guerillas at a Range Practice in the Jungle, 1974
Ink and gouache on paper mounted on mat board
19 15/16 × 24 15/16 in. (50.6 × 63.3 cm)

Red Guerillas of Zimbabwe (Rhodesia), 1974
Ink and gouache on paper mounted on mat board
19 15/16 × 24 15/16 in. (50.6 × 63.3 cm)

A Freedom Fighter of Zimbabwe, 1974
Ink on paper mounted on mat board
24 15/16 × 19 15/16 in. (63.3 × 50.6 cm)

Victory to P.A.I.G.C., 1974
Ink on paper mounted on mat board
19 15/16 × 24 15/16 in. (50.6 × 63.3 cm)

Guerilla Fighter of the M.P.L.A. Angola, 1974
Ink on paper mounted on mat board
24 15/16 × 19 15/16 in. (63.3 × 50.6 cm)

Lynn MacRitchie
Statements from the Arts Festival for Democracy in Chile, 1974
Digitized film, black and white, sound. 62:44 min.
Courtesy of Lynn MacRitchie

Artists for democracy—Chile vencera, 1975
Felt marker on rice paper
11 5/8 × 8 3/16 in. (29.6 × 20.8 cm)

Tatlin at the Funeral of Malevich, 1976
Ink and colored pencil on paper in linen-bound, accordion-folded notebook
10 × 6 9/16 × 1/8 in. (25.4 × 16.7 × 0.3 cm)

Tatlin at the Funeral of Malevich, a dramatic elegy by David Medalla, 1976
Photocopies
Seven parts, 24 × 16 3/4 in. (60.9 × 42.5 cm) each

Found Poem with a Drawing, 1976–78
Collage, felt-tip marker, ballpoint pen, graphite, and white marker on cardboard with elastic bands
9 15/16 × 7 7/8 in. (25.3 × 20 cm)

Eskimo Carver No. 1, 1977
Watercolor and China ink on paper
11 1/2 × 8 1/8 in. (29.2 × 20.7 cm)

Eskimo Carver No. 3, 1977
Watercolor, China ink, and crayon on paper
11 1/2 × 8 1/8 in. (29.2 × 20.7 cm)

James Dean and David Medalla, 1977
Acrylic on plastic, plastic strings
24 13/16 × 23 1/4 in. (63 × 59 cm)

Proust Tropicale et Marcel Maritime, 1979
Crayon and ballpoint pen on photocopy
11 11/16 × 8 1/4 in. (29.7 × 21 cm)

Rhapsody of the Dagger and Ammonia Boy, 1979
Wooden objects and acrylic on wood panel with decorative frame
26 3/16 × 25 7/8 × 1 in. (66.5 × 65.7 × 2.5 cm)

Rhapsody of the Dagger and Ammonia Boy (Interior Scene), 1979
Acrylic on wood
26 3/16 × 25 11/16 × 1 in. (66.5 × 65.2 × 2.5 cm)
Arts Council Collection, Southbank Centre, London. © David Medalla

Conversation with Jean-Paul Sartre, 1980
Acrylic and mixed media on mat board mounted on canvas
24 × 30 × 1 in. (60.9 × 76.2 × 2.5 cm)

MEDALLA SALUTA ROMA, 1980
Offset
10 1/16 × 8 in. (25.5 × 20.3 cm)

Untitled, ca. 1980
Ink on paper
16 1/2 × 11 3/4 in. (41.9 × 29.8 cm)

David Medalla with Louis Aragon, 1981
Photocopy of collage depicting an Impromptu in Paris, 1981.
6 7/8 × 6 7/8 in. (17.5 × 17.5 cm)

Untitled, 1982
Photocopies and ballpoint pen on mat board
24 13⁄16 × 19 7⁄8 in. (63 × 50.5 cm)

Le pete Paul Verlaine claire au clair de la Lune, 1982
Oil and collage on plastic
16 9⁄16 × 14 9⁄16 in. (42 × 37 cm)

Passport, 1982
Mixed media
6 1⁄2 × 4 1⁄8 × 1 in. (16.5 × 10.5 × 2.5 cm)

Untitled, 1982
Photocopies and ballpoint pen on mat board
24 7⁄8 × 19 15⁄16 in. (63.2 × 50.7 cm)

A Shot in the Dark, 1982
Photocopy
16 9⁄16 × 11 5⁄8 in. (42 × 29.6 cm)

Psychic Self-Defense, 1983
C-print
15 15⁄16 × 12 3⁄16 in. (40.5 × 31 cm)

The Naked Angel with a Bouquet of Flowers, 1983
Wax crayon and colored ink on photocopy
11 3⁄4 × 8 1⁄16 in. (29.8 × 20.4 cm)

Gay Galaxy, 1984
Ballpoint pen in notebook
8 1⁄4 × 5 7⁄8 × 1⁄4 in. (21 × 14.9 × 0.6 cm)

Un ragazetto biondo, da Venecia ("Primo Omaggio al pittore Filippo de Pisis"), 1984
Watercolor on paper
21 7⁄16 × 14 11⁄16 in. (54.4 × 37.3 cm)

Self Portrait, 1984
Mixed media on paper mounted on wood
57 × 45 in. (144.8 × 114.3 cm)
Collection of Paulino and Hetty Que

Cloud Canyons and Some Reflections on the Random in Life and Art, 1985
Ink on paper
Three sheets, recto and verso, 11 3⁄4 × 8 1⁄4 in. (29.8 × 21 cm) each
The Museum of Modern Art, New York, Gift of the Gilbert B. and Lila Silverman Instruction Drawing Collection, Detroit

Brancusi and Tatlin in Berlin—haiku sequence and ink drawings—volume one, 1985
Felt-tip marker and ink stamp on found spiral-bound notebook
11 13⁄16 × 8 7⁄16 × 5⁄16 in. (30 × 21.5 × 0.8 cm)

Binatilyong kumukuha ng ligau na bulaklak sa isla de Kalis, Coron, Palawan (Young man gathering an orchid at Kalis island, Coron, Palawan), 1986
Oil on canvas
76 × 62 1⁄8 × 1 1⁄8 in. (193 × 157.8 × 2.9 cm)

About my art, 1988
Felt-tip marker and acrylic in notebook
8 3⁄16 × 6 1⁄2 × 1⁄8 in. (20.8 × 16.5 × 0.3 cm)

Adam Nankervis
Feather Mask, 1989
Feathers, paper
21 7⁄8 × 17 15⁄16 × 3⁄16 in. (55.5 × 45.5 × 0.5 cm)

A Prophecy, 1989
Oil on canvas
82 11⁄16 × 122 1⁄16 in. (210 × 310 cm)
Arts Council Collection, Southbank Centre, London

New York Footprints No. 1, 1989–91
Oil on canvas
30 1⁄4 × 26 1⁄16 in. (76.8 × 66.2 cm)

Mondrian Fan Club
Merzman homage Kurt Schwitters Merzbarn Cumbria England, 1991
C-print
20 × 18 in. (50.8 × 46.7 cm)

Mondrian Fan Club
Untitled, 1991
C-print
20 × 18 in. (50.8 × 45.7 cm)

Mondrian Fan Club
Mondrian Fan Club no. 3, 1991
C-print
20 × 18 in. (50.8 × 46.7 cm)

Mondrian Fan Club
Mondrian Fan Club no. 9, 1991
C-print
20 × 18 in. (50.8 × 46.7 cm)

Visions after a walk in the moonlight along the East River in New York City, 1991
Ballpoint pen, China ink, watercolor, crayon, and collage on paper
11 1⁄2 × 8 7⁄8 in. (29.2 × 22.5 cm)

*Bioluminescent (*astro* Acupuncture*) Man—body art & installation by Medalla*, 1991
China ink and ink pen on paper
19 1⁄2 × 13 5⁄8 in. (49.6 × 34.6 cm)

Cosmic Propulsion by David Medalla, 1991
Crayon, ballpoint pen, and collage and scratching on Polaroid
4 1⁄4 × 3 1⁄2 in. (10.8 × 8.9 cm)

Adam Nankervis
Portrait of David Medalla, New York City, 1992
Ink on color photocopy
9 5⁄16 × 7 1⁄16 in. (23.7 × 18 cm)

Welcoming to Brooklyn, 1992
Felt-tip marker on photocopy
10 15⁄16 × 8 9⁄16 in. (27.8 × 21.7 cm)

Mondrian in Excelsis Shorts, 1993
Fabric, thread
12 3⁄8 × 18 5⁄16 in × 1.5 in. (31.5 × 46.5 cm × 3.8 cm)

Mondrian Fan Club
Mondrian in Excelsis, 1993
C-print
12 5⁄8 × 18 1⁄2 in. (32 × 47 cm)

Untitled, 1994
Felt-tip marker on photographic print
13 15⁄16 × 9 1⁄2 in. (35.4 × 24.2 cm)

Inspired by poet Octavio Paz's remark that "it is easier to discover a new planet than to find a new way of making love . . .", 1994
Photocopy and ballpoint pen on paper
10 1⁄2 × 8 3⁄16 in. (26.7 × 20.8 cm)

Mondrian Fan Club
Cypress Hills Cemetery, 1994
Inkjet on archival paper
12 5⁄8 × 18 1⁄2 in. (32 × 47 cm)
Courtesy of Ateneo Art Gallery, Ateneo de Manila University

Mondrian Fan Club
The Letter M Over Manhattan, 1994
C-print
18 1⁄8 × 12 5⁄8 in. (46 × 32 cm)
Courtesy of Ateneo Art Gallery, Ateneo de Manila University

Mondrian Fan Club
Mayflower Barn England, 1994
C-print
20 × 18 in. (50.8 × 45.7 cm)

Mondrian Fan Club
Untitled, 1994
C-print
20 × 18 in. (50.8 × 46.7 cm)

The Flying Mondrians, 1995
Offset
15 7⁄16 × 11 1⁄8 in. (39.2 × 28.3 cm)

Homage to the Reading Room of the British Museum, 1995
Ink, ballpoint pen, and collage in notebook
8 7⁄8 × 7 3⁄16 × 3⁄8 in. (22.5 × 18.3 × 0.9 cm)

Mondrian Fan Club, 1995
Book
16 9⁄16 × 11 5⁄8 × 9⁄16 in. (42 × 29.5 × 1.4 cm)

Signals, ca. 1995
Acrylic on newspaper
Two parts, 23 9⁄16 × 15 9⁄16 in. (59.8 × 39.5 cm)

Mondrian Fan Club
Untitled, 1995
Acrylic, collage, and ballpoint pen in notebook
20 × 18 in. (50.8 × 46.7 cm)

The Birth of Television, 1996
Crayon on drawing board
Two parts, 19 × 12 1⁄2 in. (48.2 × 31.7 cm) each

The Cotton Candy Sutra & Other Cosmic Propulsions, 1997
Book
8 1⁄4 × 6 1⁄16 × 3⁄4 in. (21 × 15.4 × 1.9 cm)

David Medalla and Adam Nankervis
Colour Blind, 1997
Digital video, color, sound
24:03 min.

Berlin Dialogue no. 1, 1997
Ink and collage in notebook
11 ½ × 10 ⅛ × 1 in. (29.2 × 25.7 × 2.5 cm)

David Medalla and Adam Nankervis
Drawings by David Medalla & Adam Nankervis—Berlin, 1998
Felt-tip marker in notebook
7⅛ × 16 ¼ × ⅝ in. (18.1 × 41.2 × 1.5 cm)

Mondrian Fan Club
Auf das Jahr 1998, 1998
Offset print, collage, acrylic, and ink in notebook
8 1⁄16 × 5 ⅜ × ½ in. (20.5 × 13.7 × 1.2 cm)

The Songs of Songs, 1999
C-print and collage
Two parts, 48 1⁄16 × 68 ⅛ in. (122 × 173 cm) each
Arts Council Collection, Southbank Centre, London

David Medalla and Harald Szeemann
We Can See Your Future and We Like What We See, 1999
Photocopy of a collage
11 11⁄16 × 8 ¼ in. (29.7 × 21 cm)
The Getty Research Institute, Los Angeles (2011.M.30)

Mondrian Fan Club
Mondrian Fan Club no. 13, 2000
C-print
20 × 18 in. (50.8 × 46.7 cm)

Self Portrait, 2004
Watercolor on paper
23 ⅜ × 16 ⅜ in. (59.4 × 39 cm)

Study for Cloud Canyons no. 20, 2007
Ink pen on paper
11 ¾ × 8 ¼ in. (29.8 × 20.9 cm)

1,000 Places to See Before You Die, 2008
Book
7 11⁄16 × 5 7⁄16 × ⅝ in. (19.5 × 13.8 × 1.5 cm)

I am an enigma even to myself—An Artist's Archives, 2009
Ink, ballpoint pen, and collage in notebook
6 ⅛ × 4 5⁄16 × ½ in. (15.5 × 11 × 1.3 cm)

Renata Padovan
Tulips for Iguazu, 2010
Digital video, color, sound
7:35 min.
Courtesy of the artist

Mondrian Fan Club
Tulips for Iguazu, 2010
C-print
19 11⁄16 × 19 11⁄16 in. (50 × 50 cm)

Untitled, 2011
Photo album
8 ⅞ × 13 × 1 in. (22.5 × 33 × 2.5 cm)

London Biennale 2012: The Rainbow, 2012
Paper collage, colored pencil, felt-tip marker, and clear tape on paper
13 ¼ × 9 15⁄16 in. (33.6 × 25.2 cm)

Adam Nankervis and A Stitch in Time, 2013
Acrylic on paper
27 ⅜ × 19 ½ in. (69.5 × 49.5 cm)

Making a paper mask by David Medalla, 2013
Felt-tip marker on paper
11 9⁄16 × 8 ⅛ in. (29.3 × 20.7 cm)

A Stitch in Time, 2013
Ink on paper
Two parts, 16 9⁄16 × 11 ⅝ in. (42 × 29.5 cm)

The Raven, 2013
Fake leather, feathers, safety pins, glass, acrylic, felt-tip marker
18 ⅛ × 15 ⅜ × 11 ⅝ in. (46 × 39 × 29.5 cm)

The Rainbow Bird, 2013
Woven plastic basket, tubing, acrylic, felt-tip marker, seashells, safety pins
21 1⁄16 × 18 5⁄16 × 7 ⅞ in. (53.5 × 46.5 × 20 cm)

The Bell-Ringers of the Mondrian Fan Club, 2013
Ink on paper
19 11⁄16 × 14 3⁄16 in. (50 × 36 cm)

"Maps—Mazes and Mysteries" London Biennale 2014, 2014
Ink pen and acrylic on newspaper
21 15⁄16 × 13 11⁄16 in. (55.7 × 34.8 cm)

A secular litany for Adam Nankervis, 2014
Felt-tip marker and ballpoint pen on wooden dish-drying stand
13 3⁄16 × 13 3⁄16 × 9 in. (33.5 × 33.5 × 22.8 cm)

Untitled, 2015
Collage on paper
8 ⅞ × 11 15⁄16 in. (22.6 × 30.4 cm)

Rubaiyat, 2015
Acrylic on paper
Nine parts, 24 × 16 ¾ in. (61 × 42.5 cm) each

David Medalla and Adam Nankervis
Orpheus descending, 2015
Newspaper, nylon tapestry, strings, coins, and arrow pin
18 3⁄16 × 14 ¾ × ½ in. (46.2 × 37.4 × 1.3 cm)

Stephen Hawking Mask, 2016
Paper, tinsel, masking, paper cutouts, signed cardboard box
20 × 9 in. (50.8 × 22.8 cm)

The letter B for Bologna, 2016
Inkjet on paper
19 7⁄16 × 13 7⁄16 in. (49.3 × 34.2 cm)

Mondrian Fan Club
Mondrian Mud machines, 2016
Felt-tip marker on watercolor paper
14 3⁄16 × 10 ½ in. (36 × 26.8 cm)

Cloud Canyon, 2017
Plastic, water, detergent
59 × 59 × 78 in. (150 × 150 × 200 cm)
Lito and Kim Camacho Collection

The Flame Tree at Bagong Bayan in Luneta, Manila, 2017
Ballpoint pen, felt-tip marker, and collage on photo album
11 ⅝ × 11 ¾ × 1 ⅞ in. (29.5 × 29.8 × 4.8 cm)

I was dreaming of a drunken boat—Verlaine and Rimbaud, 2017
Crayon and watercolor on paper
24 ⅞ × 36 13⁄16 × 1 ¼ in. (63.2 × 93.5 × 3.1 cm)

Adam Nankervis
David Medalla. The Fairy Mountain, a homage to Mei Lan Fang, 2017
C-print
31 7⁄16 × 23 ⅝ in. (79.8 × 60 cm)

Adam Nankervis
David Medalla in conversation with the cosmos, 2017
C-print
31 7⁄16 × 23 ⅝ in. (79.8 × 60 cm)

Adam Nankervis
David Medalla, mondrian in excelsis, 2018
C-print
31 7⁄16 × 23 ⅝ in. (79.8 × 60 cm)

Adam Nankervis
David Medalla, hunaman weaving rainbows, 2018
C-print
31 7⁄16 × 23 ⅝ in. (79.8 × 60 cm)

The Mohole Flower Blowing in the Wind in My Dreams, 2019
Watercolor, ink pen, and felt-tip marker on watercolor paper
14 ¼ × 10 ⅝ in. (36.2 × 26.9 cm)

Mondrian Fan Club
Untitled, 2019
Crayon and felt-tip marker on watercolor paper
14 3⁄16 × 10 ½ in. (36 × 26.8 cm)

Adam Nankervis
David Medalla a cloud in trousers homage to mayakovsky duchamp and man ray manila, 2019
C-print
31 7⁄16 × 23 ⅝ in. (79.8 × 60 cm)

Untitled, 2019
Crayon and felt-tip marker on watercolor paper
14 3⁄16 × 10 ½ in. (36 × 26.8 cm)

Untitled, 2019
Crayon and felt-tip marker on watercolor paper
14 3⁄16 × 10 ½ in. (36 × 26.8 cm)

A Note to Adam, 2020
Watercolor and pen on paper
11 11/16 × 8 7/8 in. (29.7 × 22.6 cm)

The Diorama, 2020
Watercolor and pen on paper
11 11/16 × 8 7/8 in. (29.7 × 22.6 cm)

In Bed with Oriol (de Quadras), 2020
Watercolor and pen on paper
11 11/16 × 8 7/8 in. (29.7 × 22.6 cm)

A Stitch in Time, n.d.
Mixed media, tin box
6 7/8 × 16 9/16 × 11 13/16 in. (17.5 × 42 × 30 cm)

A Stitch in Time, n.d.
Mixed media
6 1/8 × 10 1/4 × 2 15/16 in. (15.5 × 26 × 7.5 cm)

A Synoptic Homage to Brancusi and Tatlin, n.d.
Felt-tip marker in notebook
9 5/16 × 7 9/16 × 1/4 in. (23.7 × 19.2 × 0.6 cm)

Flotsam and Jetsam, n.d.
Photo album
5 3/16 × 7 5/8 × 3/8 in. (13.2 × 19.4 × 0.9 cm)

Grandma's Brag Book, n.d.
Magazine, newspaper, photocopy, and collage clippings
5 11/16 × 4 1/8 × 1 in. (14.5 × 10.5 × 2.5 cm)

My Life as an Artist, n.d.
Photocopied manuscript with felt-tip marker corrections
11 × 8 1/2 in (28 × 21.6 cm)

The Medalla Archives—Academic Regards, n.d.
Ballpoint pen on notebook paper
11 5/8 × 8 1/8 × 3/16 in. (29.5 × 20.7 × 0.5 cm)

Untitled (annoyance), n.d.
China ink on paper
8 × 4 15/16 in. (20.3 × 12.6 cm)

Untitled, n.d.
Ink on paper
16 1/2 × 11 3/4 in. (41.9 × 29.8 cm)

Untitled, n.d.
Ink in notebook
6 3/8 × 4 7/8 × 3/4 in. (16.2 × 12.4 × 1.9 cm)

* As of January 2, 2024

Contributors

Magalí Arriola

Magalí Arriola has been the director of Museo Tamayo Arte Contemporáneo in Mexico City since 2019. She was KADIST's lead curator for Latin America from 2017 to 2019 and curated the Mexican Pavilion for the 58th Venice Biennial (Pablo Vargas Lugo, *Acts of God*, 2019). She was chief curator at Museo Jumex in Mexico City between 2011 and 2014, where she organized exhibitions of artists such as James Lee Byars, Guy de Cointet, and Danh Võ, and curated shows contextualizing works from the Jumex Collection. As chief curator of Museo Tamayo between 2009 and 2011, she curated exhibitions and projects with artists such as Roman Ondák, Joachim Koester, Claire Fontaine, Adrià Julià, and Julio César Morales. She was a visiting curator at the Wattis Institute for Contemporary Art in San Francisco in 2006, where she curated *Prophets of Deceit*. From 1998 to 2001, she was chief curator at the Museo de Arte Carrillo Gil in Mexico City, where she worked with a generation of artists that includes Eduardo Abaroa, Francis Alÿs, Miguel Calderón, Daniela Rossell, and Pablo Vargas Lugo. Her independent projects include the 8th Panama Biennial, *The Sweet Burnt Smell of History* (2008); *What once passed for a future, or The landscapes of the living dead* (Art2102, Los Angeles, 2005); *How to Learn to Love the Bomb and Stop Worrying about It* (CANAIA [National Chamber of Art Industries], Mexico City / Central de Arte at WTC, Guadalajara, Mexico, 2003–4); *Alibis* (Mexican Cultural Institute, Paris / Witte de With, Rotterdam, 2002); *Erógena* (Museo de Arte Carrillo Gil, Mexico City / SMAK: Stedelijk Museum voor Actuele Kunst, Ghent, Belgium, 2000); and *Peter Greenaway: Painting and Artifice* (Museo Tamayo, 1997). Arriola has written extensively for books, exhibition catalogues, and publications such as *Artforum*, *Curare*, *Frieze*, *Mousse*, *Manifesta Journal*, and *The Exhibitionist*.

Nyah Ginwright

Nyah Ginwright is a curatorial assistant at the Hammer Museum in Los Angeles. She has supported exhibitions and research projects at the Museum of the African Diaspora in San Francisco and the Armory Center for the Arts in Pasadena. Her research interests include African Diasporic aesthetics and textile arts. She graduated from the University of California, Los Angeles, in the school of Arts and Architecture, where she earned a BA in World Arts and Cultures with a minor in African American studies. She currently lives and works in Los Angeles.

Aram Moshayedi

Aram Moshayedi is the interim chief curator at the Hammer Museum in Los Angeles and curator-in-residence at Museo Tamayo Arte Contemporáneo in Mexico City. Since joining the Hammer in 2013, he has organized numerous exhibitions and publications, including *Lifes*; *Paul McCarthy: Head Space, Drawings 1963–2019* (with Connie Butler); *Stories of Almost Everyone*; *Made in L.A. 2016: a, the, though, only* (with Hamza Walker); *All the Instruments Agree: An Exhibition or a Concert*; and projects by artists Lawrence Abu Hamdan, Marwa Arsanios, Andrea Bowers, Andrea Büttner, Tita Cicognani, Simon Denny, Mario García Torres, Shadi Habib Allah, David Hartt, Maria Hassabi, Ho Tzu Nyen, Jasmina Metwaly, Oliver Payne and Keiichi Tanaami, and Avery Singer. He was formerly associate curator at the Roy and Edna Disney/CalArts Theater (REDCAT) in Los Angeles, where he organized exhibitions and oversaw the production of new works by Tony Cokes, Geoffrey Farmer, Erlea Maneros Zabala, The Otolith Group, Slavs and Tatars, Jordan Wolfson, and Ming Wong. He has contributed to numerous exhibition catalogues and the periodicals *Artforum*, *Art in America*, *BOMB Magazine*, *Frieze*, *Metropolis M*, *Parkett*, *X-TRA Contemporary Art Journal*, and *Bidoun*, for which he is a contributing editor.

CJ Salapare

CJ Salapare is a Filipino American arts worker based in Brooklyn, where he is currently a curatorial assistant at the Whitney Museum of American Art in New York. He has supported exhibitions and research projects at various institutions, including the Clark Art Institute, Williamstown, Massachusetts; Getty Research Institute, Los Angeles; Hammer Museum, Los Angeles; Museum of Contemporary Art, Los Angeles; Museum of Latin American Art, Long Beach, California; and the Williams College Museum of Art, Williamstown, Massachusetts. Prior to joining the Whitney, he pursued graduate work in museum education, exhibition theory, and Philippine diaspora at the University of Cambridge, England, where he was a Herchel Smith Fellow. He received his BA, magna cum laude, in art history from Williams College, where he was awarded the Karl E. Weston Prize for Distinction in Art History.

Lenders to the Exhibition

Arts Council Collection, Southbank Centre, London
Ateneo Art Gallery, Ateneo de Manila University
Michael Chapman
David Medalla Archive
England & Co Gallery, London
The Getty Research Institute, Los Angeles
kurimanzutto, Mexico City / New York
Lito and Kim Camacho Collection
Lynn MacRitchie
The Museum of Modern Art, New York
National Fine Arts Collection of the National Museum of the Philippines
National Gallery Singapore
Renata Padovan
Paulino and Hetty Que
Thomas Dane Galley, London / Naples

Published on the occasion of the exhibition *David Medalla: In Conversation with the Cosmos*, organized and presented by the Hammer Museum, Los Angeles, June 9–September 15, 2024. On view at Museo Tamayo Arte Contemporáneo, Mexico City, November 14, 2024–March 30, 2025.

The exhibition is organized by Aram Moshayedi, interim chief curator, with Nyah Ginwright, curatorial assistant.

Major support for *David Medalla: In Conversation with the Cosmos* is provided by The Andy Warhol Foundation for the Visual Arts. Generous support is provided by Karen Hillenburg, and Christine Meleo Bernstein and Armyan Bernstein. Additional support is provided by the E. Rhodes and Leona B. Carpenter Foundation, David Regan and Edgar Cervantes, John Auerbach and Edward Tang, Beth and Ken Karmin, and Edward Lee.

The Andy Warhol Foundation for the Visual Arts

Published in 2024 by the Armand Hammer Museum of Art and Cultural Center, Inc., and DelMonico Books • D.A.P.

Hammer Museum
10899 Wilshire Boulevard
Los Angeles, CA 90024-4201
310-443-7000
hammer.ucla.edu

The Hammer Museum is operated and partially funded by the University of California, Los Angeles. Occidental Petroleum Corporation built the museum's building and established its endowment.

DelMonico Books are available through
ARTBOOK | D.A.P.
75 Broad Street, Suite 630
New York, NY 10004

artbook.com
delmonicobooks.com

Design: A Practice for Everyday Life
Copy editor: Elizabeth Pulsinelli
Proofreader: Rachel Walther
Director, exhibition and publication management: Michael Nock
Project manager: Jessi DiTillio
Color separations: Echelon, Santa Monica
Printer: Wilco Art Books, Amersfoort, Netherlands

The book is typeset in ABC Diatype and ABC Laica and printed on Munken Lynx Rough and Magno Volume.

Printed and bound in the Netherlands.

ISBN: 978-1-63681-127-7

Photographer Credits
John Arnold: 153; Mark Blower: 50; Guy Brett: 22, 75, 85, 149, 176, 189; Balthasar Burkhard © Vida Burkhard / Fotostiftung Schweiz: 97; Manuel Cristaldi: 143, 147; © Estate of John Dugger: 31, 63 (top and bottom), 93, 103, 105, 107, 125, 126; © Jane England: 95, 96, 110–12; © Mitja Hinderks: 86; © Charles Hustwick: 132–33; Rachel Inman; 156; Gerardo Landa Rojano: 67, 68; © Lynn MacRitchie Archive: 127; Adam Nankervis: 5, 159, 161–64; Andrée Navarro: 152; Paul Overy: 91; Plastiques Photography: 47; © Clay Perry: cover, 45, 51, 54, 55, 69; Mareike Tocha: 59; Mr. Bengy Toda III: 37; MM Yu: 166; unknown: 21, 81, 84, 150, 151, 157, 190.

Reproduction Credits
Courtesy of Arts Council Collection, Southbank Centre, London: 140, 167 (top); courtesy of Bonner Kunstverein, Bonn: 59; courtesy of documenta archiv: 104; courtesy of documenta archiv / Estate of John Dugger: 93, 105; courtesy of England & Co Gallery, London: cover, 87, 95, 96, 107, 110–12, 125–27, 132–33; courtesy of Getty Research Institute, Los Angeles, GRI 87-S661: 71–74; GRI 2011.M.30: 85, 91, 97, 176; GRI 44-37: 177 (bottom); courtesy of kurimanzutto, Mexico City / New York: 47, 50, 67, 68; digital image © The Museum of Modern Art / licensed by SCALA / Art Resource, NY: 60, 61; Collection of National Gallery Singapore and National Heritage Board, Singapore: 113, 115, 116–17, 118; courtesy of National Museum of the Philippines: 37; courtesy of Renata Padovan: 28, 29, 158; courtesy of Paulino and Hetty Que: 166; courtesy of Richard Saltoun Gallery: 156; works by David Medalla published in Guy Brett, *Exploding Galaxies: The Art of David Medalla* (1995): 22, 24, 48, 63, 75, 135, 153, 155, 189.

cover
Clay Perry, *David Medalla's Cloud Canyons*, 1964.

interior cover
WE FILIPINOS LIVING ABROAD CONDEMN THE FASCIST REGIME OF MARCOS AND HIS GANG OF HOODLUMS, 1972. Felt-tip marker and typed text on paper.
10 1/16 × 8 1/16 in. (25.5 × 20.5 cm).

Hammer Board